SOUTHERN BIOGRAPHY SERIES
Bertram Wyatt-Brown, Editor

JAMES HAMILTON

Courtesy South Carolina Federation of Republican Women

JAMES HAMILTON
OF
SOUTH CAROLINA

ROBERT TINKLER

LOUISIANA STATE UNIVERSITY PRESS

BATON ROUGE

Designer: Barbara Neely Bourgoyne
Typeface: Janson Text
Typesetter: Coghill Composition Co., Inc.
Printer and binder: Thomson-Shore, Inc.

Library of Congress Cataloging-in-Publication Data

Tinkler, Robert.
James Hamilton of South Carolina / Robert Tinkler.
    p.   cm. — (Southern biography series)
    Includes bibliographical references and index.
    ISBN 0-8071-2936-4 (hardcover : alk. paper)
1. Hamilton, James, 1786–1857.   2. Legislators—United States—Biography.   3. United
States. Congress. House—Biography.   4. Governors—South Carolina—Biography.   5.
Legislators—South Carolina—Biography.   6. Mayors—South Carolina—Charleston—
Biography.   7. Charleston (S.C.)—Biography.   8. South Carolina—Politics and
government—1775–1865.   9. Diplomats—Texas—Biography.   I. Title.   II. Series.

    E340.H19T56   2004
    975.7'03'092—dc22

                                                              2003027065

The paper in this book meets the guidelines for permanence
and durability of the Committee on Production Guidelines
for Book Longevity of the Council on Library Resources. ⊚

Contents

Acknowledgments

THIS BOOK IS LARGELY ABOUT DEBTS, not only James Hamilton's, but also mine. My special thanks to my graduate school adviser, William L. Barney, and to other University of North Carolina historians who helped this project along, including Harry Watson, Peter Coclanis, Don Mathews, and Joel Williamson.

Historians of the antebellum period enjoy an embarrassment of riches—scholarly if not monetary ones. Excellent archives and libraries contain mother lodes of primary documents; we're fortunate that so many archivists and librarians know these veins well and are willing to share their knowledge with us. I appreciate the assistance given me by the staffs of the Manuscripts Division of the Library of Congress, the Historical Society of Pennsylvania, the South Carolina Historical Society, the South Caroliniana Library at the University of South Carolina in Columbia, the South Carolina Department of Archives and History, the Center for American History at the University of Texas at Austin, the Texas State Library and Archives Commission, the Brazoria County Historical Museum, and Perkins Library at Duke University. My highest accolades go to the staffs of UNC's Southern Historical Collection and Davis Library's Interlibrary Borrowing and Microforms Division, all at Chapel Hill, who make research a pleasure.

Without a group of amiable fellow toilers in the graduate school vineyard, the years of dissertation writing that preceded this book would have been barren indeed. One simply could not have asked for so congenial and inspirational a crew of fellow apprentice historians as Mary Jane Aldrich-Moodie, Steve Berry, Gavin Campbell, Jeff Cowie, Tom Devine, Gary Frost, Georg Leidenberger, Marla Miller, Laura Moore, Stephen

Niven, Karen Paar, Houston Roberson, Michael Ross, Molly Rozum, Michael Trotti, and Jonathan Young. Without them, Chapel Hill, despite its many charms, would have been a dreary place. To my Austin friends, Gunther Peck and Faulkner Fox, I extend my appreciation for wonderful accommodations and great chow. My History Department colleagues at California State University, Chico, have been unfailingly gracious and supportive since I joined them, for which I am very grateful. I also thank Chuck Nelson, of Chico's Geographical Information Center, for producing the map of Hamilton's properties. Without the faith and assistance of Bertram Wyatt-Brown, editor of LSU Press's Southern Biography Series, and of Sylvia Frank Rodrigue and George Roupe, both at LSU Press, this book simply would not exist. My copyeditor, Eivind Boe, has improved this work by eliminating from it more than a few mistakes and awkward phrases. All that remain are, of course, my own responsibility.

I first learned about history from my family, and it is to them that my debts are greatest. My siblings and their spouses provided lodging on multiple research trips to Columbia, Atlanta, and Charleston. And for so much support over the years, I cannot thank my parents, William Phillips and Elsie McGill Tinkler, enough. So, instead, I dedicate this work to them.

Abbreviations

ADC	Thomas Hart Benton, *Abridgment of the Debates of Congress*
AHR	*American Historical Review*
CAH	Center for American History, University of Texas at Austin
Cong. Deb.	*Register of the Debates in Congress*
Cong. Globe	*Congressional Globe*
Duke	Special Collections, Perkins Library, Duke University
HSP	Historical Society of Pennsylvania, Philadelphia
JH	James Hamilton (1786–1857)
JHP	James Hamilton Papers
JSH	*Journal of Southern History*
LC	Manuscripts Division, Library of Congress
MVBP	Martin Van Buren Papers
NR	*Niles' Register* (occasionally *Niles' Weekly Register* or *Niles' National Register*)
RG 21	Record Group 21, Records of the District Courts of the United States, U.S. Circuit Court for the District of Columbia, Chancery Records, Chancery Dockets and Rules Case Files, 1804–1863. National Archives, Washington, D.C.
SCDAH	South Carolina Department of Archives and History, Columbia

SCHM	*South Carolina Historical Magazine* (called *South Carolina Genealogical and Historical Magazine* from its founding in 1900 through 1952)
SCHS	South Carolina Historical Society, Charleston
SCL	South Caroliniana Library, University of South Carolina at Columbia
SHC	Southern Historical Collection, University of North Carolina at Chapel Hill
State Records	William Sumner Jenkins, ed., *Records of the States of the United States of America: A Microfilm Compilation* (Washington: Library of Congress Photoduplication Service, 1949)
SWHQ	*Southwestern Historical Quarterly*
TDC	George P. Garrison, ed., *Diplomatic Correspondence of the Republic of Texas*
I	*Annual Report of the American Historical Association, 1907,* vol. 2
II	*Annual Report of the American Historical Association, 1908,* vol. 1
III	*Annual Report of the American Historical Association, 1908,* vol. 2
TSLAC	Texas State Library and Archives Commission, Austin

James Hamilton of South Carolina

TENNESSEE

NORTH
CAROLINA

ARKANSAS

SOUTH
CAROLINA

Charleston ○

MISSISSIPPI ALABAMA GEORGIA

Oswichee ■ ○
Columbus

Rice Hope &
Pennyworth Is. ■

TEXAS LOUISIANA

Houston
○
■ Retrieve

New Orleans
○

○ Mobile

Gulf of Mexico

FLORIDA

0   100   200
Miles

Chuck Nelson

HAMILTON PROPERTIES

A Death Unmourned

ONE NIGHT IN LATE NOVEMBER 1857, Alfred Huger warmed himself by a fire in the office he occupied as postmaster of Charleston, South Carolina. He had just returned from "a cold & cheerless journey" to a plantation more than ninety miles distant, where he had called on the widow of a recently deceased friend. Now, as he glanced over the newspapers accumulated during his absence, his gaze fell upon the printed message of Governor Robert F. W. Allston, delivered to the new session of the South Carolina legislature a few days before. Scanning it, Huger must have thought his nearly seventy-year-old eyes were playing tricks on him. But a closer, more deliberate reading of the governor's words convinced Huger that his vision was just fine. Governor Allston had in fact neglected to mention a particular topic. The omission bothered, even angered, Huger, an otherwise genial man whose affability had helped him retain his patronage job for over twenty years through both Democratic and Whig administrations. What Huger found so alarming was that, in all of Allston's official message, no word appeared about the death of the man whose widow he had just consoled, his old friend, James Hamilton.[1]

Allston could not be excused on grounds of ignorance of Hamilton's death, for newspapers in the state carried the sad intelligence several days before the governor gave his speech. Nor could one of his apologists claim that the news was inappropriate for an occasion of state. In fact, the speech opened by acknowledging the recent deaths of three other

---

1. Alfred Huger to William Campbell Preston, 26 November 1857, Alfred Huger Letterpress Book, Duke.

men prominent in Carolina's public life. The first few paragraphs lamented the passing of both Congressman Preston Brooks and his uncle, Senator A. P. Butler, on whose behalf and for whose honor Brooks had caned Massachusetts senator Charles Sumner the previous year. Mentioning them, Huger knew, was almost a matter of political necessity: Brooks had become a wildly popular hero by bludgeoning the detestable Sumner on the Senate floor, while Senator Butler's death left a vacancy the legislature needed to fill right away. But the governor also went on to mourn a figure not as prominent in recent years, Langdon Cheves, congressional war hawk in 1812 and president of the Bank of the United States in the 1820s. Yet Hamilton went unmentioned.[2]

"Can it be possible," Huger wrote that night, incredulous at this official snubbing, "that in the very same 'Senate House' where Hamilton decided upon the destiny of S. Carolina, they cannot find either time or feeling to notice his death?" As Huger well remembered, in the closing days of another November a quarter-century before, James Hamilton had stood at the very pinnacle of the state's political structure as governor and, even more importantly, as presiding officer of the Nullification Convention. The culmination of Hamilton's labors as governor, this 1832 convention theoretically represented the will of the state's people, and with Hamilton's guidance, that popular will expressed itself in a stunning document. The Ordinance of Nullification claimed that an individual state, in its sovereign capacity as a co-creator of the constitutional compact of 1787, could determine on its own the constitutionality of federal laws. Not content with merely asserting principle as a political protest, the Ordinance also declared the federal tariffs of 1828 and 1832 null and void in South Carolina. Moreover, the Ordinance warned federal authorities that, should they test the state's resolve, South Carolina would respond with armed force and even secession. Following the adjournment of the convention, Hamilton, brigadier general of the state militia in Charleston, readied his troops to defend the state from an anticipated invasion by land and naval forces of the federal government.[3]

For Hamilton, the crisis was a delicious moment of personal glory for

2. Hamilton died on 15 November 1857. The *Charleston Courier* carried news of Hamilton's death four days before the governor's message on 23 November. See *Charleston Courier*, 19 and 25 November 1857.

3. William W. Freehling, *Prelude to Civil War: The Nullification Controversy in South Carolina, 1816–1836* (New York: Harper & Row, 1965), 275–7.

which destiny had seemingly prepared him. Son of a Continental Army hero and grandson of a member of the Stamp Act and Continental Congresses, Hamilton inherited a dual legacy of service to the new republic created by the American Revolution. Following his father's lead, Hamilton shouldered military obligations, while, like his well-heeled maternal grandfather, he took on political responsibilities. As a young man, he eagerly volunteered for service in America's "Second War for Independence" from 1812 to 1814. With national independence assured, he assumed a seat in the South Carolina legislature, served as the intendant (or mayor) of Charleston, and eventually entered Congress, where he chaired the House Military Affairs Committee in the 1820s. Then came his greatest triumph, the Nullification Crisis of 1832–33, when, as both a political leader and a soldier, Hamilton opposed a "tyrannical" government to preserve the republican liberties and property rights guaranteed by the Revolution in which his relatives had played such important parts.

Hamilton's leadership of the Nullifiers confirmed and enhanced his impressive public stature in South Carolina. In elegant drawing rooms overlooking Charleston's Battery, Madeira-sipping gentlemen raised fine crystal in his honor, while yeomen at upcountry muster fields toasted him with more potent libations from ruder vessels. As politically popular as he was, however, his reputation rested on ground more solid than the shifting sands of political favor.

More fundamentally, Hamilton owed his position to the respect he commanded from men like himself, slaveholding cotton and rice planters. This group possessed enormous political and cultural power in the South, and especially in South Carolina. Planters not only dominated southern legislatures, but they also provided leadership in the churches, militia beat companies, agricultural clubs, and other institutions of southern white civil society. And setting the tone for Carolina's planters during the 1820s and early 1830s were a few men like James Hamilton, to whom the gentry looked for guidance in matters social as well as political. Doubtless the blue blood Hamilton inherited from his mother—she was a Lynch, a venerable, fabulously wealthy and politically powerful lowcountry Carolina family—helped him stake his claim to superior influence, but it was not sufficient. As a youth, Hamilton learned crucial lessons about how to succeed in the planter's world of masculine pride and honor. He developed an undeniable, ingratiating charm, which alternated with biting wit when required. A skilled marksman and duelist, his reputation in affairs of honor was such that, according to Charlestonian Frederick Porcher, Hamilton's word could bring a dispute among gentlemen to a conclusion all parties acknowledged as perfectly satisfactory. Even allowing for some exaggeration on Porcher's part, Hamilton clearly possessed something more valuable than mere political popularity—authority among Carolina's leading class.[4]

Within a decade after the adjournment of the Nullification Convention, though, Hamilton's position had declined considerably. Just as his fellow slaveholders had voluntarily given him their deference, they also withdrew it. Porcher went so far as to suggest that, had Hamilton died in 1833 right after the Nullification Crisis, "his memory would have been held sacred by every man in Carolina," but that "unfortunately for his reputation his life was protracted about twenty years."[5]

Why did so many Carolinians wish James Hamilton forgotten? What was it about his post-nullification years that made planters leave him unmourned at his death? In part his public standing suffered because of positions he took on public finance issues at odds with those espoused by John C. Calhoun, who emerged after 1833 as first among equals in South Carolina politics. But there was more to Hamilton's fall from grace than his opposition to the Independent Treasury. Financial overextension, highly risky land ventures, and plain bad luck—ingredients not uncommon in the lives of many southern planters—combined to drive Hamilton deeply into debt. His attempts, ultimately futile, to extinguish those debts dominated the final two decades of his life and contributed mightily to the diminution of his reputation.

That Hamilton should have become unpopular as he struggled to reverse financial setbacks must have seemed—to him, at least—a bit odd. From his perspective, he was simply trying to fulfill the legacy bequeathed him by his socially and politically prominent forebears. Restoring his personal fortune seemed an important step toward reclaiming his

4. Samuel Gaillard Stoney, ed., "Memoirs of Frederick Adolphus Porcher," *SCHM* 47 (January 1946): 43. For the role of the concept of honor in the antebellum South, see Bertram Wyatt-Brown, *Southern Honor: Ethics and Behavior in the Old South* (New York: Oxford University Press, 1982); Steven M. Stowe, *Intimacy and Power in the Old South: Ritual in the Lives of the Planters* (Baltimore: Johns Hopkins University Press, 1987), chapter 1; and Kenneth S. Greenberg, *Honor and Slavery: Lies, Duels, Noses, Masks, Dressing as a Woman, Gifts, Strangers, Humanitarianism, Death, Slave Rebellions, the Proslavery Argument, Baseball, Hunting, and Gambling in the Old South* (Princeton: Princeton University Press, 1996).

5. Stoney, ed., "Porcher Memoirs," 38.

position in South Carolina society. Yet—and here was the great irony— the methods he employed in trying to climb out of debt sullied his honor more than financial ruin ever had. Hamilton's public life from the late 1830s until his death in 1857 appeared to many friends and enemies alike to be more than a little influenced by his empty purse rather than by the sort of disinterestedness that American public men of that era, especially in the South, liked to affect. To onetime admirers, the post-nullification Hamilton, with his dubious moneymaking schemes, delinquent promissory notes, and shifting positions on protecting "southern interests," proved a terrible embarrassment. Alfred Huger knew all this. He had more than enough cause to detest Hamilton and to welcome his passing. As a Unionist during the Nullification Crisis, Huger opposed the radical states' rights philosophy that Hamilton and his allies enshrined as political orthodoxy in South Carolina. As a result, Huger relinquished his claim to political office under the flag of the Palmetto State for years to come. In the 1850s he lost patience with Hamilton—and a tidy sum of cash—when one of the former Nullifier's Texas land deals went bust. Still, when Huger reflected on Hamilton's life and death, he protested against the prevailing opinion of his old friend: "Does Misfortune really obliterate the record so thoroughly, as to leave nothing due for admitted services? Or is there nothing sacred in the ashes of Greatness?"[6]

Huger's implicit plea to remember Hamilton has largely gone unheeded by historians. Despite a long public career that shaped key episodes of antebellum history, Hamilton lies obscured today in the historiographical shadows cast by former associates such as John C. Calhoun and James Henry Hammond. A scanty record of Hamilton primary documents partly accounts for the few secondary works about him. For instance, he left neither a revealing diary like Hammond's nor a voluminous personal correspondence on the order of Calhoun's. Especially disappointing is the almost total absence of preserved correspondence between Hamilton and his wife. Except for two unpublished dissertations, one a biography finished in 1964 and the other a 1971 study of his rhetorical style, little has been written about this Carolina planter-politician. Consequently, historians know little of him other than his pro-nullification stance, for which one historian has deemed him an early

6. Alfred Huger to William Campbell Preston, 26 November 1857, Alfred Huger Letterpress Book, Duke.

southern nationalist. Yet, a commitment to states' rights and "southern nationalism" hardly defines this New England–educated planter, banker, and sometime Texas diplomat who, as lobbyist for the Compromise of 1850, stood squarely against strident supporters of "southern rights." Hamilton's story involves more complexity than historians dealing with him have heretofore recognized.[7]

To remember James Hamilton is not to offer rehabilitation to a deserving historical figure, as Alfred Huger may have wished. Remembering Hamilton, the man unmourned, offers to enrich our understanding of the antebellum South and of the internal crises the region faced as it approached the precipice of civil war.

7. John C. Calhoun, for instance, is the subject of numerous biographies, including the Pulitzer Prize–winning book by Margaret Coit, *John C. Calhoun: American Portrait* (Boston: Houghton Mifflin, 1950). For James Henry Hammond, see Drew Gilpin Faust, *James Henry Hammond and the Old South: A Design for Mastery* (Baton Rouge: Louisiana State University Press, 1982) and Carol K. Bleser, *Secret and Sacred* (New York: Oxford University Press, 1988). Hamilton's onetime law partner and nullification-era opponent is the subject of William H. Pease and Jane H. Pease's *James Louis Petigru: Southern Conservative, Southern Dissenter* (Athens: University of Georgia Press, 1995). Other works dealing with Hamilton associates include Theodore Jervey, *Robert Y. Hayne and His Times* (New York: Macmillan, 1909); Laura A. White, *Robert Barnwell Rhett: Father of Secession* (New York: Century, 1931); J. Fred Rippy, *Joel R. Poinsett, Versatile American* (Durham: Duke University Press, 1935); and Lillian Kibler, *Benjamin F. Perry: South Carolina Unionist* (Durham: Duke University Press, 1946). The Hamilton dissertations are Virginia Louise Glenn, "James Hamilton, Jr., of South Carolina: A Biography" (Ph.D. diss., University of North Carolina at Chapel Hill, 1964); and Carl Lewis Kell, "A Rhetorical History of James Hamilton, Jr.: The Nullification Era in South Carolina, 1816–1834" (Ph.D. diss., University of Kansas, 1971). For Hamilton as southern nationalist, see John McCardell, *The Idea of a Southern Nation: Southern Nationalists and Southern Nationalism, 1830–1860* (New York: W. W. Norton, 1979), 342.

CHAPTER I

The Legatee

JUST SEVEN YEARS AFTER THE LANDING of the first British colonists in Carolina, a young Irishman arrived to stake his claim to New World land and wealth. In the spring of 1677, the Grand Council of Charles Towne granted Jonah Lynch a six-hundred-acre tract on the south bank of the Cooper River. As befitted a man who claimed descent from William the Conqueror's Norman warriors, Lynch began his own kind of conquest in Carolina. In succeeding years, he added to his holdings on the Cooper and expanded into the surrounding countryside. Like other early settlers, he sought to transform Carolina's "good fat and very rich ground" into profits. For a time, Lynch, described by an agent of the Lords Proprietors as "an ingenious Planter," raised barley, "of which he intended to make Malt for brewing of English Beer and Ale, having all Utensils and Conveniences for it."[1]

To perpetuate his territorial conquests, Jonah and his wife, Margaret, began their own New World dynasty by producing two sons. The younger son, born around 1680 and named Thomas for his paternal grandfather, inherited Jonah's acquisitive streak. Thomas added to his father's landholdings and, forsaking the cultivation of silk worms and In-

1. Alexander S. Salley, Jr., and R. Nicholas Olsberg, eds., *Warrants for Lands in South Carolina, 1672–1711* (Columbia: South Carolina Department of Archives and History, 1973), 136–7. In some records, Lynch's first name is spelled "Jonack." John Crafford, "A New and Most Exact Account of the Fertiles and Famous Colony of Carolina (On the Continent of America)" (Dublin: Nathan Tarrant, 1683), 5, in *State Records*, reel 1859; "Carolina, or a Description of the Present State of That Country, by Thomas Ashe, 1682" in *Narratives of Early Carolina, 1650–1708*, ed. Alexander S. Salley, Jr. (New York: Charles Scribner's Sons, 1911), 146–7.

dian corn favored by many early settlers, planted promising new crops, rice and indigo. Taking out grants for fifteen thousand acres on the North and South Santee Rivers, located in Craven County between Charles Towne and Georgetown, Lynch exploited the labor and the technical expertise of his African slaves to establish himself as a major rice planter. By the time he died in 1738, Lynch's property holdings, in humans and real estate, encompassed nearly two hundred slaves on seven plantations.[2]

The Lynch family's position was such that Thomas's son, born around 1727 and also named Thomas, could take his place alongside the colony's leading merchants and planters in the Commons House of Assembly while still in his early twenties. Thomas Lynch, Jr., who inherited the bulk of his father's holdings when the older man died intestate in 1738, represented various parishes, off and on, for more than two decades beginning in 1752. He solidified his social position by marrying Elizabeth Allston, daughter of another prominent rice planter of the Carolina lowcountry. Before Elizabeth's death in the early 1750s, their marriage produced three children, including an only son named Thomas, born in 1749.[3]

This youngest Thomas Lynch enjoyed the genteel advantages that a fortune accumulated during two generations of rice planting afforded one in mid-eighteenth-century Carolina. After preparation at the Indigo Society School in Georgetown, fifteen-year-old Thomas III left South Carolina in 1764 to continue his education in England. At Eton and Cambridge as well as in legal studies at London's Middle Temple, he experienced life as a part of the English gentry class, whose styles his

2. Virginia Glenn Crane, "The Lynches of South Carolina: Traditional Elite and the New Family History" in *The American Family: Historical Perspectives*, ed. Jean E. Hunter and Paul T. Mason (Pittsburgh: Duquesne University Press, 1991), 42; J. Christopher Simpson and James A. Fitch, "The Lynch Family of Georgetown," Historic Georgetown Leaflet Number 11 (Georgetown, S.C.: Rice Museum and Georgetown County Historical Commission, 1978); and Walter B. Edgar and N. Louise Bailey, eds., *Biographical Directory of the South Carolina House*, vol. 2 (Columbia: University of South Carolina Press, 1977), 419.

3. Note that I have denominated the three Thomas Lynches as "Sr.," "Jr.," and "III." In many records, the one I call Thomas Lynch, Jr. (1727?–1776) is counted as "Sr.," and his son, Thomas Lynch III (1749–1779), is called "Jr." See Simpson and Fitch, "The Lynch Family," and Lynch files, SCHS. See also Edgar and Bailey, eds., *Biographical Directory*, 421–2; and Mabel L. Webber, "Death Notices from the South Carolina Gazette and American General Gazette, and Its Continuation The Royal Gazette," *SCHM* 17 (July 1916): 123.

family and their neighbors emulated back in the tidal swamps of South Carolina.

Both Thomas Lynch, Jr., and his English-educated son absorbed enough of the English gentry's sensibilities to resent, in the years immediately following the Seven Years War, parliamentary encroachments on the "ancient rights" of South Carolina's legislative body. Faced with huge war debts, the London government moved to raise revenue from those who had directly benefited from the war, namely, the residents of the British North American colonies. With a series of new taxes, beginning in 1764 with the Sugar Tax and followed shortly by the infamous Stamp Tax, British officials sought not only to collect desperately needed cash but also to reassert their authority in the internal affairs of the colonies after several decades of relatively indifferent management of their North American empire.

The privileged lowcountry residents who served in the South Carolina colonial assembly jealously guarded what they considered their right to make their own laws and to tax themselves. Refusing to accede to the new British measures, they declared that the Commons House of Assembly was not "to be subordinate to any legislative power on earth." To their minds, surrendering their "ancient" political powers to others would make them no better than slaves, a term with palpable meaning for men like Lynch, who held persons of African descent as chattel.[4]

The older Lynch became a leader in the protests against Britain's "new imperial policy," which called for a tighter rein on the North American colonies. He traveled to New York in 1765 to serve with John Rutledge and Christopher Gadsden as a South Carolina delegate to the Stamp Act Congress, the first intercolonial attempt to air common grievances against Crown and Parliament. Lynch also served on South Carolina's General Committee, a revolutionary council that supplanted the colony's royal government in mid-1774, and he was elected to both the First and Second Continental Congresses, where delegates from throughout the colonies sought to forge a common response to British initiatives.

Thomas III, on his return from England in 1772 after an eight-year absence from Carolina, joined his father in taking an active role in the

---

4. Jerome J. Nadelhaft, *The Disorders of War: The Revolution in South Carolina* (Orono: University of Maine at Orono Press, 1981), 2.

protest against encroachments on their rights. While his father represented South Carolina in the Congress meeting in Philadelphia, Thomas
III served in important political positions back home. Between 1774 and
1776, the younger Lynch served successively in the first and second pro-
vincial congresses, the constitutional commission for the new state, and
the state's first legislature, or General Assembly. His service to South
Carolina might also have been marked by military distinction had not a
permanently debilitating fever cut short that career in late 1775, only a
few months after his election as a captain of the 1st Regiment of Provin-
cial Regulars. His lasting fame would come from political rather than
military endeavors.

Neither Thomas junior nor Thomas III saw the struggle with Britain
in particularly "democratic" terms. Rather, theirs was a conservative
movement that fought to preserve the privileges and power they and
other leading Carolinians had enjoyed for a century. The idea of an independent America, which the Revolution he helped initiate seemed to be
spawning, gave Thomas Lynch, Jr., pause. "If we separate from England," he wrote in February 1776, "we shall be obliged to set up a republic, and that is a form of government . . . I think reads better than it
works." A few days later, while in New York on congressional business,
he suffered a cerebral hemorrhage that left him seriously incapacitated.
South Carolina's General Assembly sent Thomas III to join his father in
the delegation, in effect to replace the disabled older man. With his
father too feeble to participate in debates, Thomas III found himself on
July 2 voting for the independence about which his father had been so
anxious. This the younger Lynch and the rest of the South Carolina delegation did with some apprehension and only after a majority of the
states had indicated their support for severing the bond with Britain.
With the other delegates, Thomas III signed the Declaration of Independence that summer.[5]

In late 1776, with neither man's health particularly good, the Lynches
set off for home. As they rested in Annapolis en route, Thomas junior
fell victim to a second and, this time, fatal stroke. His son returned home
alone, and shortly thereafter his own poor health forced his retirement
from public life. In December 1779, in an attempt to regain his strength,

5. Thomas Lynch, Jr., to William Smith, quoted in Simpson and Fitch, "The Lynch Family," 2.

Thomas III and his wife set off for a Dutch island in the West Indies, where they hoped to book passage on a neutral ship for the south of France. But they never reached their destination. Somewhere between Charles Towne and the Caribbean islands, their ship sank without a trace.[6]

That maritime tragedy did not put an end to the Lynch family's legacy of wealth and political leadership. The Lynch heritage, however, would not be carried on by a son but was rather passed down through a daughter borne by Thomas Lynch, Jr.,'s second wife, Hannah Motte. Like Thomas, Hannah came from a politically prominent family; her father, Jacob Motte, served as South Carolina's treasurer for many years during British rule. John Adams once described her as having "the Behaviour and Appearance of a very worthy woman."[7] She bore Lynch a daughter, Elizabeth, probably in late 1756, just over a year after their wedding. The young Elizabeth, like her half-brother, enjoyed the advantages of her parents' wealth and traveled among the upper echelons of colonial society. She once entertained John Adams with her spinet playing, and even accompanied her parents to Philadelphia for the meeting of the Continental Congress.

In May 1777, just six months after her father's death, Elizabeth Lynch married John Harleston, a member of another prominent lowcountry planting family. Soon, Harleston answered the call of military duty and in 1781 near Petersburg, Virginia, died of battle wounds. John and Elizabeth Lynch Harleston produced no heirs. But just as the war took Elizabeth's husband, it would also bring her a new one so that the Lynch tradition might be perpetuated in another generation.[8]

In early 1782, Continental soldiers under General Anthony Wayne arrived in the Carolina lowcountry from the North. Fresh from Lord Cornwallis's surrender at Yorktown, Wayne's men joined General Nathanael Greene's troops in the final push against the British in their last

6. Joseph E. Fields, "A Signer and His Signatures or the Library of Thomas Lynch, Jr." *Harvard Library Bulletin* 14, no. 2: 210.

7. L. H. Butterfield, ed., *Diary and Autobiography of John Adams*, vol. 2, *Diary, 1771–1781* (New York: Antheneum, 1964), 85, 117; and Mabel L. Webber, ed., "Extracts from the Journal of Mrs. Ann Manigault, 1754–1781," *SCHM* 20 (January 1919): 63.

8. Theodore D. Hervey, "The Harlestons," *SCHM* 3 (July 1902): 172–3; Mabel L. Webber, ed., "Extracts from the Journal of Mrs. Ann Manigault, 1754–1781," *SCHM* 21 (July 1920): 114.

stronghold, lowcountry South Carolina and Georgia. Among Wayne's officers was a thirty-one-year-old major from Pennsylvania named James Hamilton. Born in rural Lancaster County in 1750, Hamilton still spoke with the Ulster brogue bequeathed to him by parents who had arrived in Pennsylvania in the early eighteenth century as part of the great Scots-Irish migration. Hamilton's father, a prosperous farmer and innkeeper, sent James, the youngest of five sons, to Philadelphia in 1774 to study medicine with the well-known physician William Shippen.[9]

The colonial capital must have been an immensely exciting place for a man in his early twenties that year. The British Empire's second largest city held numerous attractions for one accustomed to the slower pace of rural Lancaster. Moreover, Philadelphia stood at the center of the political struggle of the colonies with Britain. About the time Hamilton arrived in the city, the First Continental Congress began its deliberations there. While Thomas Lynch, Jr., and his colleagues meeting in Carpenter's Hall debated which course of action to adopt against British invasions of their rights, Philadelphia residents argued about the same issues in the city's taverns, workplaces, and streets. The political excitement rose to a crescendo in the spring of 1775. Soon after news of the bloodshed at the Massachusetts villages of Lexington and Concord reached the Middle Colonies, Philadelphians joyously welcomed delegates to the Second Continental Congress and looked to it for leadership in a conflict now officially a war.[10]

Caught up in the "rage militaire" following the skirmishes in New England, James Hamilton promptly traded his medical texts for a gun and returned to Lancaster to help raise a company of riflemen from among his Scots-Irish neighbors. His fellow volunteers in the Pennsylvania Rifle Battalion elected Hamilton first lieutenant, the unit's second

9. Samuel Prioleau Hamilton, "James Hamilton" (M–2346), JHP, SHC. This account, by the son of the subject of the present work, consists of manuscript notes and incomplete drafts for a biography of James Hamilton that S. P. Hamilton intended to publish but never did. It reports family tradition unavailable elsewhere and is therefore invaluable as a source. Because the account contains no consistent system of pagination, I have not included page numbers in my references to it.

10. Richard Alan Ryerson, *The Revolution Is Now Begun: The Radical Committees of Philadelphia, 1765–1776* (Philadelphia: University of Pennsylvania Press, 1978), chapter 5. See also Jack N. Rakove, *The Beginnings of National Politics: An Interpretive History of the Continental Congress* (New York: Alfred A. Knopf, 1979), 70–1.

highest officer, and they all headed north to get in on the fighting. By the summer of 1775, Hamilton and his comrades had joined George Washington's army encamped at Cambridge, Massachusetts.[11]

So began James Hamilton's career as an army officer, one that lasted for the duration of the War for Independence—nearly eight years—and took him through some of its heaviest fighting. Impulse and a hunger for adventure as much as commitment to certain political principles inspired the young medical student to become a soldier. When Hamilton made the decision to fight, he thought, as did many others, that the conflict would be short. When it was over, then perhaps he could return to his studies with Dr. Shippen. As the seasons changed and the years wore on, it became clear that this would be no brief skirmish. In the midst of the conflict, Hamilton discovered that he made a good soldier. In fact, although he could not have known it at the time, this hellish war would be the highlight of his life.

Over time, Hamilton rose to the rank of major in the 2nd Pennsylvania. He honed his skills as a leader of men in action that included the battles of Dorchester Heights, White Plains, and Long Island. He slogged through New Jersey with Washington in 1776 and crossed the Delaware to capture the Hessians in Trenton on Christmas Day that year and went on to command a unit at Princeton.

The long spaces between battles were filled with the everyday concerns of camp life—bone-chilling cold, sweltering heat, lack of pay, scanty food—all interlaced with plain boredom. Hamilton sought to make life more bearable for his men. Sometimes his concern for the soldiers put him in conflict with Continental military authorities as well as friendly civilians. Obtaining basic supplies such as firewood and food proved a nearly constant headache. Hamilton once complained that Governor Thomas Jefferson of Virginia "has not paid the smallest attention to what . . . I recomended [sic] on the Subject of Provisions that are deficient." On another occasion, he implored a superior officer to do

11. Martha B. Clark, "Major James Hamilton: Of the Pennsylvania Line," *Papers Read before the Lancaster County Historical Society, March 2, 1906*, vol. 10, no. 3: 71–88; John B. B. Trussell, *The Pennsylvania Line: Regimental Organization and Operations, 1775–1783*, 2nd ed. (Harrisburg: Pennsylvania Historical and Museum Commission, 1993), 28–9, 45; and Fred Anderson Berg, *Encyclopedia of Continental Army Units: Battalions, Regiments, and Independent Corps* (Harrisburg: Stackpole Books, 1972), 47–8; Ryerson, chapter 6.

something about the scarcity of meat. "[T]he little which at times is de-livered [is] very bad of its kind," he noted.[12]

Captured and held as a prisoner on Long Island for ten months during 1777, Hamilton returned to duty after his release and extracted sweet re-venge on his captors when he led the first American cavalry unit into Yorktown after Lord Cornwallis's surrender in October 1781. Major James Hamilton had the honor of raising the American colors in the last British outpost north of the Carolinas.

After the victory at Yorktown, Hamilton and his 2nd Pennsylvania unit traveled south with General Wayne to link up with General Nathan-ael Greene in lowcountry South Carolina. The Pennsylvanians arrived in January 1782 and camped near Jacksonboro, about thirty miles down the Savannah road from Charles Towne (which had been in British hands since 1780 and which locals now called by the somehow less English-sounding name of Charleston). As a special legislative session met in Jacksonboro to dispossess Tories of their land, Hamilton and his men faced relatively few of the enemy. While Wayne took units to drive the British from Savannah and destroy the resistance of Loyalists and their Indian allies in Georgia, Hamilton's outfit remained near British-held Charleston and harassed the enemy. Hamilton commanded several mis-sions in the final push to expel the redcoats from the region, and he tri-umphantly led the first detachment of Continental infantry into Charleston as the British evacuated in December 1782.

When they were not pursuing the British, Hamilton and the other soldiers spent time exploring the surrounding countryside. The low-country's deep cypress swamps, with their mysterious black water and long strands of Spanish moss, provided a marked contrast with the fields and woods of the Middle Atlantic these men knew. Local crops piqued the interest of Pennsylvanians used to corn and wheat. One officer "rode out . . . to see the Rice farms" out of curiosity "to know how the farmers raise this grain."[13] Doubtless, Major Hamilton made such a tour himself. Certainly he mingled with the local planters, some of whom dined occa-sionally with the officers in camp.

Perhaps it was at a party organized by a planter reciprocating the

12. James Hamilton to Col. Wood, 18 January 1781 and 3 June 1780, Miscellaneous Manu-scripts Collection, James Hamilton file, LC.

13. "Itinerary of the Pennsylvania Line from Pennsylvania to South Carolina, 1781–1782," *Pennsylvania Magazine of History and Biography*, July 1912, 291.

army's hospitality that he met Elizabeth Lynch Harleston. Major Hamilton, whom Lafayette supposedly called the handsomest man in Washington's army, must have caught Mrs. Harleston's eye. The young widow, still in her mid-twenties, certainly was a good catch herself. She possessed not only the Lynch family's aristocratic bearing but much of its wealth as well. Even though by the terms of her husband's will she forfeited the bulk of his property if she remarried, Elizabeth still owned several of her deceased father's plantations on the North and South branches of the Santee River.[14] As a Lynch and the stepdaughter of General William Moultrie, the state's leading Revolutionary War hero whom Hannah Motte Lynch had married after the death of her husband, Elizabeth Lynch Harleston offered Hamilton connections to the top echelons of Carolina society.

After a trip to Pennsylvania to muster out of the army, Hamilton returned to a new life in South Carolina. He and Elizabeth wed in early June 1784 at the Berkeley County plantation of General Moultrie.[15] The couple settled at Rice Hope, one of the Lynch plantations on the Santee River willed to Elizabeth. There, the Pennsylvania soldier began his transformation into a lowcountry Carolina gentleman. He learned enough about rice planting to keep the place going, and he sought refinement through reading the works of Jonathan Swift and other authors in the library his wife had inherited from her father and half-brother. Probably within a year of his marriage, Major Hamilton fulfilled a necessary requirement for assuming the position of planter patriarch when Elizabeth bore him their first child, a son named Thomas Lynch for Elizabeth's father. Unfortunately, young Thomas soon died.

Shortly thereafter, on May 8, 1786, a second boy arrived. His parents named him James in honor of the major. In time, three daughters—Hannah Motte, Elizabeth Lynch, and Harriet—joined the family, but the parents' hopes rested on their only son. As a male, James Hamilton, Jr., would assume the mantle of the Lynch tradition of political and social leadership, embellished by Major Hamilton's distinguished Revolutionary War service. It was an auspicious, if challenging, beginning.

Young James Hamilton spent his childhood in two different worlds,

14. Will Book A, 187, Probate Court, Charleston County, SCDAH.
15. Mabel L. Webber, "Marriage and Death Notices from the South Carolina Weekly Gazette," *SCHM* 18 (October 1917): 189.

the South Carolina lowcountry and the New England seaport town of Newport. The two regions, though differing in obvious ways, taught Hamilton similar lessons about society, politics, and economics.

The lowcountry depended on the production of staple crops for an Atlantic market, but at the time of Hamilton's birth, the region's economy still suffered from the lingering effects of the war. About one-fourth of all enslaved South Carolinians had deserted their masters during the Revolution, and this disruption, combined with the difficulties planters faced in obtaining credit, helped lower agricultural productivity. In the mid-1780s, exports of rice and indigo from South Carolina amounted to less than half what they had been in the early 1770s.[16]

During the 1790s, the fortunes of Carolina rice planters improved dramatically as European demand picked up and Americans established trade links with the Continent independent of Britain. By 1796 rice prices reached record highs. Throughout the region, planters responded by channeling capital and labor into new agricultural techniques. Most notably, to better irrigate their crop, more planters shifted the site of rice cultivation from inland swamps to marshes on or near tidal rivers. Some planters also began raising long-staple cotton. In 1793, the state produced 94,000 pounds of the fleecy commodity; just two years later, it shipped 1,110,000 pounds. With increased production and higher prices, lowcountry planters experienced a "golden age" around the turn of the century—with rice as king, cotton an upstart duke, and indigo a declining count.[17]

At the center of the lowcountry world sat Charleston, the region's entrepôt and marketing center, but also its social, cultural, and political capital, and the young James Hamilton early came to know the city. His family owned a house there, at the corner of East Bay and Society Streets, overlooking Charleston's magnificent harbor. It was in Charleston, too, at the socially prestigious St. Philip's Episcopal Church, rather

16. Philip D. Morgan, "Black Society in the Lowcountry, 1760–1810," in *Slavery and Freedom in the Age of the American Revolution*, ed. Ira Berlin and Ronald Hoffmann, 111 (Urbana: University of Illinois Press, published for the United States Capitol Historical Association, 1986); Richard B. Morris, *The Forging of the Union, 1781–1789* (New York: Harper & Row, 1987), 144.

17. Mark Dementi Kaplanoff, "Making the South Solid: Politics and the Structure of Society in South Carolina, 1790–1815" (Ph.D. diss., Cambridge University, 1979), 5, 7; Peter A. Coclanis, introduction to *Seed From Madagascar*, by Duncan Clinch Heyward (Columbia: University of South Carolina Press, 1993), xiv.

than in a parish church near their plantation, that the Hamiltons had their son baptized in 1790, just shy of his fourth birthday.[18]

The future for lowcountry planters seemed secure once the economy rebounded to pre-war heights. Actually, although more robust than during the war and its immediate aftermath, the region's economy was steadily declining relative to more rapidly expanding areas of the new nation. The Hamilton family, too, already was experiencing financial problems, in part from obligations related to debts of Elizabeth's stepfather. But the Hamiltons owned productive land and numerous slaves that, they hoped, might bring them returns as fabulous as those the Lynches (and their bondsmen) had wrung from the Santee plantations before the Revolution.[19]

Hamilton's other world, the Rhode Island port city of Newport, clearly differed from lowcountry Carolina, yet the two areas resembled each other in important respects. For instance, the Revolutionary War had treated Newport with an unkindness Carolinians well understood. Before the war, Newport's merchants and shipowners amassed princely fortunes by plying the Atlantic and the seas beyond to spin webs of commerce. On any given day the summer before fighting broke out at Lexington and Concord, one could have counted nearly a hundred ships in Newport's harbor. But the city's economic decline had already begun, and the war, including three years of British occupation, accelerated that process. Many residents deserted Newport during the hostilities, and its commercial fleets suffered. Much of its inland trade shifted to Providence and other towns. Denied the free flow of its commercial lifeblood, Newport's prospects appeared dim. In 1785, one traveler noted that the poverty of the town's inhabitants "will be an insuperable barrier, at least for a time."[20]

18. Samuel Prioleau Hamilton gives Charleston as James Hamilton, Jr.'s, birthplace, while Virginia Glenn reports the Rice Hope tradition. See Hamilton, "James Hamilton," and Glenn, "James Hamilton," 1. See also *Charleston City Directory*, 1807, 137, and D. E. Huger Smith and A. S. Salley, Jr., *Register of St. Philip's Parish, Charles Town, or Charleston, S.C., 1754–1810* (Columbia: University of South Carolina Press, 1971), 114.

19. Peter A. Coclanis, *The Shadow of a Dream: Economic Life and Death in the South Carolina Low Country, 1670–1920* (New York: Oxford University Press, 1989).

20. Patrick McRobert, *A Tour Through Part of the North Provinces of America: Being, A Series of Letters Wrote on the Spot in the Years 1774, & 1775, To Which Are Annex'd, Tables, Shewing the Roads, the Value of Coins, Rates of Stages, &c.* (Edinburgh: n.p., 1776; reprint ed., New York: New York Times and Arno Press, 1968), 13; Lynne Elizabeth Withey, "Population Change, Economic Development, and the Revolution: Newport, Rhode Island, as a Case Study, 1760–

Soon Newport began to recover, thanks in part to its discovery by summer visitors from the South. Before the disruptions of the Revolution, Newport had been a favorite destination for southern planters seeking respite from the heat and humidity of their plantations. South Carolinians made up the single largest cohort of these temporary Newport residents; indeed, some wags even called Rhode Island "the Carolina hospital." By the mid-1780s, southern planters and their families again journeyed to Newport for its cool breezes and gentle climate, and, as before, Carolinians led the way. Without them, an Englishman observed, "Newport would sink, as it were, into the earth."[21]

Newport's southern visitors included men like John Rutledge, Jr., South Carolina planter and Federalist congressman, who informed his father-in-law: "We have a pleasant Society here, made up of Carolinians, Marylanders & Virginians & we beguile our time with dining occasionally at each other's houses—sailing—fishing—riding—etc." The Rutledges and other southerners spent several months each year in Newport, usually from May until October. Some stayed longer. Jacob Read, South Carolina's Federalist U.S. senator, actually resided in Newport rather than the Palmetto State when Congress was not in session.[22]

The "pleasant society" of southern planters also embraced Newport families. Southerners invited their Newport friends to the frequent dinner parties they held, occasions marked by an air of casual elegance. "There is not the least fuss, or parade made about them," Rutledge's wife observed. When Sarah Rutledge hosted such a party—"it being my turn"—the festivities began around five o'clock with tea. Afterwards, partygoers played cards and nibbled on almonds, raisins, and apples, all washed down with warm punch and wine. Around ten, guests began helping themselves to cold ham, fowl, butter, bread, biscuits and porter. Sometimes, the socializing led to romance, as it did for the young John

---

1800" (Ph.D. diss., University of California, Berkeley, 1976), 111; Elaine Forman Crane, *A Dependent People: Newport, Rhode Island, in the Revolutionary Era* (New York: Fordham University Press, 1985), 24, 157; and Louis B. Wright and Marion Tinling, eds., *Quebec to Carolina in 1785–1786, Being the Travel Diary and Observations of Robert Hunter, Jr., a Young Merchant of London* (San Marino, Ca.: Huntington Library, 1943), 126.

21. Carl Bridenbaugh, "Colonial Newport as a Summer Resort," *Rhode Island Historical Society Collections*, vol. 26, 2; and Wright and Tinling, eds., *Quebec to Carolina*, 126.

22. John Rutledge, Jr., to Robert Smith, 23 August 1798, John Rutledge, Jr., Papers, SHC. George Rogers, *Evolution of a Federalist: William Loughton Smith of Charleston, 1758–1812* (Columbia: University of South Carolina Press, 1962), 347.

C. Calhoun, who met his lowcountry Carolina cousin and future wife, Floride Colhoun, while he convalesced from an illness in Newport.[23]

The family of James and Elizabeth Hamilton soon joined their fellow planters for the Newport summers. One late spring day, probably in 1791, Major Hamilton and his wife performed for the first time a ritual they repeated for the next several years as they packed up their family and belongings, and loaded everything, including their carriage and horses, onto a trading schooner bound for Rhode Island.[24]

During their sojourns in Newport, the Hamiltons often lodged with the family of a sea captain, Christopher Raymond Perry, and his wife, Sarah. The Perrys lived in a fashionable section of town called the Point, which was also home to numerous well-to-do merchants. Because Christopher was often away on long voyages to Africa and the Caribbean, the family may have kept boarders to provide adult companionship for Sarah, who oversaw a large household that included eight children by 1802.[25]

The ties between well-to-do Newporters like the Perrys and southerners such as the Hamiltons went beyond tea parties and boarding arrangements. Newport citizens who engaged in commerce in the Atlantic world shared key economic, social, and political interests with market-oriented Carolina planters. These ties, confirmed and strengthened through socializing, bound upper-class Yankees and Carolinians firmly together in support of a strong and pragmatic national government that encouraged free trade and protected the institution of slavery.

Newport's commercial success, like the lowcountry's, was inextricably linked to the slave economy. For most of the eighteenth century, Newport's impressive wealth depended heavily on the slave trade. Their mutual dependence on slavery made Yankee shippers and Carolina planters political and economic allies from the earliest days of the republic. In 1776, delegates from Rhode Island and South Carolina stood together against the anti-slavery provisions of Thomas Jefferson's draft of the Declaration of Independence. Between 1803 and 1808, as South Carolina briefly allowed further slave imports, Rhode Island ships delivered

23. Sarah Motte Smith Rutledge to John Rutledge, Jr., 6 January [1799], John Rutledge, Jr., Papers, SHC; and John Niven, *John C. Calhoun and the Price of Union* (Baton Rouge: Louisiana State University Press, 1988), 20–1.

24. Hamilton, "James Hamilton."

25. Samuel Eliot Morison, *"Old Bruin": Commodore Matthew C. Perry, 1794–1858* (Boston: Little, Brown, 1967), 12–3.

nearly 8,000 newly enslaved men and women to Charleston, with Newport captains responsible for 3,500 of them. Newport's ships also hauled
the crops grown by slave labor. After the Revolution, the city's fleet became more involved in the coasting trade that carried to market those
products, such as Major Hamilton's rice, acquired along the Atlantic sea-
board.[26]

The elites of Newport and lowcountry Carolina also supported the
federal Constitution as an instrument to protect their interests in commerce and slavery. The new charter eased interstate commerce by de-
priving the states of the power to discriminate between their own
products and those of other states. As for slavery under the Constitution,
South Carolina's Charles Cotesworth Pinckney, a delegate to the constitutional convention, argued that the new document strengthened the institution by providing for the return of fugitive bondsmen. The
Constitution, then, provided security for the economic bases of both
Newport and Carolina.[27]

Lowcountry South Carolina and New England as a whole provided
stalwart support for adoption of the Constitution and, in the 1790s, for
the Federalist Party that so identified itself with that document. At South
Carolina's May 1788 ratification convention, lowcountry delegates cast
ninety-nine votes for and only one vote against the federal Constitution.
Likewise, Newport and other commercial towns in Rhode Island
strongly favored ratification, but they faced an Anti-Federalist majority
in the state. Facing that opposition, Newport and Providence even considered seceding from the state and joining the Union on their own. By
1790, however, the state's majority conceded to the inevitability of the
new constitutional arrangement, and Rhode Island joined the other
states in a federal government already two years in operation.[28]

The Federalist *Newport Mercury* kept visitors from South Carolina
abreast of the latest political news from home in the 1790s. Carolinians
in the northern port city read toasts offered by the "virtuous and orderly
Citizens" of Ninety-Six District in support of the Alien and Sedition

26. William G. McLoughlin, *Rhode Island: A Bicentennial History* (New York: W. W. Norton, 1978), 107; and Withey, "Population Change," 109–13.

27. Jonathan Elliot, ed., *The Debates in the Several State Conventions, on the Adoption of the
Federal Constitution . . .* , vol. 4, 2nd ed. (Philadelphia: J. B. Lippincott, 1861), 286.

28. Rogers, *Evolution of a Federalist*, 154; McLoughlin, *Rhode Island*, 100–4; and Morris,
Forging of the Union, 316.

Acts, learned the results of lowcountry legislative races, and followed Charleston's Masonic elections. The activities of Palmetto State Federalists such as Congressmen John Rutledge and Robert Goodloe Harper received the sort of attention in the *Mercury*'s columns usually accorded a town's favorite sons.[29]

The Hamilton family certainly shared the Federalist outlook of the lowcountry men and their Newport allies. Federalist sympathies came naturally to someone like Elizabeth Hamilton. As a member of one of the oldest and most politically prominent families in the state, she reflected the commercial orientation and socially conservative attitudes of the lowcountry gentry. Although her politically active father and half-brother had died during the Revolution and thus missed the party conflict of the early republic, her stepfather, General Moultrie, served as a Federalist governor of South Carolina in the early 1790s. The Revolutionary War, as much as his marriage into a commercial-planting family, steered Major James Hamilton's political views towards those of his Federalist lowcountry peers and Newport friends. Serving for over seven years in battles from Massachusetts to South Carolina, Hamilton developed a cosmopolitan sense of "continentalism," the belief in the need for a strong central government to prevent the states' petty jealousies from undermining the achievement of an independent America. Moreover, on at least two occasions during his military career, Hamilton confronted unruly Continental troops and thereby gained new appreciation for the notion of social order Federalists held dear. During the mutiny of the Pennsylvania line in 1781, Major Hamilton was forced to abandon an effort to negotiate a settlement when a rebellious soldier threatened to kill him. Then, at the end of the war, he tried unsuccessfully to bring order to Philadelphia after a mob of unpaid soldiers forced Congress to desert the city for more tranquil surroundings in Princeton. These episodes raised serious reservations in his mind about rule by "the people." Doubtless, too, Major Hamilton's wartime frustrations in obtaining supplies from an uncooperative Governor Thomas Jefferson contributed to his sympathizing with Jefferson's Federalist foes in the 1790s.[30]

29. *Newport Mercury*, 11 December 1798, 5 March 1799, and 8 September 1801. For coverage of South Carolina leaders, see 6, 13, and 27 November 1798; 23 April 1799; 25 June 1799; 13 August 1799; and 25 November 1799.

30. Robert Sobel and John Raimo, *Biographical Directory of the Governors of the United States, 1789–1978* vol. 4 (Westport, Conn.: Meckler Books, 1978), 1388; Jackson Turner Main, *Political Parties Before the Constitution* (Chapel Hill: University of North Carolina Press, 1973; paper-

For several years, while his father went back to the Santee River plantation at the end of the summer season, young James Hamilton remained in Newport with his mother through the winter months. There, he attended school and made friendships that lasted well into his adult years. Other leading Carolinians sent their boys to Newport to take advantage of its good schools, so James was not the sole southerner during the school term. Hamilton also befriended Yankee boys and became especially close to two of the Perry sons whose house he shared, Oliver Hazard Perry and Matthew Calbraith Perry, later famous naval officers.

A Scot, John Frazer, taught Hamilton a smattering of Greek, Latin, mathematics, grammar, and rhetoric. Frazer's school, the only one in town offering a classical education, stood atop the hierarchy of local educational institutions. Even within this elite school, southerners such as Hamilton enjoyed a degree of privilege over their Yankee friends. While the local boys took their turns at cleaning the classroom each week, the comparatively rich—or self-consciously aristocratic—southern students often paid others to perform this chore.[31]

After three or four years of schooling under Mr. Frazer, Hamilton left Newport in the late 1790s to continue his studies in Dedham, Massachusetts. His move may have been occasioned by the departure of his surrogate family, the Perrys, from Newport in 1797, as well as by his parents' desire that he should receive special preparation for college. In Dedham, Hamilton lodged with and took lessons from a Congregationalist minister, Thomas Thacher, with a solid record for getting his students into Harvard.[32]

Under Thacher's tutelage, Hamilton learned more than Greek and Latin, for the minister was a firm Federalist. In 1788, Dedham's citizens sent Thacher to the Massachusetts convention considering the federal Constitution. There, with fellow Dedhamite and future influential Federalist congressman Fisher Ames, Thacher argued successfully for ratifi-

back ed., New York: W. W. Norton, 1974), 32–3, 385–7; and Alexander Garden, *Anecdotes of the Revolutionary War in America, with Sketches of Character of Persons the Most Distinguished, in the Southern States, For Civil and Military Purposes* (Charleston: A. E. Miller, 1822; reprint ed., Spartanburg: Reprint Company, 1972), 3:198, 2:424.

31. Channing, *Early Recollections*, 50–4; Alexander Slidell Mackenzie, *The Life of Commodore Oliver Hazard Perry*, vol. 1 (New York: Harper & Brothers, 1840), 28.

32. Joseph F. Kett, *Rites of Passage: Adolescence in America 1790 to the Present* (New York: Basic Books, 1977), 18; George Willis Cooke, *A History of the Clapboard Trees or Third Parish, Dedham, Mass.* (Boston: Geo. H. Ellis, 1887), chapter 8.

cation. Studying with Thacher, Hamilton absorbed, as he had in Newport and in the lowcountry, Federalist views about social hierarchy, the importance of unfettered commerce, and a strong national government overseen by the best men. Even when the Federalists lost support among planter families like his own because of the national party's tilt to manufacturing, Hamilton remained true to the basic lessons he had learned.[33]

Unlike most of Thacher's young scholars, Hamilton never attended college. Instead he returned to his family's home in South Carolina while in his late teens. Most likely, he did so because of family considerations. His mother died sometime just after the turn of the century, while he was still a teenager, and his father, experiencing difficulties as a planter, needed young James to take over some of the duties of plantation management.

The senior Hamilton's problems were not entirely of his own making. A series of floods damaged or destroyed crops for several seasons in the 1790s. Then, too, sometimes he diverted his financial resources from the plantation to troubled kin. His wife's stepfather, General Moultrie, faced financial difficulties after the war, and the Hamiltons stepped in to help him. Around the time of her marriage, Elizabeth had co-signed a promissory note with Moultrie so he could secure a large loan. A few years later, the Hamiltons gave Moultrie's creditor a mortgage on twenty of their slaves to "better secure" the debt. But even had Major Hamilton not been touched by natural calamities or his stepfather's debts, it is likely that little of the gilt of Carolina's golden age of rice planting would have rubbed off on him. As one of his grandsons later observed, the major was "wholly unsuited" to planting. Under his management, the value of his wife's estate declined from an estimated value of $250,000 at the time of his marriage to approximately $6,000 at the time of his death in 1833.[34]

The older Hamilton apparently became more dependent on his son, especially after a fateful incident following his wife's death. While Major Hamilton dined at his plantation with General Moultrie and John Bow-

33. Rachel N. Klein, *Unification of a Slave State: The Rise of the Planter Class in the South Carolina Backcountry, 1760–1808* (Chapel Hill: University of North Carolina Press, 1990), 257–9.

34. See petition of James Hamilton, Sr., and others to the South Carolina House of Representatives, 12 December 1795, SCDAH; Mortgage to Isaac Dubose, dated 25 August 1787, in Charleston Mortgages, 3E, p. 465, SCDAH; Hamilton, "James Hamilton."

man, his wife's brother-in-law, an unpleasant topic arose: Bowman accused Hamilton of fathering a child out of wedlock with a northern
woman. The ensuing argument, fueled by a generous consumption of alcohol, proceeded immediately to a duel without observance of the usual
protocol of notes and seconds that might have allowed the principals to
reconsider matters while sober. On the field of honor, Bowman got off a
shot that caught Hamilton just below his right knee. The severity of the
wound forced the amputation of the major's lower right leg to save his
life. The embarrassing circumstances of a drunken duel about a bastard
child led to the creation of a cover story about the incident. Major Hamilton, it was said, while overseeing the loading of rice onto a boat, had
fallen and mangled his leg between two palmetto logs on his wharf. As
far as the public knew, Hamilton lost his leg in the line of duty as a
planter. But his son knew better. It became his filial duty to preserve his
father's reputation by concealing his secrets.[35]

Ultimately, young James could not save his father. He even gave up
his claims to family property when he attained majority in 1807 so that
his father could have a free hand. Yet that was not enough. Debt and an
adverse court judgment forced Major Hamilton in 1811 to sell his remaining slaves and parcels of land, including four hundred acres granted
him by Congress for his military service. Most importantly, he parted
with his North Santee plantation, the jewel of his wife's inheritance and
the birthplace of his son. A few months after the sale, the major moved
in with his daughter, Hannah, and her new husband, Samuel Prioleau,
Jr. He spent the rest of his life in town, reliving wartime exploits with
fellow veterans on his piazza or at often bawdy meetings of the Society
of the Cincinnati.[36]

Young James Hamilton had a great legacy to live up to, but by his
early twenties, his links to the hallowed past had either been broken or
severely weakened. This heir of the Lynches stood as something of an
outsider in lowcountry society. His mother lay buried, as were all of his
male Lynch relatives. The only grandfather he ever knew, William
Moultrie, had died, too, heavily in debt. The Lynch lands and their
slaves, sources of wealth and status, were lost to him before he could
claim them as his own. His father remained his key connection to past

35. Hamilton, "James Hamilton."
36. *Charleston Courier*, 29 January and 23 March 1811; and Hamilton, "James Hamilton."

glory, but that linkage was somewhat problematic. Hamilton respected his father enormously and would later teach his own children to look upon Major Hamilton "as some superior being on account of his distinction in the Army of Genl. Washington." Yet the younger Hamilton knew the war hero's very human deficiencies, let alone his shortcomings as a lowcountry planter. It would be up to James Hamilton, Jr., to take his heritage and make something new of it himself.[37]

37. Hamilton, "James Hamilton."

CHAPTER 2

Staking His Claim

LIKE THE PASSING OF A PLEASANT DREAM, the prospect that James Hamilton might live as a Lynch heir, commanding slaves on a rice plantation, disappeared, leaving only regret that it could not be so. Upon reaching his majority, young James forfeited his claims to the South Santee place so that his indebted father could dispose of the property unencumbered. James, in his early twenties, left the plantation behind and moved to Charleston.

Bustling business activity and a diverse population characterized the Charleston that greeted Hamilton around 1807. The commercial hub of South Carolina, Charleston was the only city in the state worthy of the designation. With a total population just under twenty-five thousand, Charleston ranked as the nation's fifth largest city in 1810 and certainly, too, as one of the most cosmopolitan. Citizens with roots in all parts of western Europe called Charleston home: French Protestants, Sephardic Jews, Germans, Irish, Scots and, of course, the English. But these accounted for less than half of the city's residents. Fifty-three percent of Charlestonians looked upon Africa as their ancestral homeland; the vast majority of these black residents were chattel slaves, but many were legally free.[1]

In Charleston, Hamilton took up the law, a natural enough career for one who took pride in being related to Thomas Lynch III, a product of London's Middle Temple. Moreover, the Charleston bar enjoyed a national reputation of great distinction, and Hamilton could only be pleased to be associated with the fine lawyers who composed it. He stud-

---

1. For population figures, see Coclanis, *Shadow of a Dream*, 115–6.

ied with one of the city's leading attorneys, William Drayton, scion of an eminent tidewater family and a former Federalist state representative. In 1809, at twenty-three, Hamilton joined the bar.[2]

Hamilton quickly discovered that, while he relished the prestige of being a Charleston lawyer, he disliked the tedious work often required of an attorney. He was too restlessly ambitious and eager to make his mark in the world to spend his time poring over law books and contracts. Politics more than the law captured the imagination of this Lynch heir. In 1810, he entered politics as private secretary to Governor Henry Middleton. From this vantage point, he learned about state government and the men who made it work. And, as much as he disliked it, he continued to practice law as his main occupation.[3]

For Hamilton, the best thing about being a lawyer was that it allowed him to live in Charleston and rub shoulders, socially as well as professionally, with the "best people." He became a popular young man in Charleston society and served as a manager of the city's "bachelor ball" in 1811. His popularity stemmed partly from family connections and his striking good looks; one of Hamilton's Newport companions remembered him as "remarkable for his beauty." More important, though, were his gregariousness and a natural charm that impressed practically everyone he met. Contacts with important people and personal popularity were ingredients that, when combined with his ambition to achieve the greatness of his male relatives, laid the foundation for a promising political career.[4]

War delayed the realization of his nascent political aspirations. In 1812, the United States declared war on Great Britain after a long conflict over commerce and the rights of American sailors. The heady patri-

2. Hamilton's pride in Thomas Lynch III manifested itself in a short biographical sketch he wrote of his half-uncle for publication in a book on the signers of the Declaration of Independence. See JH to John Sanderson, 15 January 1821, Ferdinand Julius Dreer Collection, Governors of States II, HSP. For background on Drayton, see N. Louise Bailey, ed., *Biographical Directory of the South Carolina House of Representatives*, vol. 4 (Columbia: University of South Carolina Press, 1984), 164–6; John Belton O'Neall, *Biographical Sketches of the Bench and Bar of South Carolina*, vol. 1 (Charleston: S. G. Courtenay, 1859), 305–23. On age of entry in professions, see Joseph F. Kett, *Rites of Passage: Adolescence in America, 1790 to the Present* (New York: Basic Books, 1977), 35.

3. See document of appointment, 1810, JHP, SHC.

4. *Charleston Courier*, 14 March 1811. George Gibbs Channing, *Early Recollections of Newport, R.I., from the Year 1793 to 1811* (Boston: Nichols & Noyes, 1868), 59.

otism of the struggle captivated Hamilton. In a sense, this war continued
the revolutionary struggle waged by his Lynch relatives, his father, and
his step-grandfather Moultrie. Their glorious efforts established the political independence of America; now came his opportunity to help complete the Revolution by making the country economically free of Britain
as well. Young South Carolinians—John C. Calhoun, William Lowndes,
and Langdon Cheves—led the war cry in Congress and stirred the patriotic resolve of their fellow citizens back home. Hamilton responded with
alacrity to the call to arms. Just as his father and General Moultrie gained
fame in the Revolution, Hamilton wished to earn a hero's laurels upon
the battlefield.

Commissioned a lieutenant in the U.S. Army, Hamilton began his
military career with brief duty in South Carolina before joining the staff
of General George Izard in New York. In late 1813 and early 1814,
Hamilton fought in short campaigns on the Canadian frontier but spent
much time drilling or on leave. Frustrated with General Izard for not
pursuing the British more vigorously, he blamed his commander for his
lack of a chance to distinguish himself in combat. His hopes of duplicat-
ing his father's wartime achievements went unfulfilled.[5]

Hamilton found consolation for his poor martial record in a victory
of another sort. On leave in New York City in 1812, he won the heart of
Elizabeth Mathews Heyward. Born in Charleston in 1795, Elizabeth
shared with her suitor lowcountry Carolina roots. Like the Lynches, the
Heywards were a leading rice-planting family. Elizabeth's paternal
grandfather, Thomas Heyward, Jr., served with Hamilton's grandfather
in the Continental Congress and joined Hamilton's uncle in signing the
Declaration of Independence.[6]

Elizabeth never knew her wealthy, aristocratic father, Daniel; within
weeks of her birth, he died from a fever contracted on his Savannah River
plantation. Elizabeth spent her first years with her mother, born Ann
Sarah Trezevant, a woman of a more humble social background than
Daniel Heyward; Ann's father was a French-speaking Huguenot tailor
in Charleston. Mother and daughter lived in rather straitened financial
conditions following Daniel Heyward's death, as other members of the

5. Glenn, "James Hamilton," 7–8.
6. Hamilton, "James Hamilton"; and James B. Heyward, "The Heyward Family of South
Carolina," *SCHM* 59 (July 1958): 143–58.

Heyward clan legally contested Elizabeth's inheritance from Daniel. Within three years of Daniel's death, Ann married well for a second time. Her new husband, Nicholas Cruger, Jr., came from a wealthy New York mercantile family with extensive business dealings in the Caribbean. Like Hamilton's family, the Crugers had connections to South Carolina's revolutionary past, though on the "wrong" side: Nicholas's uncle commanded Loyalist forces at the backcountry village of Ninety-Six in 1781. The Crugers also enjoyed a relationship with a leading patriot figure: Nicholas's father, while handling the family business from St. Croix in the early 1770s, took a young Alexander Hamilton under his wing and helped put the future Federalist chief through King's College in New York City.[7]

Raised mainly in New York among her younger Cruger half-siblings, Elizabeth became engaged to James in late 1812 after a brief courtship. After a time at the Canadian front, James returned to New York City on leave only to discover other men vying for his fiancée's affections. He charged one of them, William Gracie, with trying to steal Elizabeth. Although Gracie's attentions were, Elizabeth later claimed, wholly innocent, Hamilton saw things differently and promptly challenged Gracie to a duel. The two met one dawn on the Long Island shore, where Hamilton inflicted a wound that left Gracie with a lifelong limp. James's right to Elizabeth firmly established, the two wed on November 15, 1813, at St. Paul's Episcopal Church in Newark, New Jersey.[8]

The marriage proved financially felicitous for Hamilton and provided the opportunity to establish himself as a lowcountry planter. By the time

7. A. S. Salley, Jr., "Daniel Trezevant, Huguenot, and Some of His Descendants," *SCHM* 3: 44–6; John S. Pancake, *This Destructive War: The British Campaign in the Carolinas, 1780–1782* (Tuscaloosa: University of Alabama Press, 1985), 209–10. Also see Robert D. Bass, *Ninety Six: The Struggle for the South Carolina Back Country* (Lexington: Sandlapper Store, 1978), esp. chapter 20. Stanley Elkins and Eric McKitrick, *The Age of Federalism: The Early American Republic, 1788–1800* (New York: Oxford University Press, 1993), 94–5; James Thomas Flexner, *The Young Hamilton: A Biography* (Boston: Little, Brown, 1978), 34–4.

8. Despite the tradition that Hamilton fought fourteen duels, his encounter with Gracie was in all likelihood both his first and last appearance as a combatant on the field of honor. Although he later served as a second in several duels, there is no evidence that he ever again participated as a principal in one of these gentlemanly rituals. The evidence to support Hamilton's alleged propensity for dueling is thin, not to say non-existent. Joseph Gregoire de Roulhac Hamilton relies on an unnamed authority, and other historians apparently rely on him. See J. G. de Roulhac Hamilton, "Among the Present: James Hamilton, Jr. of South Carolina," 4, in box 3, folder 35, JHP, SHC. For marriage date, see Hamilton, "James Hamilton."

of the wedding, the various legal contests about Elizabeth's inheritance had concluded in her favor. The property she brought to the marriage comprised three plantations and more than two hundred slaves. Hamilton's marriage restored what his father, through mismanagement and poor luck, had denied him: membership in the circle of great lowcountry planters.[9]

The couple soon moved to one of Elizabeth's plantations, located on Callawassie Island in the Colleton River, to try life as plantation master and mistress. Neither knew his or her role very well. More familiar with the salons of New York than the swamps of Carolina, Elizabeth would need time to adjust to the climate as well as to being one of the few whites in a sea of black slaves. Although familiar with the lowcountry, James, too, required a period of adjustment to his new life, for the Callawassie plantation produced short-staple cotton, not the rice he knew from his youth.[10]

Even before they moved south, they had begun a family: their first child, James, arrived in August 1814. Two other sons followed in rapid succession at Callawassie—Daniel Heyward in 1816 and Thomas Lynch in 1817. Eventually, Elizabeth bore a total of eleven children—ten boys and one girl—over a twenty-two-year period.[11]

While James entrusted the rearing of their children to Elizabeth and slave nurses, he essayed, rather half-heartedly, to be a planter. With higher cotton prices in the immediate post-war years, Hamilton might have been content to raise a profitable crop. Even before prices tumbled in the Panic of 1819, however, Hamilton had become disenchanted. A planter's life was not so pleasing as he had dreamed; he found the island boring and "exceedingly irksome."[12]

To alleviate his ennui, he occasionally visited the nearby village, Coosawatchie, located midway between Charleston and Savannah. There he traded news with other planters and met with lawyers in town to try cases at the parish courthouse. Still, to a man accustomed to the faster pace of Charleston and New York, Coosawatchie provided little stimulation. The most excitement he encountered during his years as resident master

---

9. Virginia Glenn Crane, "Two Women, White and Brown, in the South Carolina Court of Equity, 1842–1845," *SCHM* 96: 199–200.

10. Hamilton, "James Hamilton."

11. See family and genealogical papers in box 3, folder 34, JHP, SHC.

12. Hamilton, "James Hamilton."

of Callawassie occurred far to the north of the island. In late 1818, he traveled to New Jersey to serve as a second for his childhood friend, war hero Oliver Hazard Perry, in Perry's duel with Marine captain John Heth. At the same field of honor where Aaron Burr had ended Alexander Hamilton's life fourteen years earlier, Hamilton and Perry's other second, Captain Stephen Decatur, watched as Perry refused to return Heth's fire. When word spread of Perry's refusal to fire, commentators generally concurred that Hamilton's friend exhibited superior honor. Hamilton reveled in Perry's increased stature and his own role as Perry's confidant.[13]

The trip to New Jersey only compounded Hamilton's sense of isolation upon his return to Callawassie. He longed to act on a larger stage, amid the activity of Charleston. Moreover, he wanted at last to try his hand at politics in a place he knew well (perhaps inspired by visiting the nation's capital on his journey to the duel). So he resolved to relocate to Charleston, even if it meant a return to the tedium of the law as his main means of support. Consequently, during 1819 he transformed himself from a parish planter into a city lawyer. Selling his plantations and slaves, he purchased a house at the corner of Coming and Bull Streets in Charleston. Fortunately for Hamilton's plans to resume the law, William Drayton had recently given up his legal practice to accept a judicial post, and the older man arranged to steer some of his clients to his protégé. Drayton also sold Hamilton a lot in St. Michael's Alley, well placed for a law office. By the end of 1819, Hamilton was back in the thick of things in Charleston.[14]

Although the practice of law still ill suited Hamilton's temperament, he found a partner who made his professional life more bearable. During his sojourn at Callawassie, Hamilton made the acquaintance of James Petigru, a young lawyer originally from upcountry Abbeville District. The bored planter recognized Petigru's good legal mind and invited him to leave the obscurity of a country parish practice for more lucrative cases in the city. Petigru promptly accepted. Once settled into their practice, Hamilton left most of the careful legal research to Petigru, who thrived

13. Charles J. Dutton, *Oliver Hazard Perry* (New York: Longmans, Green, 1935), 248–53, 262–3.

14. Glenn, "James Hamilton," 13; *Charleston City Directory*, 1822, 46; and James Petigru Carson, ed., *Life, Letters and Speeches of James Louis Petigru, The Union Man of South Carolina* (Washington: H. L. & J. B. McQueen, 1920), 62.

on such work, while Hamilton used his contacts and charm to solicit business. Their contrasting personalities made them ideal law partners and, strangely enough, lifelong friends.[15]

Upon returning to Charleston, Hamilton became actively involved in politics. He approached elective office with a feeling of entitlement because of his family's long history of public officeholding. At the same time, he understood that the aristocratic style of politics practiced by his Lynch relatives did not play quite so well anymore. After South Carolina extended suffrage to all adult white men in 1810, gentlemen needed at least to *appear* to be catering to the masses. "You must get close to the people in order to manage them," wrote a young Federalist in 1816 in words that might have been penned by Hamilton himself. In the fall of 1819, the new resident of Charleston began his career in elective office by winning a special election for an unexpired state house seat.[16]

When Hamilton entered the legislature, he began to work closely with men who would be his allies—and sometimes foes—for years to come. A few legislators boasted pedigrees at least as distinguished as Hamilton's own. Henry Laurens Pinckney, for instance, was the son of Charles Pinckney, member of the federal Constitutional Convention, and grandson of Continental Congress president Henry Laurens. Others were men of great educational attainment, including Joel Roberts Poinsett, an Edinburgh-trained physician, and Hugh Swinton Legaré, a literary scholar and attorney. At least one legislator was a close relative, his brother-in-law, Samuel Prioleau. (Prioleau was actually Hamilton's brother-in-law twice: he married Hamilton's sister, Hannah Motte, in 1811, and then, after her death, wed another Hamilton sister, Elizabeth Lynch, in 1818.) Hamilton added legislative friends from humbler backgrounds, too, including George McDuffie of Edgefield. A poor farmboy from Georgia whom the Calhoun family had practically adopted, McDuffie became a close political ally and personal friend of the new Charleston representative. Indeed, Hamilton's charm and good graces made him popular among all of his new colleagues.[17]

15. Carson, ed., *Petigru*, 62–3.

16. Quotation from David Hackett Fischer, *The Revolution of American Conservatism: The Federalist Party in the Era of Jeffersonian Democracy* (New York: Harper & Row, 1965), 33.

17. Freehling, *Prelude to Civil War*, 182. Alexander Moore, ed., *Biographical Directory of the South Carolina House of Representatives*, vol. 5 (Columbia: South Carolina Department of Archives and History, 1992), 214–5.

Organized political parties meant little in the legislature when Hamilton entered in 1819. The once-powerful Federalist Party was practically nonexistent. Years of Jeffersonian Republican rule, defections of key Federalists, and a surprisingly good outcome to the War of 1812 hastened the anti-war Federalists' retreat into political oblivion. A burgeoning upcountry electorate proved most critical in delivering the state to the Republicans after 1800. These upcountrymen, both small farmers and new cotton-growing planters, resented the social pretensions of the low-country Federalist gentry.[18]

The very lack of an opposition party spurred factionalism among Republicans that made the state's politics as divisive as during the time of old two-party conflicts. Their partisan muscles weakened by the lack of a vigorous Federalist opposition, some of those claiming the mantle of Jefferson and Madison succumbed to ideological softness in the post-war years. A portion of Republicans found Federalist ideas less threatening with the defeat of state and national Federalist organizations, and this group of Republicans accepted policies once anathema among Jeffersonians. In the wake of the war, they advocated measures to bind the different parts of the United States more closely together for military reasons. This new nationalism also reflected their embrace of the "market revolution," that quickening and extension of capitalist enterprise that the War of 1812 encouraged. These Republicans endorsed government action not only to protect the country from external enemies, but also to create a larger, national market to accommodate a liberated entrepreneurialism.[19]

In that spirit, John C. Calhoun, Langdon Cheves, and William Lowndes, the three most prominent South Carolina congressional Republicans, labored to forge these national bonds through legislation. Calhoun's efforts especially shaped the 1816 tariff's higher duties, the bill creating the Second Bank of the United States, and the Bonus Bill, an ambitious plan of federally financed canal and road building. After leaving Congress, Calhoun continued to implement this neo-Federalist pro-

18. James H. Broussard, *The Southern Federalists, 1800–1816* (Baton Rouge: Louisiana State University Press, 1978), 295, 300.

19. For explorations of the relationship of liberal capitalism to the War of 1812 and its leaders, see Stephen Watts, *The Republic Reborn: War and the Making of Liberal America, 1790–1820* (Baltimore: Johns Hopkins University Press, 1987); and Charles Sellers, *The Market Revolution: Jacksonian America, 1815–1846* (New York: Oxford University Press, 1991).

gram as James Monroe's war secretary, while Cheves pursued it as president of the Bank of the United States from 1819 to 1822. Supporters of neo-Federalism, known as New or National Republicans, opposed Old Republicans, or Radicals, who hewed more closely to older Jeffersonian views about limited government and states' rights. The state's Radicals followed U.S. Senator William Smith of upcountry York District, and Old Republicans throughout the Union looked to Treasury Secretary William Crawford of Georgia for leadership.[20]

In South Carolina, the neo-Federalists dominated the political landscape as political leaders pursued goals on the state level akin to those that Calhoun and company supported in Washington. For instance, the state legislature proposed an ambitious network of canals, which Hamilton enthusiastically supported. The planter-dominated assembly understood the importance of improved transportation to the more efficient marketing of crops. As a Charlestonian, Hamilton especially appreciated the increased business the canal system would funnel into his city.[21]

Not only did Hamilton support the intervention of the state government in the economy, he also advocated an active federal authority. Indeed, the majority of his legislative colleagues joined him in endorsing a strong federal role in the economy, as a debate over the federal tariff of 1820 demonstrates. The 1820 tariff, which Congress narrowly defeated, called for higher duties than the 1816 law. The bill involved questions of constitutional interpretation as well as political economy. Strict constructionists condemned the bill because, as they pointed out, the Constitution does not expressly grant Congress the power to lay duties designed to protect and encourage manufacturing. The tariff also drew fire from agricultural and shipping interests, who charged that its burdens fell disproportionately on their constituencies and gave unfair ad-

20. Sellers, *Market Revolution*, 70–9, and John Lauritz Larson, *Internal Improvement: National Public Works and the Promise of Popular Government in the Early United States* (Chapel Hill: University of North Carolina Press, 2001), especially 66–9. Lowndes, who approved of federally financed internal improvements, voted against the Bonus Bill because he opposed using the federal government's "bonus" from its stock in Bank of United States as the funding source. See Carl J. Vipperman, *William Lowndes and the Transition of Southern Politics, 1782–1822* (Chapel Hill: University of North Carolina Press, 1989), 150; and *Annals of Congress*, 30:934 (1817).

21. See, for instance, Hamilton's vote for the expenditure of $250,000 in state funds on internal improvement projects. *South Carolina House Journal*, 17 December 1821, 149, in *State Records*, reel 511.

vantages to manufacturers. In several South Carolina towns, meetings of citizens adopted anti-tariff resolutions during the spring of 1820. The legislature considered the issue when Representative Pleasant May, a Smith man from Chesterfield District, introduced anti-tariff resolutions couched in strong states' rights language.

Despite opposition to the 1820 bill in the state, the house soundly rejected May's resolutions; only May supported them. With Hamilton presiding as chairman of the committee of the whole, the majority adopted a report critical of May's anti-tariff position and emphatically supportive of broad federal power. Although the report labeled the protective tariff "pernicious," it also termed the restrictive policy "premature." The use of the latter word suggested that the majority foresaw the day when the country would be ripe for protectionism. Moreover, the house explicitly recognized Congress's exclusive authority to enact "all laws relating to Commerce," including the right to pass a protectionist tariff. Legislators also criticized the introduction of the resolutions in the first place. In strong language, they decried "the practice, unfortunately become too common, of arraying upon questions of national policy, the States as distinct and independent Sovereignties, in opposition to, or, what is much the same thing with a view to exercise a control over, the General Government." South Carolina should rather, they said, "adhere to those wise, liberal and magnanimous principles" that recognized supreme congressional power to legislate "on this, as on every other occasion on which the general welfare of this Republic is in question." With these resolute words, Hamilton and the overwhelming majority of the house provided an able defense of neo-Federalism.[22]

Outside as well as within the legislative chambers, Hamilton championed broad federal power. In 1821, for instance, he endorsed the views of his legislative colleague and fellow nationalist George McDuffie when the latter became embroiled in a war of words with states' rights supporters. A series of articles, published in a Georgia newspaper and signed by "the Trio," had condemned the drift of the Monroe administration away from "pure" Jeffersonianism. When McDuffie's blistering nationalist reply appeared in pamphlet form, Hamilton provided a laudatory intro-

22. Philip Frederick Wild, "South Carolina Politics: 1816–1833" (Ph.D. diss., University of Pennsylvania, 1949), 44; and *South Carolina House Journal*, 6 December 1820, 78–9, in *State Records*, reel 511 (quotation).

duction. In praising McDuffie's views, Hamilton compared them favorably to the *Federalist* essays and to John Marshall's decision in *Cohens* v. *Virginia* of the previous year in which the chief justice held that federal courts could review certain state court decisions. Hamilton shuddered at the thought of a federal government hampered by the constraints advocated by supporters of states' rights. The Trio's constitutional vision, he wrote disapprovingly, "would limit the sphere of our National Charter merely to those suicidal efforts, which in the end would have produced its dissolution, as a matter of inevitable consequence." Hamilton's particular talent, as he demonstrated on this and other occasions, did not consist in explicating original theories or a cogent political philosophy. That he left others, especially to McDuffie and later to Calhoun. Rather, his gift lay in crafting effective propaganda, often with a sarcastic twist. For instance, he dismissed the Trio's doctrine of state sovereignty as "an ill omened blast" from "the Ancient Dominion" of Virginia, characterized by a "dull and vexatious dissonance." The young politician clearly relished his role as part of the dominant faction and as defender of the national interest.[23]

Of course, the national interest was not nearly so objective a concept as Hamilton or indeed others treated it. Personal financial interests entered prominently into decisions on questions of banks, tariffs, and internal improvements. For Hamilton, as a resident of a commercial city, government encouragement of economic expansion made perfect sense. Increased commercial traffic in Charleston could only benefit him and his neighbors. Moreover, Hamilton could well imagine fulfilling his political ambitions as a member of the political majority. One might expect that the Missouri debates of 1819–21 would have tempered Hamilton's enthusiasm for broad constructionism, yet there is little evidence it did. Indeed, his pamphlet defense of McDuffie's nationalism came on the heels of the Missouri controversy, and in a July 4 address in 1821, just months after the final Missouri vote, he engaged in unqualified nationalism. "The union can only annoy the Demagogue, who lives," Hamilton intoned, ". . . in the delusions of a distempered state of public opinion." In Hamilton's estimation, the Missouri episode was simply another in a

23. "National and State Rights, Considered by the Hon. George McDuffie, Under the Signature of One of the People in Reply to the 'Trio,' with the advertisement prefixed to it, Generally Attributed to Major James Hamilton, Jr. when published in 1821" (Charleston: W. S. Blain, 1830), iii, iv.

series of those "distempered" disagreements over slavery that ended with southerners winning what they desired, a new slave state. Cooler heads recognized that South Carolinians could still protect the state's interests in Washington's committee rooms and legislative chambers. The overriding consideration for Hamilton was that the nationalism espoused by neo-Federalist Republicans amounted to the lowcountry's interest, and his own, writ large.[24]

Hamilton's investment in post-war nationalism was more than a financial or political one, however; it was also emotional and psychological. Feeling, as much as rational calculation, shaped his views, for Hamilton's faith in expansive federal power flowed to a large degree from the Federalist influences of his formative years in the lowcountry and New England. A strong federal government supported all he held dear—and had always been supported by all whom he held dear. The lowcountry gentry, the Newport merchants, and his old Dedham teacher all championed the Constitution over the Articles of Confederation and later fought for the Federalist Party. The Federalist vision, he learned early in life, represented the culmination of the Revolution, which had enormous personal meaning for him. His self-definition in large measure consisted of being the son of a Revolutionary hero and a relative of the Continental Congress Lynches. The federal government was their legacy to Hamilton; to support and enhance its powers was his filial as well as patriotic duty.

Hamilton's first major speech as a legislator hinted at the emotional meanings nationalism held for him. Just a few months before Hamilton entered the General Assembly, Oliver Hazard Perry had died during a naval expedition to Venezuela. With florid oratory, Hamilton paid tribute not only to his old friend but also, implicitly, to the bond that linked South Carolinians to other Americans. By honoring the New England–born hero and his victory at far-off Lake Erie, Hamilton emphasized the common purpose of all Americans. Gently reminding his listeners of his personal "intimacy and acquaintance" with the dead commodore, Hamilton claimed his share of the national glory Perry exemplified. He further suggested his personal stake in this brand of patriotism as he called on the state's congressional delegation to make "a liberal enquiry of what

24. JH, "An Oration, Delivered on the Fourth of July, 1821, Before the Cincinnati and Revolution Societies" (Charleston: A. E. Miller, 1821), 19.

provision it may be proper to make for his bereaved mother, wife and children." Although providing for a hero's widow and orphans is natural enough, creating a pension for his mother seems unusual. For Hamilton, however, procuring a pension for Sarah Perry made perfect sense because of his relationship with her during his Newport years. Not precisely a surrogate mother to him, Sarah Perry certainly was a maternal presence in his life. He knew her, and that sufficed as a reason for seeking federal funds for her support. In Hamilton's view, the nation had been created by and for such persons as his family and the Perrys. It was only proper, then, that the government should grant her payment.[25]

Neo-Federalism, then, accorded with Hamilton's financial and social interests, his psychological connection to his Revolutionary heritage, and his own political ambitions. The fate of the Union was intimately linked to his own. As he would later sum up his post-war political views, he considered the federal government "magnificent . . . invincible in war, beneficent in peace, holding in exact equipose the scales of justice."[26]

Presidential politics provided Hamilton with an opportunity to demonstrate his kind of nationalism and to hone practical political skills. Shortly after Monroe's 1820 re-election, politicos turned their attention to the 1824 race to choose his successor. Numerous candidates received mention. As Hamilton observed the early jockeying among potential contenders, he approvingly noted that his state might very well cast its votes for Monroe's secretary of state, John Quincy Adams, should no leading South Carolina Republican appear electable. By the fall of 1821, however, Hamilton decided that a South Carolinian could and should be elected—Congressman William Lowndes. Not yet forty, Lowndes came from a politically active family that included older brothers who had served as Federalist state legislators and one of whom had been Charleston's Federalist congressman from 1801 to 1805. A state legislator himself before his election to Congress, Lowndes had distinguished himself in his post ever since. Following the war, of course, he supported neo-Federalist policies such as the Bank and internal improvements, although, with the proposed duties of 1820, he began to turn against higher tariffs.[27]

25. *South Carolina House Journal*, 11 December 1819, 146, in *State Records*, reel 511; and *NR* 17 (26 February 1820): 450–2.

26. *Southern Patriot*, 9 July 1830.

27. "National and States Rights," v.

Hamilton considered Lowndes sound on all of the important political issues of the day. Best of all, Lowndes was a nationalist Hamilton knew. Who would make a better president than a fellow lowcountry Republican with Federalist roots, a man who shared his own social background and from whom he had even purchased slaves? At a December 1821 legislative caucus, Hamilton spearheaded the effort that resulted in the unanimous nomination of Lowndes for the presidency, despite a considerable number of members initially preferring Secretary of War John C. Calhoun of the upcountry Pendleton District. But Hamilton and his allies convinced the majority that Lowndes gave South Carolina better hope for obtaining the executive mansion.

Before commencing his campaign for Lowndes, Hamilton neglected one crucial detail: he failed to notify Lowndes of his plans. Unfortunately for Hamilton, Lowndes displayed more than a little reluctance to run. If Lowndes harbored presidential aspirations, he kept quiet about them. He seems genuinely to have been uncertain about running and clearly unwilling to be perceived as hungry for the office. In keeping with traditional political sensibilities, Lowndes protested that the presidency was an office that should not be sought or refused. Hamilton consequently spent the next two or three months attempting to induce the congressman to accept the nomination.

As Hamilton implored Lowndes to run, he plotted political strategies to remove potential obstacles from the candidate's path. He schemed to defeat Joel Poinsett, then Charleston's congressman, should he endorse Calhoun. Hamilton also promised to "make arrangements for your having an efficient man who can take the field against McDuffie," Hamilton's nationalist ally, but by then a key Calhoun supporter in Congress. Touting his connections to the editors of all four of Charleston's newspapers, Hamilton worked to line up their support for Lowndes. As part of his press strategy, Hamilton suggested that Lowndes do a particular favor for Isaac Harby, editor of the *City Gazette*. Harby's brother, a sailor in the U.S. Navy, wanted a better assignment, and Hamilton advised Lowndes to intervene with the secretary of the navy on his behalf to ensure more favorable treatment in the *Gazette*'s columns.[28]

To Hamilton's great displeasure, Lowndes dismissed his advice and

28. See JH to Lowndes, 9, 10, and 11 January (quotation) and 4 February 1822, William Lowndes Papers, SHC.

deferred to the other, more overtly ambitious, Carolina candidate, Calhoun. As one Palmetto State political analyst assessed the situation: "Mr. Lowndes had most of the State, but Mr. Calhoun had Pendleton district *and* Mr. William Lowndes."[29]

Despite his disappointment with the reluctant Lowndes, Hamilton clearly enjoyed his taste of national politics and relished the role of political manager. Like a master military strategist, Hamilton planned the campaign and, although he did not realize his ultimate objective, he achieved a great deal. His considerable powers of persuasion, though insufficient to move Lowndes, engineered a unanimous legislative endorsement. In the process, he demonstrated practical political skills that enhanced his reputation and increased his self-confidence. With the right cause, Hamilton knew he would accomplish great things.

Although Hamilton's plans for the Lowndes campaign fizzled in the spring of 1822, his own political stock soared that summer. His rising fortunes did not result from his work for Lowndes or even from his being a state legislator, but rather from his post as the intendant, or mayor, of Charleston. Hamilton first entered city government as a warden (city council member) in 1820, took over as intendant pro tem in the spring of 1821, and was elected intendant for his first full one-year term in September 1821. At the time of Hamilton's election in 1821, the *Charleston Courier* expressed the hope that under the new intendant and council "the City may be healthy—the taxes light—the laws wise—the guard vigilant—the citizens tranquil—the markets abundant—salaries low—provisions cheap—fires seldom—and riots none." Had the wishes of the conservative, business-oriented *Courier* been entirely fulfilled, James Hamilton would have missed his opportunity for political advancement that summer. His political ascendancy, as it turned out, depended on a decided lack of tranquility among Charlestonians.[30]

On the afternoon of May 30, Hamilton may have been planning to escape to Sullivans Island, just across the Cooper River from Charleston, where the affluent found an effective antidote to summertime's heat and

---

29. Niven, *John C. Calhoun*, 93; and Harriott Horry Ravenel, *The Life and Times of William Lowndes of South Carolina, 1782–1822* (Boston: Houghton, Mifflin, 1901), 230 (quotation).

30. Hamilton was elected warden for ward 4 on 4 September 1820 (*Charleston Courier*, 5 September 1820), intendant pro-tem by the City Council (*Charleston Courier*, 24 April 1821), and intendant (*Charleston Courier*, 4 September 1821). The *Carolina Gazette*, 7 September 1822, notes Hamilton's re-election as intendant.

humidity in cool ocean breezes. Instead, Hamilton was just beginning a long stay in town during which he and other white Charlestonians would sweat a bit more than usual. Around three o'clock, Colonel John Prioleau called on Hamilton with some alarming information. One of Prioleau's slaves, Peter Desverneys, had shared with his master rumors about an intended slave uprising in the city. Hamilton immediately sent word to members of the city council to convene at five o'clock that afternoon to hear directly from Desverneys about the plot. Joined by Governor Thomas Bennett, the council listened as Prioleau's slave told how, five days earlier, a fellow slave had struck up a conversation with him in the street and hinted at a planned revolt by blacks. Some, like Bennett, found it difficult to believe that "their people" would be mixed up with something so atrocious. As further investigation over the next several days failed to discover hard evidence to confim Desverneys's story, Hamilton, too, began to doubt the slave informant. Even when the man Desverneys had fingered as the source of his original information, William Paul, broke down and confessed to Hamilton and other city authorities that the insurrection was set for a Sunday in June, Hamilton remained skeptical. On the evening of Friday, June 14, however, as Hamilton sought confirmation of Paul's allegation, John Wilson approached the intendant with corroborating information: according to one of Wilson's slaves, the revolt would begin at the stroke of midnight as Sunday, June 16, turned to Monday, June 17.[31]

31. See *South Carolina House Journal*, 11 December 1822, 138–9, in *State Records*, reel 511. In some sources Peter Desverneys appears as Devany, apparently a simplified phonetic spelling of his last name. See Larry Koger, *Black Slaveowners: Free Black Slave Masters in South Carolina, 1790–1860* (Jefferson, N.C.: McFarland, 1985), 174.

Hamilton's account of the episode is "An Account of the Late Intended Insurrection Among a Portion of the Blacks of this City" (Charleston: A. E. Miller, 1822), Duke; a second edition, published in Boston, appears in Paul Finkelman, ed., *Slave Rebels, Abolitionists, and Southern Courts: The Pamphlet Literature*, ser. 4, vol. 1 (New York: Garland, 1988), 113–62.

Most historians have accepted as fact that Denmark Vesey conspired to stage a revolt in 1822, although the notion has not gone unchallenged. For secondary accounts that express the traditional view of Denmark Vesey as a rebel leader foiled by white Charlestonians, see Herbert Aptheker, *American Negro Slave Revolts* (1943; reprint, New York: International Publishers, 1969); John Lofton, *Denmark Vesey's Revolt: The Slave Plot that Lit a Fuse to Fort Sumter* (Kent: Kent State Press, 1983; originally published as *Insurrection in South Carolina: The Turbulent World of Denmark Vesey*, 1964); Eugene D. Genovese, *From Rebellion to Revolution: Afro-American Slave Revolts in the Making of the Modern World* (Baton Rouge: Louisiana State University Press, 1979); Edward A. Pearson, *Designs against Charleston: The Trial Record of the Denmark Vesey Slave Conspiracy of 1822* (Chapel Hill: University of North Carolina Press, 1999); Douglas

Hamilton acted swiftly and decisively. On Friday night he gathered city militia officers at his home to plot strategy. Meetings about defensive arrangements continued the next day. On Sunday, under Hamilton's direction, armed volunteers guarded key positions throughout the city thought to be targets of the conspirators. Because of the whites' heightened security, the slaves apparently aborted their uprising, and an anxious peace reigned Sunday night. The next day, Hamilton and the city council appointed a special Court of Magistrates and Freeholders to investigate the conspiracy and prosecute the guilty. Within twenty-four hours, authorities arrested ten slaves. Other arrests followed as first one court and then another followed testimonial threads wherever they led. The ringleader of the whole plot, evidence indicated, was a free black man named Denmark Vesey, and his name became synonymous with the episode. All during June and July, stories of the intended depredations of Vesey and his co-conspirators circulated among Charleston's whites. According to rumors, for instance, Governor Bennett's favorite slave, Rolla, planned to murder his master and then take the governor's daughter as his reward. Charleston's whites believed that they had narrowly avoided a revolutionary massacre on the scale of Saint Domingue and, further, that Hamilton's resolution throughout the crisis had been key to the happy outcome.[32]

Among Charleston's master class, rare but notable voices of dissent sounded against the majority white view of the crisis. The chief dissenters included Governor Thomas Bennett himself and his brother-in-law, U.S. Supreme Court justice William Johnson. Although Bennett believed some sort of insurrection had been in the offing, he doubted it was

L. Egerton, *He Shall Go Out Free: The Lives of Denmark Vesey* (Madison: Madison House, 2000); and Freehling, *Prelude to Civil War*, 53–61.

Works suggesting the conspiracy existed only in the minds of paranoid white Charlestonians include Richard C. Wade, "The Vesey Plot: A Reconsideration," *JSH* (1964): 30:143–61, and Bertram Wyatt-Brown, *Southern Honor: Ethics and Behavior in the Old South* (New York: Oxford University Press, 1982), chapter 15. In a forthcoming book, Michael P. Johnson also casts doubt on the existence of a Vesey plot. For the outlines of Johnson's argument and for his trenchant criticism of the traditional interpretation of Vesey, see Johnson, "Denmark Vesey and His Co-Conspirators," *William and Mary Quarterly*, 3rd ser., 58, no. 4 (October 2001): 915–76. For responses to Johnson, both pro and con, see "Forum: The Making of a Slave Conspiracy, Part 2," *William and Mary Quarterly*, 3rd ser., 59, no. 1 (January 2002).

My view is that James Hamilton believed there was indeed a Vesey plot, and he ruthlessly sought to root it out.

32. John Potter to Langdon Cheves, 29 June 1822, Langdon Cheves I Papers, SCHS.

so extensive as to include his trusted slaves, Rolla and Batteau. As the investigation into Vesey's conspiracy proceeded, Bennett shared his opinions privately with members of the special court. Johnson, however, took his dissenting opinion public in late June by publishing a short piece in the *Courier*. Entitled "Melancholy Effect of Popular Excitement," it recounted the story of a slave falsely accused of complicity in an alleged slave rebellion in Edgefield District a decade before. The Edgefield "plot" was, Johnson implied, purely a schoolboy's April Fool's prank. Still the local Court of Magistrates and Freeholders had duly condemned and hanged the man, despite his master's protests of the slave's innocence and the total lack of solid evidence. While the purpose of Johnson's tale may have been only to imply the innocence of his brother-in-law's two slaves, some may have inferred a different moral—that the Vesey investigation had spiraled out of control, fueled by hysteria.[33]

Such opinions, heretical by white Charleston's standards, received censure from Hamilton and members of the special court. In answer to Johnson, Hamilton and the members of the court argued that the trials were as fair and impartial as they possibly could have been. Because the stakes were so high, Hamilton made clear, the situation required swift and harsh measures, including the execution of Vesey and thirty-four others. As he wrote in his official report of the Vesey conspiracy, blacks who contemplated heinous acts such as murdering their masters should know that "there is nothing they are bad enough to do that we are not powerful enough to punish."[34]

Hamilton's handling of the Vesey incident won him the plaudits of his friends and neighbors. The City Council voted him thanks on behalf of the citizens—that is, the white people—of Charleston. He easily won re-election as intendant in the September elections; his rival, former Governor John Geddes, withdrew rather than oppose the summer's hero. Running for re-election to the legislature in October, Hamilton received more votes than any of the other sixteen successful candidates.[35]

33. William W. Freehling, "Denmark Vesey's Antipaternalitic Reality," in *The Reintegration of American History* (New York: Oxford University Press, 1994), 34–58.

34. Hamilton, "Account of the Late Insurrection," 1. As Michael Johnson points out, the proceedings that led to executions fell far short of being fair trials. In fact, there is no evidence that some of the accused, including Vesey himself, actually received a trial where they heard testimony against themselves and could cross-examine witnesses. See Johnson, "Vesey and His Co-Conspirators," 933–5.

35. *Charleston Mercury*, 19 October 1822.

Hamilton's popularity extended throughout the lowcountry, and he decided to capitalize on it to advance his political career to Congress. His political ally, Joel Poinsett, held the seat from Charleston, which precluded running in his home district. Circumstances, however, created an open seat just down the road, in the Second Congressional District, comprising Beaufort and Colleton, site of his old Callawassie plantation. Hamilton's idol, William Lowndes, had represented the area in Congress since before the War of 1812, but that spring—just after his brief presidential candidacy—tuberculosis had forced Lowndes to resign so that he might seek to restore his health in Europe. A special election was set for late November, and, though he had not lived in the area for three years, Hamilton put his claim before the district's voters.[36]

Hamilton's decision to enter the race came only at the eleventh hour because of a season of travel. During September and much of October, he had been out of town for a Bank of the United States stockholders' meeting in Philadelphia and a visit to New York while voters back home re-elected him to his city and state offices. While he may have been mulling over a bid for Congress for some time, he did not decide to seek that office until soon before the Charleston press announced his candidacy on November 18. So now, just before heading to Columbia for the beginning of the legislative session, he rushed down the road to Lowndes's congressional district to re-introduce himself to his old neighbors.[37]

Before Hamilton entered the race, most observers would have wagered on the election of Dr. Richard Screven. The Beaufort physician and planter faced rather weak opposition from William Elliott, master of Pon Pon plantation and intendant of the town of Beaufort. The announcement of Hamilton's candidacy changed the political dynamics dramatically. Even though he entered the race with less than two weeks to go, his fame among slaveholders as the hero of the Denmark Vesey incident attracted strong support for his candidacy almost immediately.[38]

Even with his newfound fame, Hamilton realized his election was by no means certain. The Charlestonian knew that his not being a resident

36. Vipperman, *William Lowndes*, 261. The election took place on 25 and 26 November 1822. See Michael J. Dubin, *United States Congressional Elections, 1788–1997: The Official Results of the Elections of the 1st through 105th Congresses* (Jefferson, N.C.: McFarland, 1998), 72.

37. JH to Langdon Cheves, 10 October 1822; newspaper clipping, 12 August [1822], Langdon Cheves I Papers, SCHS; and *Charleston City Gazette*, 18 November 1822.

38. Stephen Elliott to William Elliott, 13 November 1822, Elliott-Gonzales Papers, SHC.

of the congressional district was a sore point with some; his opponents took pleasure in declaring "'that it is indeed a pretty state of things'" when voters in the district "'must *borrow a man from Charleston* to represent them.'" As Hamilton took the pulse of the district in the waning days of November, he found Dr. Screven the clear leader with only thin support for Elliott. Hamilton decided to convince the Beaufort intendant of the hopelessness of his candidacy and gain his support. Rather than charming Elliott into an endorsement, though, Hamilton informed him with brutal frankness that "even if my friends had not made me a Candidate, you could not have been elected." The main reason, Hamilton suggested, was that Elliott suffered from "the reputed sin of federalism," which defect the Screven forces were busily making known to the electorate. (Of course, Federalism tainted Hamilton's political soul as well, but he had never actually worshipped at the High Church's altar, as Elliott had.)[39]

As it turned out, Hamilton did not require Elliott's help. By the time Elliott received Hamilton's letter, and certainly by the time he replied, all the votes were in. In the wake of early indications of a Hamilton victory, Elliott, obviously stung by Hamilton's letter, wrote that "the feeling of district pride" had been wounded by the Charleston resident's election. He suggested that "this feeling, already so strongly excited, will continue alive, and produce a powerful opposition to your re-election." "I should hold it fortunate for you," Elliott went on, "if at the ensuing election you find yourself opposed by me, instead of some more formidable & popular competitor." Hamilton, oblivious to Elliott's feelings, had already rushed on to Columbia to participate in the legislative session and to await the final, official results of the congressional election.[40]

The Denmark Vesey incident very much occupied the attention of the legislature, and James Hamilton, when it convened in late November. Governor Bennett mentioned the conspiracy in his message to the body, but he openly criticized the Court of Magistrates and Freeholders. Hamilton joined the majority in preventing the publication of the governor's faultfinding message. Then Hamilton placed on the legislature's agenda a series of initiatives related to the conspiracy. He easily won legislative

39. JH to Langdon Cheves, 30 November 1822, Langdon Cheves I Papers, SCHS; and JH to William Elliott, 22 November 1822, Elliott-Gonzales Papers, SHC.

40. William Elliott to JH, 28 November 1822, Elliott-Gonzales Papers, SHC.

approval to compensate masters whose slaves the tribunal had ordered executed (at the rate of $122.44 per head). The legislature also granted Hamilton's request for a $100 annual pension to the "loyal" slave who first brought the conspiracy to the whites' attention.[41]

Hamilton also submitted a more far-reaching bill to regulate the population of slaves and free blacks. The relative freedom of slaves and free blacks in Charleston, Hamilton and other city residents believed, had created the conditions for the Vesey conspiracy. They particularly feared those African Americans, slave and free, who had not imbibed the proper respect for white authority through long residence in South Carolina. Hamilton's bill, therefore, contained two major corrective provisions for "the better government" of African Americans. First, he proposed to halt the importation of new slaves into the state and to punish masters by fine should they acquire slaves outside South Carolina. Second, he urged the expulsion from the state of any non-native free blacks who had lived in the state less than five years. Charleston's solons generally backed these elements of Hamilton's bill. To his surprise, however, Hamilton encountered significant opposition to both components from representatives of other parts of the state. Upcountry districts, where the cotton belt was still expanding, opposed any limits on their ability to import slaves. Representatives of lowcountry country parishes as well as of upcountry plantation districts apparently agreed with the rice planter Stephen Elliott that they could manage their own slaves without new regulations written by the well-meaning but misguided "Lawyers of Charleston." Their only concession to Hamilton was to assess a fifty-dollar tax on all non-native free black men between the ages of fifteen and fifty, who had lived in the state for less than five years.[42]

As Hamilton toiled to make the state's whites safer from black rabblerousers, newspapers announced the final results in his congressional race. The residents of Beaufort and Colleton had given the Charleston lawyer nearly 57 percent of the vote in the three-way contest and thus elevated James Hamilton to the United States House of Representatives. Somewhat surprised by the results and his margin of victory, Hamilton

41. Wild, "South Carolina Politics," 37–8; Pease and Pease, *James Louis Petigru,* 30; and Freehling, "Denmark Vesey's Antipaternalistic Reality," 55; *South Carolina House Journal,* 1822, 136, 138–9, in *State Records,* reel 511.

42. Stephen Elliott to William Elliott, 22 July 1822, Elliott-Gonzales Papers, SHC; *South Carolina House Journal,* 1822, 82, 122, 152–4, 166, in *State Records,* reel 511.

greeted them with satisfaction. On December 17, in a note to the Speaker of the state house, Hamilton informed his colleagues of his election and of his resignation from the legislature.[43]

Looking back over his time in Charleston, Hamilton could take justifiable pride in his accomplishments. In just three short years since leaving his plantation, Hamilton had built a substantial reputation as a nationalist Republican politician whose political skills had won him offices at the city, state, and now federal levels. As Charleston's chief executive, he had demonstrated firmness in ruthlessly protecting whites from the horrors of a slave uprising. In his personal life, he took great pride in his growing family. His domestic brood included not only James, Daniel Heyward, and Thomas Lynch, but also the newer additions, two-year-old Elizabeth Middleton and fourteen-month-old Oliver Perry. And now his wife, Elizabeth, was three months pregnant with their sixth child. As the thirty-six-year-old Hamilton bid farewell to them and departed for Washington, his head no doubt swirled with thoughts of his family, not only the one in Charleston, but also the members who had done so much to establish the national government he was going to serve.

43. Hamilton received 740 votes (56.75 percent), Screven garnered 389 (29.83 percent), and Elliott received 175 (13.42 percent). See *Charleston Courier*, 16 December 1822, and Dubin, *United States Congressional Elections, 1788–1997*, 72. For Hamilton's uncertainty about the race as he awaited the results, see JH to Langdon Cheves, 30 November 1822, Langdon Cheves I Papers, SCHS. For Hamilton's resignation, see JH to Patrick Noble, 17 December 1822, SCDAH. Despite William Elliott's warning, Hamilton was unopposed in his subsequent congressional races in 1824 and 1826. See Congressional Quarterly, *Guide to U.S. Elections*, 3rd ed. (Washington: Congressional Quarterly, 1994), 944, 947.

CHAPTER 3

The Unmaking of a Nationalist
1823–1828

WHEN HE ARRIVED IN JANUARY 1823 to take his seat in the Seventeenth
Congress, Hamilton found a capital in the midst of a slow evolution from
swamp to city. French architect Pierre L'Enfant had envisioned Washington as a three-dimensional rendering in marble, stone, and wood of
values appropriate to the capital of a nation self-consciously an heir of
republican Rome and classical Greece. But by the early 1820s, the city
had yet to fulfill its designer's grand dreams. To his daughter's plea for a
description of the capital's "eastern splendor," Ohio congressman Duncan McArthur could only offer a decidedly unromantic portrait. Washington, he admitted, contained "some prety good buildings," but "they
are in such detached clumps, and so much vacant or unoccupied ground
between them, that it scarsly deserves the name of a City." McArthur
found more than Washington's physical layout falling short of expectations; "the manners and customs of the City" provided a still greater
shock. At parties hosted by President James Monroe and Secretary of
State John Quincy Adams, the Ohio legislator observed behavior he considered unrepublican to say the least. Not only did men and women mix
too freely for his comfort, but women dressed immodestly:

> The fashionable manner of dressing, is to go half naked—the neck[,]
> breasts and sholder blades bare, and the dresses so constructed as to enable
> a person who is near and above them to see more than half way down the
> back or front of the lady, from the upper part of her dress. . . . This City,
> would be the last place, that I would wish to see a wife, daughter, or female
> relation. . . . I cannot but think, their manner of dressing, or rather

of going naked; and of crowed together, improper. It is to me truly disgusting.[1]

The gaiety Congressman McArthur so disdained had but recently returned to the city-in-the-making. Only eight years before Hamilton's arrival in Washington, British troops had sailed up the Potomac from Chesapeake Bay and set torches to the president's house, the Capitol, and other government buildings. For four years following the war, Congress met in a hastily constructed building across the street from the burned-out Capitol until repairs could be completed. Even after Congress returned to its home in 1819, working conditions inside the "people's house" remained less than ideal. McArthur complained in the mid-1820s that even "with all this expense and grandeur" the rotunda in which they met

is unfit for the purpose for which it was intended—as the debates cannot be heard by half the members, and it is seldom that a question put by the Speaker or Chairman, can be heard, or the bills or amendments read by the Clerk heard or understood by half of the members. Consequently little attention is paid to business, and some times one half of the members are engaged in private conversation. And many motions are made and questions decided on, which many of the members never hear, understand, or know anything about.[2]

Despite the appearance and manners of the nation's capital city, newly elected Congressman James Hamilton arrived with great enthusiasm for the federal Union itself, that precious legacy of his Revolution-era relatives. As a follower of neo-Federalist Republicans Lowndes and Calhoun, he came to Washington prepared to endorse expansive powers for the federal government. As he later observed, with slight exaggeration, he doubted whether there was in the early 1820s "an individual in this

1. Gordon S. Wood, *The Creation of the American Republic* (Chapel Hill: University of North Carolina Press, 1969), 48–53; Damie Stillman, "From the Ancient Roman Republic to the New American One: Architecture for a New Nation," in *A Republic for the Ages: The United States Capitol and the Political Culture of the Early Republic*, ed. Donald R. Kennon (Charlottesville: University Press of Virginia, 1999), 271–315; Duncan McArthur to Effie McArthur, 6 February 1824, Duncan McArthur Papers, LC.

2. United States Capitol Historical Society, *We, the People: The Story of the United States Capitol* (Washington, D.C.: U.S. Capitol Historical Society, 1978), 31–2. Duncan McArthur to Effie McArthur, 6 February 1824, Duncan McArthur Papers, LC.

Union more thoroughly and enthusiastically national in his politics than myself." Within a short time, however, Hamilton's nationalistic ardor cooled as he familiarized himself with Washington's ways. Just as Congressman McArthur complained about debauchery at presidential levees, Hamilton soon detected corruption even more troubling in the very halls of Congress. Contrary to republican principles, congressmen and senators sacrificed the true national interest, as Congressman Hamilton defined it, to the false gods of sectional advantage, while politicians bargained for the presidency itself. Whereas Hamilton once believed that national leaders had the best interests of all citizens, including lowcountry South Carolinians, at heart, their actions soon disabused him of that notion. Consequently, in defense of the lowcountry, his nationalism gave way to the sort of states' rights views he had previously opposed. By the close of Hamilton's congressional career in March 1829, many Carolinians looked to him as a leading champion in their struggle against what they perceived as an increasingly hostile national majority.[3]

Life in Washington followed a predictable pattern for a congressman during the 1820s. Members sought to do the nation's business as quickly as possible and leave for home in time to avoid the worst of the federal city's hot, muggy summers. The first session in a two-year congressional cycle began in December and lasted through May or perhaps into June; the second session came to order the next December, and adjourned the following March. Although most members left their families back home while Congress met, Hamilton's wife and children occasionally accompanied him to Washington. Indeed, in January 1826, Elizabeth gave birth to their seventh child, Samuel Prioleau, in the nation's capital. By Hamilton's final term, the family occupied one of the relatively grand "Seven Buildings" situated along Pennsylvania Avenue. Among the oldest structures in the federal city, the "Seven Buildings" once housed the State Department, and the largest of them served as a temporary residence for the Madisons after the British burned down the Executive Mansion.[4]

When his family was not present, Hamilton lived in one or another of

3. *Southern Patriot*, 9 July 1830.

4. See Hamilton family genealogical information, box 3, folder 34, JHP, SHC. Perry M. Goldman and James S. Young, eds., *The United States Congressional Directories, 1789–1840* (New York: Columbia University Press, 1973), 209–13. See also Constance McLaughlin Green, *Washington*, vol. 1, *Village and Capital, 1800–1878* (Princeton: Princeton University Press, 1962), 4, 78–9.

the boardinghouses, popularly known as "messes," where most congressmen and senators resided during the sessions. Hamilton kept quarters in
several different messes during his six and one-half years in the House,
preferring the Pennsylvania Avenue area west of Tiber Creek over accommodations on Capitol Hill itself. Not only did the messes provide a
place for members to eat and to rest from endless debates, but they also
served to socialize new arrivals in the ways of the congressional community. For Hamilton, his mess may have even been a locus of political re-
education.[5]

During the "Era of Good Feelings," a formal system of opposing political parties played as little role in Congress as it had back in South Carolina. Only about one-eighth of his House colleagues and just four of
forty-eight U.S. senators claimed membership in the Federalist Party
when Hamilton took his seat. The real contest was among the dominant
Republicans. The states' rights wing claimed the allegiance of many, but
most Republicans subscribed to the nationalist views associated with Calhoun, by then secretary of war, and House Speaker Henry Clay of Kentucky. Hamilton's well-known nationalism led Clay to appoint him
chairman of the House Military Affairs Committee in his first term, and
the new congressman actively advanced his faction's interests both in
Washington and at home.[6]

Even as Hamilton identified himself with the broad-construction
wing of the party, many of his messmates—men such as New York's
Churchill C. Cambreleng, Tennessee's Hugh L. White, and the Virginians William Archer, John Barbour, and Littleton Tazewell—championed
Old Republicanism. On many a cold winter's night before a blazing fire at
Mr. Kervand's or Mrs. Peyton's boardinghouse, his states' rights friends
no doubt sought to convince Hamilton of the error of his nationalist
ways. Other congressional friendships similarly influenced his political
views. He became especially intimate with John Randolph, the eccentric
Virginian and the very soul of Old Republicanism in Congress.[7]

At the outset of his congressional service, however, Hamilton re-

5. James Sterling Young, *The Washington Community, 1800–1828* (New York: Columbia
University Press, 1966), esp. chapter 5.

6. Congressional Quarterly, *Guide to Congress* (Washington: Congressional Quarterly, Inc.,
1971), 183.

7. Goldman and Young, *Congressional Directories*, 160, 170, 184, 195; and Hugh A. Garland,
The Life of John Randolph of Roanoke (New York: D. Appleton, 1851), 2:258.

mained committed to the policies he had espoused in South Carolina's assembly. As if to emphasize the continuity between his state and national legislative careers, one of his first congressional speeches echoed his earlier call for a federal pension for Sarah Perry. On issues of political economy, he paid due homage to the nationalist trinity of the Bank, internal improvements, and the tariff. But pragmatism and self-interest more than devotion to pure doctrine determined his political course. As he described his political philosophy, "metaphysical dialectics had few charms for" him, "the taper of common sense burnt with a light sufficiently steady to guide his humble steps."[8]

In the early 1820s, as a state legislator and new congressman, Hamilton embraced broad federal power because he believed it benefited his lowcountry world. For instance, the Second Bank of the United States, which Old Republicans reviled, provided essential services for planters and merchants back home, and Hamilton was "zealously devoted" to it. He assured Nicholas Biddle, Cheves's successor as B.U.S. president, that he regarded the Bank "as identical with the existence of a sound currency in our Country, & with the success & convenience of the financial operations of the Government." Personal as well as public considerations influenced his support for the Bank. Hamilton served on the board of the Bank's Charleston branch in the early 1820s, and his wife owned nearly $50,000 of B.U.S. stock until 1824.[9]

Although a Bank loyalist, Hamilton reassessed both the wisdom and constitutionality of other broad-constructionist federal policies. For example, he increasingly criticized federal spending for internal improvements. Early in his congressional career, Hamilton concurred with Calhoun about the need to "bind the nation together." Consequently, he supported appropriations for repairing the Cumberland Road and for funding surveys for a variety of road-building projects. Within a short time, though, he began to draw greater distinctions among different kinds of improvements. Congress, he acknowledged, could appropriate dollars for constructing post roads because the Constitution specifically granted it that power. As a war veteran and chairman of the Military Affairs Committee, he interpreted the military authority of Congress

---

8. *NR* 17 (26 February 1820): 451–2; and *ADC*, 8:274 (20 January 1825).

9. JH to Biddle, 22 November 1824, Nicholas Biddle Papers, LC (quotation); see also JH to Joseph Johnson, 9 October 1823, JHP, Duke.

broadly enough to allow for a federal power to build roads and even canals for the army's use. But by the mid-1820s, he rejected any arguments
for internal improvements based on the Constitution's general welfare
and commerce clauses. In addition to raising constitutional objections,
he also attacked federal aid for improvements that lacked what he considered true national importance. He complained, for example, about federal funding for the Chesapeake and Delaware Canal. He argued that
the Mid-Atlantic citizens who most directly benefited from it could easily
afford to pay for the project, which lacked national merit in his opinion.
The Catawba and Saluda Canals in his home state, he argued, were of
far greater national importance from a military point of view, yet South
Carolina was building those waterways without federal assistance.[10]

Even more than internal improvements, the protective tariff caused
Hamilton to question his nationalist faith. Higher tariffs on manufactured items required by southern agriculturalists most directly and negatively affected Hamilton and his constituents. In the early 1820s, South
Carolina's cotton planters experienced falling prices and hard times,
which many Carolinians blamed on tariff policies that increased the costs
of imported goods needed on their plantations and farms. Moreover,
Carolinians feared that Europeans would retaliate against higher American tariffs by ceasing to buy their commodities—rice as well as cotton—
and developing new sources.

Although the protective tariff did exacerbate the economic woes of
South Carolinians, it did not cause them all. Market forces more than
import laws deserved the blame. The unusually high price of raw cotton
immediately after the War of 1812 fell as trade once again flowed across
the Atlantic to satiate long-starved European demand. The Panic of 1819
then not only depressed prices but also squeezed credit-dependent cotton planters and farmers. Perhaps the greatest enemy of South Carolina's
cotton growers lay in the lands of the Old Southwest. A flood of white
settlers washed over Alabama and Mississippi after the War of 1812 and,
with their slave forces, carved plantations out of land once devoted to
small Indian farms and hunting grounds. Because of this new acreage and
spurred on by the post-war price spike, cotton production increased
fivefold between 1814 and 1826. The market price for cotton declined
because of this increased production and, especially in the early 1820s,

10. Wild, "South Carolina Politics," 203; and *ADC* 8:273–6 (1825).

the lingering effects of the panic of 1819. South Carolina's cotton growers, relying on worn-out soil, produced smaller yields than planters in
the southwestern black belt, and thus suffered disproportionately. At the
same time, South Carolina's other main export also took a hit thanks
largely to the 1819 panic. Average annual prices for rice ran as high as
6.1 cents per pound in the immediate post-war period, but in the 1820s
never rose above 3.3 cents. Although several factors contributed to tum-
bling cotton and rice prices, the tariff provided a visible target for South
Carolinians who feared for their economic lives.[11]

Right after the war, South Carolina's congressional delegation had
provided key support for higher tariffs. In 1816, Hamilton's predecessor,
William Lowndes, steered the first peacetime protective tariff through
Congress as chairman of the House Ways and Means Committee. The
1816 law set duties on most goods at 20 percent; imported cotton and
wool textiles were taxed at 25 percent of their value until 1819, when
rates would decline to 20 percent. The legislation also introduced the
"minimum-value" principle on cotton goods. Devised by John C. Calhoun and Treasury Secretary Alexander Dallas to increase protection for
New England textiles, the bill's minimum-value language provided for
taxing cheap imported cotton cloth, some costing as little as 6 cents per
square yard, as if it were actually priced at a minimum of 25 cents.[12]

Although most South Carolina representatives, following the lead of
Lowndes and Calhoun, accepted the principle that Congress could enact
a protective tariff and voted for the 1816 bill, they were not terribly enthusiastic about the policy, nor did they support protection for the sake
of the manufacturers. Instead, they regarded the protective tariff as a
temporary measure to help the nation recover from wartime dislocations
and to prepare it for another conflict. South Carolina's nationalists believed that a higher tariff would strengthen the country by filling the federal government's coffers with needed revenue and encouraging
industries useful for national defense. They also acknowledged the need
to counteract, for a brief time, the damage done to American manufacturers by the post-war dumping of British goods on the domestic market.
By 1820, a more robust federal treasury and more amicable relations with

11. Lewis Cecil Gray, *History of Agriculture in the Southern United States to 1860* (Washington: Carnegie Institution, 1941), 1026 (table 40), 697–9, 1030 (table 42).

12. Sidney Ratner, *The Tariff in American History* (New York: D. Van Nostrand, 1972), 13;
and Sellers, *Market Revolution*, 75.

Britain convinced nationalists, including Lowndes, that continued protection for manufacturers was no longer necessary and might even be harmful.[13]

Because Lowndes, Calhoun, and other southern tariff supporters, unlike Old Republicans, admitted the constitutionality of the protectionism, the question became one of raw politics: which economic interests could cut the right deals and prevail in the rough-and-tumble of the legislative process? As time wore on, the answer increasingly proved unpleasant to southerners. In the republic's earlier days, when the population of the states dominated by plantation agriculture nearly matched that of the other states, representatives of slaveholding planters exerted at least as much influence in shaping national economic policy as did those from free states. By the 1820s, however, differential population growth in the nation's sections had led to shifts in the distribution of seats in Congress. Most importantly, population levels in the burgeoning cities of the Mid-Atlantic as well as in the interior cities and farmlands of the Old Northwest increased far faster than in the South. Since regions outside the South depended on free rather than enslaved labor, the economic and social outlooks of their citizens and the legislative priorities of their representatives in Congress differed, often dramatically, from those of southerners and their spokesmen. Amid the ensuing clashes over tariff policy and related issues, some southerners began to question their faith in the rule of a national majority.

As a congressman, Hamilton began questioning just how well the interests of South Carolina's commercial planters meshed with those of other powerful economic sectors represented on Capitol Hill. Enthusiasm for increased protection, without any concern for its effect on the rest of the country, continued unabated among representatives of the Middle Atlantic and New England states. Meanwhile, southern congressmen, their states' economies reeling, decried further tariff increases as insults gratuitously laid upon quite real injuries. Spokesmen for southern planters, such as Virginia's John Randolph, claimed that planters already suffered from decreasing profits and that higher tariffs on textiles only exacerbated the problem by raising the cost of clothing their slaves.[14]

13. Vipperman, *William Lowndes*, chapter 7; Norris W. Preyer, "Southern Support of the Tariff of 1816—A Reappraisal," *JSH* 25 (August 1959): 306–22; and Wild, "South Carolina Politics," 140.

14. *Annals of Congress*, 42:2256 (1824).

These arguments took on a more personal meaning for Hamilton as he once again entered the ranks of the lowcountry planters. In 1824, he purchased a Savannah River rice plantation from his wife's bankrupt stepfather, Nicholas Cruger. The property, a few miles upriver from the city of Savannah in Carolina's St. Luke's Parish, shared its name with the old Lynch plantation of Hamilton's childhood, Rice Hope. His purchase also included Pennyworth Island, approximately one hundred acres of prime real estate located in Georgia waters, just across the "back river" from Rice Hope. There, on the island, Hamilton established a dwelling built on stilts from which he could survey his rice duchy.[15]

Higher tariffs, moreover, reminded Hamilton of the disruptions Jeffersonian economic policy had caused in southern commerce with Europe. The embargo and non-intercourse laws had transformed the lowcountry's golden age, through a perverse Midas touch, into an era of cheap brass. Almost certainly, Hamilton blamed his father's failure as a planter partly on those earlier restrictive trade policies. Now, once again master of his own plantation, Hamilton feared for his own financial well-being should tariffs raise his costs and discourage Europeans from purchasing his crops. So Hamilton, defender of the 1820 tariff as a state legislator, in 1824 took the free trade, anti-tariff baton once carried by William Lowndes.[16]

In early 1824, John Tod of Pennsylvania, Speaker Henry Clay's hand-picked chairman of the House Committee on Manufactures, presented a tariff bill that called for yet higher duties on a variety of imported goods. Not only did the Tod bill increase the tariffs on manufactured iron and lead goods to please businessmen in eastern states, but in a bid to gain the support of certain agricultural constituencies, it also protected raw wool (important in parts of New York) and hemp (key particularly in Clay's Kentucky). Continuing efforts made four years earlier by congressmen from textile districts, the bill raised rates on cotton and woolen goods to 33 1/3 percent of their value. Moreover, it extended Calhoun's 1816 principle of minimum valuation to finer grades of cotton cloth than previously covered and applied it to woolens as well.

The bill Tod forged in his protectionist-dominated committee met

15. JH to Nicholas Biddle, 22 November 1824, Nicholas Biddle Papers, LC; and JH to Langdon Cheves, 31 January 1823, Langdon Cheves I Papers, SCHS.

16. Kaplanoff, "Making the South Solid," 225–6; and Coclanis, *Shadow of a Dream*, chapter 4.

Clay's specifications for providing incentives to American manufacturers, and the Speaker praised it as the cornerstone of what he dubbed the American System. As Clay envisioned it, high tariffs would help create a home market for budding American industries as well as provide the funds to build a national system of roads and canals. Meanwhile, Tod's bill infuriated Hamilton and other southern representatives, as well as some New Englanders who represented shipping interests rather than factory owners.

Though Ohio's Duncan McArthur observed that the many long speeches on the tariff "command but little attention," Hamilton took to the floor on April 6 to deliver a two-hour oration outlining his objections to the Tod bill. For the most part, the speech was Hamilton at his best— well-informed, pragmatic, and witty. He demonstrated a thorough knowledge of classical liberal economics and frequently paid homage to Adam Smith, whom he more than once called "the master." Most importantly, the speech marked a clear public turning point in his journey from nationalism to a more decidedly states' rights position.[17]

Hamilton opened by tipping his rhetorical hat to Daniel Webster, the brilliant orator and Massachusetts congressman, who previously had risen to denounce the Tod bill. Speaking on behalf of his Massachusetts constituency of merchants and shippers, Webster had blasted the special privileges the bill accorded manufacturers at the expense of not only the commercial and agricultural sectors, but also consumers. Iron manufacturing, centered in Pennsylvania, drew the New Englander's special scorn. Under the Tod bill, Webster charged, Americans would pay increased duties of $1,125,000 on iron goods *"to support a business that cannot support itself."*[18]

Fully endorsing Webster's views, Hamilton countered Clay's contention that America should follow the British model and pursue wealth through protective trade regulations. Britain's economic and political power, Hamilton argued, resulted not from protectionist legislation but from its natural resources, colonies, and military might. Free trade, he pointed out, had already proven its value by building New York and Boston into great metropolises and stimulating the expansion of the republic

17. Duncan McArthur to Nancy McArthur, 25 February 1824, Duncan McArthur Papers, LC; and *Annals of Congress*, 42:2177–209 (1824).

18. Webster, quoted in Ratner, *Tariff in American History*, 110.

since the Revolution. Against Clay's demands for greater protection, James Hamilton cited the authority of the original American tariff proponent, Alexander Hamilton. Secretary Hamilton had never advocated duties as high as those proposed by Clay, Congressman Hamilton claimed. Moreover, Alexander Hamilton rejected the sort of perpetual protection Clay seemed to support. The earlier Hamilton believed that if a product could not be made in America without the aid of a high tariff, it was unwise to continue efforts to manufacture it.

In practical terms, Congressman Hamilton pointed to the problems the tariff posed for his constituents, particularly the sea island cotton planters. They had already suffered greatly as cotton prices had fallen from 60 to 25 cents per pound, and, Hamilton argued, they had just as much claim to government assistance as the manufacturers and wheat farmers who would benefit from the tariff. Not only did cotton planters face higher prices for manufactured goods under the proposed tariff, but also if Congress raised duties on imported goods, Hamilton asked, "what inducements do we leave to Great Britain to take our cotton?" He feared that the British would seek new suppliers in Brazil and Egypt. Earlier in the debate, Clay had argued that southern planters did not need foreign buyers for their crops because soon American textile makers would be in a position to consume all the South's cotton. Even if that rosy scenario materialized, Hamilton asked, where would all these cotton goods be sold? Certainly not in the United States. To Clay's suggestion that South American customers would buy surplus U.S.-made textiles, Hamilton had a ready retort. If American manufacturers feared meeting the British head-on in our own country without the benefit of a high tariff, how could they expect to compete successfully with British textile makers, backed by the British navy, in marketing finished goods to Latin America? Southern planters needed European, especially British, buyers for their commodities, Hamilton concluded, and therefore they justly feared the consequences of the proposed duties.[19]

Hamilton's speech also revealed a clear movement away from his earlier almost unquestioned nationalism. In a statement reflecting classic states' rights doctrine and strict constructionism, Hamilton declared: "We are independent States and our league merely looks to a common

19. *Annals of Congress*, 41:1518–9 (1824) (quotations); and Gray, *History of Agriculture*, 692–3.

defence, external and internal commerce, an army, navy, judiciary, and the powers necessary to carry these objects into effect. No one member of this Confederacy could have contemplated joining a Union in which 'the common defence and general welfare' meant a sacrifice of any part of it, under fanciful and arbitrary considerations of 'the good of the whole.'"

As his speech reached a crescendo with the introduction of the states' rights motif, Hamilton's demeanor shifted from that of a dispassionate disciple of Adam Smith to one befitting an angry, besieged man. In his overheated excitement he ungenerously attacked Congressman Tod for "gross ignorance of the operation, bearing, and character" of the proposed tariff. He ended his two-hour appeal by labeling the tariff as "unjustifiable in its principles, offensive in its character, and pernicious in its consequences." Upon concluding his oration, a still irate Hamilton exchanged "sharp words" with Congressman Henry C. Martindale and challenged him to a duel, which the New Yorker declined on religious grounds. The next day, a cooler Hamilton apologized to Tod for having questioned the chairman's grasp of the issues, but his opposition to the tariff remained red-hot.[20]

Tod's bill squeaked through the House by a five-vote margin, despite the efforts of Hamilton, Webster, and other foes of protection. The entire South Carolina delegation opposed the bill, quite a contrast from eight years before, when a majority of Palmetto State representatives had endorsed the Tariff of 1816. Carolinians would argue that they were not being inconsistent, because the purpose of the tariff had changed. In any case, this congressional debate clarified one key point: South Carolina's politicians no longer controlled national economic policy. Instead, Henry Clay and his alliance of easterners and westerners now constituted a majority and could dictate terms.[21]

Although Hamilton attacked the tariff on states' rights grounds, he had not abandoned his nationalist ideals entirely. Rather, he applied strict construction principles selectively. He still favored the Bank, for instance. But Hamilton certainly understood Carolinians' anger and where it might lead. In ominous terms, he warned Charles K. Gardner,

20. *Annals of Congress*, 42:2207-8 (1824); Charles F. Adams, ed., *Memoirs of John Quincy Adams, Comprising Portions of His Diary from 1795 to 1848* (Philadelphia, 1874-1877; New York: AMS Press, 1970), 6:282; and Wild, "South Carolina Politics," 83.

21. Wild, "South Carolina Politics," 213-4.

a New York editor and old army comrade, that the tariff would send the southern states into ruin or disunion. For the moment, those alternatives raised equally horrific specters in Hamilton's imagination.[22]

Disappointed with the drift of federal policies on the tariff and internal improvements, Hamilton still trusted the political process and looked toward the election of a new president in 1824 to steer the ship of state back to its proper course. As the election approached, each Republican faction focused on winning the White House for its own leader. Old Republicans rallied around Treasury Secretary William H. Crawford of Georgia. Competing cliques of National Republicans saw potential champions in War Secretary John C. Calhoun, House Speaker Henry Clay of Kentucky, and Secretary of State John Quincy Adams of Massachusetts. War hero Andrew Jackson, a senator from Tennessee, attracted still others, especially westerners who admired his skill in fighting their twin enemies, the British and the Indians.[23]

In the 1824 scramble for the White House, South Carolina politicians cast around before deciding on their favorite candidates. Radicals led by Senator William Smith supported Crawford, but nationalists like Hamilton might reasonably have endorsed any of the remaining contenders. With the death of Hamilton's favorite, the diffident William Lowndes, the young congressman threw his support to Calhoun. Long before the balloting, however, Calhoun recognized the dimness of his prospects and sought the less-contested vice presidency instead. His withdrawal from the presidential race left his followers in South Carolina puzzled over whom to support. Some Palmetto State politicos hinted that Calhoun's adherents might back John Quincy Adams. Touting the New Englander as the only candidate opposed to the increasingly unpopular tariff, several newspapers in the state took up his cause. Hamilton himself fueled this speculation by confiding to Massachusetts congressman John Reed that Andrew Jackson's support for the 1824 tariff in the Senate would deprive the Old Hero of South Carolina's electoral votes. Reed inferred that the state would therefore back Adams, but Adams himself put "no faith in" this political intelligence. With keener political instincts, Adams assured Reed "that nothing was to be expected from South Carolina."[23]

22. JH to Nicholas Biddle, 22 November 1824, Nicholas Biddle Papers, LC; and JH to C. K. Gardner, 27 April 1824, JHP, SCL.
23. Wild, "South Carolina Politics," 222–3; and Adams, ed., *Adams Memoirs*, 6:316.

As Adams knew, Calhoun was forging an alliance with Jackson. Indeed, in several states, Jackson forces nominated the Carolinian for the second spot on their ticket. As a Calhoun ally, Hamilton therefore prepared to support the general for the presidency. Undoubtedly, Hamilton's high regard for the military predisposed him to support the great war hero, but he did not know the candidate very well before the election. As Charleston's intendant in 1821, Hamilton had welcomed a proposal from Jackson to visit the city, but the Tennessean, then governor of Florida Territory, did not actually make the trek. Hamilton did not become personally acquainted with Jackson until the autumn of 1823, when the Old Hero entered the Senate. By then, the potential presidential candidate was "courted by the Great as well as the Sovereign folks," thus leaving little opportunity for Hamilton to achieve much political or personal intimacy with him.[24]

In the fall 1824 balloting, Calhoun handily won the vice presidency and Jackson commanded an impressive plurality of the presidential popular vote. He garnered 43 percent to 30 percent for second-place Adams, while Clay and Crawford each received around 13 percent. Still, the Tennessean did not receive the majority of electoral votes needed to win the race. This left the decision about the next occupant of the Executive Mansion to the House of Representatives, which would choose from among the candidates—Jackson, Adams, and Crawford—with the three highest numbers of electoral votes. As the Constitution specified, each state would cast a single vote, and the successful candidate needed a majority of states to win.

In the weeks before the February 1825 House vote, speculation about members' leanings filled Washington's boardinghouses and the Capitol's hallways. That Hamilton and the other South Carolina representatives would back Jackson was a foregone conclusion, given the Tennessean's alliance with Calhoun and the fact that the state earlier had awarded him its electoral votes. The votes of members in certain states remained unclear, and candidates and their friends tirelessly lobbied swing voters. Lobbying on behalf of Jackson, for instance, George McDuffie and Pennsylvania's Samuel Ingham pressed hard on Daniel P. Cook, who, as

24. JH to Jackson, 7 March 1821, in *The Papers of Andrew Jackson*, ed. Harold D. Moser et al. (Knoxville: University of Tennessee Press, 1980), 5:475; and Samuel Houston to Abram Maury, 13 December 1823, Samuel Houston Papers, LC (quotation).

the sole member from Illinois, would cast the vote for the entire state. No one, however, carried more influence with undecided congressmen than Henry Clay, especially with those members from the three states— Missouri, Ohio, and Kentucky—he had carried in the fall. A few days before the election, he publicly threw his support to Adams, but had, in fact, privately pledged his support to the Massachusetts candidate a month earlier. Clay's endorsement worked wonders for Adams's ailing candidacy. Although under instructions from their legislature to back Jackson, Kentucky congressmen followed Clay's advice and voted for Adams. Several other delegations, including Illinois (despite McDuffie's best efforts), also switched to Adams. When all the dust settled, the House had elevated the secretary of state to the presidency over the frontier general.[25]

These events shocked Hamilton. Not only were tongues set to wagging about Adams's unusual come-from-behind victory, but also the subsequent selection of Clay as the administration's secretary of state reeked of corruption. Moreover, the choice of Clay for the plum cabinet post portended the full-scale adoption of the Kentuckian's "American System" with permanently high tariffs. Hamilton and other tariff opponents had a new focus: to oppose the incoming Adams administration.

Leaving the alleged corruption of the capital behind soon after the inauguration of President Adams in early March, Hamilton returned to Charleston and happier duties. Congress would not begin its new session until December. Until then, he would be able to survey his new plantation. He also devoted time to his growing family. Indeed, soon after Hamilton's arrival at home, Elizabeth conceived their seventh child.

In the public highlight of Hamilton's visit home, the congressman welcomed the Marquis de Lafayette to Charleston in mid-March as the aging Revolutionary War hero made his triumphal tour of the United States. The two men had become acquainted earlier in the year, when the South Carolina delegation invited Lafayette, then in Washington, to grace their state with a visit, and Hamilton assisted in planning the Frenchman's Palmetto State itinerary. When they met, Lafayette must have greeted Congressman Hamilton with special warmth, for Hamil-

---

25. Samuel Flagg Bemis, *John Quincy Adams and the Union* (New York: Alfred A. Knopf, 1956), 39–41; and Henry Clay to Francis T. Brooke, 28 January 1825, in *Andrew Jackson versus Henry Clay: Democracy and Development in Antebellum America*, ed. Harry L. Watson (Boston: Bedford/St. Martin's, 1998), 158.

ton's father had served under the marquis in the War for Independence. Lafayette even credited Major Hamilton with having saved his forces from disaster at the Battle of Green Springs during the Yorktown campaign. So the general was especially delighted to accept South Carolina's invitation, and he looked forward to seeing his old comrade-in-arms when he arrived in Charleston for a three-day visit.[26]

Like the many other cities along Lafayette's route, Charleston staged elaborate festivities in his honor. As a public official, Hamilton toasted the city's guest at a grand dinner held at City Hall. More personally satisfying for Hamilton, though, were those occasions that demonstrated the particular regard in which Lafayette held his father and, by extension, Hamilton himself. Lafayette made a special trip to see Hamilton's father at his residence, for the old major rarely left home now because of his injury. With Charleston's leading citizens in tow, Lafayette ran up to the piazza where Major Hamilton sat and greeted his fellow veteran with a kiss on each cheek. That delighted the crowd, but startled the old Scots-Irishman unaccustomed to such a Gallic custom. Then Congressman Hamilton hosted a party for Lafayette attended by Charleston's elite. When it was time for the marquis to move on from Charleston, Hamilton accompanied him on the next leg of his journey, to Savannah. On the way, the pair stopped at Edisto Island in Hamilton's congressional district, so that Hamilton could present Lafayette to his constituents and bask in their accolades for the marquis and himself.[27]

Lafayette's visit provided more than an entertaining diversion for the busy politician; it also served to reinforce Hamilton's personal connection to the Revolutionary past. The attention that Lafayette lavished on the old major reconfirmed the younger Hamilton's legacy as a true heir of the founding generation. That this confirmation was public as well as personal gave Hamilton great satisfaction. His sense of Revolutionary rectitude renewed, he returned to Washington that fall ready to take on the Adams administration.

As soon as the new Congress gathered in December 1825, the opposi-

26. Henry P. Johnston, *The Yorktown Campaign and the Surrender of Cornwallis, 1781* (New York: Harper & Brothers, 1881), 56–70; and Hamilton, "James Hamilton."

27. Edgar Ewing Brandon, ed., *A Pilgrimage of Liberty: A Contemporary Account of the Triumphal Tour of General Lafayette through the Southern and Western States in 1825, as Reported by the Local Newspapers* (Athens, Ohio: Lawhead Press, 1944), 64–88; and Hamilton, "James Hamilton."

tion to Adams began to coalesce as members considered the president's annual message. One of Adams's proposals in particular provided live ammunition for the president's new opponents to use against him in the emerging partisan warfare. Adams announced that he had accepted an invitation from the governments of Colombia, Mexico, and Central America to send representatives to an "Assembly of Plenipotentiaries" scheduled to meet in Panama in 1826. As proposed by Simon Bolívar, the great Latin American Liberator, this Panama Congress would allow for cooperation and consultation on a number of issues among the newly independent governments of the Americas. Secretary of State Clay heartily endorsed the idea as a way of incorporating the new southern republics within a hemispheric version of his American System, something of which he had dreamed at least since 1820. As a congressman that year, Clay had urged the creation of "a *system* of which we shall be the *centre*, and in which all South America will act with us." He imagined a future in which the United States would occupy an economic position relative to Latin America analogous to the place of dynamic New England within the Union. "Let us become real and true Americans," said Clay, encompassing the entire hemisphere within the term "American," "and place ourselves at the head of the American system."[28]

The congressional response to the Adams announcement and to his subsequent nomination of two representatives to the Panama meeting hardly matched the enthusiastic embrace hoped for by the president and his secretary of state. Crawfordites, Jackson loyalists, and Calhoun men all viewed American participation at Panama with suspicion or outright hostility.

James Hamilton expressed his opposition publicly, on the floor of Congress, before any other member. Shortly after the reception of the president's message, Hamilton introduced a resolution calling on Adams to deliver to the House any documents related to the Panama invitation; he "tartly expressed" this request, noted Massachusetts congressman Edward Everett, an Adams ally. The president's backers saw Hamilton's resolution, with its implicit threat of a congressional investigation, as part of a purely partisan strategy to embarrass the administration. Adams himself speculated that this issue was "apparently the first measure in

28. Joseph Byrne Lockey, *Pan-Americanism: Its Beginnings* (New York: Macmillan, 1920), chapters 8 and 10; and Garland, *John Randolph*, 2:249 (quotation).

which the opposition are endeavouring to array themselves" and that Hamilton was merely the "organ" of a nascent party. Although, to be sure, the anti-Adams leaders sought to use this issue to rally their troops, Hamilton's reservations went deeper than mere partisanship. The Panama Congress proposal revealed to the South Carolinian yet further dangers that nationalistic policies posed to his home state.[29]

Hamilton rested his objections to the Panama Congress on two grounds. First, he argued that it threatened U.S. sovereignty. He feared that the conference organizers intended it to be a precursor to some kind of confederation of American states rather than simply a one-time diplomatic conclave. Indeed, Bolívar had more than a simple alliance in mind when he initially proposed the meeting, though his interests lay in uniting the newly independent Spanish-speaking republics. Still, some of the planning documents for the Congress indicated its conveners intended uncomfortably close policy coordination among the participants. At the very least, Hamilton charged, the Panama Congress would involve the sort of entangling alliance about which Washington had warned the country. More troubling, it might compromise American sovereignty by committing the United States to joining its southern neighbors in a common foreign and commercial policy enacted by an inter-American "Cortes": "Sir, this is consolidation, indeed, in its most potent and undisguised form, when the rights of the several States of this Union can be so far merged into one great empire . . . and be represented in an assembly beyond our territory, to which the General Government has arrogated to itself the power to transfer a portion of the sovereignty of the People."[30] The idea of creating a new supernational entity with any claims to sovereignty—and potentially with the power to regulate trade—deeply concerned Hamilton. If broad construction of federal power had resulted in a tariff policy harmful to South Carolina, what deleterious consequences might arise from Clay's bi-continental American System overseen by a remote, permanent Panama Congress? South Carolina was losing influence in Washington and would certainly have less in the inter-American union Hamilton feared would spring from the proposed diplomatic conference.

Yet a more profound and immediate matter weighed on Hamilton's

29. Adams, ed., *Adams Memoirs* 7:94–5, 102–3.
30. *Cong. Deb.*, 2:2135–66 (quotation, 2144) (1826).

mind as he considered American participation at Panama. Very likely, the assembled diplomats would endorse recognition of the black-led republic of Haiti. Independent of France for more than two decades, Haiti still did not enjoy diplomatic relations with its fellow American nations. Hamilton shuddered to think of American emissaries attending "an assembly composed of the Deputies of Republics which have colleagued with all colors and complexions" to acknowledge Haitian independence. "If we assent, in the Congress of Panama, to a recognition, however qualified," he added ominously, "it shakes the South to its centre." Even the hint of American approval of Haitian independence presented a grave threat. "Sir, it is proper, that, on this occasion, I should speak with candor, and without reserve; that I should avow what I believe to be the sentiments of the Southern People on this question; and this is, that Haytien Independence is not to be tolerated in any form."[31]

Haiti was problematic because there free blacks ruled. Southern whites considered the presence of free blacks in their own midst troubling enough. Neither chattel—as the logic of racial slavery demanded—nor truly free persons, they occupied an anomalous position in the South. Free blacks, to whites' way of thinking, posed a danger because they served as living reminders to enslaved southerners of the unnatural condition of their bondage. A nation of free blacks so close to southern shores, especially one born in violence against masters and baptized in the blood of whites, alarmed Hamilton. Memories of the disaster that nearly befell white Charleston in 1822 haunted Hamilton as he pondered the Haitian question. It had taken only one free black man, Denmark Vesey, to incite the slaves of Charleston to near rebellion. What terrible hopes might a free black country, recognized by the United States, inspire among South Carolina's enslaved masses? By exchanging diplomats with Haiti, the United States would be legitimizing a slave insurrection and thereby encouraging new Denmark Veseys to arise. *That* prospect shook the South to its core.

South Carolina's slaveholding leaders, Hamilton believed, could handle their black population—slave and free—if the federal government would simply leave the state to its own devices. Although the state's official response to the Vesey incident had not gone as far as Hamilton had wished, South Carolina had demonstrated its control over blacks in its

31. Ibid., 2:2150.

judicial and legislative actions. Moreover, the federal government had generally acquiesced in the state's actions. True, South Carolina had squabbled with a federal judge (embarrassingly enough, Charleston's own William Johnson) about one post-Vesey law designed to restrict blacks, the Negro Seamen Act, but federal authorities had offered little resistance to its enforcement. But now, as Hamilton saw it, Adams and Clay threatened slaveholders' control by involving the United States in the Panama Congress. And, because that Congress was hopelessly entangled with the administration's American System, Hamilton redoubled his efforts to oppose the president and to ensure that he would serve but one term.[32]

In the course of the debate on Panama, Hamilton's friend, John Randolph, now in the Senate, fired a blazing shot in the rhetorical war between the two emerging congressional parties. In a long, rambling, alcohol-fueled speech, the quintessential Old Republican castigated the administration for the "corrupt bargain" by which it had gained power. Repeating charges made earlier by a Pennsylvania congressman, Randolph alleged that Clay threw his support to Adams in order to obtain the coveted office of secretary of state, frequently a stepping stone to the Executive Mansion, and he referred to the administration as a coalition of "the Puritan and the black-leg." Calhoun, presiding over the Senate, refused to call Randolph to order, but instead allowed the Virginian's anti-administration tirade to roll on. Understandably, Randolph's words upset Henry Clay. Many Washingtonians advised him to ignore Randolph's performance as the intoxicated rantings of a madman, but the Kentuckian felt compelled to challenge the senator to meet him on the field of honor.[33]

Randolph took up the gauntlet and asked that Hamilton and Georgia congressman Edward Tattnall serve as his seconds. Hamilton's selection symbolized more than his personal relationship with Randolph or his reputation in matters of southern honor; it also represented the new

32. Donald G. Morgan, *Justice William Johnson, the First Dissenter: The Career and Constitutional Philosophy of a Jeffersonian Judge* (Columbia: University of South Carolina Press, 1954 and 1971), 192–6; and Arthur P. Whitaker, *The Western Hemisphere Idea: Its Rise and Decline* (Ithaca: Cornell University Press, 1954), 46.

33. Robert V. Remini, *Henry Clay: Statesman for the Union* (New York: W. W. Norton, 1991), 292–5; Bemis, *John Quincy Adams*, 57; and Henry Adams, *John Randolph* (1882; reprint, Greenwich, Conn.: Fawcett Publications, 1961), 186–7.

political realities in John Quincy Adams's Washington. Old Republicans and Calhounites were joining forces publicly to do battle, quite literally, with the administration. Fortunately for the duelists, none of the bullets struck its mark, though one of Clay's ripped a hole in Randolph's coat. Despite the happy outcome of this honorable affair, however, warfare between the pro- and anti-Adams men was just beginning.[34]

Friends of Vice President Calhoun in Congress soon began to identify themselves more publicly not just as opponents of Adams, but also as supporters of Andrew Jackson as the man to replace Adams in 1828. Hamilton enlisted as a loyal lieutenant in the cause to elect the Tennessean. This brought him into a common enterprise with Jackson men from Tennessee, such as James K. Polk and John Eaton, as well as with Calhoun's important Pennsylvania backer, Samuel Ingham. In May 1826, just after the Panama Congress debates, Hamilton pledged $300 to help begin a pro-Jackson newspaper in Washington. Edited by Duff Green, the *United States' Telegraph* soon emerged as the authoritative voice for the Jackson party in the nation's capital.[35]

Hamilton's closer association with Jackson also drew him into the circle of Senator Martin Van Buren of New York, whose reputation for successful political machinations had already earned him the nickname "the Little Magician." A Crawford supporter in 1824, Van Buren decided by late 1826 to throw his considerable political weight behind Jackson as the best means of defeating Adams in the next presidential contest and thus ensuring the implementation of his Republican vision. The Jackson movement, Van Buren believed, would be the best way to realize his longtime goal of reuniting the "plain republicans" of the North with southern planters in a revitalized Jeffersonian party.[36]

To create a united anti-Adams coalition under the Jackson banner and prevent another debacle like 1824, Van Buren needed the cooperation of

34. Thomas Hart Benton, *Thirty Years' View; or, A History of the Working of the American Government for Thirty Years, From 1820 to 1850* . . . , vol. 1 (New York: D. Appleton, 1854–56), 70–77 (quotation from 77); Remini, *Henry Clay*, 293–5; Garland, *John Randolph*, 2:258–60; and William Cabell Bruce, *John Randolph of Roanoke, 1773–1833*, vol. 1 (1922; reprint, New York: Octagon Books, 1970), 518–23.

35. John Spencer Bassett, ed., *Correspondence of Andrew Jackson* (Washington: Carnegie Institution, 1928–31; reprint, New York: Kraus Reprint Co., 1969), 3:301–2.

36. Donald B. Cole, *Martin Van Buren and the American Political System* (Princeton: Princeton University Press, 1984), 150–2; and Richard H. Brown, "The Missouri Crisis, Slavery, and the Politics of Jacksonianism," *South Atlantic Quarterly* 65 (winter 1966): 55–72.

Calhoun and his allies, including Hamilton. Creating an alliance between the New York senator and the vice president would not be easy, even with their common antipathy for administration measures. Their past political differences and their conflicting ambitions for higher office presented enormous challenges, yet, in the end, the common goal of defeating Adams allowed them to put those considerations aside, at least temporarily. The two spent the Christmas 1826 holidays together as guests at the Virginia plantation of Calhoun's friend, William Henry Fitzhugh. Eyeing each other warily, they discussed their common political interests. Van Buren proposed winning the support of other Crawfordites for a Jackson-Calhoun ticket in 1828 if Calhoun would clearly separate himself from Adams. Calhoun agreed, and the deal was struck. Van Buren set about recruiting for the Jackson cause influential Crawfordites such as North Carolina congressman Romulus Saunders and Thomas Ritchie, editor of the *Richmond Enquirer*. Against sometimes strenuous objections, he also convinced his fellow Old Republicans to accept Calhoun, the father of the Second Bank of the United States and of federal internal improvements, as their vice presidential candidate.[37]

Hamilton played a key role in cementing the Calhounites to the new Jacksonian edifice Van Buren undertook to construct. In the spring of 1827, he agreed to accompany the New York senator on a tour through the South, during which Van Buren hoped to become better acquainted with his new allies. The men met in Richmond in May just after the adjournment of Congress. Two other members of Congress joined them: C. C. Cambreleng, Manhattan's North Carolina–born congressman, and William Drayton of Charleston, both of whom shared Hamilton's Pennsylvania Avenue lodgings. They planned no public appearances until Charleston, where Van Buren looked forward to being shown "all that is good in S.C." by his new allies. During the long trip through the Virginia and Carolina countryside, the party talked and strategized. Once the group arrived in Charleston, the Carolinians lavished warm southern hospitality on the New Yorker at a dinner honoring Senator Robert Hayne. Van Buren reciprocated with a toast to state sovereignty, a concept receiving greater emphasis by South Carolina Calhounites. Then

---

37. Cole, *Martin Van Buren*, 150–1; John Niven, *Martin Van Buren: The Romantic Age of American Politics* (New York: Oxford University Press, 1983), 179–80; and Robert V. Remini, *Martin Van Buren and the Making of the Democratic Party* (New York: Columbia University Press, 1951; reprint, New York: W. W. Norton, 1970), 129–33.

Hamilton accompanied Van Buren and Cambreleng as far as Savannah, probably giving the pair a personal tour of his nearby rice plantation before they continued on their way. A crucial mission still awaited the New Yorkers on this journey. After leaving Hamilton, they traveled to the Georgia interior for an audience with William Crawford himself to obtain his blessing on the union of his followers with the Calhounites and Jacksonians. They succeeded, with some difficulty.[38]

Mutual admiration between Van Buren and Hamilton ripened during their travels, and after returning home, Van Buren praised the South Carolinian as "one of the best men in the nation." They became personal friends as well as political allies, and over the next few years exchanged warm letters and visits.[39]

Hamilton's new relationship with Van Buren earned the South Carolina congressman an even more prominent role in the Jackson movement. In preparation for the convening of the first session of the Twentieth Congress in December 1827, Hamilton and Van Buren worked in tandem to organize the House to their liking. Hamilton chaired a pro-Jackson steering committee in the House, which now boasted an anti-Adams majority. The Jacksonians' first order of business was to defeat the pro-Adams Speaker from the previous Congress and elect one of their own men. They settled on Andrew Stevenson, an Old Republican from Virginia, and lined up enough support to elevate him to the Speaker's chair. According to William Rives, a Virginia congressman who buttonholed members on behalf of another Old Republican candidate for Speaker, Stevenson backers had beaten him to the punch. The plan to elect Stevenson, Rives explained to his wife, "had been too long and too deeply laid by certain master-workmen, to be broken up altogether."[40]

Flush with his success in the Speaker's election, Hamilton flexed

38. Cole, *Martin Van Buren*, 152–3; Remini, *Martin Van Buren*, 138–42; and Niven, *Martin Van Buren*, 182; Goldman and Young, *Congressional Directories*, 184; Martin Van Buren to James A. Hamilton, 28 January 1827 (quotation) and 15 February 1827, Martin Van Buren Correspondence, Manuscripts and Archives Division, New York Public Library; JH to F. D. Petit DeVillers, 21 March 1827, Emmet Collection, Miscellaneous, New York Public Library.

39. Martin Van Buren to Edwin Croswell, 25 December 1827, MVBP, LC.

40. Kell, "Rhetorical History," 28; William C. Rives to Martin Van Buren, 31 October 1827, William C. Rives Papers, LC; George Raymond Nielsen, "The Indispensable Institution: The Congressional Party During the Era of Good Feelings" (Ph.D. diss., University of Iowa, 1968), 272 (quotation); and *Cong. Deb.*, 4:811 (1827).

political muscle worthy of a "master workman" as the House went on to organize committees. He informed Navy Secretary Samuel Southard that the triumphant Jacksonians intended to use their new strength in the House "liberally," implying that administration measures faced tough going on the Hill. Seeking to establish himself as a formidable but magnanimous force in Washington politics, Hamilton offered to place on the Naval Affairs Committee a member of Southard's choice. "It seems Hamilton disposes of the places on committees as if he were himself the Speaker," President Adams acidly observed. Indeed, Hamilton exerted significant influence in committee appointments. Not only did he reclaim chairmanship of the Military Affairs Committee for himself, but he also helped South Carolinians receive plum assignments at the expense, primarily, of members from Adams-dominated New England. Seven of the nine Palmetto State congressmen secured seats, including two chairmanships, on the most important committees, while the thirteen members from Massachusetts accounted for only four spots on those committees.[41]

As a party leader, Hamilton presented a series of initiatives designed to galvanize the Jacksonians. Containing little legislative substance, Hamilton's initiatives brimmed with symbolic importance. This strategy was not entirely new. In the previous Congress, Hamilton had, for instance, charged Secretary of State Clay with handing out lucrative government printing contracts as rewards to pro-Adams newspaper publishers. In the Twentieth Congress, he joined a wider and more organized effort to embarrass the Adams administration and its congressional supporters in order to build the Jackson party.[42]

For instance, Hamilton resurrected the Sedition Act as a political issue. Passed by a Federalist Congress and signed into law in 1798 by John Quincy Adams's father, the Sedition Act penalized individuals for printing material critical of the president, cabinet officials, and members of Congress. With the Alien Act, which permitted the president to expel foreign nationals without a trial in peacetime, the Sedition Act provided Jeffersonians with evidence of Federalist abuse of constitutional liberty. The two laws became a focus for Republican Party organizing and in-

41. Adams, ed., *Adams Memoirs*, 7:378 (quotation); Nielsen, "Indispensable Institution," 274; and Goldman and Young, *Congressional Directories*, 98–199.

42. *Cong. Deb.*, 3:929–35 (1827).

spired Jefferson and Madison to pen those touchstones of states' rights doctrine, the Kentucky and Virginia Resolutions.

One person convicted under the Sedition Act, South Carolina's own Thomas Cooper, petitioned Congress in 1825 for reimbursement of the four-hundred-dollar fine he had paid a quarter century before, and Hamilton took up his cause. Aiding Cooper, now the septuagenarian president of South Carolina College and a leading Smithite radical, offered dual benefits to Hamilton. Not only did it link John Quincy Adams with an unpopular policy of his father's Federalist Party, but it also served to mollify the politically influential Cooper. Long suspicious of Hamilton's nationalism—just a year before Cooper considered the congressman an Adams man—the college president wielded considerable influence in South Carolina and was an ally of Hamilton's new political friend, Van Buren. By backing Cooper's claim, Hamilton could ingratiate himself with a critic at home while needling President Adams in Washington.[43]

Hamilton first presented his resolution calling for the refund of Cooper's fine in 1826, but the House, dominated then by Adams men, voted 80 to 72 not to consider it. In 1827, he made greater headway, but could not muster a majority. Although he did not win back Cooper's fine, he managed to win over Cooper himself. Moreover, Hamilton's efforts on Cooper's behalf helped solidify the Calhounites' alliance with the Van Buren wing of the party. As the New Yorker observed in the midst of the Cooper debate, "It is gratifying to meet the Republicans of the South upon the old platform which was laid by Jefferson."[44]

To infuriate the Adams men further, Hamilton proposed on January 8, 1828, the thirteenth anniversary of the Battle of New Orleans, that Congress commission a painting of General Jackson's most famous triumph to adorn a vacant panel in the Capitol rotunda. Hamilton presented this as the most non-partisan of resolutions, one that honored American martial genius rather than a particular hero. A painting of the battle that ended the War of 1812, that "beautiful chef d'oeuvre in the science of war," would nicely complement the artistic rendering of Yorktown, the final major engagement of the Revolution whose depiction already graced a Capitol wall. An American painter of distinction should execute the commission, and Hamilton suggested for the job one of the nation's most universally acclaimed artists, Washington Allston. Despite

43. Thomas Cooper to Mahlon Dickerson, 18 January 1825, in *AHR* 6 (July 1901): 727.

44. *Columbia Telescope*, 1 February 1827; Thomas Cooper to Mahlon Dickerson, 18 January 1829, in *AHR* 6 (July 1901): 731; *ADC*, 9:621–2 (1827); Martin Van Buren to Edwin Croswell, 25 December 1827, MVBP, LC (quotation).

its patriotic trappings, the proposal's partisan purpose of advancing Andrew Jackson's candidacy and embarrassing the Adams men, many of
whom as Federalists had opposed the War of 1812, was apparent to
everyone on the House floor. Even Hamilton's choice of an artist born
in South Carolina, Jackson's home state, reeked of politics. John Quincy
Adams noted that "Hamilton, who fancies himself equal to five Ciceros,
flourished in a speech about Allston's restoring the Augustan Age of
Painting," but the president observed that the "picture was part of the
canvass for Jackson."[45]

Hamilton's proposal stirred lively debate for the better part of two
days. George Kremer, a dependable Jackson man from Pennsylvania,
carried Hamilton's idea a step further by suggesting that Congress authorize a second painting to celebrate yet another event from the close
of the war—the Federalist-dominated Hartford Convention. The Jacksonians enjoyed this thinly veiled insult to the Adams men, while the administration forces responded with amendments to divert attention from
the latest war with Britain by honoring more deserving Revolutionary
War battles. Henry Storrs Randolph of New York, chairman of the
Naval Affairs Committee in the previous Congress, weighed in with a
proposal to commemorate American naval victories. Hamilton agreed
that Congress should show its respects for a certain maritime battle, his
friend Commodore Perry's Lake Erie success, but he opposed changes
in his resolution. Should, however, the purity of his proposal be violated
by amendment, Hamilton urged his fellow Jacksonians, in language
bared to its partisan core, to stick by it "as the man whom they desire to
honor by its passage, did to his country in the hour of her utmost need."
When the vote finally came on Hamilton's original resolution, the measure lost narrowly, 103 to 98. Victory in this legislative skirmish, as in
the Cooper matter, however, was beside the point. Hamilton's eye was
fixed on the final battle of the war, the presidential election that autumn.
By embarrassing the administration's supporters and whipping up the
Jackson troops, Hamilton had achieved his purpose.[46]

A few weeks after the battle over the painting, Hamilton sparred with
the Adams men again over a matter related to Jackson's military career.
This time, however, Hamilton found himself on the defensive in a situa-

45. Edgar P. Richardson, *Washington Allston: A Study of the Romantic Artist in America* (New
York: Thomas Y. Crowell, 1948), 28–9; and Adams, ed., *Adams Memoirs* 7:399.
46. *Cong. Deb.*, 4:930–9, 950–3 (1828).

tion possibly detrimental to the Old Hero's presidential hopes. Earlier, a Philadelphia editor had published the story of Jackson's approval of the execution of six Tennessee militiamen during the Creek War in 1814. According to the account, distributed in a handbill illustrated with six large, black coffins, the men had simply wanted to return home at the end of their enlistments. Instead, Jackson court-martialed them and ordered them killed. When this news reached Washington, Ohio congressman John Sloane demanded that Congress obtain any and all War Department documents relating to the incident. The Adams forces meant to expose Jackson as a murderous despot wholly unsuited to the presidency. They could, it seemed, play the propaganda game as well as Hamilton.[47]

When the House received the documents, Speaker Andrew Stevenson referred them to Hamilton's Military Affairs Committee for consideration. In early February, Hamilton brought the House a committee report exonerating Jackson. Hamilton's report laid out evidence of the complicity of the six militiamen in a mutiny against their officers in September 1814. The report charged that, having convinced many of their fellow soldiers that their unit's three-month tour of duty was illegally being doubled, the six led an attack on the commissaries' storehouse at Fort Jackson near Mobile. The War Department records, however, clearly showed that the governor of Tennessee had indeed called the men up for six months, not three, so that they were legally obliged to serve at the time of the Fort Jackson incident. A court-martial in January 1815 cleared most of the mutineers of crimes, or meted out light sentences, because they had been misled by the six ringleaders. In keeping with federal military regulations on mutiny, however, the court ordered the execution of the six, and Jackson, as commanding general, simply approved the sentences. Jackson was not a callous murderer of innocent men; rather, he was a general following proper military procedure to maintain discipline in wartime.[48]

Adams partisans howled in outrage at Hamilton's report. Thomas Whipple of New Hampshire objected to the report's being "scattered over the country" before all members could examine the documents

47. Robert V. Remini, *Andrew Jackson and the Course of American Freedom, 1822–1832* (New York: Harper & Row, 1981), 122.

48. *NR* 34 (22 March 1828): 55–7.

themselves and determine the accuracy of Hamilton's conclusions. Whipple and other Adams supporters wanted to distribute the documents to the public without a report, especially one written by a Jackson party leader. What Jackson man, taunted a pro-Adams congressman, would "say that the naked truth shall not go forth until his friends had prepared a commentary to accompany it? . . . that papers must, of necessity go to the world with a commentary and argument to teach his fellow-citizens how to understand the record." Jackson's enemies strongly implied, without evidence, that Hamilton had simply whitewashed the whole affair.[49]

Although the Adams forces continued to invoke the "six militiamen" to indict Jackson as a "military chieftain" unfit for the presidency, Hamilton seriously undermined their efforts. His report clearly and dispassionately recounted the facts of the incident, and those facts backed Jackson. As the anger of the Adams men testified, Hamilton trumped their hand by demonstrating the Old Hero's innocence.[50]

During the winter of 1827–28, Hamilton continually demonstrated his political skill and his loyalty to the Jackson cause. The Tennessean represented the best means to defeat Adams and the consolidationism that Hamilton increasingly considered injurious to South Carolina's interests. Still, precisely what policies a President Jackson would favor remained a matter of speculation. The Old Hero himself pronounced conveniently vague political sentiments, while his backers in different regions of the country offered conflicting visions of his potential administration. Hamilton trusted that Jackson would recognize the contributions that he, Calhoun, and other like-minded Carolinians were making to the campaign. Their advice would, he hoped, mold a Jackson presidency to their liking. Yet, as winter turned to spring in 1828, Hamilton became less certain of the Carolinians' influence over a future Jackson administration. He soon doubted the soundness of the party he had worked so hard to create, as some of his closest allies—Van Buren chief among them—lent their support to a policy Hamilton considered entirely detrimental to his constituents. More importantly, that policy strained his once fervent faith in the national government to the breaking point. The repercussions of his disaffection threatened to shake the foundation of the Union.

49. *Cong. Deb.*, 4:1495, 1490 (quotation) (1828).
50. James K. Polk to Andrew Jackson, 13 April 1828, *Correspondence of James K. Polk*, vol. 1, ed. Herbert Weaver (Nashville: Vanderbilt University Press, 1969), 175.

CHAPTER 4

The Making of a Nullifier

EVEN AS MARTIN VAN BUREN WAS assembling the Jackson coalition with the assistance of James Hamilton, the changing American economy brought into sharp relief key differences between northern and southern members of the emerging Democratic Party. Northern Jacksonians could hardly ignore the appeal of Clay's American System to swelling numbers of market-oriented farmers, entrepreneurs, and artisans in their region. They wished to oblige New York's raw wool producers and Pennsylvania's budding iron manufacturers, for instance, who desired more, not less, tariff protection for their products. Of course, Hamilton's opposition to the American System had led him to ally with the northern Jacksonians in the first place. If they, too, succumbed to the fever for higher tariffs, what charm did their alliance hold for him? During his final years in Congress in the late 1820s, Hamilton cooperated with Van Buren and company on matters of common interest but objected vigorously to their drift on the tariff. When his protests failed to persuade the Jackson leadership, Hamilton became convinced of the necessity for stronger measures.

South Carolinians shared Hamilton's concerns with the direction of national tariff policy, with important consequences for the state's political alignments. Ever since the passage of the protectionist 1824 act, the state's planters and farmers had almost universally opposed higher tariffs. More fundamentally, increased import taxes and federal appropriations for internal improvements outside the state prompted South Carolinians to challenge the Calhounites' nationalist doctrines more vigorously. Senator William Smith and his followers, consistently the champions of states' rights and strict construction, took advantage of this discontent to dislodge the Calhounites from their position of political dominance.

The tide began to turn against nationalist doctrine with Governor John Wilson's December 1824 message to the legislature. A Smithite, Wilson directed legislators' attention to "the alarming extent to which the Federal Judiciary and Congress have gone towards establishing a great consolidated government, subversive to the rights of the States, and contravening the letter and spirit of the Constitution." Although disturbed by some "consolidationist" trends the governor identified, neo-Federalist legislators hardly enjoyed this Radical's lecture. Endorsing Wilson's views implied that their nationalist program had spawned the ills the governor described. A special house committee, chaired by Hamilton's brother-in-law, Samuel Prioleau, therefore issued a report in early 1825 that downplayed the governor's concerns. Prioleau's neo-Federalist committee majority confessed that, even if Wilson's warning merited investigation, it could not "discover any where that the state Legislature have any legitimate authority to originate any procedure for the redress of such evils, except that which would lead to an application to Congress, for a call of a convention to amend the constitution." But Prioleau's report came too late in the session for the house to act, so that the position of legislators on "consolidation" could not be gauged with official accuracy.[1]

In the next session, however, William Smith himself, now a member of the state's lower house, led a successful assault on neo-Federalism. Directly challenging George McDuffie's "One of the People," which expressed nationalist sentiments that Hamilton had enthusiastically endorsed, Smith proposed resolutions condemning federally funded internal improvements and protective tariffs. A clear majority of Smith's fellow legislators, holding the tariff responsible for the state's feeble economy, passed the resolutions. With that vote, South Carolina's political leaders began not merely a new chapter in state politics, but a whole new volume. Nationalism no longer held a privileged place in the Palmetto State; states' rights views became official doctrine for the remainder of the antebellum period. This shift at the state level prodded the

1. *Columbia Telescope*, 13 January 1826.

Calhounites, already displeased with the drift of their allies in Congress, to move with greater alacrity towards states' rights views.[2]

Even as a growing consensus at home emboldened Calhounite congressmen to eschew neo-Federalism, western agricultural interests and northeastern manufacturers continued to push their agendas. Confrontation, not compromise, loomed as Vermont congressman Rollin Mallary proposed a bill in January 1827 to raise duties on raw wool and woolen goods. Virginia's Andrew Stevenson condemned Mallary's bill as more "obnoxious and unjust . . . than the one of 1824, under which the Southern and Southwestern country were now bleeding at every pore."[3]

Hamilton shared Stevenson's sentiments. The 1824 tariff, Hamilton declared during the debate over the woolens bill, had shaken "this Union to its centre," and now he warned of the threats the proposed bill posed to sectional harmony. By essentially prohibiting the import of woolen goods, it would raise the cost of the "fabrics. . . principally worn by the poor, who can least bear the burden." Left unsaid was that planters balked at paying more to clothe the poorest of the South, their slaves. As in 1824, Hamilton also argued against the constitutionality of protective tariffs. The framers, he reminded his audience, had specifically refused to grant Congress "the power to promote and encourage the useful arts"—including industries—"by bounties."[4]

The pleas of Hamilton and his anti-tariff colleagues failed to sway the majority; the House passed the woolens bill, 106 to 95. Although the bill died in the Senate when Vice President Calhoun cast the tie-breaking vote against it, anti-tariff men could take little comfort in the disregard pro-tariff forces had shown for southern economic distress.[5]

The woolens bill—even after its defeat—stirred up yet more opposition in South Carolina to protectionism and to neo-Federalism more generally. Anti-tariff gatherings of Calhounites and Smith men met throughout the state for a soon-to-be-familiar ritual of listening to speeches and adopting resolutions of protest. Still, a truly effective re-

2. Ibid., 13, 19, and 24 January 1826. For Hamilton's support of "One of the People," see chapter 2.

3. Edward Stanwood, *American Tariff Controversies of the Nineteenth Century* (Boston: Houghton, Mifflin, 1903), 255; and *Cong. Deb.*, 3:783 (quotation) (1827).

4. *Cong. Deb.*, 3:780–1 (1827).

5. Stanwood, *American Tariff Controversies*, 257; and Charles M. Wiltse, *Nationalist, 1782–1828*, vol. 1 of *John C. Calhoun* (Indianapolis: Bobbs-Merrill, 1944), 351.

sponse to the pro-tariff majority in Congress remained elusive. Of what use would be more protests to Congress, or even a regional or national free trade convention? As South Carolinians mulled those options, some prominent men recommended more drastic measures.

Thomas Cooper of South Carolina College shocked some and delighted others with his pronouncement at a Columbia anti-tariff meeting in July 1827 that the time would soon come for the state to "calculate the value of our union; and to inquire what use to us is this most unequal alliance." Privately and frankly, the college president warned Van Buren about the seriousness of his state's opposition to protectionism. Should higher tariffs pass, he predicted, within a year "South Carolina will be an independent State. . . . I count upon all this with full assurance."[6]

More hints of disunion came that summer in a series of essays penned by Robert Turnbull, a planter and former lawyer. For Turnbull, the American System placed the state in a profound crisis, one whose import most South Carolinians did not perceive. The tariff was but a symptom of a more virulent disease that threatened the South. The very security of slavery, he believed, was at stake.

The same broad constructionism that permitted protective tariffs and national roads also allowed for creeping emancipation, Turnbull argued, in the guise of federal support for the colonization of free blacks. Some slaveholders, particularly in the Upper South, regarded colonization as a potential boon because it promised to reduce the nation's "troubling" free black population. Turnbull, however, considered colonization a first step toward abolition. The successful colonization of blacks outside the United States would obviate the argument that emancipation necessarily would create a large, permanent, and dangerous population of freed slaves in the white republic. If colonization were a viable option, planters might be more willing to let their slaves go, thus weakening support for the peculiar institution. Turnbull and others were alarmed when, as Congress considered the woolens bill, the American Colonization Society petitioned for federal aid to remove free blacks to Africa.

Both of South Carolina's U.S. senators opposed the Society's petition. Robert Hayne declared that "of all the extravagant schemes that have yet been devised in this country, I know of none more wild, impracticable,

---

6. Freehling, *Prelude to Civil War*, 130 (first quotation); and Thomas Cooper to Martin Van Buren, 5 July and 31 July (second quotation) 1827, MVBP, LC.

or mischievous, than this of Colonization." His longtime political adversary, William Smith, concurred. Smith, defeated by Hayne for the Senate in 1822 but returned to that body in 1826, perceived malicious motives behind the colonizers' efforts, motives so terrible "he did not wish to touch upon" them. Colonization "was an entering wedge." He left to his listeners' imaginations what would follow this wedge to split the republic.[7]

In Turnbull's series of essays, collected in a pamphlet entitled *The Crisis*, he made explicit what Smith only hinted at, that there was an intimate, insidious connection between implied powers and emancipation. An anti-slavery congressional majority imbued with broad-constructionist principles could declare emancipation "necessary and proper," he pointed out, and then proceed to free the slaves. By allowing Congress to build roads and lay tariffs to encourage northern industries, southern slaveholders were setting down the precedents for their own destruction.

Turnbull's essays prompted Hamilton to think more deeply about the connections between nationalist policies and the security of slavery. "The Crisis," Hamilton later wrote, "was the first bugle-call to the South to rally." As recently as 1824, Hamilton had been amenable to colonization. That year, when Virginia congressman Charles Mercer, a leading proponent of colonization, sent Hamilton a colonization petition for his review, the Carolinian did not upbraid his fellow southerner for weakening slavery. Rather, he complimented Mercer for the petition's "tone of philanthropy," and remarked that he had "not made up my mind conclusively" about the policy. Between 1824 and 1828, however, several congressional debates that linked broad constructionism to looser racial control, such as the discussion of the Panama Congress, turned him against colonization and drew him further from neo-Federalism.[8]

Even as he retreated from his earlier nationalist positions, Hamilton failed to adopt states' rights views wholesale. Before 1828, he occasionally sacrificed ideological consistency to achieve pragmatic political ob-

---

7. *Cong. Deb.*, 3:289 (Hayne) and 296 (Smith) (1827).

8. JH, "An Eulogium of the Public Services and Character of Robert J. Turnbull, Esq. Delivered in St. Philip's Church, Charleston, on the 22d day of November, 1833, After the Laying of the Corner-Stone of the Monument Erected by the State Rights' Party to His Memory" (Charleston: A.E. Miller, 1834), 15; and JH to C. F. Mercer, 3 July 1824, Miscellaneous Collection, SCHS.

jectives. For instance, Hamilton continued to support the Bank of the United States, that bane of Old Republicans everywhere. Although he sometimes complained about the Bank, he considered it necessary and constitutional. The notion that an entity so popular with voters and so useful to his lowcountry constituents might be opposed on the basis of overly sensitive constitutional scruples that he did not wholly share bordered on the ridiculous. He feared, too, that the anti-Bank rhetoric of a few of his allies posed a threat to Jackson's election in 1828. During a December 1827 debate on an anti-Bank resolution presented by Philip Barbour, a Virginia Old Republican, Hamilton exclaimed that "many an old fundholder, roasting his feet before the fire, will tremble in his flannel for his plum, and no doubt exclaim—there, you see how it is the moment these Jackson men have got possession of the House; away goes the bank of the United States 'sky-high,' and we shall next see the 'military chieftain' after his election, making his way, sword in hand, into the vaults of the Bank, and seizing its coffers as his especial portion of the booty after the strife and victory." Hamilton assured his audience that the Jacksonians "do not mean to run our heads against the Bank of the United States." Barbour's resolution went down in utter defeat, thus vindicating Hamilton's position that the Bank was—for the moment at least—safe with Jackson men in charge.[9]

If the pragmatic Hamilton did not wholly share the doctrinaire views of Turnbull and the states' rights men, he certainly concurred with their view that higher tariff duties would hopelessly cripple South Carolina and might even constitute the "entering wedge" of forced emancipation. He therefore resolved to fight efforts by protectionists to shape a new tariff during the spring of 1828.

For their part, supporters of higher tariffs, stung by the defeat of the woolens bill in the previous Congress, vowed to succeed in 1828. When Congress convened in late 1827, Rollin Mallary, the pro-Adams chair of the Committee on Manufactures, began working on legislation for a high tariff. Jacksonians dominated the committee, however, and the bill that emerged reflected their political needs more than Mallary's. Particularly, it catered to the demands of northern and western farmers to protect raw wool, hemp, and flax, while forging high iron duties to curry favor in

9. *Cong. Deb.*, 4:854 (1827); and Thomas Payne Govan, *Nicholas Biddle: Nationalist and Public Banker, 1786–1844* (Chicago: University of Chicago Press, 1959), 108–9.

Pennsylvania. Meanwhile, the party's southern wing was led to believe that their northern and western colleagues had no intention of letting the bill pass. Rather, Jacksonians would load it up with such high rates on iron, hemp, and molasses, that Adams's allies, representing unhappy New England shipbuilders, distillers, and machine makers, would join southerners in killing it. As George McDuffie later remembered the Jacksonian strategy, "we determined to put such ingredients in the chalice as would poison the monster and commend it to his own lips." Pro-tariff Jacksonians from the North and West could claim they did their part to produce a protectionist bill, while southern Jackson men could go back home and take credit for laying it to rest. The only thing the bill would encourage, as John Randolph cogently expressed it, was "the manufacture of a President of the United States."[10]

Hamilton maintained silence during the debate and voted as Jackson strategists envisioned. He joined other southerners to defeat efforts to lower duties on molasses, in the hopes of "poisoning the chalice" for New England rum distillers. Hamilton also supported an amendment that replaced the woolens duties favored by Mallary with slightly less protectionist ones. Still, the taxes on woolens he approved topped those that stirred such controversy the year before. Under the legislation, rates on woolen goods immediately rose from 33 1/3 percent to 45 percent and would increase to 50 percent after a year; moreover, they were also subject to an additional tariff of four cents per pound.[11]

As a final vote approached in the House, it became clear that enough Adams men would join some Jacksonians to pass the bill. At that point, Hamilton supported a motion to postpone the vote indefinitely. He genuinely regretted, he said, his difference of opinion with pro-tariff Jacksonians, who had been "stimulated into a mistaken, but honest zeal, for interests that only require to be let alone to thrive." He wasted little time, though, trying to convince them of the error of their ways. Instead, he concentrated on the injury the tariff inflicted on South Carolina and his state's possible response.[12]

    10. David Franklin Houston, *A Critical Study of Nullification in South Carolina* (1896; reprint, New York: Russell & Russell, 1967), 34–5, n. 3 (first quotation); Wiltse, *Nationalist,* 369; and Stanwood, *American Tariff Controversies,* 290 (second quotation).

    11. *NR* 35 (20 September 1828): 52–7; and Sidney Ratner, *The Tariff in American History* (New York: Van Nostrand, 1972), 17.

    12. *ADC,* 10:111, 113 (1828).

Using language laced with references to the American Revolution and to the compact theory of the Constitution, Hamilton argued vehemently against passage. Echoing Thomas Cooper, Hamilton advised his colleagues "that it is the clearly ascertained 'authentic sense of public opinion' in South Carolina that from an irresistible physical and moral destiny, we consider you are coercing us, to inquire, whether we can afford to belong to a confederacy in which severe restrictions, tending to an ultimate prohibition of foreign commerce, is its established policy."[13] He hoped "that in our firmness and enlightened patience—not base submission—and in your returning sense of justice, we shall find our remedy and relief." But he frankly warned that should the protective policy continue, "South Carolina will be found on the side of those principles, standing firmly, on the very ground which is canonized by that revolution which has made us what we are, and imbued us with the spirit of a free and sovereign people." The time was fast approaching, he added ominously, "when resistance itself becomes a virtue."[14]

The tariff's passage in May 1828 enraged Hamilton. As he saw it, his reasoned arguments on free trade, constitutional interpretation, and basic justice to planters had apparently merely echoed through the drafty House chamber without entering his listeners' ears. Whereas once Hamilton had believed nationalism meant a concern for the good of the whole, the term now simply masked the desires of a majority intent on achieving a narrow self-interest. In the emerging battle of sectional interests, the majority appeared opposed to southern concerns, perhaps irreversibly so.

Van Buren's role in crafting the successful bill especially infuriated Hamilton. In the Senate, the New Yorker voted for a key amendment that assured the bill's passage by making it more palatable to New England's wool manufacturers. It appeared Van Buren had supported the bill all along, no matter what southerners believed the Jacksonian game plan to have been. From Van Buren's perspective, the vote's outcome made perfect sense. He knew his South Carolina allies desperately wanted to replace Adams with Jackson; they simply needed to recognize that a higher tariff was the price of securing the necessary electoral votes. Clearly, Van Buren gambled that, as objectionable as the Calhounites

13. Ibid., 112.
14. Ibid., 114.

judged the tariff, these men, so recently distinguished by their nationalism, would never permit the realization of Thomas Cooper's secessionist
fantasies. Unfortunately for the party he was attempting to create, Van
Buren failed to appreciate the magnitude of South Carolina's opposition
to the protective policy.[15]

Nor did Van Buren understand his friend Hamilton very well. The
Carolinian characterized the course pursued by pro-tariff Jacksonians as
"marked by circumstances of unkindness, not to say bad faith" that filled
him and the rest of the South Carolina delegation "with indignation and
dismay." For Hamilton, the tariff was no mere party-building measure,
akin to the proposed painting of the Battle of New Orleans or Cooper's
Sedition Law petition. Rather, the tariff damaged South Carolina's vital
interests, and that Van Buren should have ignored such a crucial fact
after all Hamilton and other South Carolinians had done for the Jackson
party amounted to betrayal.[16]

Still, while the tariff controversy strained the personal and political
bonds between Hamilton and Van Buren, it did not immediately break
them. Hamilton considered the leader of the Albany Regency too important an ally to dismiss so quickly. Moreover, Hamilton also felt a genuine
fondness for the man, whom only a year before he had accompanied on
the triumphant party-building southern tour. A tone of personal warmth
and political trust continued to suffuse Hamilton's letters to Van Buren
for some time. In Hamilton's mind, Adams and Clay, not his Jackson
friends like Van Buren, remained the major corrupters of national
politics.

Stunned by the passage of a bill they had believed unpassable, upset
with some of their "political friends," and embarrassed by their own
naive complicity in making the new law, members of the South Carolina
delegation gathered to plot a response. The tariff united political adversaries; now Smithite congressmen—William Martin, John Carter, and
Thomas Mitchell—joined Hamilton and other Calhounites—Robert
Hayne, William Drayton, and George McDuffie—to seek common
ground. They met at Hayne's Washington lodgings to discuss a formal
anti-tariff protest to be entered into the official congressional journals.

15. Niven, *Martin Van Buren*, 199.
16. *NR* 35 (22 November 1828): 202.

Hoping for a sectionally united response, they appointed several participants to enlist other southern congressmen in the effort.[17]

Although discussion of the formal protest constituted the evening's main business, the meeting also allowed Hamilton to vent his anger. Convinced that "the south [was] in substance, on this question of taxation, without any representation, and the form might as well be dispensed with," Hamilton proposed vacating his congressional seat. He vowed "not to return again to witness the remonstrances of my constituents insulted, and their interests trampled upon, unless" they instructed him to do so. His fellow members counseled against this move, but Hamilton remained resolute. Only after another series of meetings the next morning did Hamilton finally relent.

At a follow-up meeting at Hayne's, frustration turned to rage as the group learned of divisions among other southern delegations about so simple a matter as placing their official protest on the record. Deeply disappointed with his fellow southerners, McDuffie wondered aloud at their reticence. Certainly they felt the oppressiveness of the tariff as much as the South Carolinians did? Could they not see that those oppressions would inevitably force free men to disunion? Why not act now, by a strong and manful protest, to convince the tariff states of their error and so save the Union?[18]

17. The following account of the two meetings at Hayne's house in May 1828 is based on statements issued by participants after a public flap over the purpose of the meetings. The statements do not precisely distinguish between the events of the first meeting and those of the second. See *NR* 35 (22 November 1828): 199–203. For factional affiliations, see Wild, "South Carolina Politics," 302.

18. The South's diversity in 1828 largely accounts for varying degrees of acceptance of and opposition to protective tariffs throughout the region. Not all areas depended so much on cotton for their economic health, or if they did, their soil was better than South Carolina's. Kentucky hemp growers and Louisiana sugar producers actually benefited from tariff protections for their crops, while the newer black belt regions of Alabama and Mississippi raised cotton profitably. Moreover, in Georgia and the Old Southwest, many looked to the federal government to aid them in their struggles against Indians. Then, too, few were as touchy about the potential dangers to slavery of a strong federal government as white South Carolinians, particularly those lowcountry whites outnumbered by slaves. As noted earlier, key Upper South leaders considered emancipation and colonization a positive idea.

For discussions of South Carolina's uniqueness in the antebellum period, see Freehling, *Prelude to Civil War*; James M. Banner, Jr., "The Problem of South Carolina," in *The Hofstadter Aegis: A Memorial*, ed. Stanley Elkins and Eric McKitrick (New York: Alfred A. Knopf, 1974), 60–93; and Lacy K. Ford, Jr., *Origins of Southern Radicalism: The South Carolina Upcountry,*

Hamilton took McDuffie's thoughts several steps further. The federal government, he began, would never attempt to enforce an unconstitutional law through use of arms. If it attempted to, however, he assumed South Carolina would leave the Union. Not stopping for comment, Hamilton charged on. Should Washington "recruit an army from the power-looms of the manufacturers" to use against the state, Hamilton trusted that Virginians and North Carolinians would not allow soldiers to march through their territories in order to subdue the Palmetto State. But if, by some miracle, the federal army reached South Carolina's soil, the state would be ready. As defiant as his Lynch grandfather decrying British trespasses on American rights, Hamilton declared South Carolina could count "on the spirit of a free and gallant people, and in the holy enthusiasm of a just cause; and if our altars and firesides were invaded, we would have to meet our invaders like men, and I have little doubt we would re[en]act, with considerable improvements, the victories of the 10th of June, Eutaw and Cowpens."

The room stilled as colleagues recovered from Hamilton's blast of Revolutionary rhetoric. They did not know quite how to react to this stirring but seditious speech. The casualness with which Hamilton appeared to accept disunion alarmed some present. If others concurred with him, they remained silent. Then William Drayton spoke up. Seeking to calm his old law student, Drayton acknowledged the horrible injustice of the tariff. Everyone could agree on that. But disunion, he insisted, was far worse. Perhaps the old Federalist believed the reason for this was too obvious to mention, that all knew it in their bones: secession equaled civil discord, even war, which would inevitably spawn slave revolts of epic proportions. The tariff may well have been the entering wedge of abolition, but secession would swiftly strike a fatal blow to the peculiar institution.

Heads nodded in assent, Hamilton silently fumed, and the Carolinians turned their attention to their next steps. They agreed that, on returning home, they would keep one another informed about public reaction to the tariff within their districts. Further, because the members suspected the Adams forces would use anti-tariff excitement in South Carolina

---

1800–1860 (New York: Oxford University Press, 1988). A work emphasizing antebellum southern diversity is Freehling, *The Road to Disunion: Secessionists at Bay, 1776–1854* (New York: Oxford University Press, 1990).

against the Jackson-Calhoun ticket in pro-tariff states, they agreed to discourage overheated rhetoric—like Hamilton's—at public meetings. Finally, if necessary, they would meet in Columbia at the beginning of the next legislative session, just after the presidential election, to direct the state's response.

Before the close of the congressional session, Hamilton decided not to seek re-election that fall. True to his promise to Hayne and the others, he would serve out his term through March 1829. However, as he informed his constituents in a public letter published before he headed home that spring, he could serve no longer than that.

Publicly, he credited his decision to "the claims of a large family to a more uninterrupted application of my time to their interests." He indeed had a large family—seven children by early 1828, and Elizabeth would bear their eighth just after the November election. The income to support this large crew came largely from his Rice Hope plantation, where over 150 slaves planted, tended, harvested, and processed the estate's white gold. To his slaves, Hamilton was an absentee master more often than not. Although he had competent overseers and an excellent factor in the reliable and efficient F. D. Petit de Villers of Savannah, Hamilton sometimes missed more direct management of his holdings. He longed especially for Pennyworth, his Savannah River island, of which he had grown quite fond since acquiring it in 1824. There, from his house built on stilts, he could survey his vast domain of rice and slaves, and truly feel the planter he was born to be. Yet, congressional service kept him in Washington during the winters and early springs, the healthiest times to spend on the marshy island. It was time to go home.[19]

As compelling as his publicly stated reasons were, Hamilton's disgust with Washington politics certainly contributed to his decision to leave the national legislature. It had been thrilling to participate in Congress in his early years of optimistic nationalism, when his idea of South Carolina's interests paralleled the national interest as articulated by leading political figures from around the United States. Even after discovering what he considered the perfidy of Adams and Clay, Hamilton had found a purpose in Congress: to champion the Revolutionary faith of property

19. *Speech of Mr. Hamilton, of S. Carolina on Mr. Randolph's Motion Indefinitely to Postpone the Tariff Bill: Delivered in the House of Representatives of the United States, 19th April, 1828* (Washington: Green & Jarvis, 1828), 3.

and national harmony by opposing the Republican apostates who formed the administration. As a leader in that struggle, he proved himself the true heir of his revered Lynch relatives. Then, with his principles poised on the verge of victory, the evil of the American System appeared among his own allies. His hopes frustrated, Hamilton realized that Congress was no place for the politically pure of heart, which he considered himself.

Hamilton's decision to leave Congress disappointed Andrew Jackson. Urging Hamilton to reconsider, Jackson wrote that "you cannot be spared from the councils of the nation; your services are still necessary to aid in bringing back the administration to the virtuous precepts of a Washington and Jefferson, in renewing the land marks of the constitution, between the states and general government, and to aid in the necessary amendments of the constitution." As cheered as he may have been by those kind words, Hamilton found Jackson's tariff views, which the candidate outlined in the remainder of the letter, too equivocal for his taste. The Tennessean, to be sure, paid homage to a tariff that would spread its benefits and burdens equally throughout the Union. But then he added, "Whether the late act will operate equally upon every section of the union, can only be, tested by experience." Hamilton must have despaired when reading those words, for he believed South Carolina's planters and farmers had amassed all the experience they possibly needed. In his view, the 1824 tariff had harmed them quite enough, and now came the even more abominable 1828 law. Jackson's letter brought Hamilton little comfort. The old man himself, like Van Buren, seemed to be in the grips of the American System.[20]

As Hamilton returned home, he found widespread opposition to the tariff. Precisely what Carolinians should do, other than complain, became the chief topic of debate on sale-days and at militia musters. One popular response was the non-consumption pact. With Revolutionary resolve, South Carolinians pledged not to buy products from pro-tariff states. Numerous Carolinians made it a point to spurn livestock and produce proffered by drovers hailing from pro-tariff Kentucky. Meanwhile, a people who began to perceive New England textile manufacturers as enemies wore homespun as a badge of patriotic honor.[21]

20. Andrew Jackson to JH, Jr., 29 June 1828, in *Correspondence of Andrew Jackson*, ed. John Spencer Bassett (Washington: Carnegie Institution, 1931), 3:411–2.

21. *Charleston Mercury*, 1 October 1828; and *NR* 35 (4 October 1828): 82–3.

Other tariff opponents drew different lessons from the Revolution. Rather than endorsing unenforceable, private non-consumption pacts, they demanded public action to protect the people's rights. Robert Barnwell Smith, a young legislator from Hamilton's congressional district, led the way. On June 12, Smith's constituents in the Colleton District town of Walterborough unanimously approved two documents Smith wrote, an address to the people of the state and another to the governor. Smith laid out familiar anti-tariff themes, but expressed them more insistently. The corruption of the Constitution had proceeded to the point, he said, where "All the resources of this union are under the control of congress for internal regulation. All the property we possess, we hold by their boon; and a congressional majority in congress, may, at any moment, deprive us of it and transfer it northward, or offer it up on the bloody altar of a bigot's philanthropy."[22] Clearly, Turnbull's warnings about the threats to slavery had taken effect here. To counteract the congressional majority, Smith called for "open resistance to the laws of the union" by the state of South Carolina, for, as he declared, "our attachment to this union can only be limited by our superior attachment to our rights."[23]

Although Smith clearly defined the problem posed by the tariff, he failed to specify precisely what form "open resistance" should take. To be sure, the Colleton Address urged the governor to convene the legislature or a state convention, but after that, what? What should or could a legislature or convention do to oppose a federal law? The absence of a well-articulated plan for action led many, both within the state and without, to hear in Smith's rhetorical blast a barely disguised call for secession. Smith's constituents wanted action, or the appearance of it, so they unanimously adopted Smith's Colleton Address, as ill defined as the document's remedy might have been.

With one accord, those gathered also expressed their appreciation for "the talents and zeal" of their congressman, James Hamilton. They passed resolutions expressing their regret with his decision not to seek re-election, and they invited him to attend a public dinner in his honor at a time of his convenience.

Smith's rhetoric fit Hamilton's foul mood perfectly, but during the summer he abided—for the most part—by the congressional delegation's

22. *NR* 34 (28 June 1828): 287–9.
23. Ibid.

agreement not to stoke the fires of protest. Although disappointed with Old Hickory's apparent acquiescence to the tariff, Hamilton remained committed to the Jacksonian ticket and guarded his comments lest he jeopardize his party's chances. Still, at his only public appearance of the summer, the June 28 celebration of the anniversary of General William Moultrie's successful defense of Charleston in 1776, he expended no effort to cool the tempers of his lowcountry friends. For instance, comparing Moultrie's battle of June 28 to the fight over the tariff of June '28, C. C. Pinckney declared, "Let *New* England beware how she imitates the *Old.*" Hamilton even allowed himself a provocative toast. "[A] proud memorial of what South Carolina *was,*" he said of his step-grandfather's victory, "and a cheering token of what she *will be, whenever* called upon to defend her rights, her interests, and her honor." Following this public outburst of defiance, Hamilton maintained a "sullen silence" on the tariff for the duration of the summer. While other lowcountry planters delighted in the cool of the Carolina foothills, the Virginia springs, or points north, Hamilton stayed on Sullivans Island, site of Moultrie's long-ago battle, and contemplated his state's—and his own—political future.[24]

A possible political opportunity presented itself soon after his return home. In June, Columbia's *State Gazette* endorsed Hamilton for governor, a post the legislature would fill in early December. Other papers followed suit as anti-tariff meetings around the state praised Hamilton's strong free trade stand. The governorship, although a weak, mainly honorific office, held some attraction for the retiring congressman. It would require that he neglect his private affairs only during the two-month annual meeting of the legislature in Columbia; the rest of the year he could attend to his few official duties while at home in Charleston or even at his plantation. Yet, as he told Van Buren, to whom Hamilton sent half a barrel of hominy that summer as a sign of continuing friendship, he really did not want the office. Hamilton kept his reasons to himself. Perhaps he wished to remain available for a Cabinet post in the event Jackson won; certainly he wanted to be in Washington, not Columbia, early the next year to advise the presumptive new president on appointments.[25]

24. *NR* 34 (26 July 1828): 352; and JH to Martin Van Buren, 7 September 1828, MVBP, LC.

25. Wild, "South Carolina Politics," 359–60. See a toast, for instance, made at a 13 September meeting in Barnwell, in *Charleston Mercury,* 1 October 1828; and JH to Martin Van Buren, 28 July 1828, copy in JHP, SHC.

THE MAKING OF A NULLIFIER

A gubernatorial campaign would also distract him from thinking about how best to resist the tariff. Like Robert Barnwell Smith, he wanted more vigorous action than non-consumption agreements, which made their signers feel virtuous but were only mildly effective at best. A possible mode of resistance had occurred to Hamilton, one based on a thirty-year-old document John Randolph had placed in his hands—what the Virginian believed to be the only extant copy of Jefferson's original draft of the Kentucky Resolutions of 1798.[26]

Jefferson's resolutions provided a constitutional basis for circumventing the corrupt majority. They argued that the U.S. Constitution was a compact by which the states created a federal government of specific and limited powers. If the federal government ever exercised undelegated powers, a single state, as an equal party to the original compact, could declare such an exercise of power unconstitutional and refuse to enforce it. As Jefferson put it, "every State has a natural right in cases not within the compact . . . to nullify of their own authority all assumptions of power by others within their limits."[27]

In the heat of a lowcountry summer, Hamilton mulled over Jefferson's words and reviewed James Madison's companion piece, the Virginia Resolutions. The 1798 resolutions struck him with the force of truth and called him all the way back from neo-Federalism. His tortuous journey from nationalism to states' rights views now over, Hamilton embraced the doctrine of nullification with the fervency of the newly converted.

As the summer days shortened and autumn elections approached, Hamilton plotted with political allies an anti-tariff course for the state. Although sensitive to his state's budding reputation for hotheadedness, Hamilton could bear silence and inaction only a little longer. "The moment you are out of the wood," he told Van Buren, whose candidacy for governor of New York Hamilton did not want to endanger by taking any embarrassing action, "then I mean to come out & we will then indicate the course our state will take under this system of iniquity & injustice." Struck down with a painful case of dengue fever for the better part of a week in September, Hamilton rose from his sickbed to accompany Robert Hayne on a political journey into the upcountry. Hamilton had two

26. Glenn, "James Hamilton," 112.

27. Thomas Jefferson, "The Kentucky Resolutions," in *The Portable Thomas Jefferson*, ed. Merrill D. Peterson (New York: Viking Penguin, 1988), 286.

objectives for the trip. First, he wished to dissuade allies from nominating him for governor. Second, he wanted to discuss Jefferson's nullification theory with others and determine whether it could provide a workable plan for the state's resistance to the tariff. The first goal he could accomplish on his own as he talked to local politicians and other influential men in the region. The second required his traveling to the extreme northwestern corner of the state—to Clergy Hill, the Pendleton plantation of Vice President Calhoun.[28]

On their way to Pendleton, the lowcountry travelers stopped in the village of Abbeville to make a public appearance and release a trial balloon. There on September 25 in the small courthouse town, a crowd of more than four thousand denounced the tariff and praised their congressional guests for leading the fight against protectionism. After Abbeville's congressman, George McDuffie, harangued the masses for over three hours about the evils of the tariff, the event's organizers offered resolutions suggesting a course of action for the state. In words that echoed Jefferson's Kentucky Resolutions and bore Hamilton's unmistakable influence, Abbevillians claimed that a state could judge whether any particular federal law violated the Constitution and could refuse to allow the enforcement of any it deemed to violate that document. Moreover, in an elaboration of Jeffersonian compact theory, the Abbeville resolutions asserted that a state's declaration of a law's unconstitutionality would stand unless reversed by three-fourths of the states, the proportion required to amend the Constitution. With the adoption of these resolutions, a group of South Carolinians had for the first time publicly endorsed nullification (although they did not use that word). The day's events delighted Hamilton.[29]

The pair of Charlestonians continued their journey north to Pendleton. There, in shadow of the Blue Ridge, the three politicians spent days sharing their ideas about resistance to the tariff and their newfound respect for states' rights. They all agreed that, once the election was over, the state should be ready to stake out an official position. Hamilton no doubt excitedly told Calhoun about the enthusiastic reception the resolutions had received in Abbeville. Hamilton was pleased to learn that Calhoun, too, had been reading the resolutions of 1798. Calhoun confided

28. JH to Martin Van Buren, 7 September 1828, MVBP, LC.
29. Wild, "South Carolina Politics," 341.

that he was working on a document, at the request of Columbia legislator William Preston, which elaborated on the 1798 documents. Calhoun's essay, later called the "South Carolina Exposition," would lay out a theoretical basis for nullification, which the vice president preferred to call a state veto or interposition. The "Exposition" would help legislators translate the theory into practice if the need arose. South Carolina, thanks to the great metaphysician, had the antidote to high tariffs, and Hamilton headed back to the lowcountry to spread the good news.[30]

He picked the perfect spot to begin—Walterborough, where the Colleton Address had been issued a few months before. Colleton District's white residents were ripe for action, and Hamilton came to town with a plan. On October 21, Hamilton's constituents hosted the dinner they had promised him in June, and the congressman addressed them on the crisis confronting them.[31]

Hamilton painted a verbal picture of despair the lineaments of which his auditors well knew. The American System, he argued, was nothing more than a system of organized bribery that had corrupted the majority in Congress. As he explained it, lobbyists for avaricious northern manufacturers bought the support of western congressmen for high tariffs by agreeing to fund canals and roads in the West. Completely ignoring the constitutional objections raised by southerners, the congressional majority declared the American System the settled policy of the country so that they could continue to reap their corrupt harvest. And these were not the only "abuses which must result from a confederate government exercising among its members an internal legislation, unauthorised by the compact of their union," as Turnbull had well taught Carolinians. Not even the election of so noble a man as Andrew Jackson could reverse the trends, for he could not repeal the laws already adopted. There seemed to be no hope for South Carolina or indeed the South.[32]

Just as it seemed the dark hues of corruption would dominate his portrait, Hamilton splashed bright and hopeful colors on his canvas. South Carolina did have a solution to its constitutional conundrum, a conservative principle that could check the abuses of the federal government. In state sovereignty lay the answer, for, as Thomas Jefferson and James

30. Wilson, ed., *Calhoun Papers*, 10:424; Kell, 47; and Margaret Coit, *John C. Calhoun, American Portrait* (Boston: Houghton Mifflin, 1950), 185.

31. *NR* 35 (22 November 1828): 203–8.

32. Ibid., 204.

Madison argued in the Kentucky and Virginia Resolutions of 1798, the states have the right to protect their citizens from "a deliberate, palpable, and dangerous exercise of powers" not granted by the Constitution. Relying on Madison, Hamilton declared that a state was the proper authority to judge whether power had been exercised unconstitutionally. Once the state had made that determination, what was its next step? For the answer, Hamilton referred to Jefferson's defiant first draft of the Kentucky Resolutions: "A NULLIFICATION . . . of all unauthorized acts . . . is the rightful remedy."[33]

Elaborating on the Abbeville resolutions and informed by his conversations with Calhoun, Hamilton then explained what would happen should South Carolina choose to nullify the Tariff of 1828. Following an official declaration of the tariff's unconstitutionality, state authorities would declare the tariff null and void. A regular meeting of the legislature could do that, or a special convention might be required; Hamilton cared not which. Next, should the federal government challenge the nullification, the question would be submitted to a convention of the states. There, three-quarters of the states would have to back the law; otherwise the nullifying state would be upheld. If the convention of the states did pronounce the tariff constitutional, then South Carolina would be faced with a momentous, but perfectly legal decision, "to determine whether she can or cannot belong to a confederacy, in which the prohibitory system is sanctified by the very constitution of the union."[34]

He presented this process as the proper—and peaceful—way that a dispute between a state and the federal government over the constitutionality of the tariff, or any law, should be handled. Of course, the federal government could respond differently to nullification, he pointed out. Washington might do nothing. Such inaction was unlikely, however, given the customs revenue it derived from the state. More probably, the federal government would resort to force. If it did so, it would be solely to blame for the consequences, including the inevitable secession of the aggrieved state. But a federal attack would never accomplish its purpose. Before his Colleton audience, Hamilton repeated the prediction he had made at Hayne's lodgings that spring: federal military forces would more

33. Ibid., 206–7. Hamilton did not quote Jefferson precisely, but he certainly got the gist of it.

34. Ibid., 207.

than meet their match in South Carolina's brave neighbors and the state's own people. The choice then lay with the federal government—either abide by Hamilton's peaceful nullification process, or use force in an attempt sure to end in ruin and disunion.[35]

It was a breathtaking performance. Hamilton's speech marked the first time a leading South Carolinian publicly uttered the word "nullification." More importantly, to the cheers of his audience, he had forcefully laid out how nullification could solve the crisis caused by self-interested congressmen and senators.

Proudly, Hamilton dispatched a copy of his remarks to James Madison, the surviving author of the 1798 Resolutions. Surely, he would approve of the use to which Hamilton had put Jefferson's and his own ideas. Shortly the former president honored Hamilton with a reply. Madison opened by praising the "intellectual power & impressive eloquence" of Hamilton's speech. If the Carolina congressman beamed at such laudatory words from the Father of the Constitution, the rest of the note provided him little pleasure indeed. Hamilton's remarks, Madison added as gracefully as possible, embraced "doctrines in which I can not concur, & an indulgence of feelings which I cannot but lament." Madison suggested that Hamilton had not understood the Kentucky and Virginia Resolutions, perhaps because he had not seen them "in their ancient form." Obligingly, the aged man enclosed a copy of the original texts. His ego bruised, Hamilton dismissed Madison as senile.[36]

Others joined Madison in denouncing Hamilton's doctrine of nullification. Opponents of nullification pointed out its connection to disunion and revolution, especially given the ominous hints dropped by Cooper, Turnbull, Robert Barnwell Smith, and Hamilton himself. Nullification, its critics charged, masked secession.

Even in South Carolina, arguments about the disunionist nature of nullification gained ground that fall, largely thanks to the publication of

35. Ibid.

36. James Madison to JH, 13 December 1828, copy in JHP, SHC. Madison's resolutions constituted the fraternal, not identical, twin of Jefferson's. Jefferson declared a state's right of nullification, using that word, while Madison argued that a state could interpose its authority between an unconstitutional federal law and its citizens in order to protect the latter. He failed to specify the practical meaning of interposition. Until shown an original draft of the Kentucky Resolutions after his correspondence with Hamilton, Madison did not believe Jefferson had employed the term "nullification." See Drew R. McCoy, *The Last of the Fathers: James Madison and the Republican Legacy* (Cambridge: Cambridge University Press, 1989), 143–4.

a letter in a Georgetown newspaper. An anonymous source close to Congressman Thomas Mitchell (probably Mitchell himself) made public a summary of the discussions held at Senator Hayne's earlier in the year. Specifically, the article accused Hamilton of having openly advocated disunion. Although Hayne and several other participants rose to Hamilton's defense, the characterization of nullification as essentially destructive to the Union persisted—as did the image of Hamilton as a disunionist conspirator.[37]

Hamilton's Walterborough speech came too late in the campaign season to damage Jackson's chances, and voters handed Jackson and Calhoun a decisive victory. Still, as word spread of Hamilton's remarks, the party faithful around the country worried about such talk emanating from Jackson leaders in South Carolina. Calhoun, who in 1828 was more interested in asserting the right of nullification than in exercising it, tried to reassure his out-of-state friends. Though the American system "tends to alienate our [southern] people from their brethren, and from our political institutions," Calhoun wrote a New Yorker, "yet I feel a thorough conviction that the Southern people still remain devotedly attached to the Union. I do not think they look to revolution for redress, but to the Constitution; . . . any other interpretation of Majr Hamilton's speech, to which you refer, would do his motives great injustice." Despite Calhoun's efforts, the Walterborough speech raised suspicions among Jacksonians about Hamilton's intentions.[38]

Family matters provided a brief respite from Hamilton's politically active fall. On November 17, Elizabeth Hamilton gave birth to their eighth child, a seventh son. The delighted father continued his tradition of naming sons for men he admired. This time, Hamilton chose to honor his friend John Randolph. After bestowing the name of the states' rights purist on his youngest, Hamilton left his wife and family behind so that he might promote states' rights principles in the state capital. The legislature was set to open just a week after the birth, and there was much to be done before the opening gavel fell.

Once in Columbia, Hamilton went to work with his allies to shape the legislature, using political skills honed the previous year at the opening

37. See NR 35 (22 November 1828): 199–203.

38. John C. Calhoun to [John A.] Dix, 2 January 1829, Calhoun Papers, ed. Wilson, 10:541–2.

of the Twentieth Congress. Hamilton's influence could be detected in the complaint of Beaufort's William Elliott about all the "maneuverings of party politicians" in the capitol. Elliott, Hamilton's electoral opponent in 1822 and now a skeptic about nullification, lamented that "a private cabal" had "arranged before hand all the play of the machinery" of government. Not only did they decide who should be Speaker, but they also fixed the gubernatorial election. Hamilton, Elliott understood, had agreed not to oppose the Smithite Stephen Miller for the state's chief executive post, provided that Miller convince his friends not to oppose Hayne's re-election to the U.S. Senate. Legislators easily elected Miller and Hayne once the session began.[39]

Hamilton enjoyed less success in convincing legislators to adopt nullification. The theory was simply too new and radical to be widely embraced. Even among legislators friendly to the idea, there was a decided lack of consensus about the nuts-and-bolts of the process. Could an ordinary legislature nullify a federal law, or was a convention akin to that which had ratified the Constitution required? Hamilton believed the legislature had the power to nullify, but Calhoun's final draft of the "Exposition," which circulated among legislators as the session got under way, insisted nullification was no mere legislative act. Rather, it was an expression of the will of the people acting in their sovereign capacity, and thus it required a convention. Some moderate tariff opponents favored yet another petition to Congress expressing their outrage over higher rates, while others suggested a meeting of anti-tariff states. Moderates also could point to the language of the "Exposition," which argued that South Carolina should assert the theory of nullification without implementing it. Instead, the "Exposition" called on the state to give the newly elected president a chance to redress their grievances. (Most legislators did not realize that the author of those words was Vice President Calhoun, who wished to give Jackson an opportunity to push tariff reform; Calhoun's authorship remained secret for the next two years.)[40]

39. William Elliott to Anne Hutchinson Smith Elliott, 24 November 1828, Elliott-Gonzales Papers, SHC. For rumors about Hamilton's unwillingness to be governor, see Job Johnston to Stephen D. Miller, 20 August 1828, Henry L. Pinckney to Stephen D. Miller, 23 August 1828, and James A. Black to Stephen D. Miller, 15 September 1828, all in Chesnut-Miller-Manning Papers, SCHS.

40. William Elliott to Anne Hutchinson Smith Elliott, 29 November 1828, Elliott-Gonzales Papers, SHC. For a lucid explanation of the constitutional theories underlying these two

The feuding among supporters of nullification in addition to the opposition to this radical new idea by others convinced William Elliott by
early December that "Nothing violent I think will be done on the tariff."
He was right. The most radical proposal, Andrew Pickens Butler's resolution calling for a state convention, went down in defeat, with two-
thirds voting against it. That resolution called for a convention a year
hence, in December 1829, thus allowing time for the new Congress and
administration to repeal the protectionist law while holding the threat of
nullification over their heads. Hamilton doubtless was disappointed that
Butler's measure failed, for only such firm action, he believed, could
bring members of Congress to their senses. Instead, the house approved
a formal protest against the tariff. As for the "Exposition," the legislature
refused to sanction it as official policy, though it ordered five thousand
copies of the document printed.[41]

Hamilton returned to Washington for the short session, his final as a
member of Congress. A few pieces of business, some lingering from the
spring, some new, awaited him there. Hamilton got in one last jab at the
Adams administration by issuing a report of a special retrenchment committee he chaired. Appointed during the previous session, the committee
hardly had found the profligate spending with which Jacksonians had
charged the administration. Still, since the spring, the committee's work
had generated its share of propaganda for the election, and with the defeat of Adams, the actual report was rather anticlimactic.[42]

Then there was the matter of the South Carolina Canal and Railroad
Company. A group of Palmetto State investors petitioned Congress in
early 1829 to obtain federal aid for their planned railroad from Charleston to Hamburg, a relatively new village midway up the Savannah River
on the Carolina side. Designed to divert upcountry cotton from Savannah to Charleston, the railroad would, its boosters claimed, prop up the
state's flagging economy. The petitioners asked that Congress authorize

different methods of nullification, see Freehling, *Prelude to Civil War*, 159–73. The drafts of
the "Exposition" by Calhoun and the legislative committee appear on facing pages in Wilson,
Calhoun Papers, 10:444–534. For Calhoun's desire to give Andrew Jackson a chance to lower
the tariff, see John C. Calhoun to William C. Preston, 6 November 1828, ibid., 10:429.

41. William Elliott to Anne Hutchinson Smith Elliott, 10 December 1828, Elliott-Gonzales Papers, SHC. *South Carolina House Journal*, 15 December 1828, 127, in *State Records*, reel
513. Freehling, *Prelude to Civil War*, 175.

42. Adams, ed., *Adams Memoirs*, 7:432.

the federal government to purchase 2,500 shares of their company's stock. Despite the potential benefits to their state, Hamilton and other members of the South Carolina delegation arranged to table the measure. They could not abide the hypocrisy of seeking federal aid for a state project in the midst of their battle with the broad constructionists.[43]

In the weeks before Jackson's inauguration, the composition of the incoming president's Cabinet rather than congressional business occupied much of Hamilton's attention. His concerns focused on the secretary of the treasury, for that officer would potentially exert enormous influence on the course of the administration's tariff policy. A solid anti-tariff man might yet be able to bring Jackson to his senses. Hamilton and his South Carolina colleagues decided that the post should go to Langdon Cheves, the former Palmetto State congressman. He held impeccable credentials, which included service as Speaker of the U.S. House of Representatives and president of the Bank of the United States. Moreover, he now lived in Pennsylvania, so that state, so important to Jackson's election, would be honored by his appointment. Louis McLane of Delaware stood second on their list to head the department. For the other Cabinet seats, Hamilton favored his friend Van Buren for State, John McLean of Ohio for War, Pennsylvania's Samuel Ingham for postmaster general, and either William Barry of Kentucky, James Barbour of Virginia, or New Hampshire's Levi Woodbury for attorney general. "This I believe would be the strongest Cabinet which the Old Man could call to his aid . . . if he was to ransack the whole Country."[44]

There was one other person whom Hamilton believed deserved a top administration position—James Hamilton himself. He entertained thoughts of being secretary of war, an office for which he believed himself particularly well suited. Hamilton's qualifications, including service in the late war with Britain and as chairman of the House Military Affairs Committee, surpassed those of Calhoun when Monroe had appointed him a dozen years before. Hamilton, however, did not press for an appointment, but waited, in good old republican style, for an offer.

Hamilton and the South Carolinians, of course, were not the only Jackson supporters seeking a share of victory's spoils. Hamilton naturally

43. William H. Pease and Jane H. Pease, *The Web of Progress: Private Values and Public Styles in Boston and Charleston, 1828–1843* (New York: Oxford University Press, 1985), 57. See also *Charleston Courier*, 24 February 1829.

44. JH to Martin Van Buren, 23 January 1829, MVBP, LC.

considered the pro-tariff Jacksonians his greatest adversaries in the bid for influence in the new administration. Characterizing them as "small men with narrow & interested views," Hamilton confided to Van Buren that he feared Jackson would succumb to their arguments "that gratitude for [Pennsylvania] should even surpass what is due to the rest of the Country." His fears would soon be realized.[45]

Once the president-elect arrived in Washington on February 12 for his March 4 inauguration, office seekers and dispensers of free advice immediately swarmed around him. Not wishing to appear too demanding, Hamilton left a message for Jackson suggesting a meeting between the president-elect and his "southern friends." Mainly, though, he and his colleagues kept a respectable distance. Still, Hamilton hardly wanted to yield the field to his political opponents, so he passed advice on to Jackson through their mutual friend, Senator Hugh L. White of Tennessee. James A. Hamilton, who was son of Alexander Hamilton and was a Van Buren operative, served as another crucial conduit for information. It was through the northern Hamilton that the southern Hamilton got a second and slightly more insistent message to Jackson that the South Carolina delegation wished to see him. On February 17, Jackson informed Calhoun that he would meet with the group, and, the following evening, Hamilton and three other Carolinians—Hayne, McDuffie, and Drayton—had their audience with the Old Chief. A fifth Carolinian, Calhoun, attended as a strangely silent figure.[46]

Beforehand, Hayne, the senior member of the congressional delegation, had appointed Hamilton to the "office of breaking the Ice." Hamilton commenced the conversation by urging that Jackson appoint a truly distinguished Cabinet. The expected nomination of Van Buren for secretary of state was "highly acceptable" to his colleagues, Hamilton said, but he frankly expressed their anxiety about rumored candidates for other posts, especially for the Treasury Department.[47]

Jackson naturally anticipated the Carolinians' concerns and interjected that he wished neither an extreme pro-tariff man nor an extreme anti-tariff man as treasury secretary. He then broke the news to them that he had already promised the Pennsylvanians that he would appoint

45. Ibid.
46. James A. Hamilton to Martin Van Buren, 19 February 1829, MVBP, LC.
47. JH to Martin Van Buren, 19 February 1829, MVBP, LC.

one of their own, Samuel Ingham, to the post. An awkward silence ensued. On the surface, Ingham seemed an acceptable candidate for Hamilton and his friends. Long a Calhoun supporter, he had voted with the Carolinians for the most part during House consideration of the tariff. Yet, on final passage, he had abstained. So although Ingham's apparent neutrality made him a logical choice as Jackson's top tariff advisor, his abstention—and his being a Pennsylvanian—rendered him suspect in the minds of the Carolinians. Old Hickory sensed his guests' discomfort, not to say anger, so he sought to reassure them by sharing the three goals of his administration, with which he knew they would agree: quieting the tariff controversy, paying the public debt, and reforming administrative abuses. In that case, Hamilton interjected, not so subtly ignoring the intelligence about Ingham, the perfect treasury secretary would be Langdon Cheves. Jackson praised Cheves's qualifications, but responded that the Pennsylvanians hardly considered him representative of their interests. Hamilton then suggested his alternative candidate, Senator Louis McLane of Delaware. Unfortunately, Jackson countered, the appointment of McLane would create a Senate vacancy, which the pro-Adams majority in the Delaware legislature would fill with one of its own. No, Jackson declared, McLane was too valuable as a U.S. senator.[48]

The meeting ended with a clear understanding that Jackson could not accommodate the South Carolinians, thus confirming in Hamilton's mind his fears about the trajectory of the administration. Following the delegation's meeting with Jackson, Hamilton confided his feelings to Van Buren, whom he still considered a close ally. "I assure you as Sir Anthony Absolute says," he wrote, referring to a character in a popular eighteenth-century play, "'I am perfectly cool—damn cool—never half so cool in my Life.'"[49]

Hamilton met with Jackson once more before the inauguration. In a "long and feeling talk," the president-elect tried to smooth things over with his Carolina ally. Jackson informed Hamilton that he had considered the Carolinian for "a seat in his political household," but that the political pressures on him made that impossible given Hamilton's "ultra tariff violence." Hamilton graciously thanked Jackson "for the honor he

48. For Ingham's votes on the tariff, see *NR* 35 (20 September 1828): 56.

49. JH to Martin Van Buren, 19 February 1829, MVBP, LC. Sir Anthony Absolute appears in "The Rivals" (1775) by Richard B. Sheridan.

had intended" to give him, but "confessed that the *cause* of my exclusion I regarded as the highest compliment of my life."[50]

The events of March 4 did little to dispel Hamilton's growing gloom about the new order in the nation's capital. The day began on a cheery note with President Jackson's inaugural speech, to which Hamilton applied a string of very positive adjectives: "excellent, chaste, patriotic, sententious & dignified." But he had only scorn for "the *sovereigns*" who celebrated the day with "a regular Saturnalia" at the White House. "The Mob broke in," as he described the scene, "in thousands—spirits black yellow & grey, poured in in one uninterrupted stream of mud & filth, among the throng many subjects for the penetentiary and not the fewest among them [were] Mr Mercer['s] tyros for Liberia. It would have done Mr Wilberforce's heart good to have seen a stout black wench eating in this free country a jelley with a gold spoon at the Presidents House."[51]

Before Hamilton's very eyes, his worst nightmares about the Jackson administration were taking on flesh in scenes that could have cheered only British abolitionists and American colonizers. The president seemed to be overwhelmed by the "miserable Ale House or what is worse Whiskey House" crowd, a daunting prospect for a representative from aristocratic South Carolina. Moreover, Hamilton frankly thought Jackson too weak to withstand the pressures brought to bear by the great unwashed and the self-interested. Jackson had practically admitted as much in their final interview before the inauguration. The central committee that had run the campaign—mostly tariff men—had, Hamilton believed, "taken the Old man under their parental guardianship." The administration was theirs to rule.[52]

As Hamilton headed home to Charleston in early March, only two men seemed to be able to prevent the Jackson administration from ending in democratic disaster. Fortunately they were both friends of his, men he could trust. Yes, they had differed with each other in the past, but surely they would be able to join forces to return the nation to its proper republican course. Hamilton felt sure he could depend on Calhoun and Van Buren.

50. JH to Martin Van Buren, 5 March 1829, MVBP, LC.
51. Ibid.
52. JH to Martin Van Buren, 23 January and 5 March 1829, MVBP, LC.

CHAPTER 5

The Chief Nullifier
1829–1833

"I LOOK BACK UPON MY RECENT EXCITEMENT in politicks as a dream of insanity," wrote James Hamilton in the spring of 1829 from Pennyworth Island, far from the tariff battles and Cabinet intrigues of the national capital. Back home among his fields and slaves, he threw himself into spring planting, which provided a brief but needed diversion from Washington warfare. Soon he headed north to spend the summer with his family in Northampton, Massachusetts. There, where his three oldest boys—James, Dan, and Lynch—had recently begun studies at the Round Hill School, he took a well-deserved rest from the dizzying months of politics. He also made an excursion to the resort town of Ballstown, New York, where he enjoyed the conviviality of other seasonal visitors from the South as well as the occasional Yankee. Mainly, though, during his New England summer, Hamilton experienced "an intolerable fit of ennui which translated into plain english means nothing but sheer laziness." For a month, he could only "loll on a soffa" and read in a leisurely fashion. Apparently, Hamilton had awakened from his political dreams to the typical lowcountry planter's reality of slave management, rice yields, and indolent summers up North.[1]

Notwithstanding his protestations, however, Hamilton was not

1. JH to Martin Van Buren, 28 April 1829, MVBP, LC (copy in JHP, SHC) (first quotation). JH to John C. Calhoun, 10 May 1829, in Clyde N. Wilson, ed., *The Papers of John C. Calhoun* (Columbia: University of South Carolina Press, 1979), 11:43. JH to Martin Van Buren, 16 July 1829, MVBP, LC (second and third quotations). "Ballstown" was the early-nineteenth-century spelling of the New York township known today as Ballston. The resort village of Ballston Spa, where Hamilton probably spent his time, is within the Town of Ballston.

through with politics. In fact, he was embarking on the most important
phase of his public life, the nullification controversy. Over the next five
event-packed years, he led the creation of the most extensive and influential political organization in his state's history while marching South
Carolina to the brink of secession and war. Although his efforts earned
Hamilton the scorn of some Carolinians and former allies such as Andrew Jackson, the adulation showered on him by the majority of the
state's white men more than made up for those ill feelings. Most importantly, South Carolina politics from Hamilton's retirement from Congress in 1829 through 1834 resembled nothing so much as a battlefield,
and his leadership in the struggle over nullification allowed him finally
to live up to his own expectations of himself as an heir of the Revolution.
No single individual bore greater responsibility than James Hamilton for
this constitutional showdown between the federal government and South
Carolina, and he would always consider it the high point of his life.

During the summer of 1829, tariff politics never strayed far from the
center of his thoughts. Before leaving the humid, unhealthy lowcountry
for the summer, Hamilton instructed pro-nullification Charleston editors "to keep up the Fire on the tariff." He wanted his lowcountry neighbors unfortunate enough to remain at home that summer to remember
the oppressive legislation while he enjoyed New England's temperate
clime. Once he arrived in Northampton, he focused his reading on the
tariff while Elizabeth and the family slaves kept the eight rowdy Hamilton youngsters—ranging in age from six months to sixteen years—from
disturbing him.[2]

As Hamilton took the measure of the new administration that summer, he discerned few hopeful signs. Hamilton imagined that Jackson's
relatively advanced age and lack of experience in high office rendered
him so insecure as to be simply the puppet of a cabal of unsound advisors.
Precisely who was advising the president that summer Hamilton could
not say with certainty, since he was far removed from official circles. He
knew that the vice president exerted little influence. He hoped John
Eaton, the new war secretary, did not fill that role. Not only had Eaton
generated social and political scandal in Washington by marrying his
paramour, Margaret O'Neale Timberlake, soon after the apparent sui-
cide of her husband, but as a Tennessee senator he had been the only

2. JH to John C. Calhoun, 10 May 1829, Wilson, ed., *Calhoun Papers*, 11:44.

southern Jacksonian to support the Tariff of Abominations. Hamilton could abide another rumored chief advisor, Martin Van Buren, although the New Yorker had disappointed him. Hamilton kept in contact with him, not only because he might emerge as Jackson's right-hand man, but also because Hamilton genuinely liked him. Moreover, Hamilton hoped—vainly it turned out—that the new secretary of state would appoint his brother-in-law to a minor diplomatic post.[3]

No matter who had Jackson's ear, Hamilton believed the president would be easily dissuaded from a course of thoroughgoing reform. To be sure, the administration had begun prosecuting corrupt holdovers from the Adams administration, beginning with a Treasury Department auditor accused of embezzlement. But Hamilton wanted Jackson to do more than punish the occasional "poor pilferer." He demanded nothing less than the full dismantling of the American System. "If the Old Veteran does not accomplish this, it were better that we had permitted him to remain in a retirement so full of dignity and comfort at his own Hermitage. For God knows we did not make him president, even to work the miracle of making Mrs E[aton] an honest woman." Even should Jackson ever propose scrapping the protective tariff and federally financed internal improvements, Hamilton was certain the president would back down the moment "Harry Clay" held "up a dreadful Bugaboo."[4]

Traveling home with his family in late September, Hamilton stopped in Manhattan to confer with Churchill Cambreleng, the New York congressman who had accompanied Van Buren on his southern tour two years before. With Cambreleng, Hamilton shared his deep misgivings about the administration's probable tariff policies and his thoughts about South Carolina's likely response. Later, a shaken Cambreleng wrote Van Buren: "I feel much solicitude that we should not lose so excellent and honorable a friend—but I have my apprehensions that if he returns home with his present impressions he will be unconsciously driven into an opposition repugnant to his feeling and hostile to his permanent political interest." This "crisis in the political career of our friend," Cambreleng

3. On the Eaton affair, see John F. Marszalek, *The Petticoat Affair: Manners, Mutiny, and Sex in Andrew Jackson's White House* (New York: Free Press, 1997). JH to Martin Van Buren, 16 July, 2 and 9 October, 16 November 1829; 8 and 21 March, 20 April, 27 May 1830; John Randolph to Martin Van Buren, 2 April and 21 May 1830; all in MVBP, LC.

4. Remini, *Andrew Jackson and the Course of American Freedom*, 186–7; and JH to Martin Van Buren, 16 July 1829, MVBP, LC (quotations).

warned Van Buren, might very well drive the Carolinian "into violent measures in opposition to the tariff."[5]

Despite this warning, Van Buren did nothing to soothe his South Carolina ally. Less concerned with Hamilton's complaints than was the southern-born free trader Cambreleng, Van Buren concentrated on satisfying his own pro-tariff constituencies. Moreover, the Little Magician was already scheming to sour relations between the president and vice president as part of his plan to position himself as Jackson's favorite and heir apparent. In that larger power play, Hamilton, whom Van Buren erroneously considered primarily a Calhoun loyalist, was expendable. Had he appreciated that Hamilton's concern lay with the tariff and not Calhoun's political fortunes, the two might have cut a mutually satisfactory deal that spared the nation the showdown of 1832–33. One can imagine an arrangement by which Hamilton would have delivered the support of a substantial portion of Carolina's growing "state's rights" party to Van Buren in exchange for the New Yorker's cooperation in lowering the tariff and channeling federal patronage in the state through Hamilton.

Hamilton returned home resolved to pursue the solution he believed within the state's power: nullification. Achieving it would require great political unity among state leaders because calling a convention necessary to nullify a federal law required the concurrence of two-thirds of the legislature. The resounding vote in the previous legislative session against a convention demonstrated nullification's unpopularity. Hamilton knew, too, that more than legislative arm-twisting would be required to change perceptions of nullification. Although South Carolinians lived under the most oligarchic constitution in the nation, the state had undeniable democratic strains. Public opinion mattered.

Unhappily for Hamilton, "the mass of the people" were, in his view, ignorant "of the operations of the General Government on the interests of the South" and languished in "an apathy in regard to the proper means of preserving their rights." He needed to convince Carolinians that their problems could be traced to the tariff and that their only remedy lay in nullification. In seeking to forge a pro-nullification majority, Hamilton relied on a state political culture that, while democratic in that all white men could vote, remained highly deferential. "The people *expect*," Ham-

5. C. C. Cambreleng to Martin Van Buren, 25 September 1829, MVBP, LC.

ilton observed, "that their Leaders in whose honesty & public spirit they have confidence will think for them, and that they will be prepared to *act* as their Leaders *think*." Public opinion could be molded, and Hamilton looked forward to shaping the state's response to the tariff.[6]

South Carolina's existing means of political mobilization were inadequate to the task of changing the collective mind on so controversial an issue as nullification. The state boasted no mass political party that was even a pale shade of Van Buren's disciplined New York Bucktails. Instead, the various Republican factions of the post-1815 era, including the most important ones headed by Calhoun and William Smith, resembled not well-oiled machines but fragile webs of influence. Emanating from Calhoun and Smith, delicate threads connected key state legislators and judges, newspaper editors, militia officers, and other assorted leading men. Individuals enmeshed themselves in one faction or the other based partly on their constitutional views and partly on the personalities of the leaders. In rural areas where the vast majority of ordinary voters lived, the political predilections of local notables often held sway with their neighbors on election day. By the late 1820s, the blurring of constitutional differences between Calhoun men and Smithites meant that, with the exception of a handful of merchants and their allies in Charleston and a few inland market towns, almost all South Carolinians had deep reservations about the tariff and the rest of Henry Clay's American System. By 1829, such Calhounites as Hamilton and McDuffie opposed the tariff by championing the reserved rights of the state as vociferously as the Smithites did. Only personal loyalties to Calhoun and Smith remained as the major dividing line between the state's two main Republican factions. The state was ripe for a new system of political connections.[7]

Soon after Jackson's inauguration, Hamilton and a few of his allies, most notably Robert Hayne, George McDuffie, and Henry L. Pinckney, began to redraw the lines of political association in the state. Because most politically active Carolinians agreed on the problem—the tariff— the only disagreement concerned the remedy. Hamilton and company put forward nullification as the only proper and effective response to the

6. JH to Stephen D. Miller, 7 August 1830, Chesnut-Miller-Manning Papers, SCHS.

7. Wild, "South Carolina Politics"; Lacy K. Ford, Jr., *Origins of Southern Radicalism;* and Freehling, *Prelude to Civil War.*

protective tariff, and that question of nullification destroyed the old Calhoun and Smith factions and gave rise to new political organizations. It
was a revolutionary change that gave the state the deceptive appearance
of a highly democratic political system in the early 1830s.

The new nullification-era parties, though more popularly based than
the old factions, clearly lay under the control of their leaders. In a top-
down fashion, the leaders set the political agenda and defined the choices
for the electorate. For the pro-nullification forces, Hamilton assumed
the role of master strategist and almost embodied the cause. Handsome
and gregarious, he employed his personal charm and excellent oratorical
skills to good effect. Using public spectacles and mass meetings, a well-
organized system of political clubs, and a press strategy that diffused the
nullification message throughout the state, he channeled economic discontent and social anxiety among South Carolinians into anger at the
tariff and support for his party. Hamilton appealed to his fellow citizens
not only as rational economic actors, but also as heirs of the Revolution,
as South Carolinians, and as men. He succeeded spectacularly by winning a majority of Carolinians to his cause, staring down Andrew Jackson, and amassing enormous power for himself. Hamilton's first step in
the long march to nullification came with his 1830 gubernatorial campaign. Winning the governorship meant gaining a majority in the state
legislature, for that body selected the state's chief executive as well as the
other constitutional officers. Also, only the legislature could authorize a
convention of the people.[8]

Months before the legislative elections, Hamilton was widely considered the likely successor to Governor Stephen Miller. Throughout the
state, citizens hailed the "fearless" Hamilton, "defender of Southern
Rights," as their choice for South Carolina's chief executive. Even nullification opponent Joel Poinsett, who had been in Mexico as U.S. minister, knew the scuttlebutt as early as May. Stopping in Washington on his
way home, Poinsett shared with John Quincy Adams his prediction that
Hamilton—"the most violent man they had"—would be the next
governor.[9]

The rumors of the likely election of Hamilton, increasingly viewed as
a hothead outside the state, combined with rumblings of discontent from

    8. Banner, "The Problem of South Carolina," 60–93.
    9. *Charleston Mercury*, 17 July 1830; and Adams, ed., *Adams Memoirs*, 8:227.

other Palmetto State politicians finally caused Van Buren to take notice
of the political situation down South. That winter, Senator Hayne's spirited defense of nullification during a senatorial verbal battle with Daniel
Webster had alarmed many Jacksonians as well as their opponents. Then,
in April, Calhoun first openly hinted at his nullification sympathies when
he countered Jackson's unionist toast at a Jefferson Day dinner. In May,
Van Buren, anxious to hold the Jackson coalition together, urged Hamilton to adopt a course of "*unexpected moderation*" should he win the governor's race. Hamilton responded in a firm but friendly way to the man
emerging as the president's main advisor. His friends in Washington had
nothing to fear from South Carolina's version of state sovereignty, Hamilton said. "When it comes to the pinch . . . if there is judgment & discre-
tion on both sides," Hamilton assured Van Buren, nullification would
encourage a settlement between South Carolina and the federal government "not only without shedding a drop of blood, but with eminent benefit to those conservative principles of united interest & concord without
which the Union itself would be . . . either a withering despotism or a
rope of sand." Still, Hamilton let Van Buren know that he valued some
things even above the Union. "[I]f you think that this confederacy either
can or ought to last under the conjoint operation of the tariff & internal
improvements, understood & enforced as Mr Clay & Mr Adams
doctrines would justify," he wrote, "I can only say that we differ in
opinion."[10]

During the summer of 1830, Hamilton stayed on Sullivans Island near
Charleston to plot political strategy. The island offered the prospect of a
pleasant retreat after a trying winter during which his rented house in
Charleston had burned to the ground; fortunately, no one had died.
Hamilton found the family's new island accommodations cramped, and
the noisy activities of his young children grated on his nerves. "My father
was of a peculiarly mercurial temperament subject to fits of elation and
gloom," remembered one of the Hamilton boys later, "a northeasterly
wind with rain would always give him the blues and more especially if
confined to the house with a number of his sons." To keep his children
out of his way, Hamilton kept them confined for much of the day and
hired a tutor to occupy them. Ironically, this leading exponent of southern states' rights employed as a tutor an economically disadvantaged

10. JH to Martin Van Buren, 27 May 1830, copy in JHP, SHC.

College of Charleston student named John Charles Frémont. A quarter century later, after gaining fame as an explorer in the far West, Frémont was the first presidential nominee of a new Republican Party decidedly unfriendly to "southern rights."[11]

As Hamilton began organizing his campaign, he portrayed all white South Carolinians as members of a large, undifferentiated State Rights Party. In reality, political alliances fluctuated as divisions over nullification emerged. During the late spring and summer, the seeds of two new parties began germinating in Charleston as Daniel Huger, a longtime Calhounite nationalist, decided to oppose William Smith for the U.S. Senate. While some Calhounites rallied to support one of their own against the leader of the opposition, Hamilton discouraged Huger's candidacy. On the surface, Hamilton's behavior seemed odd. Huger had long been a political ally as well as a good friend whose Savannah River plantation bordered Hamilton's own Rice Hope. Personal considerations, however, could not stand in the way of larger ideological matters. Quite simply, because Huger opposed nullification, Hamilton helped to abort his candidacy.

Huger's candidacy frustrated Hamilton's plans to encourage Smithites to join his nullification crusade. By 1830, the contest, Hamilton believed, pitted supporters of the state against champions of a consolidationist federal government, and all who opposed the tariff had to support nullification. Suspicious of Hamilton and other adherents of nullification long identified as nationalists, Smith and his friends were loath to enlist in the nullification cause. One circumspect Smithite warned an ally to beware of their opponents' attempts "to out Doctor Cooper Doctor Cooper." They suspected that Hamilton and his allies simply wished to capitalize on rising states' rights feelings to advance their own interests.[12]

If Hamilton could not convince all Smithites to accept his leadership, he certainly could persuade some. Demonstrating political skill worthy of his friend Van Buren, Hamilton flattered onetime opponents into

11. *Charleston Courier*, 22 and 23 February 1830; Wild, "South Carolina Politics," 418, Hamilton, "James Hamilton" (quotation); and Allan Nevins, *Frémont: Pathfinder of the West* (New York: D. Appleton Century, 1939), 14.

12. Thomas Harrison to Stephen D. Miller, 6 September 1828, Chesnut-Miller-Manning Papers, SCHS. Dr. Thomas Cooper, as noted in chapter 4, was the Smithite who hinted at secession in 1827.

joining his cause. Two years before, Hamilton had stepped aside and allowed the election of the Smithite Stephen Miller as governor. Now, in
1830, he worked to recruit Miller as a candidate to oppose Senator
Smith's re-election. The defeat of Smith, known as lukewarm toward
nullification, would severely damage the organization of traditional
states' rights supporters and permit Hamilton to lead a new pro-nullification coalition comprising former Smithites and Calhounites.

Accordingly, Hamilton and his allies set about to reel in Miller. Robert Barnwell Smith urged Miller to put aside his loyalty to Senator Smith
so that the state might achieve the greater good of overturning the oppressive tariff. Barnwell Smith offered his own behavior toward Daniel
Huger as an example of how one should eschew the politics of personal-
ity for the politics of principle. As the lowcountry legislator told Miller,
he had publicly opposed the senatorial ambitions of his friend and ally
because of their differences over a convention. For the same reason, he
could not support William Smith's re-election. "I shall only do towards
Judge Smith," Barnwell Smith informed the governor, "what I shall do
to all my best or dearest friends"—clearly an invitation for Miller to do
the same.[13]

Over the summer, Hamilton continued to pressure Miller, through
flattery and by raising suspicions about Smith's reliability on the tariff.
Hamilton gleefully spread a rumor that Smith owned a Louisiana sugar
plantation and thus raised a tariff-protected crop. Smith, Hamilton suggested sarcastically, "means to resist the tariff by enjoying its benefits."
The senator's forbearance toward the federal government, Hamilton
predicted, "will in the end amount to submission."[14]

As Hamilton sought to subvert Miller's loyalty to Smith, he also tried
to hold as many tariff opponents together as possible. Emerging differences over nullification as the proper remedy to the state's ills, however,
threatened his efforts. There was, for instance, the matter of a potential
duel between James Blair, a Smithite congressman and ardent tariff opponent, and James Hammond, the young editor of the pro-nullification
Columbia Southern Times. When President Jackson issued the Maysville
veto, which struck down federal support for some internal improve-

13. Robert Barnwell Smith to Stephen D. Miller, 10 July 1830, Chesnut-Miller-Manning
Papers, SCHS.

14. JH to Stephen D. Miller, 7 August 1830, Chesnut-Miller-Manning Papers, SCHS.

ments, Blair had touted it as proof that ordinary political processes would kill the American System. Nullification, in Blair's view, was wholly unnecessary. Hammond then attacked Blair as insufficiently committed to states' rights while gratuitously mocking the congressman's constituents. Verbal exchanges and mutual insults led to a call for a settlement by arms. While some in Hamilton's camp egged Hammond on, Hamilton himself did not. A duel would only inflame old factional wounds. Hamilton urged friends of the potential combatants, both of whom he considered valuable to the state's cause, to work for peace. He even offered to "ride 500 miles through any hazards from sickness" in order to serve on a "court of honor" to avert violence. Fortunately, the would-be duelists settled their differences amicably. Hamilton's direct intervention proved unnecessary, but the episode demonstrated his increasing stature throughout the state. Both Blair and Hammond prized Hamilton's expressions of concern for them.[15]

That spring and summer, as Hamilton sought to create a new statewide alliance, he also worked to consolidate his forces in Charleston. A July public dinner he arranged played an important role in this effort. Ostensibly, the event welcomed Senator Hayne and Congressman Drayton back home following a momentous congressional session. Charlestonians naturally wished to honor Hayne for having bested Webster in the debate over Foote's resolutions and to thank both Hayne and Drayton for their efforts, though unsuccessful, to lower tariff rates. But more was on the evening's agenda than acknowledging the legislators' exertions on the state's behalf. Hamilton let it be known that attendees would by their presence "declare themselves in favour of some interposition of State Sovereignty."[16]

Though most participants warmly toasted nullification, not everyone endorsed the radical views. The most conspicuous dissenter was honoree William Drayton. Hamilton knew his former congressional colleague harbored serious reservations about nullification, but he hoped the evening's festivities might persuade him to reconsider. Instead, in remarks that evening, Drayton pointedly took issue with the efficacy, logic, and peacefulness of nullification. A majority of Americans, Drayton noted,

15. JH to Stephen D. Miller, 17 August 1830, JHP, SHC. See also Faust, *James Henry Hammond*, 50–54.

16. Freehling, *Prelude to Civil War*, 192–6. I. W. Hayne to James Henry Hammond, 29 June 1830, quoted in ibid., 201.

clearly supported the protective tariff policy, and he doubted they would yield "to the menaces of a single State." Moreover, he regarded as patently absurd the idea that a state could remain in the Union after nullifying a federal law. He also argued that nullification would almost certainly spawn disunion and "that direst of national calamities—civil war." "For my own part, I feel no hesitation in avowing," Drayton continued, "that I should regard the separation of South Carolina from the Union, as incalculably more to be deplored, than the existence of the law which we condemn." Defiantly, he concluded with a toast praying that the star-spangled banner would always wave "with undiminished lustre, over free, sovereign and *united* States."[17]

As Drayton sat down amid merely polite applause, Hamilton arose to counter his onetime mentor. Hamilton reminded the audience that when he first entered Congress, no one in the country had been "more thoroughly and enthusiastically national in his politics than myself." He now publicly confessed his past errors of constitutional construction. Seven years before, he had been merely "a young man whose estimates of life were as sanguine as his knowledge was imperfect and limited." Soon he grew into political maturity and put aside his youthful ways. Congressional experience had convinced him that "the government of this confederacy" had become "nothing more or less than an organ of indefinite power" used to tax the South unconstitutionally for the benefit of "the Tariff and Internal Improvement parties." It behooved southerners to employ a constitutional remedy to fight this gross abuse of power and return the government to its true basis—nullification.[18]

The disagreement between Drayton and Hamilton that evening underscored the lack of unanimous support for nullification in Charleston. Although many residents backed the theory, others remained skeptical or outright hostile. Some, like Drayton, argued that a convention inevitably meant nullification, which equaled secession and war. Hamilton admitted that his own allies gave ammunition to this view. By voicing "some indiscreetly warm Toasts & sentiments" at the July dinner, supporters of nullification allowed their opponents "to raise the war whoop of disunion against us." In addition to Drayton's allies, others argued for a state or regional convention as a means of protesting but not nullifying laws.[19]

17. *United States' Telegraph*, 30 July 1830.
18. *Southern Patriot*, 9 July 1830. See also Carson, ed., *Petigru*, 78.
19. JH to Martin Van Buren, 20 September 1830, MVBP, LC.

As the elections approached—Charlestonians would select city officials in early September, state legislators and a congressman a month
later—local political leaders divided into two camps. While Hamilton
organized a slate of pro-nullification "State Rights" candidates for the
September city elections, opponents of a convention and nullification responded by forming their own party organization. In August, nationalists
such as Daniel Huger, James Petigru, and Joel Poinsett launched the
State Rights and Union Party of Charleston. Determined to oppose
Hamilton's "Ultra State Rights Party," whom they derisively termed
Nullifiers, the Unionists nominated their own candidates for city offices.
Like Hamilton's group, they opposed the tariff and genuflected toward
state sovereignty, but they denounced nullification as a threat to the integrity of the Union. Oddly for a party seeking to portray itself as anti-
tariff as well as pro-union, it nominated for intendant James Pringle, the
federal collector of customs who enforced the detested tariff law in
Charleston. For Hamilton, Pringle's nomination simply demonstrated
the corruption of the Charleston Unionists. It certainly illustrated the
poor political instincts Unionists frequently displayed over the next few
years.[20]

To Hamilton's dismay, after a spirited campaign the Unionists pre-
vailed at the polls. Pringle garnered 52 percent of the vote to defeat the
incumbent, *Mercury* editor Henry L. Pinckney, and the Unionists swept
the city council. The results stunned Hamilton and his party. The Unionist victory necessitated a change in Nullifier strategy. The Unionists
had persuaded a majority of the electorate that the overriding issue was
union versus disunion. Hamilton hoped to reshape the discourse, to convince voters that their choice was instead between an effective, peaceful
means of resistance to an unconstitutional law and none at all.[21]

The legislative campaign allowed Hamilton to try out his new strategy. In an early September party meeting at the Carolina Coffee House,
he began to moderate his party's image and took pains to pledge his party's fealty to the Constitution and Union. Hardly were they the disunionist "jacobins" or inexperienced youths of Unionist oratory,
Hamilton insisted. Instead, the wisdom of years and the pure principles
of the American Revolution guided them, a case Hamilton made not only

20. JH to Stephen D. Miller, 7 August 1830, Chesnut-Miller-Manning Papers, SCHS.
21. *Charleston Courier*, 7 September 1830.

rhetorically but also by having Revolutionary War veteran Keating Simons chair the meeting and by prominently displaying his own father, the revered associate of Washington and Lafayette. Hamilton also claimed for the Nullifiers the mantle not only of Jefferson, author of the practically sacrosanct Kentucky Resolutions of 1798, but also of Andrew Jackson. As he would argue throughout the fall campaign, his followers included the real "old Hickorites" of 1824, not just the post-1828 recruits. Supporters of nullification even designated themselves the "State Rights and Jackson party."[22]

After the meeting, party leaders continued efforts to widen their appeal through deliberate obfuscation. Although Hamilton and his clique favored legislative candidates who would vote for a convention that would then nullify the tariff, many South Carolinians remained unconvinced of the propriety of that course. Therefore, for now, the best way to achieve the party's goal was to be unclear about it. Thus, in a September 28 gathering to unveil candidates whom leaders had selected for the October races, Hamilton retreated into vague declarations of support for the Jeffersonian principles of '98. The party's official line, Hamilton indicated, was that its candidates were not pledged to nullification, or even to a convention. Defending a convention in principle, he argued that legislators should be free to devise whatever remedy they deemed proper. The party's nominees for Charleston's sixteen house seats even included several who also ran with Unionist blessing. The party also endorsed the re-election of Congressman Drayton despite his very public opposition to nullification. As Hamilton saw it, nominating Drayton involved no sacrifice for his party because, although the congressman was "privately so much esteemed," he was "destitute of influence." By backing the politically harmless Drayton, the party avoided alienating those who might oppose the State Rights ticket if Hamilton's party put up a candidate against the congressman.[23]

Even as Hamilton sought to blur any differences between the two parties on specific policies, he drew an important distinction between them in his September 28 address. The State Rights Party, he said, would only nominate candidates "whose feelings and principles would tend to re-

22. "Address of the State Rights' and Jackson Party," [Charleston, 1830], Duke; and JH to Martin Van Buren, 20 September 1830, copy in JHP, SHC (quotation).
23. JH to Martin Van Buren, 20 September 1830, copy in JHP, SHC.

move the odium, that this Metropolis is the mere vassal trading-market of Northern Capitalists." Their opponents, he insinuated, were beholden to outsiders; Unionists constituted the "yankee party." By so defining his opponents, Hamilton planted the seeds for a one-party state in which political dissent became tantamount to treason.[24]

In a letter to organizers of a September State Rights dinner in Columbia, Hamilton provided compelling reasons that true sons of Carolina should support the strongest possible action against the tariff. First, he cleverly linked a convention to aspirations for expanding democracy. The state constitution, Hamilton noted, barred some "of the most talented and patriotic citizens of our State" from serving in the legislature because of property qualifications. Because no such rules applied to a convention, men of humble means would participate and add "a vast amount of wisdom and public spirit . . . to our counsels." He then emphasized the peacefulness and moderation of a potential convention. Through its actions, the state could "put the points at issue between her and the general government on such a basis that our difficulties must be compromised." In that case, Hamilton continued, with a nod to President Jackson, "it will be the glorious destiny of that hero who saved our country by the valor of his arms, again to preserve it by the mediatorial interposition of his wisdom, moderation, and virtue."[25]

But Hamilton's letter made yet more powerful and revealing points about the ultimate stakes of the tariff struggle for his state and region. "I have always looked to the present contest with the government, on the part of the Southern States, as a battle at the out-posts, by which, if we succeeded in repulsing the enemy, *the citadel would be safe.*" The citadel, of course, was slavery, and the threat to it was not a Haitian-style uprising but broad interpretation of the federal Constitution's general welfare clause. Echoing Robert Turnbull's essays, he argued that the failure to challenge misreadings of that provision would allow "the federal government to erect the *peaceful* standard of servile revolt, by establishing colonization offices in our State, to give their bounties for emancipation here, and transportation to Liberia afterwards." If South Carolinians failed to stand up against tariffs and internal improvements, Hamilton considered such an internal assault on slavery almost certain.[26]

24. "Address of the State Rights' and Jackson Party," [Charleston, 1830], Duke (quotation); and *Charleston Courier*, 8 September 1830.
25. *Charleston Mercury*, 29 September 1830.
26. Ibid.

Although Hamilton tipped his rhetorical hat to greater democracy, the campaign he managed gave ordinary voters few, if any, opportunities to influence the position of his party. A party committee secretly selected candidates and announced them just a week before the election, which gave ordinary voters little time to question them. Instead, Hamilton insisted that voters recognize his as a "holy cause" and proceed in an "unbroken phalanx" to the polls, vote a straight party ticket, and thus protect "LIBERTY, THE CONSTITUTION AND THE UNION." Similarly, Unionist leaders laced their voter appeals with identical militant motifs: "March with the energy and compactness of the Macedonian phalanx, to the polls, and prove by your votes for 'The State Rights and Union Ticket,' that you are indeed for 'UNION AND LIBERTY— ONE AND INDIVISIBLE.'"[27]

When the results came in, Hamilton's Nullifiers bested their previous showing in the city elections but still trailed their opponents. The Unionists captured eight seats to the Nullifiers' five; three other winners appeared on both tickets. The Unionist candidate for the sole contested state senate seat, Hamilton's former law partner, James Petigru, lost, but trailed the winner by only twenty-five votes. Moreover, the victorious State Rights candidate, planter Richard Cunningham, was actually on record as opposing a convention. In the rest of the state, results were similarly mixed, although a regional pattern emerged. Anti-conventionists completely carried at least seven upcountry districts and captured three of four seats from an eighth. Coastal areas surrounding Charleston more generally favored convention candidates. Still, with even Charleston's Nullifiers not officially endorsing nullification, making predictions about the actions of the next legislature would have been inexact indeed.[28]

As legislators gathered in Columbia, Hamilton, "the Master Spirit" as one Unionist described him, "was busy enough" persuading lawmakers to approve a convention and make him governor. The results of Hamilton's efforts soon became apparent as solons shed the Smithite and Calhounite designations and began voting as convention and anti-convention men.[29]

The legislature's election of a U.S. senator demonstrated the destruc-

27. "Address of the State Rights' and Jackson Party," [Charleston, 1830], Duke; and *Charleston Courier*, 8 October 1830.

28. *Charleston Courier*, 14, 16–21 October 1830.

29. John Ravenel to Eliza Ravenel, 29 November 1830, John Ravenel Papers, SCL.

tion of the old factions. The race pitted incumbent William Smith against his onetime chief lieutenant, Stephen Miller. Their rivalry revealed not only the divisions within the Smith faction but also demonstrated that the convention issue was responsible. Rumors that Smith opposed a convention and nullification had received confirmation in early November when the senator issued his anti-nullification "Yorkville Address." Meanwhile, the efforts of Hamilton and other Nullifiers had succeeded in persuading Miller to run against Smith. As Smithites divided over this race, the Calhounites also split, with Hamilton's followers supporting Miller while other disciples of the vice president, including Daniel Huger, backed Smith. Huger's endorsement of Smith, whom he had hoped to unseat only months before, demonstrated the rapid shift that had occurred in Carolina politics. "Never before," wrote an observer, "has there, in my knowledge, been such intense and bitter excitement in the Legislature." To the dismay of Smith, Huger, and other convention opponents, Hamilton's forces proved strong enough to hand Miller a narrow victory.[30]

Miller's election boded well for Hamilton's personal political future, but not for nullification's immediate prospects. In early December, the legislature chose Hamilton over Richard Manning, a former Calhounite governor, by a vote of 93 to 67. Despite their majority, Hamilton and his allies fell well short of the two-thirds necessary to call a convention. Unless economic conditions seriously worsened, it was doubtful that there would be a convention during the life of this legislature. The new governor, then, began planning for the legislative elections of 1832.[31]

During the first few months of 1831, Hamilton did relatively little to advance the cause of nullification. The birth in February of his ninth child, Henry Cruger, named for Elizabeth's half-brother, diverted him somewhat. Then, too, Hamilton and his allies were closely watching the unfolding political drama in Washington and considering its implications for their own cause. In brief, the relationship between Calhoun and Jackson, already strained under the weight of the Margaret Eaton affair, was

30. *Camden Journal*, n.d., reprinted in *Charleston Courier*, 12 October 1830; "Yorkville Address" appears in *Charleston Courier*, 14 and 15 November 1830; and *Charleston Courier*, 3 December 1830 (quotation).

31. For the gubernatorial vote, see *Charleston Courier*, 13 December 1830. In the state house, 60 favored and 56 opposed a convention. In the senate, 23 supported the convention and 18 opposed it. Ibid., 20 December 1830.

collapsing. The cause was Calhoun's ill-advised publication of documents detailing his criticism of Jackson's advances against the Seminoles back in 1818, when the South Carolinian was the then-general's superior. Dredging up this episode infuriated Jackson and led to a purge of Calhoun's associates from the Cabinet that spring.[32]

Hamilton knew that he needed to act in order to create and sustain public interest in nullification. "I am fully aware of the great peril of permitting public feeling to collapse because the inference made is that the cause is not worth supporting or the party unworthy of supporting it," Hamilton wrote to James Hammond, who was eager to carry on the battle for public opinion in the *Southern Times*. "We must have a rally on some firm ground & then stand manfully to our arms."[33]

The opportunity came in May when Hamilton organized a Charleston dinner to honor Congressman George McDuffie. On that occasion, McDuffie delivered a nearly three-hour-long speech focusing on what might be considered dull economic theory. Yet he captivated his audience, for the fiery Abbeville representative and leading Nullifier orator made his points with homespun examples. Most famously, he pushed the forty-bale theory, which held that it was cotton farmers and planters, not consumers as a whole, who paid the full cost of import duties on cotton, woolen, and iron goods. After whipping his listeners into a froth over the oppressive tariff, McDuffie justified nullification as the appropriate response of aggrieved citizens of a sovereign state. To "our adversaries, and their coadjutors amongst us," who resisted nullification out of fear of disunion and civil war, McDuffie had a ready retort. It was they— those who "exclaim in the most patriotic agonies, the Union, the Union, the Union is in danger"—who were the problem. By valuing the Union more than liberty, opponents of nullification allowed a tyrannical congressional majority to oppress all South Carolinians. "The Union, such as the majority have made it, is a foul monster," he declared. Claiming to be a sincere Union man, McDuffie left no doubt that he preferred secession to worshipping the "false idol," the "monster-god," that had spawned the tariff. Better to be prepared to resort to arms than to suffer continued outrages.[34]

---

32. See genealogical papers, box 3, folder 34, JHP, SHC; and Remini, *Andrew Jackson*, 2:306–10, 315–8.

33. JH to James Henry Hammond, 3 May 1831, copy in JHP, SHC.

34. *Charleston Mercury*, 25 May 1831.

The speech electrified the audience. It inspired defiant toasts from the men of Charleston: "South Carolina . . . should do her duty, and leave the consequences to God." The tenor of the proceedings delighted Hamilton. Such sentiments were just the thing the Nullifiers needed to propel them forward, he believed, and he helped McDuffie ready the speech for publication so that soon the congressman's words reached readers nationwide. Outside the state, the speech confirmed the image of the Nullifiers as radical disunionists. More importantly for Hamilton, it helped smoke out Calhoun.[35]

In Washington, the vice president still harbored hopes of succeeding Andrew Jackson. By the summer of 1831, it was clear that Calhoun would do so, if ever, only over Jackson's strenuous objections. Still, Calhoun believed "I never stood stronger" with the public, and he hoped to capture the presidency by striking the right deals with various groups, including northern manufacturers. He favored a lower tariff, of course, but to win over the nation's budding industrialists, he supported a "liberal protection" on "some of the most important articles." McDuffie's speech disturbed and alarmed him; the last thing Calhoun needed was a group of hotheads back home threatening secession over any kind of protectionist legislation.[36]

To preserve his presidential prospects, Calhoun tried to rein in his allies in Charleston, but to no avail. Duff Green, Calhoun confidant and editor of Washington's U.S. Telegraph, "civilly asked" Hamilton if the Nullifiers "were all crazy at McDuffie's dinner." He urged the Carolinians to back off from nullification or risk harming Calhoun's presidential prospects. Hamilton replied that the Nullifiers would "abate not one jot of our Zeal in the support of our principles which we would sacrifice to the elevation of no man on earth." Even when Calhoun himself chastised Hamilton about the "imprudent" nature of McDuffie's speech, the governor forthrightly responded "that the State rights party will not be diverted for one moment from the prosecution of their cause by the presidential question." Fearful of losing his South Carolina supporters, a reluctant Calhoun that fall publicly embraced the theory of state interpo-

35. JH to James Henry Hammond, 21 May 1831, in *AHR* 6 (July 1901): 746.
36. Freehling, *Prelude to Civil War*, 221 (quotation); and James Henry Hammond, "Memorandum," 18 March 1831, in *AHR* 6 (July 1901): 744.

sition in his Fort Hill Address. The Nullifiers had finally snagged the most respected South Carolina political figure for their cause.[37]

In the wake of McDuffie's speech, Hamilton charged ahead with plans to establish his party statewide. He envisioned an organizational push following the Independence Day celebrations in Charleston. "After this festival is over we shall go to business in good earnest & endeavour to unite our party thoroughly throughout the state," he wrote to Stephen Miller, from whom he sought information about political affairs in his region. "What has been done & what is doing in the northeastern portion of the State? Is Blair making head? How can we aid you? We [would] like to have our State Rights associations thoroughly organized by the 1st Augst & will accord much useful matter into that corner of the State."[38]

On July 4, the Charleston Nullifiers celebrated their links to the Revolution, a theme they emphasized during the entire course of their struggle with the Unionists. Several patriotic organizations, including the Society of Cincinnati, over which Hamilton's octogenarian father presided, joined party members to hear the day's main speaker, Senator Robert Hayne. In his remarks, the senator paid special tribute to old Major James Hamilton, Sr., who, Hayne noted, bore "a *name, doubly dear* to our hearts." Soaring to great oratorical heights, the senator praised both Hamilton *père* and *fils:* "Happy father! . . . it is thy *living* Ossory [*sic*], whom thou wouldst not exchange 'for any son in christendom,' and whom thou hast lived to see elevated to the first office in the gift of Carolina, and standing first in the confidence and affections of his countrymen."[39]

While the Nullifiers toasted the Hamiltons and Revolutionary ideals, Charleston's Unionists sponsored a separate celebration featuring a speech by Congressman Drayton. The highlight of the Unionist fete

37. JH to James Henry Hammond, 11 June 1831, copy in JHP, SHC (first quotation); John C. Calhoun to Samuel D. Ingham, 16 June 1831, *Calhoun Papers,* ed. Wilson, 11:404; and JH to Stephen Miller, 25 June 1831, JHP, SCL (second quotation). See also the Fort Hill letter *Calhoun Papers,* ed. Wilson, 11:413–39; and John C. Calhoun to Francis Pickens, 1 August 1831, ibid., 445.

38. JH to Stephen D. Miller, 25 June 1831, JHP, SCL.

39. Robert Y. Hayne, *An Oration, Delivered in the Independent or Congregational Church, Charleston, Before the State Rights & Free Trade Party, the State Society of Cincinnati, the Revolution Society, the '76 Association, and Several Volunteer Companies of Militia; on the 4th of July, 1831, Being the 55th Anniversary of American Independence* (Charleston: A. E. Miller, 1831), 38, Duke.

came with the reading of a letter from President Jackson, whom the party had invited to be their guest of honor. Although disappointed Old Hickory could not attend, Unionists cheered his letter, which declared that he would put down nullification "at all hazards."[40]

Jackson's letter destroyed the Nullifiers' allegiance to the president. For some time, Nullifiers had been distancing themselves from the White House, as Jackson continued signing legislation "tainted" by the American System. While publicly remaining friendly to the administration, Hamilton had privately cheered that spring's Cabinet shake-up, which he hoped signaled the end of the old man's chances for a second term. By Independence Day, Nullifiers had replaced "Jackson" with "Free Trade" in their party's official name. Now Jackson's open, unambiguous tirade against nullification proved that he was not the states' rights man they once had believed. That fall a Nullifier-dominated legislative committee condemned Jackson's letter as "a manifest and most unauthorized interference of the Executive of the Union with the domestic parties of a separate state." David McCord succinctly expressed the prevailing attitude of Nullifiers toward the president by late 1831: "Our party do not care a damn for him."[41]

In the months following that Independence Day, Hamilton directed the formation of pro-nullification clubs, called State Rights and Free Trade Associations, in towns, villages, and rural areas all over South Carolina. The governor intended the local associations to "make 'Nullification easy'" by spreading the nullification gospel and creating grassroots support for its doctrines. But this would be no true movement from below; Hamilton and other Nullifier leaders carefully provided central direction for the associations. At the local level, the deferential nature of South Carolina's hierarchical society checked the populist potential of the associations. Slaveholders, large and small, mingled with the slaveless, all joined in a common enterprise to restore the republic to its proper constitutional basis. For the more humble, the opportunity to rub

40. William W. Freehling, *The Nullification Era: A Documentary Record* (New York: Harper Torchbooks, 1967), 120 (quotation).

41. JH to James Henry Hammond, 3 May 1831, copy in JHP, SCL; *Charleston Mercury*, 10 June 1831; Governors' Papers, 1831, SCDAH; *Charleston Mercury*, 17 December 1831; and David J. McCord to Stephen D. Miller, 11 December 1831, Chesnut-Miller-Manning Papers, SCHS. McCord was married to Louisa McCord, the pro-slavery writer and daughter of Langdon Cheves.

shoulders with local aristocrats helped to mitigate some of the social tensions in white society. "Many persons have joined the rank of the nullifiers in order to get into a company a little above their accustomed circle," Greenville Unionist Benjamin Perry asserted.[42]

As the party organization infiltrated districts across the state that fall, Charleston Nullifiers, led by Governor Hamilton, tested their strength against the Unionists in a bid to win back the city government. Party leaders established a special campaign newspaper, edited by John Stuart, Robert Barnwell Smith's brother-in-law, "to fire on the enemies [sic] lines." Hamilton himself helped to bankroll this new publication and guide its editorial policy. He also took special care in staging pro-nullification meetings and rallies. Often these public events stressed the links between nullification and the Revolutionary heritage of resistance to tyranny. "To night I have put the party up to having a thundering meeting in honor of Old Sumter," he wrote of a mass meeting featuring the wizened Revolutionary War general Thomas Sumter, "which will communicate a few shocks from our State Rights electrical battery which cannot fail to invigorate for" election day.[43]

In addition to press pleas and mass rallies, the Nullifiers—and their opponents—also employed more colorful practices to sway voters. Each side targeted sailors and other transients with bribes of alcohol, and party leaders often kept them locked in designated houses until party agents could march the hungover voters to the polls. Hamilton's opponents even accused him of carrying his campaign into "houses of ill fame."[44]

Although both parties used these tactics, the Nullifiers developed greater proficiency in them, and, unlike their opponents, they used such methods without apology. As the Unionist Petigru put it, the Nullifiers "possess a greater degree of impudence than our folks." The Unionists, for instance, used alcohol to buy votes, but complained that the Nullifiers went further and dishonorably bribed "those that were sold before." One anecdote making the rounds reported that one of Hamilton's subordinates came to him after dragging a gang of bribed voters to cast their ballots at three of Charleston's four polling places. When the campaign

42. JH to James Henry Hammond, 21 May 1831, in *AHR* 6 (July 1901): 746; and Freehling, *Prelude to Civil War*, 228–30 (quotation from 229).

43. JH to Waddy Thompson, 3 September 1831, JHP, SCL. See also *United States' Telegraph*, 26 July 1831.

44. JH to Stephen D. Miller, 1 September 1831, Chesnut-Miller-Manning Papers, SCHS.

worker asked whether he should take them to the fourth, the governor barked affirmatively, "Sir, this is no time to mince matters!" Apocryphal or not, the story captures the Nullifiers' aggressiveness that autumn. The Unionists, Hamilton believed, possessed numerous advantages, including a widespread distrust of nullification, their control of the city government, and deeper pockets. From the Nullifiers' perspective, the need to overcome the Unionist edge and the very nature of their struggle to preserve South Carolina from hostile external forces justified their less-than-honorable electoral techniques. The Nullifiers' "impudence" paid off, as they swept all the city warden positions and again crowned Henry L. Pinckney as intendant. The conservative James Petigru decried the victory engineered by his old law partner: "The day . . . has really come, when passion is openly preferred to reason, and as long as they can play the part of patriots and resist the constituted authorities at the cheap rate of blustering and bawling, I believe they will continue to draw more fools into their circle."[45]

Surveying the political situation that autumn, Governor Hamilton determined the state was not yet ripe for nullification. "What stand our Party ought to take next Winter in the Legislature must depend on the State of public Sentiment," he wrote to his Greenville ally, Waddy Thompson. "*Discussion* should always be in advance of public opinion, *action* in the rear of it." He was willing that "our friends in the Legislature take the strongest ground public opinion will justify but let *them not go beyond it.*" As he knew from his contact throughout the state, South Carolina's voters still needed convincing. So, too, did state legislators. Indeed, during that legislative session, some members aligned with Hamilton's party favored a convention as a means of protesting the tariff but still opposed nullification. Hamilton needed time to bring those lawmakers around to his way of thinking, and he opposed holding what he knew would be another unsuccessful vote on a convention that year.[46]

Although Hamilton did not advocate a convention during the legisla-

45. James L. Petigru to William Elliott, 7 September 1831, James L. Petigru Papers, LC (first, second, and last quotations); Stoney, ed., "Porcher Memoirs," *SCHM* 46 (January 1945): 37 (third quotation); JH to Waddy Thompson, 3 September 1831 and 31 August 1832, JHP, SCL.

46. JH to Waddy Thompson, 3 September 1831, JHP, SCL; JH to Stephen D. Miller, 25 June 1831, JHP, SCL; William Elliott to Anne Hutchinson Smith Elliott, 1 and 5 December 1831, Elliott-Gonzales Papers, SHC; and *Charleston Mercury*, 3 December 1831.

ture's meeting, he did present solons with disturbing evidence of threats that might persuade them to assert state sovereignty more boldly. South Carolinians, white and black, knew of Nat Turner's bloody rampage through southern Virginia earlier in the year. Indeed, many whites had feared the Turner contagion would spread south from the Old Dominion into the Carolinas, and many masters near the North Carolina line spent sleepless nights as rumors spread of servile rebellion in their midst. Even as the governor publicly cast doubt on reports of disaffection among South Carolina's slaves, he urged his fellow citizens to remain vigilant regarding any challenges to their control of their bondsmen. In that spirit, he passed on to legislators an anti-slavery letter he had received in the wake of Turner's revolt. A correspondent from Hartford, who identified himself only as "Ethiopia," had mailed Governor Hamilton a copy of William Lloyd Garrison's new publication, *The Liberator*, accompanied by a polite request that Hamilton encourage the South Carolina legislature to enact a general emancipation. Had the letter ended there, no doubt the governor would have tossed aside this product of an obviously demented mind. But the remainder of the letter contained ominous words. "Ethiopia" warned "that as true as there is a god above if you do not emancipate the people they will certainly break the yoke themselves and hurl tyrants into ruin," a threat made more credible by Turner's recent deeds. Governor Hamilton submitted this letter as conclusive evidence that external forces endangered slavery. It portended not the slow decay of the peculiar institution by means of colonization agents, as bad as that mode of destruction might be. Rather, it demonstrated the growth of a hostile anti-slavery movement outside the state, one that might spark an internal, sanguinary revolution. Surely, the existence of that threat justified nullification, for such a show of state sovereignty would demonstrate South Carolina's firm resolve to control its own affairs and protect its citizens from ruin.[47]

While the legislature pondered the plans of abolitionists, the pace of partisan organization accelerated as Hamilton organized two statewide party conventions. The first met in conjunction with the legislative session in December. Another, larger gathering, chaired by Hamilton and boasting delegates from at least thirty-six local associations, met in

---

47. Governor's Message #2, 6 December 1831, and "Ethiopia" to JH, 31 July 1831, Governors' Papers, 1831, SCDAH.

Charleston during February when many planters visited for the social events surrounding the annual horse races. Hamilton had high expectations for the February event: "I believe it will be one of the most important assemblies in its probable influence on public opinion and public measures that has ever convened in the State."[48]

The February conclave focused on creating an efficient party propaganda machine. "Our only battery is a free press," Hamilton told delegates, and he exhorted the party to print and distribute greater numbers of pro-nullification publications. At his urging, the party published a series of "more popular and less abstract" pamphlets to explain the Nullifiers' economic and political theories in terms simple enough, as Hamilton put it, for "every freeman in the South who is able to read what it so behooves him to learn." Ten thousand copies of each of at least a dozen separate pamphlets rolled off printing presses for distribution through the local State Rights and Free Trade Associations. In addition, Hamilton played a major role in the creation of several new pro-nullification newspapers, including Charleston's *State Rights and Free Trade Evening Post*, which he partly owned. Edited by John Stuart, the *Evening Post* began operations in Charleston just after the 1831 city elections. Hamilton also encouraged the publisher of the pro-nullification Columbia *Southern Times* to purchase the Unionist *Columbia Telescope*. When finalized in mid-1831, that deal denied the Unionists a press in the state capital. Then, in order to "carry the war into the enemy's country as vigorously as possible," Hamilton helped establish Turner Bynum as the editor of a Nullifier sheet, the *Southern Sentinel*, in Unionist stronghold Greenville during the summer of 1832. Most importantly, he advised editors on the messages they should be sending to their readers.[49]

Hamilton himself became one of the best tools of Nullifier persuasion. State law required the governor to inspect local militia units. With extraordinary panache, Hamilton complied by touring muster fields from the dark swamps of the coastal parishes to villages nestled among the

48. See *Charleston Mercury*, 10 December 1831 and 24, 25, 27, and 28 February 1832. JH to James Henry Hammond, 16 January 1832, in *AHR* 6 (July 1901): 748.

49. *Charleston Mercury*, 25 February (first and second quotations) and 28 February 1832; Kell, "Rhetorical History," 95–100; John Hammond Moore, *South Carolina Newspapers* (Columbia: University of South Carolina Press, 1988), 62–3; JH to Waddy Thompson, 8 June 1832, JHP, SCL (last quotation); and JH to James Henry Hammond, 24 August 1830, in *AHR* 6 (July 1901): 738.

gentle hills of the piedmont. The governor traveled in a grand style meant to impress the militiamen. He crisscrossed the state in a small military carriage, behind which rode a mounted slave leading Hamilton's parade horses. At the muster grounds, Hamilton, resplendent in his official gubernatorial uniform with gold epaulets and a sword by his side, inspected his troops.[50]

Whereas previous governors had made such tours, even ones touched with pomp and circumstance, Hamilton's was different. His journey allowed him to identify the doctrine of nullification with the martial spirit of Carolina's white male population. Deferential upcountry farmers and sons of lowcountry planters listened attentively as this war veteran and son of a Revolutionary War hero addressed them on the dangers South Carolina faced. Echoing themes of eighteenth-century American Whigs, he preached resistance to tyranny and readiness to back up their words with force. Although Hamilton failed to win over all those serving in the militia—men in upcountry districts such as Greenville and Spartanburg proved especially suspicious of their lowcountry governor—his tour helped to galvanize support for defending the state's sovereignty from federal usurpations.[51]

The dinners that invariably accompanied the militia musters on Hamilton's journey provided opportunities for the public demonstration of the links among resistance, manliness, and nullification. The greatest of these events took place that May in Hamburg, a village on the banks of the Savannah River opposite Augusta, Georgia. The location allowed Georgians, involved in their own struggle with federal authority over Cherokee lands, to attend and add their voices to Hamilton's crusade. Billed as a "grand festival of Nullification," the occasion seamlessly blended the martial with the political. Local militiamen vied for marksmanship awards, while cavalrymen delighted the crowd with demonstrations of their skills. Governor Hamilton arrived mid-day to the salute of gunfire and soon took his place at the sumptuously laid out main table in a riverside warehouse some 300 feet long and 50 feet wide. As a band

50. Hamilton, "James Hamilton."

51. James Brewer Stewart, "'A Great Talking and Eating Machine': Patriarchy, Mobilization, and the Dynamics of Nullification in South Carolina," *Civil War History* 27 (September 1981): 197–220; and Stephanie McCurry, *Masters of Small Worlds: Yeoman Households, Gender Relations, and the Political Culture of the Antebellum South Carolina Low Country* (New York: Oxford University Press, 1995), especially chapter 7.

dressed in white uniforms and blue silk sashes played patriotic airs, the mass of diners—nearly two thousand at two seatings—enjoyed the largest public dinner yet given in either South Carolina or Georgia.[52]

To feed this multitude, organizers had fattened, slaughtered, and cooked twelve sheep, fourteen lambs, forty shoats, six pigs, four calves, and an indeterminate number of turkeys. As awe-inspiring as the victuals was the setting itself, a veritable visual celebration of nullification. Cotton bales, rice tierces, intertwined portraits of prominent South Carolinians and Georgians, palmetto trees, and pines decorated the warehouse and announced the theme of the dinner—the united interests of Georgia and South Carolina. Banners sported nullification slogans, while from the center of one wall a full-length, floor-to-ceiling portrait of George Washington offered the great patriot's blessing.[53]

After diners had stuffed themselves with pork, mutton, and beef, the wine freely flowed and the seventy-six toasts began. The guest of honor naturally received the warmest praise. "A patriot, without fear, and without reproach," the Committee of Arrangement's special accolade to the governor began. "He has generously devoted himself to the defence of Southern Rights and Southern Interests, and is qualified for every crisis. And Southern people will support him in the great cause, in every peril, and at every hazard." Hamilton rose and responded with a three-hour oration characterized by "brilliancy of wit, playful humor, and cutting sarcasm, so peculiar to its author," according to one admirer.[54]

Hamilton's tour not only built up support for nullification, it also affirmed his sense of importance and power. When Hamilton reported to Greenville Nullifier Waddy Thompson that "[w]e had a glorious day of it at Hamburg," the glory was not all for the great cause. He reveled in the adulation he received along the way.[55]

The exuberant crowds at Hamburg and elsewhere on Hamilton's tour betokened an upsurge in popular support for nullification. Recognizing

52. For a good overview of the state of Georgia's disputes with the Supreme Court over matters of state sovereignty and Indian policy, see Richard E. Ellis, *The Union at Risk: Jacksonian Democracy, States' Rights, and the Nullification Crisis* (New York: Oxford University Press, 1987), 25–32, 112–20; and *Charleston Mercury*, 26 May, 31 May (quotation), and 1 June 1832.

53. *Charleston Mercury*, 1 June 1832.

54. Ibid (quotation). See also Kell, "Rhetorical History," 119–20.

55. JH to Waddy Thompson, 8 June 1832, JHP, SCL.

the Nullifiers' momentum, some Unionists endorsed a convention of southern states as an alternative to their opponents' designs. Hamilton feared that some of his forces might fall for this Unionist "straw man," which he considered merely a distraction thrown up by his enemies to prevent the realization of his dreams. Hamilton instructed Nullifier editors to "open fire vigorously" on the southern convention, "this thief of time & public honor." Soon blistering attacks on the convention rolled off pro-nullification presses. Pinckney's *Mercury*, for instance, criticized a southern convention on two grounds. If such a convention were meant to form a confederacy of anti-tariff states, then it must be stopped before it led to inevitable disunion. On the other hand, if a southern convention produced only further memorials to Congress, it was pointless, for the Free Trade Convention in Philadelphia the previous autumn had already pursued that option to no avail. Criticizing a southern convention as either radically disunionist or too weak, the Nullifiers presented their own course of action as the moderate, reasonable, and effective one.[56]

Unionists hoped that Congress would kill the nullification movement by lowering the tariff. They praised the tariff passed in July 1832 as a step in the right direction and rightly noted that it eliminated the minimum valuation principle that inflated duties. The state's three Unionist congressmen—James Blair, Thomas Mitchell, and William Drayton— joined a majority of southern representatives in passing the bill, and Unionist editors offered it as proof of improving conditions.[57]

Although the new law lowered average rates to 25 percent, it failed to abandon the concept of protection. Moreover, it kept high duties on precisely those imports—woolens, cottons, and iron—that Nullifiers claimed were most often exchanged for raw Carolina cotton. Nullifiers naturally condemned the new tariff as a further assault on the Constitution and the rights of South Carolinians. Hamilton's party pressed ahead for a state convention to nullify the new law, and it urged citizens to be prepared to go further. "If you are determined to be free," a Nullifier tract advised Carolinians that summer, "say so at the ballot box in Octo-

56. JH to William C. Preston, 6 May 1832, JHP, SCL; and *Charleston Mercury*, 25 May 1832.

57. John D. Macoll, "Representative John Quincy Adams's Compromise Tariff of 1832," *Capitol Studies* (fall 1972): 41–58; Ratner, *Tariff in American History*, 18–9; Stanwood, *American Tariff Controversies*, 384.

ber: and if it be necessary afterwards, say so with your musket on your shoulder, and the cartouch box at your back."[58]

After Hamilton returned to Charleston in mid-August following a short respite at his Pendleton estate, the fall campaign for nullification got into full swing as the governor busied himself, as one Unionist contemptuously put it, "among his infatuated Crew." The rampant corruption evident in the two preceding annual elections only intensified as the city elections approached in early September. One observer commented that it was "unnecessary to speak about Bribery and Corruption, Suffice it to say, there never was so much excitement exhibited and the most disgraceful acts resorted to by both parties sufficient to cause the most awful visitations from a just & offended God." An incident just before the city elections, however, gave leaders of both parties pause. Because during the previous campaign season the Nullifiers had successfully bought off many voters whom the Unionists had already bribed, the Unionists made a greater effort in 1832 to confine their "rented" electors until they could be marched to the polls. An inebriated man in Unionist custody, Peter Staunton, either fell or jumped to his death from a third-story window. A riot nearly ensued before leaders of both parties, realizing that matters had gotten out of hand, agreed to release all voters whom they held.[59]

The Nullifiers won the city elections handily, then pushed ahead toward the main prize—capturing a two-thirds majority in the legislative races. Having traveled throughout the state for much of the year, Hamilton now concentrated his efforts on Charleston.

Because the stakes were so high, so, too, was the potential for violence. On more than one occasion angry armed mobs of political opponents nearly came to blows or worse. One night in a dark Charleston street, a group of Unionists led by Petigru happened upon Hamilton and some Nullifiers. The opponents bumped one another while hurling mutual insults. Suddenly, a Nullifier knocked Petigru down into the street. Petigru's compatriots surged forward, and a deadly fight seemed certain. Thinking quickly, Petigru called out to Hamilton, "I slipped!" As Hamil-

58. Freehling, *Prelude to Civil War*, 248–9; and "An Appeal to the People on the Question What Shall We Do Next?" Political Tract Number 12 (Columbia: Free Trade and State Rights Association, 1832), 4.

59. Timothy W. Johnson to William E. Storrs, 17 August 1832, Timothy W. Johnson Papers, SCL; Jacob Schirmer Diary, 2 and 4 September 1832, SCHS; and *Charleston Courier*, 3 September 1832.

ton bent down to help his friend up, the Unionist leader whispered to him, "For God's sake, move on!" Instantly complying, Hamilton led his men away and thus avoided bloodshed.[60]

There were similar close-calls in Charleston, but the only casualty of the campaign (besides the accidental death of the unfortunate Peter Staunton) occurred outside Charleston. In Greenville in early August, Turner Bynum of the pro-nullification *Southern Sentinel* derided Unionist editor Benjamin F. Perry as "a treacherous Dalilah" for lulling the people of that district into submitting to the 1832 tariff. Perry, accustomed to dealing with Nullifier threats, challenged the twenty-five-year-old Bynum to a duel. The two met for combat on an island in the Tugaloo River between South Carolina and Georgia, accompanied by their retinues of surgeons, seconds, and friends (Bynum's coterie included another fiery editor, James Hammond). They faced each other armed with dueling pistols borrowed from Hamilton's nearby Pendleton retreat. With a single bullet from a Hamilton gun, Perry ended Bynum's life.[61]

Despite this loss for the Nullifier cause in the mountains, Hamilton confidently expected an overwhelming victory for his party throughout the state that fall. He matter-of-factly informed a Georgia friend in August that the Nullifiers would indeed capture two-thirds of the legislature, assemble their convention, declare the tariff null and void, and adopt appropriate enforcing legislation. Just before voting began, Hamilton sent trusted lieutenants copies of a proclamation calling the new legislature into session a month earlier than usual. The recipients were to deliver the proclamations to their local newspapers as soon as the polls closed. He instructed them to keep the proclamation secret until then "as a knowledge of it might enable your opponents to cry out their 'civil war' was at last approaching and thus have an unfavorable influence on your elections with some timid & weak minded voters."[62]

Hamilton's years of political organizing paid off as the Nullifiers garnered well over two-thirds of the legislative seats. Pursuant to the gover-

60. Francis Lieber to Edward Everett, 22 October 1863, copy in JHP, SHC. Lieber reported that Hamilton and Petigru told him this story in 1835.

61. Kibler, *Benjamin F. Perry*, 124–36; quotation from *Southern Sentinel* on 128. See also JH to Waddy Thompson, 31 August 1832, JHP, SCL; and Hamilton, "James Hamilton."

62. JH to Edward Harden, 31 August 1832, Edward Harden Papers, Duke; JH to Patrick Noble, 9 October 1832, JHP, SCL (quotation); see also James L. Petigru to Hugh Legaré, 21 December 1832, in *Petigru*, ed. Carson, 112.

nor's now public proclamation, legislators gathered in Columbia on October 22 and quickly got down to business. Just four days later, Hamilton triumphantly signed his long-sought convention bill into law. According to the statute, the convention would open on November 19, just one week after elections for delegates. Moreover, representation at the special conclave would be based on both property and population, just as in the legislature, thus preserving the disproportionate power of the slave-rich lowcountry. Not unexpectedly, Nullifiers swept the elections for convention delegates; Unionists carried only eight districts, mainly clustered in the northeastern and northwestern corners of the state. In Charleston, where the Unionists clearly could not win—and even in some coastal parishes where they stood a chance of election—the opponents of nullification failed to make a stand. By mid-November, the Nullifiers stood poised—finally—to meet in convention and work their will.[63]

Between the meeting of the legislature and the commencement of the convention, Hamilton dashed down to St. Peter's Parish, site of his Savannah River plantation, to run for convention delegate. At Pennyworth he prepared for the convention by filling two demijohns with "fine Old Sherry & Madeira 15 years old to comfort us poor abused Nullifiers at Columbia." Unfortunately, the jugs seemed prone to leaking, so he sent a trusted slave to his factor in nearby Savannah on a Sunday to obtain new ones. Hamilton realized his factor might have difficulty procuring the wine vessels on the sabbath, but he humorously insisted that "if you have to break open a store you must send me the Demijohns—for the Nullifiers must have their wine." The next morning, with his wine presumably safe in new crockery, Hamilton steamed on to Charleston as his neighbors in the parish voted to send him to the convention.[64]

On November 19, the representatives of the sovereign people gathered in Columbia; 136 of them favored nullification, only 26 opposed it. Among the delegates sat eighty-two-year-old James Hamilton, Sr., one of two Revolutionary War veterans present. As much as Carolinians revered the old major, they revered his son even more. This was James Hamilton, Jr.,'s convention, and delegates acknowledged his primacy by

63. The state house of representatives passed the convention bill 96 to 25, and the state senate agreed, 31 to 13. For the convention enabling legislation, see *Charleston Mercury*, 26 and 27 October 1832; and Freehling, *Prelude to Civil War*, 260.

64. JH to F. D. Petit Devillers, 11 November 1832, JHP, LC.

electing him convention president. Taking the reins, Hamilton appointed a special committee to recommend measures to the convention as a whole. Although four Unionists sat on the committee, key Nullifiers, including Congressman George McDuffie, Senator Robert Hayne, pamphleteer Robert Turnbull, Senator Stephen Miller, and state Appeals Court judge William Harper, dominated its proceedings. By November 22, the committee had drafted an Ordinance of Nullification, largely the work of Harper, as well as several accompanying reports that set forth the rationale for exercising the state veto.[65]

Although severely outnumbered, the Unionists tried to frustrate the Nullifiers' proceedings. Indeed, as soon as the committee reported the proposed Ordinance, sixty-two-year-old Henry Middleton, the former governor who had given Hamilton his start in politics back in 1810, presented a resolution declaring the convention incompetent to act on behalf of the sovereign people. The problem, Middleton averred, was that all free white men were not represented equally in the historic assembly. He acknowledged that although a system of representation based on a combination of property and population favoring the wealthier coastal parishes "may be, and probably is" appropriate for the legislature, that method was "by no means adequate . . . to the exercise of the highest attributes of sovereignty." As disingenuous as this protest in the name of expanded democracy may have been coming from a lowcountry aristocrat who owned hundreds of slaves, it made for good politics. Faced with the embarrassing resolution, McDuffie immediately moved the question. Unionist Daniel Huger requested that his Nullifier colleague withdraw the motion so "that the resolution might be freely discussed." Because a formal debate would have allowed Unionists officially to question the legitimacy of the convention, McDuffie refused to budge. The Nullifier-dominated convention quickly swept away Middleton's objections and proceeded to consider the Ordinance of Nullification and three accompanying documents that made the case for nullification.[66]

On November 24, the convention approved the Ordinance as expected by a vote of 136 to 26. As of the first of February 1833, the tariffs of 1828 and 1832 would be null and void in South Carolina. Moreover,

65. *State Papers on Nullification* (Boston: Dutton and Wentworth, 1834), 309–15; *Journals of the Conventions of the People of South Carolina, Held in 1832, 1833, and 1852* (Columbia: R. W. Gibbes, 1860), 11; and Freehling, *Prelude to Civil War*, 261.
66. *State Papers on Nullification*, 305–7.

should the federal government seek to use the army or navy to enforce them, the state's connection to the Union would be dissolved. In addition, the convention decreed that the state require of all state officials, including militia officers, judges, and jurors, a pledge "to obey, execute and enforce this Ordinance." Then, before adjourning later that evening, the delegates empowered Hamilton to reconvene them later to consider any federal response to the ultimatum their Ordinance represented.[67]

When the convention adjourned and the legislature came back into session, Governor Hamilton laid out the steps his overwhelming majority in the General Assembly should take to enact the convention's measures. Among other things, he proposed changes designed to beef up the militia and suggested the legislature formally request that President Jackson remove the federal troops then stationed in the city's military garrison known as the Citadel. (Seeking to avoid any provocations, the president soon complied with that request.) Most of the work of putting nullification into practice rested on Hamilton's successor, Robert Hayne, whom legislators elected governor in early December. Meanwhile, the legislature tapped Calhoun to replace Hayne in the Senate. The lame-duck vice president resigned the nation's second-highest executive office on December 31 so that he could accept his new position and take an active role in seeking a congressional compromise to end the crisis.[68]

While Calhoun took up his new duties in Washington, state lawmakers approved legislation implementing nullification. In essence, they made nullification voluntary. An importing merchant could, if he chose, pay duties and suffer no pain of law. If, however, he refused and the customs collector confiscated the imported goods, the importer could sue the collector under a writ of replevin. This legal device required the collector to defend the confiscation in state court and allowed the importer to use the tariff's unconstitutionality as the basis for his non-payment. With a judge and jury sworn to uphold the Ordinance under the oath prescribed by the convention, theoretically the importer was sure to win and nullification would triumph.[69]

As the Nullifiers worked furiously to put their theory into practice, they received with approbation President Jackson's initial statements fol-

67. Ibid., 28–31 (quotation, 30), 318.

68. Message of 27 November 1832, Governors' Papers, 1832, SCDAH; *Charleston Mercury*, 30 November 1832; and *Charleston Courier*, 22 February 1833.

69. Freehling, *Prelude to Civil War*, 271–3.

lowing the Ordinance. In his annual message to Congress delivered in early December, Jackson for the first time as president condemned a protective tariff. Moreover, he recommended lowering the duties he had signed into law only five months earlier. Praising the message as reflecting "high honor on the Executive," the *Charleston Mercury* suggested that Jackson now embraced "genuine Carolina Doctrines" about the nature of federal powers. South Carolina's pressure seemed to be working. For a few days in early December, Nullifiers believed that Jackson would acquiesce in their official nullification of the tariff just as he had allowed Georgia's unofficial nullification of Chief Justice John Marshall's *Cherokee Nation* decision.[70]

Their optimism soon evaporated. On December 10, Jackson issued a special proclamation on nullification that quite clearly drew the lines between himself and Hamilton's party. Nullification, the president now firmly declared, amounted to a constitutional absurdity. Relying on a nationalist interpretation of the Constitution, he claimed the central government had been created by the people, not the states, and that the states did not retain "their entire sovereignty." A threat of coercion accompanied this seeming constitutional about-face of the president's. "The laws of the United States must be executed—I have no discretionary power on the subject," Jackson declared in a direct appeal to South Carolinians. "Those who told you that you might peaceably prevent their execution, deceived you—they could not have been deceived themselves. They know that a forcible opposition could alone prevent the execution of the laws, and they know that such opposition must be repelled."[71]

Although Jackson's Nullification Proclamation won praise from some

70. *Charleston Mercury*, 10 December 1832.

71. *State Papers on Nullification*, 75–97 (quotations, 88 and 94). In adopting a nationalist construction of the Constitution so at odds with his previous commitment to states' rights, Jackson was putting the greatest possible distance between himself and the Nullifiers. His response to the Ordinance was guided less by constitutional views than by his borderline-paranoid antipathy for Calhoun. Convinced that his first-term vice president longed to head up a southern confederacy, Jackson believed that Calhoun had corrupted his old South Carolina friends, including Hamilton. In short, Jackson misread the situation in South Carolina because of his personal hatred of Calhoun. See Richard B. Latner, "The Nullification Crisis and Republican Subversion," *JSH* 43 (February 1977): 19–38; Andrew Jackson to Martin Van Buren, 17 December 1831, *Correspondence*, ed. Bassett, 4:383–5; John Randolph to Andrew Jackson, 28 March 1832, in ibid. 4:429.

quarters—Daniel Webster, for instance, even contemplated joining the president in a new party—its nationalist tone shocked many of his allies, especially in the South. Even important northern Jacksonians, including Vice President–elect Martin Van Buren, found its belittling of traditional Jeffersonian states' rights rather disturbing. The Nullifiers, of course, reacted most negatively of all, with the *Charleston Mercury* labeling the proclamation a "DECLARATION OF WAR" against South Carolina.[72]

The Nullifiers' reaction to the president's pledge to enforce the tariff increased the possibility of armed conflict that had been haunting Carolinians all that autumn. Even before the Nullification Convention, South Carolina Unionists, fearing violence from their foes, had requested an increased federal military presence in Charleston. In response, President Jackson had sent a special agent in November to gather military intelligence about the forts in Charleston Harbor, and he ordered more ships and troops into the area. Once the Ordinance passed, the Nullifier-led South Carolina government heightened its military readiness. Legislators in December approved the recommendations of Governors Hamilton and Hayne for a new force of volunteers to meet the potential armed threat from the federal government. The state also purchased over $100,000 worth of new arms and ammunition in a three-month period.[73]

Hamilton played a leading role in the state's push for preparedness beyond his earlier inspection tour and legislative proposals for militia reform. Back in May 1832, while still governor, he had run for brigadier general of the militia's 4th Brigade, comprising Charleston District's four regiments, when the previous commander had died suddenly. In a special election of the brigade's officers, Hamilton captured a narrow victory, 97 to 95. Allegations of illegal votes for both candidates forced a new election, which Hamilton won in a race most Unionists boycotted. By whatever means, James Hamilton was by late 1832 a full-fledged general, and he commanded the militia in the very place where the first shots of a new independence movement might soon be fired. His new rank— higher than that held by his revered father—became an integral part of

72. Merrill D. Peterson, *The Great Triumvirate: Webster, Clay, and Calhoun* (New York: Oxford University Press, 1987), 216; and *Charleston Mercury*, 17 December 1832.

73. Joel R. Poinsett to Andrew Jackson, 16 October 1832, and Andrew Jackson to George Breathitt, 7 November 1832, *Correspondence*, ed. Bassett, 5:482–2, 484–5. Freehling, *Prelude to Civil War*, 275.

his name and identity for the rest of his days. It was heady stuff, indeed, for the man who longed for military glory.[74]

Hamilton's promotion inspired him to new heights of brashness. In late December, he and other Nullifiers steamed up the Savannah to Augusta in a risky move to capture arms from a federal arsenal. Precisely how Hamilton and his small company hoped to proceed against the facility remains clouded in mystery. Most likely, they planned to slip in and take the weapons without challenge from the normally small guard. Someone, however, leaked word of the intended attack, the arsenal's guard stood ready, and nothing came of the Nullifiers' plans.[75]

The Augusta mission was as far as Hamilton was prepared to go to challenge the federal government by force. Although some in the Nullifier entourage favored secession, Hamilton did not. Buoyed by popular acclaim and by his new rank, Hamilton may have indeed been tempted that winter by the thought of leading a Carolina independence movement, but his pragmatic streak won out. The martial attitude he adopted and the dark hints he dropped about secession were meant to extract concessions from the federal government, for, in the end, he wanted to destroy the protective tariff, not the Union. Hamilton blustered to rally the troops at home and to create the appearance of a credible threat, but the new general recognized that South Carolina could hardly go toe-to-toe with Old Hickory. Hamilton knew the incredible odds stacked against the Nullifiers. First, they needed support from other southern states, but by late January that had failed to materialize. Indeed, in the wake of the Nullification Convention, state legislatures across the South passed resolutions declaring their opposition to South Carolina's interpretation of the Constitution. Just days after the Ordinance's adoption, Georgia legislators condemned nullification in strong language. Terming the doctrine of nullification "revolutionary," both Alabama and North Carolina deplored its disunionist tendencies. South Carolinians, the Mississippi legislature suggested, had acted "with a reckless precipitancy

74. *Charleston Mercury*, 22, 23, and 28 May, 19 November, and 1 December 1832. See also Jean Martin Flynn, *The Militia in Antebellum South Carolina Society* (Spartanburg: Reprint Co., 1991), 108, 111.

75. Bernard C. Steiner, ed., "The South Atlantic States in 1833, As Seen by a New Englander, Being a Narrative of a Tour Taken by Henry Barnard," *Maryland Historical Magazine* 13, no. 4 (December 1918): 365; Silas Wright to Martin Van Buren, 13 January 1833, MVBP, LC.

(originating we would willingly believe in delusion)." Even Virginia, long defender of the reserved rights of the states, declared that its revered Resolutions of 1798 could not sanction the Palmetto State's form of state interposition. These states also pledged their fealty to the Union in terms that left grave doubts about their support for South Carolina in any violent clash with federal forces. Alabama's legislature, for example, "urgently recommend[ed]" that its neighbor "abstain from the use of military power, in enforcing her Ordinance, or in resisting the execution of the revenue laws of the United States."[76]

Not only did Nullifiers lack widespread support in the South, they also faced firmer opposition from Jackson than Hamilton had anticipated. The president no longer appeared the weak, vacillating old man of Hamilton's imagination. The popularity of his veto of the Bank of the United States recharter bill, his resounding re-election, and his firm Nullification Proclamation demonstrated political skills and backbone enough to enforce the tariff with ordnance if necessary. Looking out into Charleston Harbor, Hamilton could see the USS *Natchez* and other vessels—tangible proof of Jackson's preparedness to support federal laws. In addition to the sailors and soldiers in and around the Harbor, Hamilton fully expected troops from Kentucky and Tennessee to pour into the Palmetto State to help vanquish his own Nullifier army.[77]

If the specter of South Carolina's confronting a federal military assault alone were not bad enough, the state suffered serious divisions. For months, the Unionist leadership had been so slow, disorganized, and downright inept that many Nullifiers believed the Unionist opposition would simply collapse and that their onetime foes would "go with the state" once nullification became a fait accompli. But Unionist stubbornness exceeded Nullifier expectations. Even as the Nullifier legislature met in December to implement the Ordinance, 184 Unionists convened at Columbia's Presbyterian Church to protest the state's actions.[78]

Unionists also used this occasion to plan their own statewide military organization to support federal authority once nullification took effect—or should the state secede. From mid-December through February, Unionists recruited as many as ten thousand men into paramilitary

76. *State Papers on Nullification*, 274, 222, 201–2, 230, 195–7, 225.
77. JH to Thomas Butler King, 11 April 1833, Thomas Butler King Papers, SHC.
78. *Charleston Courier*, 13 December 1832; *The Report of the Committee of the Convention of the Union and State Rights Party, Assembled at Columbia, 10th December, 1832* (n.p., n.d. [1832]).

"Union Societies" at the district level, with Joel Poinsett serving as overall commander-in-chief. The Paris Mountain Union Society in Greenville exemplifed the defiant spirit of these would-be warriors: "Resolved, that in defence of the Federal Union, *we have drawn our swords and flung away the scabbards* . . . we have but two words by way of reply to the Nullifiers, which are these: *'Come on.'*" Unionists elsewhere demonstrated equal determination, including in Hamilton's own Charleston, where the local Unionist force accounted for roughly 35 percent of the militia-aged white male population. In short, General Hamilton knew his state was sorely divided.[79]

As the Ordinance's February 1 deadline for the implementation of nullification approached, Hamilton pushed for a peaceful compromise with the federal government. In his last message as governor, Hamilton urged legislators "to apply specially and specifically in the manner prescribed by the Constitution, for a General Convention of the States." Only such a new constitutional convention, he suggested, could resolve this crisis in federalism. By late January, as he contemplated a new complication with the introduction of the Force Bill, which granted the president authority to use the military to execute tariff laws, Hamilton agreed with Calhoun that "we must not think of secession, but in the last extremity." The former governor held out hopes for the passage of the lower tariff introduced by New York congressman Gulian Verplanck. Timing was crucial; Congress would probably not complete its work by February 1.[80]

On January 21, Nullifiers at a Charleston mass meeting listened as Hamilton urged patience while Congress considered lower rates. He seconded a series of resolutions offered by the party leadership that, while thumbing South Carolina's collective nose at Jackson, also provided Congress more time. Nullification would still be effective as of February 1, but "all occasion of collision between the Federal and State authorities should be sedulously avoided" until national legislators had finished their work on a new tariff. This amounted to an agreement among Nullifiers to postpone nullification until Congress had acted. In the meantime, pro-nullification importers could follow Hamilton's own example. As he

79. Kibler, *Perry*, 150 (quotation).
80. *Charleston Mercury*, 12 December 1832 (first quotation); and Freehling, *Prelude to Civil War*, 291 (second quotation).

explained, he had shipped rice to Havana to be exchanged for a cargo of sugar. When the sugar arrived, Hamilton planned to let it sit in James Pringle's customs house and await the outcome of the debates in Washington. Should Congress lower the tariff, Hamilton would gladly pay the new, non-protective duty. But if not, he said he knew "that his fellow-citizens *would go even to the death with him for his sugar.*" This statement earned him sustained applause from the Nullifier audience, and snickers from Unionists, who dubbed him "Sugar Jimmy."[81]

Just to make sure his opponents in Washington—and his Charleston audience—did not get the impression that party leaders were backing down, Hamilton ended his conciliatory speech on a defiant note. If Congress passed the Force Bill, Hamilton declared he would immediately recall the convention delegates and "submit to them THE QUESTION OF SECESSION." No one "could doubt what their choice would be," he continued. "If we were deprived by the Government of the United States the right of peaceably seceding, we would then triumph in asserting it, or die in the attempt." Amid the cheering, perhaps no one noticed that Hamilton had not actually endorsed secession, although he came close. Rather, this was yet another bluff in Hamilton's high-stakes game with the federal government.[82]

The "fatal first" of February passed without incident as Nullifiers awaited congressional action. The failure of the Verplanck bill paved the way for two recent enemies, Clay and Calhoun, to join forces behind a bill the Kentuckian devised. Meanwhile, the Virginia legislature dispatched a commissioner to calm down the South Carolinians. Arriving in early February, Benjamin Leigh requested that the state convention reassemble to consider Virginia's solution to the crisis, resolutions demanding a lower tariff but rejecting nullification. On February 13, Hamilton complied by issuing a call for delegates to gather again the following month in Columbia. Not only would they be able to receive Leigh's report, but Hamilton expected they would be able to review Congress's completed work by then.[83]

A day before Hamilton's proclamation, Clay introduced his new tariff bill and Calhoun immediately rose in its support. The measure failed to

81. *Charleston Mercury*, 23 January 1833; and Freehling, *Prelude to Civil War*, 288–9.
82. *Charleston Mercury*, 23 January 1833.
83. Freehling, *Prelude to Civil War*, 290; and *Charleston Mercury*, 18 February 1833.

end protectionism immediately, but gradually reduced average rates to 20 percent by 1842. The bill passed Congress, as did the Force Bill, and Jackson signed both in early March. While they cursed the Force Bill, most Nullifiers welcomed the new tariff as a way out of their predicament.

On March 11, President Hamilton opened the second session of the Nullification Convention with a calming speech. Rather than recommending secession as a response to the Force Bill, Hamilton urged delegates to accept the compromise tariff. He acknowledged its shortcomings but defended it as providing "an early, though gradual amelioration of that system." He did call on conventioneers to nullify the Force Bill, which they did, although even the radical McDuffie thought that an empty gesture. Following his speech, Hamilton yielded the convention presidency to Governor Hayne.[84]

Not all of his allies adopted Hamilton's conciliatory position. Robert Barnwell Smith denied that he was, as the convention address claimed of South Carolinians, ardently "attached to the Union." Rather, he boldly proclaimed his preference for a southern confederacy in which slaveowners could "hold their destinies in their own hands." Hamilton sparred with his lieutenant over those remarks before Smith sulked into silence. Another irate Nullifier, seventy-year-old Robert Turnbull, declared he would not be reconciled to the Unionists until they provided evidence of their loyalty to the state. A young Unionist, Chesterfield's Philip Phillips, jumped to his feet and questioned the right of Turnbull, well known as a Federalist opponent of the War of 1812, "to challenge the loyalty of anyone." As Phillips's stinging words reverberated throughout the hall, a delegate called for adjournment so that heads might cool. Some younger Nullifiers proposed challenging the brash Phillips to a duel for his cutting criticism of Turnbull, but Hamilton intervened to bring peace. Hamilton, "recognized as the highest authority" on challenges of honor, argued that Turnbull's words gave Phillips a "right to a severe retort," and that, besides "allowance should be made for the impetuosity of youth and the excitement of the times." Nullifiers let the matter lie, and Hamilton's moderation won out over the Smiths and Turnbulls.[85]

84. *Speeches Delivered in the Convention, of the State of South-Carolina, Held in Columbia, in March, 1833* (Charleston: E. J. Van Brunt, 1833), 13; and Perry, *Reminiscences*, 228.

85. *Speeches Delivered in the Convention*, 24–7 (quotation on 27); and Philip Phillips, "Summary of the Principal Events of My Life," 14, Phillips-Myers Papers, SHC.

After the assembly had accepted the tariff and nullified the Force Bill, some radicals wanted simply to adjourn rather than to dissolve the convention, so that delegates might be recalled on short notice to deal with other abuses of federal power. One delegate argued that Georgia would appreciate the support of the South Carolina convention should it butt heads with Washington over the Cherokee land issue. Wanting to close this chapter in his state's political history, however, Hamilton convinced the others to dismiss the convention for good and return sovereignty to the people.[86]

When the final gavel fell, Hamilton returned home to celebrate the conclusion of his long and successful struggle for nullification—and to welcome the latest addition to his family. On March 12, while Hamilton was in Columbia urging fellow delegates to accept the new tariff, in Charleston his thirty-seven-year-old wife gave birth to their tenth child, Lewis Trezevant Hamilton. Later that month, while Elizabeth recuperated, her husband joined in the public ceremonies marking the end of the crisis. On an early spring evening, Charleston Nullifiers, splendidly attired in their military finest, escorted their ladies fair into the city's arsenal, the Citadel. There among the unused swords, rifles, and gunpowder, they held an impressive victory gala. While Carolinians claimed to have forced their enemies into retreat—and certainly felt enormous relief that the clouds of war had passed them by—their celebration did not erupt into triumphant mayhem. The festivities bore not a trace of the passionate and overly democratic debacle Hamilton had witnessed four years before at Jackson's first inaugural. Instead, South Carolina's gentry displayed its most dignified and restrained aristocratic bearing that evening. In the center of the celebrations stood James Hamilton himself. Dressed in his general's uniform, surrounded by adoring women and admiring men, the former governor looked, as a visitor from Maine put it, like the "Emperor of the South . . . far less humble than Napoleon."[87]

And why indeed should Hamilton have not felt the conqueror? With skillful planning, incredible political talent, and unyielding perseverance, he had waged war against the tariff and onetime political allies for more than four years. His efforts led directly to congressional action to undo,

86. *Speeches Delivered in the Convention*, 78–9.

87. Quotation from the *Portland Advertiser*, reprinted in the *Charleston Mercury*, 27 April 1833.

if gradually so, what Henry Clay and his manufacturing friends had insisted was the "settled policy of the country." Moreover, Hamilton had shown himself to be a true Lynch heir by creating the first real statewide party in South Carolina's history and ascending to the very heights of political power in the Palmetto State. As political impresario, governor, and convention president, he had wielded more influence than any of his peers. To top it all off, he now held the rank once bestowed on his heroic step-grandfather. Surely, James Hamilton had demonstrated his worthiness of the legacy left to him by his Revolutionary forebears. New worlds now awaited conquest by this "Emperor of the South."

CHAPTER 6

An Enterprising Gentleman
1834–1839

THE MONTHS AND YEARS IMMEDIATELY following South Carolina's acceptance of the Compromise Tariff marked a time of transition for former governor Hamilton. Following the tariff crisis, contemporaries acknowledged his preeminence in South Carolina society. His friend William Preston observed in 1833 that "all love and admire" the former governor "beyond any other man in our borders." Although surely the state's Unionists hardly shared that opinion, even they appreciated Hamilton's role as peacemaker at the March convention. Despite the power and position the nullification controversy afforded him, by the close of the decade Hamilton's standing in the Palmetto State had been seriously compromised.[1]

Bad luck accounted for many of his post-nullification troubles, but in large measure, he brought them on himself. Hamilton, the perceptive Preston noted, possessed what their mutual friend, the classical scholar Hugh Legaré, might have identified as a tragic flaw. Hamilton's "foible," Preston believed, "was an over anxiety to exhibit himself strikingly to the public eye." The great Nullifier's desire for public acclaim and his willingness to take risks proved a formula for misfortune in the 1830s.[2]

The March 1833 convention ended South Carolina's confrontation with the Jackson administration over the tariff, but despite Hamilton's efforts at compromise it failed to heal the wounds nullification had in-

---

1. William C. Preston to Waddy Thompson, 15 October 1833, Waddy Thompson Papers, LC.
2. Ibid.

flicted within the state. Members of the State Rights and Free Trade Party considered their opponents traitors to South Carolina, while Unionists regarded Nullifiers as tyrants bent on the destruction of basic rights. Months of heated rhetoric, occasional street brawls, and the near clash of arms could not be so easily forgotten or forgiven. But Hamilton soon realized the necessity of making peace. Continued political warfare, he discovered, made it difficult for him and his peers to maintain control over the mass political movement they had built.

In Charleston, elites such as Hamilton, not ordinary voters, had always determined the course of the Nullifiers. The party's victory celebrations neatly reflected the leaders' control of the movement. Before Hamilton organized his party, each winner of a city or legislative race in Charleston would treat "the mob" to food and drink at his own house. By doing so, a victorious candidate risked property damage at the hands of drunken revelers. The Nullifiers solved this problem by "clubbing" their festivities under one roof, usually at a theatre called the Circus. By carefully organizing these events, party leaders not only kept their homes intact but also reinforced their influence over their less socially advantaged followers. Spatial arrangements inside the Circus, for instance, emphasized the leadership of Hamilton and his friends. According to one Nullifier, "the more respectable part of the company" occupied the stage, reflecting higher status as compared with the ordinary white Charlestonians, who milled about in "the Pit" below. As voters enjoyed their beef, veal, and claret down in the Pit, they thus remained under the watchful eyes of their social and political betters. From the leaders' perspective, a single celebration had the added attraction of solidifying the loyalty of voters to the party itself rather than to any individual candidate.[3]

The controversy over the test oath, the most divisive political issue in South Carolina from the close of the convention through 1834, demonstrated the limits of aristocratic influence. Many Nullifiers, Hamilton included, considered the test oath a perfectly reasonable means of excluding Unionists from certain state offices as punishment for their "betrayal" of South Carolina during the nullification winter. Acting under authority granted by the March convention, the legislature in December 1833 passed a test oath requiring all militia officers to swear alle-

3. Entries for 6 September 1832 and 6 September 1833, John Berkley Grimball Diary, SHC. See also McCurry, *Masters of Small Worlds*, 270–1.

giance to South Carolina. The precise meaning of "allegiance" became a
sticking point. Whereas Unionists argued that allegiance to the state did
not preclude their offering allegiance to the federal government as well,
Nullifiers insisted it meant exclusive loyalty to South Carolina. In the
upcountry, militia general Waddy Thompson found himself surrounded
by "disloyal" Unionist officers. Egged on by the young and militantly
Unionist editor of the *Greenville Mountaineer*, William Lowndes Yancey,
these officers and their anti-Nullifier foot soldiers refused to follow orders from anyone taking the oath. In other districts, the refusal of Unionists to take the oath led to legal disputes that ended up before the state
Court of Appeals in May 1834. The two Unionist judges on the three-
man bench struck down the militia oath. Nullifiers responded by pledg-
ing to win a two-thirds legislative majority that fall so they could incor-
porate a test oath directly into the state constitution.[4]

During that 1834 legislative campaign, an event in Charleston convinced Hamilton of the dangers to patrician-led politics of continuing
the struggle with the Unionists. On the evening of the first of two days
of polling, three or four hundred unruly Nullifiers—not commanded by
their leaders—attacked Unionist headquarters. The Unionists showered
the surging mass with a barrage of buckshot that wounded six and sent
the Nullifiers scurrying off in search of arms. Hamilton and Governor
Robert Hayne rushed to the scene as the Nullifiers reassembled. The
governor spoke first, but the revenge-obsessed mob felt little disposed to
heed Hayne's pleas for peace, which they attributed to cowardice. This
constituted a crisis of authority, not simply for Governor Hayne, but for
the entire Nullifier leadership. Thinking quickly, Hayne suggested that
if they doubted his own courage they should "ask Hamilton, whom no
one could doubt," what to do. The unquestioned hero of nullification
then spoke up and persuaded the angry crowd that the law should punish
the trigger-happy Unionists.[5]

Although Hamilton had successfully averted any further violence that
evening, the episode shocked him into abandoning his support for a pu-
nitive test oath. Controversial issues, he knew, required the mobilization
of the mass of voters. During his 1830–32 campaigning, he encouraged

4. On the test oath controversy, see Freehling, *Prelude to Civil War*, 309–20. Also see JH
to Waddy Thompson, 23 May 1834, JHP, SHC.

5. James L. Petigru to Hugh Legaré, 26 October 1834, *Petigru*, ed. Carson, 162–3 (quotation from 163); Pease and Pease, *Web of Progress*, 81.

wide participation because he needed "the people." The risk of democratic insurgents taking over his movement, slight as it was given the reigning political culture of deference, was well worth the reward of achieving his convention. But Hayne's near loss of control of the Charleston mob demonstrated that agitation of the masses had gone far enough. Further appeals for manly political action might lead in directions about which Hamilton dared not to think. The leaders of the two parties needed to reach an accommodation before things got out of hand.

Elected to the state senate with only 52 percent of the vote in a hotly contested race against Henry Middleton, Hamilton pushed for a mutually satisfactory settlement with Unionist leaders. During the legislative session, he hammered out a deal with Petigru, recently defeated for the lower house but still a Unionist power. The two former law partners agreed to solve the problem by having the legislature adopt a report specifying that the oath simply required that allegiance every citizen owes to the state consistently with the U.S. Constitution. Such a vague formulation allowed both Unionist adherents of dual sovereignty and Nullifier believers in supreme state sovereignty to take the oath in good conscience. Petigru and Hamilton then returned to their respective party caucuses and successfully lined up the votes to pass the report and the oath.[6]

The test oath controversy marked the end of Hamilton's years of active political management. For five years, the nullification movement had dominated his life. Now he turned the reins over to others, such as Henry L. Pinckney, Charleston's new congressman, and Barnwell Smith, the Walterborough legislator. Calhoun, from his senate seat in Washington and his plantation seat near Pendleton, superintended the State Rights Party Hamilton had built. Having been forced by Hamilton to embrace nullification openly in 1831, the sage of Fort Hill became the party's supreme theorist and strategist. Calhoun's famously "metaphysical" approach to politics, rather than Hamilton's more pragmatic style, dominated South Carolina public life thereafter. Under Calhoun, the state's leaders staked out the most advanced position on the protection of slavery and allowed for nothing that might theoretically threaten their peculiar institution.

6. *Charleston Courier*, 16 and 17 October 1834; and James L. Petigru to Hugh Legaré, 15 December 1834, *Petigru*, ed. Carson, 169–70.

Concerns other than politics largely drew Hamilton's attention after 1834. His family assumed a higher priority than before. Perhaps the death of his eighty-three-year-old father in November 1833 influenced his domestic turn. Although not yet fifty, Hamilton became more conscious of his own aging; doubtless, he wished to be more of a paternal presence in his children's lives. In addition to his own ten children (his eleventh and last, Arthur St. Clair, named for a general under whom his father served in the Revolution, arrived in 1836), Hamilton also served as the guardian for the eight children of his dead distant cousin, John Middleton. As a good patriarch, he saw to their educations and even willingly endured criticism for sending his children to northern boarding schools during the nullification controversy. He also made sure they married well. Indeed, two of Hamilton's children married two of his Middleton wards who came with substantial property. His only daughter, Elizabeth, became the bride of Jacob Motte Middleton, while son Dan took Rebecca Middleton as his spouse.[7]

As important as his family was to him, business became Hamilton's obsession after 1834. Charleston shared in the national economic boom of the mid-1830s as increasing cotton and rice prices enriched planters and those city-based factors and merchants who serviced them. Prosperity fueled speculation of all kinds. In a single day in April 1836, for instance, the value of one Charleston property shot up 50 percent.[8]

The potential for economic gain mesmerized Hamilton, and he grabbed opportunities to diversify his personal finances. His first foray outside the familiar world of planting took him into banking. Not that banking was wholly unknown to him, for in the early 1820s he had served on the boards of two banks and represented Charleston stockholders at B.U.S. meetings in Philadelphia. When a group of Charleston merchants announced plans in 1834 to organize a new Bank of Charleston, Hamilton jumped at the chance to get involved.[9]

With the city's B.U.S. branch set to expire in late 1835, the new bank

---

7. JH to Martin Van Buren, 24 June 1837, MVBP, LC; Langdon Cheves, "Middleton of South Carolina," *SCHM* 1 (July 1900): 237–8; JH to Charles Manigault, 30 April 1836, JHP, SHC; and Jacob Schirmer Diary, entry for 31 March 1841, SCHS.

8. Gray, *History of Agriculture*, 1030–1; and Pease and Pease, *Web of Progress*, 51.

9. *Charleston Courier*, 14 March and 6 December 1821, and *Carolina Gazette*, 7 December 1822, clipping in box 4, folder 47, JHP, SHC. George W. Williams, *History of Banking in South Carolina from 1712 to 1900* (Charleston: Walker, Evans & Cogswell, 1900), 11–2.

would perform the functions Biddle's bank had previously discharged, particularly regarding the business of foreign exchange so crucial to the state's export economy. In December 1834, Senator Hamilton successfully obtained a legislative charter that authorized the bank to be capitalized at $2,000,000, which made it twice the size of any other South Carolina bank.[10]

Potential investors looked upon the new bank as a good investment—or at least a sure speculative venture. The commissioners responsible for organizing the bank announced in the spring of 1835 that a subscription for 20,000 shares of stock at one hundred dollars per share would be held in June. All signs indicated far more interest in the new bank than there were shares to go around. Under the terms of the stock offering, then, the commissioners allowed individuals to buy as much as they wanted. After the two-day subscription closed, the amount of stock each person received would be pro-rated based on the total subscribed. If, for example, investors put in orders for double the total amount of stock, each investor would receive only half the amount he had ordered. "Consequently," one insider told a friend, "if you want five Hundred shares you had better subscribe for more." Checks for stock purchases— and only checks were accepted—would not be cashed until it was known how much stock a subscriber would actually receive. Moreover, the commissioners required only one-fourth of the purchase price in June, with the remainder due in installments over the next eleven months.[11]

All of these conditions contributed to what the conservative *Courier* termed an "extraordinary mania for speculation." A month before the stock went on sale, investors from as far away as Boston, New York, and Philadelphia had already put in orders for well over twice the bank's authorized 20,000 shares. When the subscription books officially opened on June 1, Charlestonians wrote checks for many more shares than they intended to buy. On the final subscription day, individual investors not uncommonly subscribed for half a million dollars' worth of stock. When

10. James G. Lindley, *South Carolina National: The First 150 Years* (New York: Newcomen Society of the United States, 1985), 9; Robert Hayne to Nicholas Biddle, 18 December 1834, Nicholas Biddle Papers, LC. "Exchange" in this context means the business of handling financing of long-distance commerce. See Peter Temin, *The Jacksonian Economy* (New York: W. W. Norton, 1969), 29–40.

11. *Charleston Courier*, 7 May 1835; and [John Haslett?] to John Potter, 9 May 1835, Nicholas Biddle Papers, LC (quotation).

it was all over, checks for nearly $90,000,000 filled the new bank's cof-
fers—forty-five times the bank's authorized level of capitalization. Each
investor therefore received only one share of stock for every forty-five he
had supposedly purchased. Nicholas Biddle, for instance, put in for 4,000
shares but ended up with only 88. (A true speculator, Biddle sold his
shares for a 100 percent profit within the month.) Although the stock
frenzy enriched and empowered some, the *Courier* complained that the
new bank amounted to "a complete monopoly in favor of the large capitalists" that made "the rich richer . . . leaving the poor in their poverty."[12]

James Hamilton certainly was among the wealthy who benefited from
the bank's creation, and not only as a stockholder. A faction favoring his
election as bank president and another supporting Unionist Thomas
Bennett vied with each other for control of the institution at its incep-
tion, thus contributing to the extreme speculation. Allies of each man
marched into the subscription room at the Fire and Marine Insurance
Company to vote for the bank's future leadership with their checkbooks.
Hamilton hovered in the company's offices, keeping track of how much
stock each side had purchased. Just before the books closed on June 2, he
pulled a check from his pocket and placed it before the commissioners.
It bore the signature of his wife's millionaire kinsman, planter Daniel
Heyward. The staggering amount of the check—$5,000,000—assured
Hamilton's election as the first president of the Bank of Charleston.[13]

The day after the B.U.S. branch officially closed in November 1835,
the Bank of Charleston opened for business in the branch's old offices,
with many former B.U.S. employees performing their accustomed jobs.
From the beginning the institution was successful, largely because of the
business it inherited from the B.U.S. branch and the role it assumed as
the Philadelphia bank's Charleston agent. In addition, Hamilton had the
audacity to ask Jackson's treasury secretary to select the Bank of Charleston as a federal deposit bank. Because of the new bank's size and importance, Secretary Levi Woodbury complied. In the midst of the Bank

12. *Charleston Courier*, 2 June (first quotation) and 3 June 1835 (second quotation); Peter
Bacot to Nicholas Biddle, 3, 6, and 24 June 1835; John Potter to Nicholas Biddle, 13 June 1835,
all in Nicholas Biddle Papers, LC.

13. J. Mauldin Lesesne, *The Bank of the State of South Carolina: A General and Political History* (Columbia: University of South Carolina Press for the South Carolina Tricentennial Commission, 1970), 143–4; Stoney, ed., "Porcher Memoirs," *SCHM* 47 (January 1946): 35; Carson,
ed., *Petigru*, 175; *Charleston Courier*, 5 May 1835.

War, then, Hamilton positioned his institution as both the successor to Biddle's Bank in Charleston and a Jackson pet. The Nullifier financier further showed his political acumen by soothing Unionist stockholders with the appointment of James Petigru as the bank's attorney. Under Hamilton's conservative and politic management, the Bank of Charleston soon filled its vaults with specie, generated tidy profits and, before the end of its first year of operation, declared the unheard of semi-annual dividend of five dollars per share.[14]

In addition to heading up Charleston's newest bank, Hamilton also became a cotton merchant and factor. For too long, he believed, Carolina planters had allowed northerners to control the trade in the state's own staples. Hamilton hoped to capture the wealth of Yankee middlemen for himself. As early as 1836, Hamilton & Company operated a wharf along Charleston's waterfront. He sent his oldest son, James, off to Europe to learn the ropes of transatlantic commerce. In 1837, twenty-three-year-old James returned to Charleston to join his father in a merchant firm reorganized as James Hamilton & Son Company. At the same time, the elder Hamilton dispatched another son, Lynch, to Le Havre with the intent that he be educated "as a thorough merchant." Hamilton shared the dream of his friend Robert Hayne, who set up his own son in a Charleston import firm, "to rear up a brood of Carolina Merchants . . . to put our Southern Commerce on a right footing." Hamilton turned down re-election as president of the Bank of Charleston that fall so that he could devote more attention to his mercantile firm. With the younger James's European "commercial connections & correspondence of no small value" and Hamilton's own contacts throughout the region and nation, the new cotton merchant expected his company "to do business to any extent we may desire."[15]

Hamilton gained quite a reputation as a knowledgeable businessman.

14. Lindley, *South Carolina National*, 9. For an early suggestion that the Bank of Charleston would buy B.U.S.'s Charleston property, see John Potter to Nicholas Biddle, 13 June 1835, Nicholas Biddle Papers, LC. Pease and Pease, *Web of Progress*, 47; *Reports of the Secretary of the Treasury* (Washington: Blair & Rives, 1837), 3:754; Pease and Pease, *Petigru*, 87–8; *Charleston Mercury*, 25 May 1837.

15. *Charleston Courier*, 1 July 1836 and 7 January 1837. See also Glenn, "James Hamilton," 274; Pease and Pease, *Web of Progress*, 51; Hamilton, "James Hamilton"; Robert Hayne to James Henry Hammond, 18 June 1839, copy in JHP, SHC; and JH to Nicholas Biddle, 17 October 1837, Nicholas Biddle Papers, LC.

Franklin Elmore, a budding Carolina industrialist and soon president of the state-owned bank, listed Hamilton as one of the state's three prominent business figures who could convince northern capitalists to invest in the Nesbit Manufacturing Company that Elmore headed. Later, Elmore also depended on Hamilton to make contacts with English and Dutch bankers to benefit his enterprises.[16]

A leading banker and businessman, Hamilton also devoted himself to a variety of commercial projects during Charleston's boom years of the mid-1830s. He became associated with one of the city's major building projects as a founding director of the Charleston Hotel Company. With Gazaway Buggs Lamar of Georgia, he started the Savannah and Charleston Steam Packet Company by purchasing an English steamer in 1836 for $50,000. They planned for the ship, which they christened the *Pulaski*, to engage in direct trade between southern ports and Liverpool—again showing Hamilton's interest in ensuring for southerners (especially himself) a larger share of the profits of southern commerce. Perhaps most importantly, he joined the board of directors of the Louisville, Cincinnati, and Charleston Railroad Company (LCC), which sought to make Charleston the main port not only for South Carolina but also for a vast region of the central South, from Kentucky to Georgia.[17]

While he busied himself with these various projects, Hamilton also expanded and improved his planting empire during the decade. He purchased Fife, a St. Peter's Parish rice plantation near Rice Hope, in late 1835. He also sought to make his holdings more profitable by modernizing his operations. To his rice mill, which cleaned his crop and also the crops of his neighbors, such as Langdon Cheves, Hamilton added a mechanical rice-thresher. The machine's Yankee inventor credited Hamilton with popularizing the device among lowcountry planters by establishing one at Pennyworth. Hamilton even hired a Connecticut mechanic to take care of the plantation machinery. "Everything is going on

16. Franklin Harper Elmore to Gentlemen [Nesbit Manufacturing Company investors], 27 December 1838, and JH to Elmore, 3 June and 20 July 1840, Franklin Harper Elmore Papers, LC.

17. Pease and Pease, *Web of Progress*, 52; Gregory Allen Greb, "Charleston, South Carolina, Merchants, 1815–1860: Urban Leadership in the Antebellum South" (Ph.D. diss., University of California, San Diego, 1978), 156; JH to Langdon Cheves, 16 September 1837, Langdon Cheves I Papers, SCHS; and Samuel M. Derrick, *Centennial History of the South Carolina Railroad* (Columbia, S.C.: State Company, 1930).

prosperously," Hamilton reported of his agricultural duchy in 1836. "Our staples are selling high & property is generally advancing."[18]

Succeeding admirably in his enterprises during the mid-1830s, Hamilton enjoyed the material advantages befitting a member of the upper echelon of southern society. His crops yielded thirty to forty thousand dollars annually. In addition, he earned a good salary from the Bank of Charleston. In 1837, he moved his family into the elegant Gadsden mansion on Charleston's fashionable East Bay, where liveried slaves served the Hamiltons. Slaves on a small Hamilton farm just outside Charleston supplied the family with fresh produce. When the master of the house went about town, an Irish coachman drove him through Charleston's streets.[19]

Hamilton impressed visitors during these years. Francis Lieber, the German-born academic whom Hamilton helped attract to the South Carolina College faculty in 1835, characterized the former governor as "uncommonly kind." Lieber felt "more attracted [to Hamilton] than to any American before." The English writer Harriet Martineau, despite Hamilton's pro-slavery views that she despised, found the man himself absolutely charming. Although she believed Hamilton less well known to her readers than former senator Robert Hayne, Martineau considered the ex-governor "a yet more perfect representative of the Southern gentlemen [sic]. He is handsome, and his manners have all the grace, without much of the arrogance of the bearing of his class." Despite his well-deserved reputation for graciousness, Hamilton was not terribly gregarious in his middle years. Indeed, he enjoyed spending time at Pennyworth, alone or perhaps with a few of his sons. Still, even on his small rice island, he extended generous hospitality from time to time. On one occasion at his house on the marsh, he impressed Francis Lieber with a fine dinner, which included "four different meats," served by barefoot slaves.[20]

18. Mortgage of Daniel Heyward Hamilton to Bank of Charleston, 6 January 1844, Charleston Mortgages, Book 4B,176, SCDAH; D. H. Hamilton to John W. Bass, 17 April 1854, William Pitt Ballinger Papers, CAH; Robert F. W. Allston, "Rice," *DeBow's Review*, April 1846, 341–2; Hamilton, "James Hamilton"; and JH to Charles Manigault, 30 April 1836, JHP, SHC (quotation).

19. Hamilton, "James Hamilton."

20. Thomas Sergeant Perry, ed., *The Life and Letters of Francis Lieber* (Boston: James R. Osgood, 1882), 104–5 (first and third quotations); and Harriet Martineau, *Retrospect of Western Travel* (London: Saunders and Otley, 1838), 2:80–1 (second quotation).

The expanding economy that accounted for Hamilton's prosperity, based so much as it was on speculation, could not last forever. As early as the spring of 1836, signs of economic weakness began appearing throughout the country, particularly in the Northeast. In March 1837, the *Charleston Mercury* reported to its readers on a "GREAT COMMER-CIAL CALAMITY" in New York, the failure of an important banking house. That spring, hundreds of businesses in that metropolis went bust, and in early May, New York banks suspended specie payments. If nothing were done to alleviate the distress, one New Yorker predicted, "Blood will flow in our streets and a civil war will be the consequence."[21]

"At the last the Bubble burst and great is the explosion," a Charlestonian observed in the aftermath of the bad news from the North. Charleston suffered, too, though not as badly as major cities farther up the coast. Whereas many northern merchants failed, only a few Charleston businesses went under in the first half of 1837. All of Charleston's banks, including Hamilton's, suspended specie payments, but none of the institutions actually went out of business.[22]

Even so, the citizens of Charleston were not spared rumors of financial ruin in their very midst. Throughout the spring of 1837, as ill tidings arrived from the North, Charlestonians shared with one another fevered stories of impending devastation. Word spread that the city's banks verged on collapse. The Bank of Charleston's directors, Hamilton included, supposedly had gambled away the institution's funds in disastrous Mississippi land speculations. When city officials called a public meeting to quell these rumors, Hamilton was off at Pennyworth. His absence on the eve of the meeting led to fears that he had escaped to Texas to avoid the consequences of his bank's destruction.

Fortunately, Hamilton arrived in Charleston in time for the public meeting, where he allayed concerns about his bank's solvency and defended his reputation. He offered a financial statement that put to rest tales of his bank's imminent collapse; indeed, the institution was in fine shape. He also denied the rumors of the bank directors' use of deposits for land speculation. Acknowledging the country's fall "from a high and palmy state of prosperity" to one more bleak, Hamilton offered an opti-

21. *Charleston Mercury*, 24 March 1837 (first quotation); Glyndon G. Van Deusen, *The Jacksonian Era, 1828–1848* (New York: Harper & Row, 1963), 116–8; Samuel Swartwout to William C. Rives, 2 August 1837, William C. Rives Papers, LC (second quotation).

22. Jacob Schirmer Diary, 30 June 1837, SCHS; and Lesesne, *Bank of the State*, 40.

mistic assessment of the future. "But who doubts," he said, "the solvency of this great country—that its resources vastly transcend its indebtedness, or that any paralysis on its industry must be essentially fugitive and temporary? We shall come out of the struggle wiser from its inflictions." With Hamilton's calming words, the meeting succeeded in restoring Charlestonians' confidence in the city's banks.[23]

The meeting also inspired an effort to solve the nation's crisis. This took the form of a letter-writing campaign by Charleston's bank presidents to their counterparts in other major cities. They hoped to coordinate with other bankers the resumption of specie payments. Each president wrote several of his banking colleagues. To Hamilton went the assignment of contacting Nicholas Biddle, which he did by means of a private letter followed by a public one.

In his public letter to Biddle, widely reprinted in the nation's press, Hamilton offered a clearheaded and evenhanded analysis of the nation's economic plight as well as suggestions for a solution. Hamilton attributed the nation's underlying ills to the explosion of banks that had issued far too much currency. Showing rather remarkable restraint for an old Nullifier, he absolved the Jackson administration of blame for the crisis. The downturn would have occurred with or without the B.U.S. veto and the removal of the deposits, he said, although he considered those actions quite harmful. He expressed sympathy with the Democratic hard money position, but thought it should be introduced much more gradually than administration policymakers did. Like Biddle and the emerging Whig Party, Hamilton recognized the necessity of paper currency in a healthy, growing economy. Therefore, his long-term solution lay in re-creating a national bank with the power to regulate denominations of bills. To satisfy the strictest constructionists, he proposed amending the Constitution to authorize such a bank. Once the amendment passed, Hamilton hoped Congress would simply recharter B.U.S. as the nation's central bank. Because that permanent solution would take time and the country needed immediate help, Hamilton also suggested a temporary fix. He urged Biddle to convene a meeting of the nation's leading bankers in order to develop a plan for resuming specie payments and for making other recommendations to Congress.[24]

23. *Charleston Mercury*, 25 May 1837.
24. Ibid., 16 June 1837.

Hamilton's proposal won praise from many quarters. The *Philadelphia Inquirer* labeled his letter "the ablest article . . . that we have yet met with upon the subject." The paper also commented favorably upon Hamilton's "patriotism" and lack of "political bigotry" in the way he presented his views. Although his forbearance toward the administration drew accolades, it disappointed Whigs who wished to build their new political party by attacking the Jacksonian financial record. Henry Clay considered the Hamilton letter "a manly production . . . worthy of its high minded author," but complained that it let Old Hickory and his minions off the hook too easily.[25]

Partisanship, however, did not suit Hamilton's needs in 1837. He wholly agreed with neither of the two major parties competing for national political power. Harriet Martineau put his political stance in positive terms when she noted "his generous appreciation of the powers and virtues of the great men of every party at Washington." Although partisan imperatives pushed the Nullifiers into coalition with the anti-Jackson Whigs and Hamilton's financial views closely approximated those of Clay's party, he also agreed with the Democrats on the need for more hard money and a low tariff. Moreover, as president of a pet bank, he could ill afford to heap ridicule on the party in power. As a banker and not so much a politician, he put faith in financiers like himself rather than the Washington crowd.[26]

Hamilton made more than one trip up the East Coast that summer in an effort to garner support for his idea of a national bankers' convention. Although the leaders of some New York banks also issued a call to meet, Nicholas Biddle, the most influential financier in the country, remained unconvinced. In a meeting with Hamilton, the B.U.S. president prophesied that resumption "would prove a fallacy and an abortion. It could not be maintained a week." Without Biddle's support, Hamilton's proposal for solving the resumption problem died. Although bankers from across the country never gathered as Hamilton hoped, eighty representatives from Georgia and South Carolina banks met in Charleston the following spring to adopt a regional version of Hamilton's plan. The delegates, in-

25. Reprinted in *Charleston Mercury*, 30 June 1837; and Henry Clay to Waddy Thompson, 8 July 1837, in *The Papers of Henry Clay*, ed. James F. Hopkins and Mary W. M. Hargreaves (Lexington: University Press of Kentucky, 1988), 9:57.

26. Martineau, *Western Travel*, 81; and JH to Hugh Legaré, 17 December 1837, Hugh Swinton Legaré Papers, Duke.

cluding Hamilton representing the Bank of Charleston, agreed their institutions would resume specie payments by the first of January 1839.[27]

Hamilton's permanent settlement of the crisis—a new national bank—fell victim to politics. Having killed one "Monster," Democrats hardly would consent to another, although they would have loved for the Whigs to embrace such a Hamiltonian solution. Whigs themselves, having been pilloried by their opponents over Biddle's institution, denied they really wanted a central bank. By the fall of 1837, even Hamilton himself had rejected his own suggestion. Instead, he favored a revised pet bank system under which the federal government kept accounts in selected state banks—such as the Bank of Charleston.[28]

During the summer of 1837, his search for a resolution to the economic crisis led Hamilton to approach his old friend, the new president, Martin Van Buren. The Carolinian dangled in front of Van Buren the prospect that, in return for his cooperation with Hamilton, the president might receive backing from the Nullifiers. Old Kinderhook, however, had other ideas. As it turned out, Nullifiers would cooperate with Van Buren's plans, much to the consternation of their former leader.[29]

Van Buren offered a simple solution to the nation's economic ills. Acting on the premise that banks were the problem, the president proposed the Independent Treasury plan, under which the federal government would sever all its connections with banks. Instead, federal authorities would deposit customs and land revenue in one of several regional "subtreasuries" controlled by the Treasury Department. According to Jacksonian Democrats, only such a divorce of bank and state could shield government from the corrupting influence of private financial interests.

To Hamilton, Van Buren's plan—"that infernal scheme of mischief the subtreasury Humbug"—amounted to lunacy, and most prominent South Carolina business and political figures agreed with him. The commercial planters of the Palmetto State had never shared the agrarian distaste for banks exhibited by Jacksonians. Moreover, the Nullifiers' Whig coalition allies opposed the subtreasury. Not surprisingly, then, seven of

27. Adams, ed., *Adams Memoirs*, 9:364; and *Charleston Mercury*, 22, 25, 26 May 1838.

28. John M. McFaul, *The Politics of Jacksonian Finance* (Ithaca: Cornell University Press, 1972), 75–6; John C. Calhoun to James Edward Colhoun, 27 October 1837, *Calhoun Papers*, ed. Wilson, 13:628.

29. JH to Martin Van Buren, 24 June 1837, MVBP, LC.

the state's nine congressmen voted against the Independent Treasury bill in September 1837.[30]

Despite the overwhelming opposition to the subtreasury in the state, however, Calhoun decided to use the issue as an opportunity to break ranks with the Whigs. Unhappy with his broad constructionist partners in the anti-Jackson alliance, Calhoun believed the time had arrived for rapprochement with the Democrats. By aligning with the administration, Calhoun could also help heal the rift between Jacksonian Unionists and his own Nullifiers at home. On September 18, Calhoun shocked friends and foes alike by announcing his support for Van Buren's financial measures.[31]

Hamilton's old friend James Petigru happened to be in the Senate gallery when Calhoun made his pro-subtreasury speech. The oration raised the Unionist leader's hopes that Calhoun's endorsement of "the Divorce of Bank and State" would result in "a divorce of Calhoun from his little party" in South Carolina. It was not to be. Although important Carolina politicians besides Hamilton opposed the subtreasury—including Robert Hayne, George McDuffie, and Waddy Thompson—Calhoun succeeded in winning a majority to his side.[32]

During the legislative session that fall and winter, Hamilton led a lonely fight against the subtreasury in the state senate. In a sense, he was reaping the harvest of what he himself had sown earlier in the decade. Thanks in large part to his efforts, many Carolinians viewed federal power as tyrannical. Consequently, he smoothed the way for Calhoun and his friends to persuade the state's residents of the dangers of the union of the federal government and the banks. Moreover, Hamilton had popularized the principle that the state spoke with one voice and had created a disciplined party to express the proper views. Only now, Hamilton neither headed that party nor gave the orders; Calhoun did. In the legislature, Robert Barnwell Smith, who had recently adopted his mother's maiden name of Rhett, executed Calhoun's instructions with as much efficiency as he had when serving as Hamilton's lieutenant. Rhett lined up

---

30. JH to Hugh Legaré, 17 December 1837, Hugh Swinton Legaré Papers, Duke; and Ernest Lander, "The Calhoun-Preston Feud, 1836–1842," *SCHM* 59 (January 1958): 24–37.

31. For Calhoun's discomfort as an ally of Henry Clay and Daniel Webster, see Calhoun to Duff Green, 26 June 1837, *Calhoun Papers*, ed. Wilson, 13:516–7. For the text of Calhoun's speech, see Wilson, ed., *Calhoun Papers*, 13:546–71.

32. James L. Petigru to Thomas Petigru, 18 September 1837, *Petigru*, ed. Carson, 191.

the votes of old Nullifiers to endorse the subtreasury. The Jacksonian Unionists, who naturally supported the policies of Old Hickory's successor, joined Rhett's Nullifiers to make an unbeatable combination.[33]

As the state senate prepared to pass resolutions endorsing the Independent Treasury, Hamilton offered a series of counter-resolutions. Reflecting his frustration as a member of the minority, Hamilton attacked the administration's proposal in language much less temperate than one might have expected from his letter to Biddle that spring. He criticized the "unwise tampering and pernicious experiments of the government with the currency of the country—experiments conceived in a blind ignorance of the ordinary principles of finance, and prosecuted with a daring exercise of power, unparalleled in the previous history of our country." He decried the pet bank system—never mind the fact that it included the Bank of Charleston—and the specie circular. He regarded "with absolute dismay the seemingly meditated hostility to the Banks, both by the Government and its supporters." Such hostility could only result "in the general bankruptcy of the whole country."[34]

Hamilton's fellow senators would hear none of it. They overwhelmingly tabled Hamilton's resolutions on a motion by Rhett; only two other senators endorsed Hamilton's sentiments. The senate then proceeded to approve the house's pro-subtreasury resolutions. The state officially went on record as backing the Van Buren administration.[35]

That spring, disaster diverted the attention of Charlestonians from the subtreasury struggle. On the evening of April 27, what "proved to be the largest and most distressing fire that we have ever had in the City" began at the corner of King and Berresford Streets. Coming after a period of very dry weather, the fire "burnt with fury for 12 hours and nothing could arrest it." The conflagration claimed the lives of several residents and consumed at least three churches, a synagogue, the Masonic Hall, Seyle's Long Room—site of so many Unionist meetings during the nullification struggle—and even the new hotel in which Hamilton had invested. The blaze left the city a "melancholy ruin."[36]

33. George C. Rogers, Jr., "South Carolina Federalists and the Origins of the Nullification Movement," *SCHM* 71 (January 1970): 30; and A. S. Salley, Jr., "Historical Notes," *SCHM* 30 (October, 1929): 257–8.

34. *South Carolina Legislative Journal*, 1837, 64–6, *State Records*, reel 480.

35. Ibid., 15 December 1837, 70.

36. Jacob Schirmer Diary, 27 April 1838, SCHS (first two quotations); and Stoney, ed., "Porcher Memoirs," *SCHM* 47 (April 1946): 83 (last quotation).

In late May, right after the Charleston banking conference, Hamilton headed to Columbia for a special legislative session called to consider relief measures for the ruined city. It soon became clear, as Hamilton informed a friend, that in the senate chamber he stood "between two fires—the conflagration of our city & the Sub Treasury." Supporters of the Calhoun-backed financial plan announced their intention to seek passage of yet more resolutions in its favor. They wanted, first, to declare that a majority of South Carolinians supported the subtreasury and, second, to instruct the state's congressional delegation to vote for it that summer. Subtreasury backers aimed their instructions at the few holdouts—including Senator William C. Preston and Representatives Waddy Thompson and Hugh Legaré—who refused to follow Calhoun's lead on the issue. Hamilton did his best to snuff out the subtreasury fire by offering a motion requiring legislators to confine their work to providing relief to Charleston. He withdrew the motion when its failure became obvious, but he defended his position vigorously.[37]

In his speech on the motion, Hamilton gave a vintage performance. The resolutions before them, he asserted, originated in "a preliminary Caucus." He denied the truth of the first resolution, which claimed a majority of Carolinians supported the subtreasury. Certainly, he said, with a "few clap traps and cant phrases" and some party discipline, a majority might be persuaded to go for Van Buren's plan. "At present," however, he sarcastically noted, "the people of South-Carolina have regarded the Sub-Treasury scheme with about as much indifference as they have the popular humbugs of Animal Magnetism and Phrenology." He therefore could not vote for such a resolution "without violating my own sense of veracity."[38]

The second resolution, which instructed members of Congress, he considered not so much ridiculously false as dangerously unrepublican. He specifically defended Senator Preston, whom he understood to be the special target of the subtreasury men. Already they had branded the Virginia-born Preston as an outsider whom Carolinians could not trust. Alluding to Preston's contributions to his adopted state, Hamilton chided

37. JH to Thomas Gilmer, 3 June 1838, *William and Mary Quarterly*, 1st ser., 21 (October 1912): 83 (quotation); and *Charleston Mercury*, 30 May 1838.

38. The speech, paraphrased and quoted from in this paragraph and the next, may be found in *Charleston Mercury*, 18 June 1838.

his opponents for attacks that violated the "hospitality of South Caro-lina—that sentiment which is the very religion of our hearth-stones."

Hamilton's remarkable speech was precisely the sort a Unionist might have made in 1832. All of the techniques about which he complained in 1838—resolutions predetermined by caucus, the branding of opponents as suspicious outsiders, demands for unity—he himself had employed during his crusade for a nullification convention. His efforts now, like those of his Unionist opponents in former days, failed. Hamilton and one other senator did enter a protest against the subtreasury in the senate journal; anti-subtreasury house members placed an identical protest in the official record of their proceedings. In terms Hamilton might have used five years before, the *Charleston Mercury* derided this protest "against the action of THE STATE" by likening it to "the last cry of a child against being put to bed in the dark."[39]

Because of his subtreasury stance, Hamilton's political standing in South Carolina declined precipitously. The *Richmond Whig*, sympathetic to Hamilton's views, commented on the sea change in Palmetto State politics: "The flightiest fancy . . . could never, in its wildest dreams, have deemed it among the things possible, that the Charleston Mercury would be found denouncing James Hamilton, because he would not sing hosan-nas to Martin Van Buren! The annunciation of the fact stuns the brain, and the imagination reels in the effort to grasp and realize it."[40] The sub-treasury episode effectively ended Hamilton's political career; his speech against the resolutions was his last ever as an elected official. Although he did not know that in 1838, he did decline to run for re-election so that he could concentrate on his business career.

That summer, Hamilton put politics behind him and took on an excit-ing financial project. The legislature had granted the LCC banking privi-leges as the Southwestern Railroad Bank, and the company's directors dispatched Hamilton to England to procure a two-million-dollar loan to start the institution. His connections developed while president of the Bank of Charleston and as a merchant-factor made Hamilton a logical choice for the mission.

Hamilton narrowly avoided personal disaster at the beginning of the

39. *South Carolina Legislative Journal*, 1838,10–14, in *State Records*, reel 480; *Columbia Tele-scope*, 2 June 1838; *Charleston Mercury*, 5 June 1838 (quotation).

40. *Richmond Whig*, reprinted in *Columbia Telescope*, 7 July 1838.

trip, but the catastrophe adversely affected his infant shipping company. Hamilton and his partner in that enterprise, G. B. Lamar, had converted the *Pulaski* into a passenger ship to carry southerners up north for the summer; the panic had scotched their plans for immediately instituting direct trade between southern ports and Europe. In mid-June, he booked passage on the steamer to take him on the first leg of his journey to England. He planned to board when the *Pulaski* stopped in Charleston to pick up a cargo of lowcountry aristocrats as it made its fourth voyage from Savannah to Baltimore. Lamar himself was aboard, accompanied by his wife and seven children. But business affairs detained Hamilton in Charleston, and the *Pulaski* left without him. Then on the night of June 14, as the ship steamed along the coast near the border of the Carolinas, its boiler exploded. The accident killed a number of the socially prominent passengers, including Lamar's wife and several of his children. Although Hamilton had the good fortune to miss the boat, the sinking of the *Pulaski* ended his budding career as a shipping magnate.[41]

Later in the summer, he safely traveled up the coast and on July 7 departed New York City for Liverpool. His first transatlantic crossing took more than two weeks, during which he prepared for his talks with English financiers. In Britain, he met with prominent London bankers, including John Horsley Palmer, former head of the Bank of England. With the assistance of his new "financial friends & correspondents," Hamilton was, as he himself put it, "exceedingly successful" in the loan negotiations. Soon, the first of two expected million-dollar shipments of specie left England bound for the vaults of Charleston's Southwestern Railroad Bank.[42]

While in England, Hamilton also became embroiled in an international incident in which he defended the honor of southern slaveholders against Daniel O'Connell, Irish member of Parliament and abolitionist. In a fiery speech to an anti-slavery gathering in Birmingham, O'Connell hurled insults at American slaveholders, singling out Andrew Stevenson, the U.S. minister to Britain, for special scorn by labeling him a "slave

41. *Charleston Mercury*, 20 June 1838; George White, ed., *Historical Collections of Georgia* (1855; reprint, Baltimore: Baltimore Genealogical Publishing Co., 1969), 353–64; and Rebecca Lamar McLeod, "The Loss of the Steamer Pulaski," *Georgia Historical Quarterly*, June 1919, 63–95.

42. JH to Mirabeau Buonaparte Lamar, 11 October 1838, *The Papers of Mirabeau Buonaparte Lamar*, ed. C. A. Gulick et al. (Austin: Texas State Library, 1922), 2:245.

breeder." Stevenson, whom Hamilton had helped elect Speaker of the U.S. House of Representatives in 1826, called on his old ally for guidance. Hamilton then turned to American friends in London for advice on handling the situation. One was Captain Matthew Calbraith Perry, brother of his old chum, Oliver Hazard Perry. The younger Perry, in England on U.S. Navy business, and another American acquaintance convinced Hamilton to seek clarification from O'Connell as to whether he meant to defame Stevenson's character. Before Hamilton could contact him, the Irish politician issued a public statement asserting he had intended no insult to the American minister. That should have ended the episode. But Hamilton wrote a letter, subsequently published in several American newspapers, that expressed his clear contempt for O'Connell. The Carolinian declared he had been prepared to "stop [O'Connell's] wind" if necessary in order to defend Stevenson's honor. Upon docking in New York, Hamilton discovered his intemperate letter had stirred controversy. His mentioning of Perry's minor role in the affair caught the attention of Congressman John Quincy Adams, who called for an investigation into the activities of the naval officer and the old Nullifier. Adams's demands produced nothing, but Hamilton also faced criticism from Irish immigrants for his denunciation of O'Connell. In a notice published in the *New York Gazette*, Hamilton disavowed any disrespect on his part toward the Irish. Having made amends to the Irish, an important constituency in Charleston, he felt great satisfaction with having, at least in his own mind, bested an abolitionist.[43]

A terrible misfortune overshadowed any satisfaction he might have derived from his victory over O'Connell. Soon after returning to the United States, Hamilton received word of the death of his oldest son, twenty-four-year-old James. Forced to remain in Charleston during the worst yellow fever epidemic in over a decade, the young man had succumbed to the disease. Not only was the younger James's death a hard emotional blow to the fifty-two-year-old father, but it also had business ramifications. Hamilton had relied on his son's business acumen and considered judgment, two qualities the father did not always possess in great measure. "This dreadful event has deranged my whole affairs here,"

43. See newspaper clippings enclosed in JH to Andrew Stevenson, 3 October 1838, Andrew Stevenson Papers, LC; Morison, *"Old Bruin,"* 137–8; and Matthew C. Perry to Andrew Stevenson, 16 February 1839, Andrew Stevenson Papers, LC.

Hamilton confessed to Langdon Cheves. The grieving father ordered Lynch home from Europe to take his brother's place in the firm, but Hamilton's company never quite recovered.[44]

Deranged business affairs threatened many southern planters and merchants as the economic depression lingered and credit tightened in the late 1830s. During 1837 and 1838, southerners received largely inadvertent assistance from Nicholas Biddle as the B.U.S. president worked to prop up the price of cotton. He intended to correct a large trade deficit with English manufacturers by procuring the highest possible rates for the nation's leading item of trade. Biddle sent agents to southern markets to buy cotton or make advances to planters on their crops. He then consigned all of his purchases to a single firm in Liverpool that he founded. The Liverpool merchants, Humphreys & Biddle, kept the cotton off the market until demand reached such a point in the autumn of 1838 that they could sell it profitably. Biddle's intervention brought Anglo-American trade back into balance, while also putting money into planters' pockets. The following spring, Biddle retired from the Bank and ceased his efforts in the cotton market.[45]

As cotton prices fell in 1839, Hamilton and another planter-banker, John Gamble of Florida, met in New York to consider their own plans for artificially inflating cotton prices. Hamilton had been marginally involved with Biddle's efforts the previous year by supplying the Philadelphia banker with information about the cotton supply. Inspired by Biddle, Hamilton and Gamble in June 1839 anonymously issued a "cotton circular," which proposed cooperation among southern banks, merchants, and planters to raise cotton prices by carefully controlling sales to English textile mills. The following month, Hamilton and Gamble issued another circular signed by fourteen planters from all the Deep South states. It fleshed out their ideas and issued a call for an October commercial convention in Macon, Georgia, to consider their plan. In the

44. J. D. B. DeBow, *The Industrial Resources, Statistics, Etc., of the United States, and more particularly of the Southern and Western States . . .* , 3rd ed. (New York: D. Appleton, 1854), 1:248. See also Jacob Schirmer Diary, "Remarks" for August 1838, SCHS; JH to Langdon Cheves, 12 November 1838, Langdon Cheves I Papers, SCHS.

45. Thomas Payne Govan, "An Ante-Bellum Attempt to Regulate the Price and Supply of Cotton," *North Carolina Historical Review* 17, no. 4 (October 1940): 303–4; Leland Hamilton Jenks, *The Migration of British Capital to 1875* (New York: A. A. Knopf, 1927), 91; and Mays Humphreys to Nicholas Biddle, 20 and 30 November 1838 and 7 January 1839, Nicholas Biddle Papers, LC.

meantime, the signers authorized an agent to go to Liverpool and Le Havre to scout out a mercantile firm willing to take the consignment of cotton they hoped to control. Although the circular left out the name of the agent, the planters designated James Hamilton to do their bidding in Europe.[46]

The cotton circulars of June and July 1839 caused quite a stir. Because the first, anonymous circular had been issued from the office of a New York mercantile agent connected to Biddle, many English manufacturers imagined it yet another scheme of the former B.U.S. president. They obviously opposed any effort to restrict their supply of raw materials or hike prices. But many southerners also expressed opposition to the plan. Some planters suspected the circular constituted a merchant's plot designed to somehow harm growers. A Mississippi newspaper condemned the circular's interference with free trade, while that state's fall Democratic convention labeled it a speculative bubble.[47]

Charlestonians also greeted the circular with skepticism. Robert Hayne found a "great difference of opinion as to its merits, objects, and probable effects" among his friends and colleagues. Hayne himself distrusted attempts to influence prices. "The thing is very difficult to accomplish," he sagely observed, "and if effected, does in general, at least as much harm as good, while the failure of the attempt is positively injurious." Although Hayne objected to the plan for economic reasons, he noted that the rumored author of the first circular turned some Charlestonians against it. "It is said that our friend Hamilton is at the head of the combination, & this of course renders the measure peculiarly obnoxious to some persons here." Hamilton himself had become an issue, an object of resentment for at least a portion of his Charleston neighbors. His wealth and his pursuit of more, his political stands, and his undeniable imperiousness all contributed to the negative way in which some viewed him.[48]

With little care about the cracks in his reputation or the sort of cau-

46. See extracts of letters to JH enclosed in Nicholas Biddle to Edward C. Biddle, 20 November 1838, Nicholas Biddle Papers, LC; and Govan, "Ante-Bellum Attempt," 305. The July circular appears in Samuel Hazard, *United States Commercial and Statistical Register*, July 1839, 91–2, and Hamilton's report on his duties as agent in *NR* 57 (15 November 1839): 185.

47. Govan, *Nicholas Biddle*, 357–9; and Govan, "Ante-Bellum Attempt," 307.

48. Hayne refers here to the first, unsigned cotton circular of early June 1839. Robert Hayne to James Henry Hammond, 18 June 1839, copy in JHP, SHC.

tion Hayne counseled, Hamilton charged ahead. Acting as the agent of the Cotton Planters' Association created by the circular, he took a cargo of cotton from his own plantations and his merchant house to England that summer. Arriving in mid-August, he discussed his Association's plans with representatives of Liverpool cotton firms and then went to Le Havre for more meetings. European cotton buyers expressed little interest, however, because demand slackened considerably even as Hamilton and his associates plotted to drive up cotton prices. That summer, some English textile factories began working only four days per week and others shut down altogether. "We have just received dreadful news from England & may look out for the *worst* in financial matters. Cotton down & c," observed Charlestonian Hugh Legaré in July. Soon thereafter, as the enormity of the situation became apparent, Legaré remarked that "the fall of cotton involves, unfortunately, some of our most active & public spirited people, I am sorely afraid Hamilton is ruined by it. I have been told he will lose $250,000! & that at a time when the depreciation of all property at Charleston which will probably not fall far short of 50 per ct. will proportionately diminish his means of making payment. There may be exaggeration in those evil bodings—but certain it is, the effects already produced by them are sufficiently disastrous."[49]

In early October, Hamilton returned to the United States, where a new round of specie payment suspensions greeted him. Hurrying on to Macon for the cotton convention, he remained publicly optimistic despite the bad economic news and his own recent cotton losses. In Macon, he reported on his contacts with the European firms but, significantly, could say nothing of their interest in the Association's plans. The convention, chaired by Georgia congressman Thomas Butler King, proceeded to make elaborate plans to control the supply of cotton. Nothing, however, came of them. The suspension of payments forced banks to call in their old loans rather than to make new advances to planters as called for by the convention.[50]

Just as his unsuccessful cotton speculation imperiled his private fortune, his public image received a damaging blow as well. New informa-

49. "The Manifesto of the Cotton Spinners," *Manchester Guardian*, 3 July 1839, reprinted in Samuel Hazard, *United States Commercial and Statistical Register*, July 1839, 90. Hugh Legaré to William C. Rives, 26 July (first quotation) and 7 August 1839 (block quotation), William C. Rives Papers, LC.

50. *NR* 57 (15 November 1839): 184–7; and Govan, "An Ante-Bellum Attempt," 310–2.

tion revealed that the previous year he had misled the LCC directors about the Southwestern Railroad Bank loan. Everyone assumed that Hamilton had sold the bank's bonds in England. In fact, he had not. Concerns about risky investments in American internal improvement projects had made that nearly impossible, given the state of the post-panic money market in 1838. Instead, Hamilton had deposited the bonds with brokers, who advanced him the million dollars in specie for the bank. He gambled that improved financial conditions would allow for later bond sales, but that did not happen. Thus, the Southwestern Railroad Bank could not draw on its second million when it needed to in late 1839. With the exposure of his lie, Hamilton "sank fearfully in public estimation."[51]

In the five years from the test oath controversy until the end of the decade, James Hamilton experienced the best and worst of times. Setting out to conquer the business world as he had the political one, he achieved great success as a banker and merchant. But then came a series of reverses with astonishing rapidity—the *Pulaski* sinking, his son's death, his unsuccessful battle against the subtreasury, the large cotton losses, the Southwestern Railroad Bank scandal. These touched his private life and seriously eroded his personal fortune. Moreover, they affected how others viewed him. The increasingly negative way his peers perceived him wounded this man so anxious about appearing "strikingly to the public eye." But Hamilton, like the proverbial riverboat gambler, had an ace up his sleeve, one that could win him back his reputation and his fortune: a new revolutionary republic called Texas.[52]

51. Stoney, ed., "Porcher Memoirs," *SHCM* 47 (January 1946): 39.
52. William C. Preston to Waddy Thompson, 15 October 1833, Waddy Thompson Papers, LC.

CHAPTER 7

Texas and the Diplomacy of Debt
1837–1842

IN A NOVEMBER 1836 MESSAGE TO THE South Carolina legislature, Governor George McDuffie addressed a topic of great interest to his constituents—Texas. Ever since the first salvo of the Texas Revolution reverberated across the continent the previous year, American political leaders had debated the possible annexation of the new republic by the United States. President Andrew Jackson wanted to bring the Lone Star Republic within the constellation of the Union, but felt constrained by northern opinion not to do so. An increasingly vocal though still quite small group of abolitionists opposed the admission of yet another slave state, and the president could not risk a sectional division within Democratic ranks that might damage Martin Van Buren's chances to succeed him. While Jackson refused even to recognize Texas in 1836, some southern congressmen maneuvered to welcome the former Mexican state to the family of nations as a first step toward its adoption by the United States.[1]

Governor McDuffie made clear his opposition to both annexation and independence as options for Texas, but he spoke as neither an abolitionist nor a Jackson apologist. Instead, he offered a slaveholder's case for official American neutrality in the struggle of Texas against Mexico. McDuffie maintained that strict neutrality best accorded with southern interests. South Carolina's slaveholders, who insisted on controlling their own internal affairs, should oppose interfering in the domestic concerns "of all

---

1. Robert V. Remini, *Andrew Jackson* (1966; reprint, New York: Harper & Row, 1969), 179; *NR* 52 (4 March 1837): 12.

other states, foreign or confederate." If they advocated the rogue prov-
ince's independence or its incorporation into the Union in contravention
of Mexican rights and wishes, South Carolinians would weaken the principle of non-interference and "commit an offence against their own institutions, by impairing the sanctity of their surest guaranty against foreign
intrusion." By observing the national integrity of Mexico, McDuffie argued, South Carolinians would strengthen their dearly held principle of
a state's right to regulate its own domestic institutions.[2]

For those unswayed by his legal argument, McDuffie offered more
practical ones. An American war with Mexico, he predicted, would almost certainly result from U.S. support for the Texas revolutionaries.
Then Mexico, "aided by some great European power," might "hoist the
standard of servile insurrection in Louisiana and the neighboring states."
Even if one discounted the possibility of a massive slave revolt, still this
was no time for war. "We are now engaged in a fearful and doubtful
struggle to reform our federal system of government, by throwing off
the corruptions under which it is rapidly sinking," McDuffie reminded
legislators. "In this state of things a war with any country would be the
greatest of calamities; for we could scarcely hope to come out of it with
any thing but the mere wreck of a free constitution and the external
forms of a free government."

Clearly, siding with the Texans involved perils for Carolinians; it
would erode their states' rights principles, possibly cause a slave uprising,
and upset the Nullifiers' efforts to restore the Union to its proper constitutional basis. Was the Texan cause worth the risk? McDuffie thought
not. He saw no reason to prefer the Texans over the Mexicans in their
conflict. To the argument that the Texans deserved support because
many of them came from the United States, McDuffie countered that
"by their voluntary expatriation . . . they have forfeited all claim to our
fraternal regard." He dismissed most of the Texans as "mere adventurers" who had gone west in hopes of seizing land for selfish purposes. If
the Texans had once been liberty-loving Americans who now suffered
under a despotic government, McDuffie asserted, they knew what they
were getting themselves into when moving to Texas "and deserve their
destiny." Surely such men did not merit the sympathy of South Carolini-

2. Quoted in *NR* 51 (10 December 1836): 229–30. All McDuffie quotations are from this
source.

ans, nor did any reason for assisting them outweigh the potentially disastrous consequences of intervening on their behalf.

The governor's logic convinced the state's house of representatives, which formally endorsed McDuffie's views. In the upper chamber, however, the governor's sentiments got a cooler reception because of the efforts of Charleston's senator, James Hamilton. As chair of the senate's Federal Relations Committee, Hamilton presented a report adopted by the entire body that conceded the wisdom of U.S. neutrality in the Texan Revolution but pointedly differed with the governor on his characterization of the revolutionaries. Hamilton agreed that the state should be neutral in deed, but he refused to concur that South Carolinians should be neutral in thought. His report defended the Texans from McDuffie's charge that they were "mere adventurers" interested in speculation. Instead, Hamilton argued that loftier purposes motivated them. "The cause of Texas," he insisted, "is identical with the cause which severed the colonies of North America from the parent country." Even as he claimed the sacred legacy of the American Revolution for the Texans, Hamilton also drew an implicit analogy between the Texas Revolution and South Carolina's struggle with the once benevolent, now corrupt and consolidated, federal government in Washington. In language well understood by Nullifiers, Hamilton explained that the Texans revolted only after their constitutional liberties had been stamped out by a "consolidated central despotism" that replaced the "confederacy of provinces" many Texans had given their lives to create in Mexico's Revolution of 1821. Just as in 1832 South Carolina threatened to disrupt the Union in order to return the United States to sound constitutional principles, the Texans in 1836 sought to restore liberty through revolution. If South Carolinians were, as they claimed, the defenders of the limited government and liberty won in the American Revolution, they could not possibly regard the Mexicans and Texans as moral equals. Carolinians had to side with the Texans.[3]

Yet another reason existed for South Carolinians to sympathize with the Texans: Both were slaveowning peoples increasingly subject to attack by anti-slavery zealots. Texas, Hamilton pointed out, "has already been threatened with the hostility of Great Britain and the opposition of some of the free states of our own union" because its new constitution pro-

3. Hamilton's quotations in this and the succeeding paragraph are from his report printed in ibid., 31 December 1836, 277.

tected slavery. Given ongoing disputes with northerners regarding abolitionist pamphlets in southern mailbags and the reception of anti-slavery
petitions in Congress, Hamilton's listeners needed no reminders about
the problems slavery's critics posed. A frank appraisal of their situation
as slaveholders besieged by hostile forces should convince Carolinians
that they had a fundamental stake in the Texans' struggle. "Let us,"
Hamilton said, "attend to the duty of looking well to our own interests:
of husbanding the good will and nourishing the sympathy of those who
may be in alliance with us on the vast and momentous relations of property, and social and political organization, which may be destined to be
touched by the hand of ruthless ambition . . . guided by the madness of
a blind and pernicious fanaticism, by reason of these very institutions
which have been engrafted in her new constitution." Governor McDuffie's official neutrality might be prudent public policy for the federal government, but the self-interest of slaveholding Carolinians required that
their hearts be with the Texans.

A land of liberty-loving, slaveowning revolutionaries held a strong attraction for James Hamilton, southern master and son of the American
Revolution. The Charleston legislator had already begun practicing the
support for Texas that he preached to his fellow solons. A few months
earlier, he contributed $500 to its courageous but cash-strapped army.
For Hamilton, though, Texas represented more than an idealized land
linked to America by a common revolutionary fervor. Nor was it simply
a place "out there" where some unknown slaveholders might re-create
the golden age of Carolina planters, this time unencumbered by powerful
non-slaveholding fellow countrymen. More immediately important for
Hamilton was the potential wealth Texas offered him, poised as he was
to be one of the greatest of the "mere adventurers" McDuffie derided.
Initially, he speculated in Texas land as a wealthy planter and businessman with money to spare. As his personal financial situation worsened in
the late 1830s, however, Texas represented his main chance to escape the
disgrace of debt. Moreover, the young republic appreciated Hamilton's
instinct for political management, talent largely ignored in his native
state after the subtreasury fight. Soon, Hamilton's promotion of his financial interests became so completely interwoven with his advocacy of
Texas policy that the individual strands could not be disentangled. Although he unquestionably helped prop up an independent Texas, his own

investments so colored his sense of public duty that he ultimately served his newly adopted republic very poorly indeed.

When Texans claimed their independence in 1835, their new republic excited the imagination of planters in the southeastern states who felt the pull of better lands and grander opportunities to the west. "Nature seems to have formed Texas for *a great* agricultural, manufacturing and commercial country," exulted one of the numerous guides designed to lure new settlers. Boosters particularly touted the region as a North American Andalusia, whose rich soil and Mediterranean-style climate would yield olives and grains reminiscent of Spain or Italy. But the potential of Texas for producing high-quality cotton most tantalized planters from the American South.[4]

The heightened interest in Texas among southerners meant that an enterprising man could profit handsomely buying cheap property there and then selling it at higher prices to settlers. Speculators went wild, and this frenzy attracted Hamilton's attention. The Texas activities of his Charleston neighbor, Joel Poinsett, may have influenced Hamilton. Political enemies during the Nullification Crisis, Poinsett and Hamilton were drawn together again by their common interest in Texas. Like Hamilton, Poinsett spoke out against Governor McDuffie's position on Texas during the December 1836 legislative session. Before the Texas Revolution, exploiting connections developed while U.S. minister to Mexico in the late 1820s, Poinsett invested in lands granted to his "old and valued friend," the Mexican politician and empresario Lorenzo de Zavala. Fortunately for Poinsett's purse, Zavala supported the Revolution and served as vice president under the Republic's first, interim government.[5]

Almost as soon as the ink was dry on the Texas Declaration of Independence, Hamilton began cultivating his own potentially useful connections with the highest levels of the new republic's government. Not long

4. "Letter to Mr. Moseley," quoted in David Woodman, Jr., *Guide to Texas Emigrants* (1835; reprint, Waco: Texian Press, 1974), 143.

5. Andreas V. Reichstein, *Rise of the Lone Star: The Making of Texas*, trans. Jeanne R. Willson (College Station: Texas A & M University Press, 1989), esp. chapters 4 and 7. Joel Roberts Poinsett to James Butler Campbell, 3 June 1835 and 21 December 1836, in Samuel Gaillard Stoney, ed., "The Poinsett-Campbell Correspondence," *SCHM* 42 (July 1941): 127 and (October 1941): 154; and Certificate of Galveston Bay & Texas Land Company to Joel Roberts Poinsett, 16 October 1830, Joel Roberts Poinsett Papers, Duke.

after the decisive Battle of San Jacinto in April 1836, Barnard Bee, a gubernatorial aide to Hamilton, relocated to Texas. He carried a letter of introduction from Hamilton to Mirabeau B. Lamar, a Georgia native prominent in Texas and cousin of Hamilton's shipping partner, G. B. Lamar. Soon Bee joined the Cabinet of the interim Texas president, David Burnet. Serving as Burnet's treasury secretary and then secretary of state, Bee began a decade-long career of public service in Texas that positioned him to do favors for his old friend and employer.[6]

By mid-1836, Hamilton had become identified with the cause of Texas independence in both Texas and the United States. He spent part of the summer "feeling the pulse of the Capitalists" in Philadelphia and New York about potential Texas investments. In New York, Hamilton occupied the seat of honor at a public dinner for "friends of Texas."[7] Meanwhile, a leading Texas newspaper endorsed him to head the army once Sam Houston assumed the presidency:

[I]n James Hamilton, of South Carolina, we believe Texas would find a general worthy to lead her army; and one who would not only lead her to victory and independence, but would throw a degree of lustre around her that would soon make our country the abode of talent, wealth and chivalry. The gallant heroes of the south and west and north would be proud to be marshalled under his banner; and that moment the congress of Texas shall declare that General James Hamilton is commander of her forces, that moment the independence and future prosperity of the country will be placed on a basis which all the attacks of despotism cannot shake.[8]

In December, Congress voted to offer Hamilton the command, and President Houston, despite his personal misgivings about the South Carolinian stemming from their disagreements over nullification, wrote to make the request official. Hamilton turned down Houston's overture,

6. Bee and Hamilton had long been friends, and Bee purchased Hamilton's Pendleton home, probably in late 1833. See Mary Elizabeth Cheves to Mrs. Ann Lovell, 28 November 1833, in "Pendleton in the Eighteen Thirties," *SCHM* 47 (April 1946): 73.

7. Sam P. Carson to David G. Burnet, 3 July 1836, *Papers of the Texas Revolution*, ed. John Jenkins (Austin: Presidial Press, 1973), 7:346 (first quotation); Madge Evalene Pierce, "The Service of James Hamilton to the Republic of Texas" (master's thesis, University of Texas at Austin, 1933), 14 (second quotation); and B. R. Brunson, *The Adventures of Samuel Swartwout in the Age of Jefferson and Jackson* (Lewiston, N.Y.: Edwin Mellen Press, 1989), 74–5.

8. *Telegraph and Texas Register*, 19 October 1836 (quotation); and JH to Stephen F. Austin, 28 June 1836, *Texas Revolution*, ed. Jenkins, 7:303–4.

tempting and flattering though it was. Hamilton's successful South Carolina business ventures, including his commercial house and the Bank of Charleston, were too lucrative in 1836 to justify leaving the state even for so grand an adventure as leading a revolutionary army.[9]

For the time being, Hamilton preferred to pursue his Texas prospects from the comfort of his Charleston home. He began buying Texas real estate as early as mid-1836. Then, in early 1837, Hamilton took the lead in organizing a group dominated by prominent South Carolinians to speculate in Texas lands. By June, he had recruited all the investors in what they named the South Carolina Land Company. The ten individuals who joined Hamilton in this enterprise included some of the most influential figures in the state. Five men in addition to Hamilton each owned one-eighth of the company: Wade Hampton, one of the South's largest slaveholders; Baylies J. Earle, a leading planter in Greenville District; Pierce Butler, who had recently succeeded McDuffie as governor; Paul Fitzsimmons, a merchant from Augusta, Georgia, and brother-in-law of Congressman James Hammond; and Isaac Holmes, a lawyer and planter soon to take office as Charleston's congressman. Five others owned smaller portions of the remaining one-quarter of the company. These included Robert Hayne, the former senator and governor; Langdon Cheves, retired president of the Bank of the United States; Alfred Huger, Charleston's postmaster; Benjamin Huger, Alfred's brother; and Benjamin F. Dunkin, a Massachusetts-born Charleston merchant. Since only citizens of Texas could legally own land in the Republic, Hamilton arranged for titles to be taken out in the names of his Texas friends such as Lamar and Bee. In August, Hamilton purchased on the company's behalf some 30,080 acres at a price of 50 cents per acre. Actually, for its $15,040 investment, the company received land scrip, which gave the partners the right to claim lands within the public domain of Texas. Hamilton expected the company's investment to pay off handsomely once it had staked out choice acreage. He enlisted Barnard Bee, by then secretary of war under President Houston, to find a good judge of lands to make the selection for the company. Hamilton planned to visit Texas

9. Joint resolution of the Texas Congress, 22 December 1836, Madge Williams Hearne Collection, CAH. See also Ernest William Winkler, ed., *Secret Journals of the Senate, Republic of Texas, 1836–45* (Austin: Texas Library and Historical Commission, 1911), 315; and Sam Houston to Thomas Jefferson Green, 1 January 1837, *Writings of Sam Houston*, ed. Amelia W. Williams and Eugene C. Barker (Austin: University of Texas Press, 1939), 2:32.

with Hampton and Cheves in the spring of 1838 to see the territory for himself. "I hope to fix upon a Tract of Country which in five years will make the Capital of our Company $300,000 from $15,000." He did not consider a 1,900 percent increase in value extravagant if one condition were satisfied—the firm establishment of "the independence & pacification of Texas."[10]

Assuring a stable Republic of Texas became Hamilton's chief goal for the next several years. Devoting most of his time and energy—and a good deal of his fortune—to the task, Hamilton threw himself into a fit of activity with vigor unmatched since his organization of the Nullifiers. This time, though, his stage more befitted his ambitious new role as financier of a nation. From the hill country of central Texas to Continental capitals, he negotiated, schemed, and cajoled for four years with a cast of kings, government ministers, bankers, and the occasional shady operator. In short, Hamilton was in his element.

To realize his Texas dreams, Hamilton worked to assist the struggling Republic onto its feet. As an experienced businessman and banker, Hamilton concentrated on putting the Republic's financial house in order. Texas possessed potential riches, but its national coffers contained little money. Moreover, the Republic inspired abysmally low confidence in financial markets. On a good day, its currency might bring thirty cents to the dollar in the closest important commercial center, New Orleans. With sound finances, Texas could defend its borders and continue to attract settlers willing to buy land from Hamilton and his fellow speculators. Were the new nation to fail, Hamilton's land scrip would be worthless.[11]

The Panic of 1837 frustrated Hamilton's financial plans for Texas. His proposal to create a Bank of Texas failed when potential backers in Philadelphia and New York withdrew. Hamilton then joined in efforts of the Houston administration to obtain a loan for the Texas government under terms of a November 1836 law authorizing the president to pursue negotiations with potential lenders for up to five million dollars. Following

10. Glenn, "James Hamilton," 287; JH to Francis Lieber, 4 June 1837, Francis Lieber Papers, SCL; JH to Mirabeau B. Lamar, 29 March 1837, *Lamar Papers*, ed. Gulick et al., 1:542; Deed of South Carolina Land Company, 12 December 1837 (copy dated 5 January 1838), Langdon Cheves I Papers, SCHS; and JH to Langdon Cheves, 16 September 1837, Langdon Cheves I Papers, SCHS (quotation).

11. Barnard Bee to James Webb, 6 July 1839, *TDC* II, 456.

rejection by the Bank of the United States (its resources strained by Jackson's removal of federal deposits), Texans looked to Europe for assistance. Hamilton provided $15,000 to finance a foreign loan-hunting trip by James Pinckney Henderson, a young North Carolina native who had previously served as Houston's secretary of state.[12]

Hamilton's involvement in the search for the Texas loan soon deepened primarily because negotiating the loan promised to be lucrative. The loan law provided that the two commissioners who landed the money would share a 10 percent commission. For a five-million-dollar loan, that meant Hamilton's portion would be one-quarter of a million dollars. At first, in late 1837, Hamilton became an assistant loan commissioner to two other financially Whiggish southerners like himself, Thomas Gilmer of Virginia and Albert Burnley of Kentucky. But Gilmer soon left the service of Texas to pursue politics in Virginia (and eventually to become President Tyler's navy secretary), and Hamilton replaced him as Burnley's full partner. Hamilton shortly assumed the position as the senior partner, despite his later appointment, because of his greater reputation as a politician and businessman. Soon, Hamilton proved his effectiveness by convincing Nicholas Biddle to extend Texas a half-million-dollar loan from the Bank of the United States. That agreement strengthened the possibility that European lenders would look more favorably on the young Republic.[13]

With a shot of legitimacy from the B.U.S., Texas leaders anticipated a successful loan mission to Europe despite some difficulties. No European lender was likely to provide credit to Texas until the Republic received official diplomatic recognition from at least one Old World power. The prospect that Texas might be annexed to the United States dampened European enthusiasm, too. Hamilton stood squarely with those opposing

12. JH to Nicholas Biddle, 24 April 1837, Nicholas Biddle Papers, LC (microfilm); Samuel Swartwout to Thomas Jefferson Green, 22 October 1837, Thomas Jefferson Green Papers, SHC; Edmund Thornton Miller, *A Financial History of Texas*, Bulletin of the University of Texas, no. 37 (Austin: University of Texas Press, 1916), 59–60; Statement of J. Pinckney Henderson, George S. McIntosh, John K. Allen and B. T. Archer, dated 16 August 1837 (copy dated 4 April 1838), TSLAC.

13. Dubois de Saligny to Dalmatia, 24 June 1839, in *The French Legation in Texas*, trans. and ed. Nancy Nichols Barker (Austin: Texas State Historical Association, 1971), 101; JH to Henry Smith, 5 April and 11 October 1838, Treasury Papers of the Republic, TSLAC; and JH to Thomas W. Gilmer, 3 June 1838, John Tyler Papers, LC (microfilm, ser. 2, reel 2); and Miller, *Financial History*, 60.

annexation and championing full independence. He urged Mirabeau Lamar, shortly before his December 1838 inauguration as president, to withdraw the Republic's application for annexation. Hamilton advised that this best served Texas interests. Hamilton's reasoning went beyond the loan. "Indeed what have you to expect or hope from us by Union," he asked, "but a marriage to the Fanaticism of abolition and the huge monopoly of an oppressive tariff strangling your infant industry in the Cradle?" Lamar needed no convincing. Dedicated to an independent republic, he relied on Hamilton's success with the loan to ensure the attainment of his national dreams.[14]

Set to make his first major trip to Europe as a diplomatic representative of Texas in the summer of 1839, Hamilton had yet to visit the infant country; his proposed 1838 trip never occurred. Finally, in the spring of 1839, he journeyed to Texas with a small company that included former South Carolina governor (and fellow land speculator) Pierce Butler.[15]

They traveled to Texas aboard the steamship *Charleston*, which Hamilton had arranged to buy from a Philadelphia company earlier that spring at the request of acquaintances acting on behalf of the Texas navy. Up to that point, these naval agents had been unsuccessful in their attempts to purchase a ship in the United States. Hamilton then convinced Nicholas Biddle and English merchant James Holford to join him in buying the *Charleston*, with the understanding that Texas would pay them back in its bonds.[16]

On March 11, the party arrived at Galveston, a coastal town little more than a year old. As he viewed the rough-hewn but burgeoning settlement, Hamilton must have felt as his great-great-grandfather Jonah Lynch did when that Irishman first encountered a tiny frontier outpost along the Ashley River in 1677. Like Carolina then, Texas in the late 1830s was a new world where the aspirations of ambitious white men might be realized through the labor of enslaved blacks.[17]

14. JH to Mirabeau B. Lamar, 3 November 1838, *Lamar Papers*, ed. Gulick, 2:277. See also Stanley Siegel, *A Political History of the Republic of Texas, 1836–1845* (Austin: University of Texas Press, 1956), 91.

15. Note that former governor Pierce Butler was not the same Pierce Butler who owned plantations on St. Simon's Island, Georgia. For Hamilton's arrival in Texas, see *Telegraph and Texas Register*, 20 March 1839.

16. See agreement between JH and the Texas naval agents Albert Burnley and Samuel Williams, 24 October 1838, Albert T. Burnley Papers, TSLAC.

17. Dubois de Saligny to Mole, 17 April 1839, *French Legation*, ed. Barker, 75.

Hamilton found even more reason for cheer as he traveled upriver to an official greeting more splendid than he could have ever imagined. Guns saluted his arrival in the capital city, Houston, on March 19, just the beginning of more than a week of banquets, patriotic meetings, and military reviews honoring him. A European observer, impressed by the outpouring of patriotic fervor for Hamilton, remarked that the South Carolinian enjoyed greater popularity in Texas than did newly inaugurated President Lamar.[18]

Moved by the grand reception, Hamilton reciprocated with a soaring appraisal of the future of Texas. In a speech delivered in the Republic's humble one-story Capitol building, he flattered his hosts with extravagant praise for the high state of civilization—marked by schools, churches, newspapers, and even two theatres—they had already achieved in their frontier town, less than two years old. But Hamilton most thrilled the listeners packed into the cramped Senate Hall with his vision of a Greater Texas. He suggested that Mexico, "a country which by comparison dwarfs the imaginary nations for which Alexander sighed" and which stretched over more varied lands "than the sword of Caesar ever measured in his boasted conquest of the world," would inevitably fall into their laps. Hamilton foresaw a day "when the language of Shakespeare and Milton shall be spoken from the spot where I utter these few and feeble words, to the Pacific . . . embalming the memories of those who fell at the Alamo, and giving a fresh and enduring immortality to those who conquered at San Jacinto." In endorsing the Republic's manifest destiny, Hamilton claimed Texans as good fellow Anglo-Saxons, whom he unapologetically lauded as "the greatest Land Robbers on the face of the earth." They had a right, indeed a duty, to take Texas from the Mexicans and transform its woodlands and prairies into the prosperous plantations and flourishing trade centers of true civilization.[19]

In his two-week visit, Hamilton accomplished a great deal. Not only did he meet the leaders for whom he would be working, he also completed the sale of the *Charleston* (later known as the *Zavala*) to Texas au-

18. Dubois de Saligny to Mole, 26 March 1839, quoted in Mary Katherine Chase, *Negociations de la Republique du Texas En Europe, 1837–1845* (Paris: Librairie Ancienne Honore Champion, 1932), 36 n. 1; and 38.

19. *Telegraph and Texas Register*, 27 March 1839.

thorities. Texas paid Hamilton in bonds, half of which went to James Holford while Hamilton himself and Biddle each received a quarter.[20]

Fresh from his triumphant visit, Hamilton gushed with enthusiasm for Texas upon his return to the United States. He advised his friend Francis Lieber, the German-born professor at South Carolina College, to prepare to move to Texas where "you may make your fortune in three years in that astonishingly growing Country" through a "scheme" at which Hamilton only hinted. His excitement about Texas stemmed not only from purely pecuniary motives. The public adulation accorded him in Houston affirmed Hamilton in a way he had not known since the glory days of the Nullification Crisis. As he made his way during the next several months to New York, where he would embark later that summer for England to press for the loan, Hamilton spread the gospel of Texas with evangelical fervor at every opportunity.[21]

Even at Charleston's commercial convention in April 1839, where the agenda concerned improving the economic health of the South by cutting out northern middlemen and increasing direct trade between southern ports and Europe, Texas preoccupied him. At a convention banquet, Hamilton delivered an impromptu paean to Texas. Calling the republic he now served "the most beautiful country in the world," Hamilton painted a verbal picture of its inexhaustible, fertile soil and abundant resources. At the risk of slighting his audience of Carolinians and Georgians, Hamilton extolled the Texans as "the noblest and most glorious people in the world." Rather than taking offense, his listeners seemed rapt by what observers called "an eloquent speech" and the evening's most memorable words.[22]

After leaving Charleston for New York, Hamilton stopped in two cities to consult with former adversaries from the nullification struggle whom he now considered allies on Texas. In Washington, he met with

20. Hamilton's deeding of the *Charleston* to Texas, 23 March 1839; R.G. Dunlap to Albert Burnley and William Branker, n.d.; and *Zavala* Passenger List (401–1265), all in Adjutant General, General Correspondence, Navy Papers, TSLAC. See also William Wetmore letter with memorial of James Hamilton, RG 100-OS box 10, TSLAC.

21. JH to Francis Lieber, 29 April 1839, Francis Lieber Papers, SCL.

22. Frederic Trautmann, "South Carolina through a German's Eyes: The Travels of Clara Von Gerstner, 1839," *SCHM* 85 (July 1984): 227 (first and second quotations); *Charleston Courier*, 19 April 1839 (last quotation).

Joel Poinsett, the old Unionist military chief. The onetime foes already had joined forces in the state senate to oppose McDuffie's sentiments on the Texas Revolution. Now, as secretary of war under President Van Buren, Poinsett could exert greater influence on behalf of the Texas interests he shared with Hamilton. Poinsett briefed Hamilton on his talks with Mexico's Washington minister that sought to persuade the Mexicans to accept American mediation of their country's disputes with Texas. Although the Mexican government had not agreed to mediation, Hamilton was certainly cheered to know of his Charleston friend's efforts to bring peace to the country he represented.[23]

Then, in Philadelphia, he conferred with an even more unlikely ally, Daniel Webster. Not one to let differences in political philosophy get in the way of his financial interests, Hamilton eagerly sought to enlist the influence of this archnationalist. Webster knew people who could provide crucial assistance in Hamilton's mission. Not only did he represent Nicholas Biddle's bank as an attorney, but Webster soon would be visiting England where, Hamilton hoped, he might exploit his good connections with leading Britons to pave the way for diplomatic recognition of Texas and say a good word about the loan. Webster cooperated with Hamilton because he, too, preferred that Texas maintain its independence rather than become a new U.S. state. The Carolina slaveholder gladly played on Webster's concerns about admitting another slave state to the Union in order to secure the Yankee senator's support for propping up a slaveholding republic.[24]

Before leaving the United States, Hamilton attended to diplomatic details to ensure the success of his European mission. The first involved Mexico, which Britain considered an important ally as a counterweight to the United States. Moreover, British investors held a substantial portion of Mexico's debt. Consequently, Lord Melbourne's government was unlikely to come to terms with Texas so long as the Mexicans considered it a rogue state. Hamilton therefore considered an accommodation between Texas and Mexico essential to his work in England, and he set about to accomplish it. In New York, Hamilton made the acquaintance of James Treat, whom Poinsett had recommended as a negotiator. A

23. JH to Mirabeau B. Lamar, 22 June 1839, *TDC* II, 450–2.

24. JH to Daniel Webster, 29 April 1840, *The Papers of Daniel Webster*, ser. 1, *Correspondence*, vol. 5, *1840–1843*, ed. Charles M. Wiltse and Harold D. Moser (Hanover: University Press of New England, 1982), 32.

businessman and onetime resident of Mexico, Treat enjoyed good relations with key Mexican officials. Moreover, Treat also possessed personal financial motives for becoming a peacemaker; he, too, speculated in Texas lands.[25]

In letters to Lamar, Hamilton urged the president to employ Treat to assist Barnard Bee, then the Texas government's point man on Mexico, in a scheme worthy of a man familiar with plantation debt financing. The plan involved convincing the Mexican government, through its financial agent, Lizardi & Company in New Orleans, to accept American or British mediation of its differences with Texas. Then, in exchange for Mexican recognition of the Texas Republic, Bee and Treat would arrange for Mexico to receive a payment of between three million and five million dollars. This money would then be used to redeem the Mexican bonds held by British investors. In one fell swoop, the plan granted peace and independence to Texas, compensated Mexico for the loss of territory, retired part of the Mexican debt, and satisfied important British creditors. With the backing of Hamilton and others, Treat set off for Texas to confer with Lamar, who dispatched him to Mexico with proper credentials later in the summer.

Hamilton also discussed Franco-Texan affairs with a French diplomat then in New York, Jean Pierre Isidore Alphonse Dubois—known popularly by his illegitimately claimed title, Dubois de Saligny—a junior member of his country's legation in Washington. Having just completed a fact-finding tour of Texas for his government, Dubois de Saligny was headed home to report. The French foreign ministry's talks with J. P. Henderson in Paris were on hold pending Dubois de Saligny's arrival, and his report would be a key factor in the government's decision about whether to establish diplomatic and trade relations with Texas. Back in March, Hamilton and Dubois de Saligny had spent time together when both were in Houston, and the South Carolinian clearly had impressed the French diplomat. Indeed, Dubois de Saligny believed Hamilton en-

---

25. For British policy, see J. Fred Rippy, "Britain's Role in the Early Relations of the United States and Mexico," *Hispanic American Historical Review* 7, no. 1 (February 1927), 2–24; and J[ohn] B[ackhouse] to [Palmerston], 4 November 1840, FO Texas, I, LC. On Treat and his speculations, see Articles of Association for New Washington, 23 October 1835 (copy dated 21 February 1903), Samuel Swartwout Papers, CAH; see Ron Tyler et al., eds. *The New Handbook of Texas* (Austin: Texas State Historical Commission, 1996), 6:557–8; Reichstein, *Rise of the Lone Star*, 107–8; *TDC* II, 451 n. a; and ibid., Bee to Webb, 26 July 1839, 466.

joyed "unlimited" influence over President Lamar. In their June meeting in New York, Hamilton arranged with Dubois de Saligny for a "secret service fund" of $50,000 to be used to bribe key French officials in order to grease the loan.[26]

Leaving New York in August, Hamilton traveled first to Liverpool, where he pursued the business of the Cotton Planters' Association before going on to Paris to join Henderson's negotiations. In 1838, Henderson and the French had agreed on an informal commercial arrangement (like that between Texas and Britain, which did not require official diplomatic recognition), and now in the summer of 1839 they were close to an agreement on full diplomatic and trade relations. Still, there were sticking points, and the ministry refused to finalize any agreement until hearing from Dubois de Saligny.[27]

Dubois de Saligny reached Paris a few weeks ahead of Hamilton. Although enthusiastic about Texas, he urged his government to delay signing any formal agreement. The Texans desperately wanted French recognition, Dubois de Saligny informed his country's negotiators, and he advised they await Hamilton, whom he believed carried further trade concessions from Lamar. French negotiators then demanded of Henderson further tariff reductions on certain products. Henderson refused, and the talks stalled.

When Hamilton arrived in Paris, he worked to conclude the diplomatic discussions so that he could proceed to loan bargaining. First, he urged Henderson to accede to French demands. If Texas were not to receive French recognition, he impressed upon Henderson, the chances of obtaining the loan the Republic so desperately needed became very dim indeed. At the same time that he sought to soften Henderson's position, Hamilton contacted Marechal Soult, the foreign minister, to do his own backchannel negotiating. In a demonstration of his self-importance, Hamilton promised the foreign minister that he would persuade the Texas Congress to grant France more desirable trade terms than the treaty would provide. Hamilton assured Soult "that I shall be able to ob-

26. Dubois de Saligny to Mole, 26 March 1839, in Chase, *Negociations*, 38. On the secret service fund, see David Burnet to JH 19 August 1839, *TDC* III, 873. Apparently Hamilton spent $30,000 of the authorized $50,000. See Ashbel Smith to Thomas Lynch Hamilton, 27 March 188[5?], and Hamilton Prioleau Bee to Samuel Prioleau Hamilton, 6 September 1887, JHP, SHC.

27. Chase, *Negociations*, 27–9, 39–40.

tain in the liberal intercourse of the two Countries more than Genl. Henderson has been able to grant by Treaty stipulations." Of course, a skillful negotiator would never have let on that his side might be open to even greater concessions than those already on the table. The French now had no reason to lessen their demands in their talks with Henderson; indeed, they had reason to press the young diplomat even harder. But Hamilton cared little how his actions might subvert Henderson's position. More important for his purposes, his talk with Soult produced a verbal assurance that "the Govt. of France would say a good word in furtherance of," as Hamilton significantly phrased it, "my Loan." Pressured by Hamilton directly and secretly undercut by him, Henderson dropped his objections to the French demands and signed a treaty of amity, navigation, and commerce with Soult on September 25, 1839.[28]

With French recognition in his pocket, Hamilton headed immediately to London. His failure to follow up with French officials about the loan at that point seems puzzling. Perhaps French lenders wished confirmation of ratification before they acted, or maybe Hamilton hoped to begin a bidding war between British and French bankers for the privilege of loaning several million dollars to Texas. In any event, he engaged in unofficial talks with British foreign minister Lord Palmerston at the minister's London residence. In earlier discussions with Henderson, Palmerston had reached informal agreements about trade upon which Hamilton wished to build. Now with French recognition assured, certainly the British would want to formalize their relations with Texas. Hamilton sweetened the deal for Palmerston by mentioning the plan to pay an indemnity to Mexico that would then be transferred to bondholders in England. Palmerston made no decision, and Hamilton headed back across the Atlantic in the early autumn.[29]

On returning to North America in October 1839, Hamilton attended the Cotton Planters' Convention in Macon, Georgia, before speeding on to Texas to confer with leaders there. It was December by the time he arrived in Texas, and as he crossed the prairie from the coast to the new capital at Austin on horseback, his spirits soared. Enraptured by the tall, lush grasses and the magnificent live oaks as far as the eye could see, Hamilton knew his loan would help this new country prosper. He enter-

28. Ibid., 42; and JH to Marechal Soult, 8 September 1839, ibid., 185.
29. See *TDC* III, 850–60, passim; and JH to Palmerston, 10 February 1840, ibid., 887.

tained his traveling companions—his old friend, Barnard Bee, now Texas envoy to Mexico, and a new acquaintance, Ashbel Smith, a North Carolina native and former surgeon general of the Texas army—with stories of his journeys and of the famous men he knew. Smith was quite taken with Hamilton. The Yale-educated physician described Hamilton as "one of the most amiable, kindhearted and agreeable men in the world. He has been and doubtless will continue to be of immense importance to this country and to the cause of free and good institutions everywhere." The party lodged one evening in a humble dwelling on the banks of the Colorado. There, the diplomat who only weeks before had mingled with ministers and bankers in European capitals, slept beside Smith "on the floor in double off hand sort of bed." With his feet toward the fire, Hamilton slept, dreaming, no doubt, of national glory for Texas and appropriate rewards for himself.[30]

In Austin, politicians shared Smith's assessment of Hamilton. Pleased with the novice diplomat's performance in Europe, Congress granted him Texas citizenship. In addition, the Lamar administration increased the scope of Hamilton's official duties by making him the Republic's confidential agent to Great Britain charged with seeking recognition and negotiating a treaty of amity and commerce. Further, Hamilton received responsibility for negotiating with Mexico, using British mediation, a treaty of peace that would establish the Rio Grande as the national border. Lamar also authorized Hamilton to negotiate with the British holders of Mexican bonds. With these powers, Hamilton could accomplish tasks necessary to clear the way for the loan.[31]

Hamilton lost no time in setting things in motion as he began preparing for his return to Europe. In a letter to Richard Pakenham, Britain's minister to Mexico, Hamilton offered the British positive incentives veiled with a threat. He made it plain that the five million dollars that Texas was offering Mexico would actually wind up in the hands of British bondholders. But he also suggested the limited life of this offer. Mexican

30. For discussion of the Cotton Planters' Meeting, see chapter 6. Ashbel Smith to unknown, 5 [possibly 6] December 1839, copy in the Barnard Bee Papers, CAH (quotations); and Ashbel Smith to Thomas Lynch Hamilton, 29 March 188[5?], JHP, SHC.

31. Mirabeau B. Lamar to Palmerston, 21 December 1839, TDC III, 877; Mirabeau B. Lamar to Palmerston, 21 December 1839, TDC II, 516. (This letter may be the same as the previous one; it is difficult to be certain because neither TDC volume contains a full copy of either letter.)

Federalists were courting Texas for support in their disputes with the ruling Centralists, he said. A Texas-Federalist alliance would certainly spell trouble for Britain's Centralist friends in Mexico City. Texas was waiting to see whether British mediation would solve their dispute with Mexico and thus obviate an alliance with the Federalists.[32]

While he gently threatened the British, Hamilton also moved on the French front. He contacted Dubois de Saligny, now the French chargé d'affaires in Austin, to sweeten the Texas proposal for French assistance in obtaining the loan. If Mexico did not respond to Lamar's peace offers, he told the Frenchman, Texas would almost certainly take the Santa Fe region by force—and with it, all of its vaunted gold and silver mines. Hamilton proposed a secret treaty between their two countries under which Texas would share the mineral wealth of New Mexico with France in exchange for French help in arranging the loan. To whet the French appetite for New Mexico, Hamilton also passed along tantalizing information about its resources to a French mining engineer writing a book about the region. Clearly intrigued but unauthorized to commit his country to a course jeopardizing its relations with Mexico, Dubois de Saligny reluctantly refused the offer.[33]

In addition to working through diplomatic channels, Hamilton sought and received the support of prominent Americans in his Texas efforts. While Hamilton's partner, Albert Burnley, contacted fellow Kentuckian Henry Clay for letters of introduction to key European officials, Hamilton sought similar endorsements from South Carolinians Joel Poinsett and John C. Calhoun. Having obtained from them letters "speaking of Texas in the strongest confidence—of the certainty of her maintaining her independence," Hamilton requested that Daniel Webster, too, write to his "financial friends either in England or on the Continent who you think might help us." Webster obliged with at least two

32. JH to Richard Pakenham, 2 January 1840, *TDC* III, 882. See also Richard Pakenham to JH, 12 December 1839, and JH to Pakenham, 3 January 1840, *TDC* III, 879–81, 884. For background on Mexican politics in this period, see Michael P. Costeloe, *The Central Republic in Mexico, 1835–1846: Hombres de Bien in the Age of Santa Anna* (New York: Cambridge University Press, 1993).

33. See JH to James H. Starr, 8 February 1840, Treasury Papers of the Republic, TSLAC. See also Dubois de Saligny to Dalmatia, 4 May 1840, *French Legation*, ed. Barker, 136–44 (quotations from 137–8), and Chase, *Negociations*, 57–8. On Hamilton's contribution to the engineer's book, see Thomas D. Clark, ed., *Travels in the Old South: A Bibliography*, vol. 3, *The Antebellum South, 1825–1860* (Norman: University of Oklahoma Press, 1959), 130.

letters that helped open doors for Hamilton, one to Baron Johan Verstolk van Soelen, the Dutch foreign minister, and another to Samuel Jones Loyd, a leading British merchant and a Bank of England director.[34]

As Hamilton made careful preparation for another assault on European politicians and bankers, his personal financial situation influenced his increasingly aggressive, even desperate pursuit of the Texas loan. When he first became involved in Texas diplomacy in 1837, he sought to ensure a steady flow of immigration in order to increase the value of his speculative land investments in the young Republic. But matters in the spring of 1840 stood very differently. This Texas business was no longer just a way to enhance an existing fortune. His resources depleted by his unsuccessful cotton speculation the previous year, Hamilton's economic survival hinged on obtaining a share of the 10 percent loan commission. In the meantime, Hamilton borrowed heavily to keep his plantations afloat as well as to bankroll his upcoming trip to Europe. To obtain personal loans, he imposed on friends and fellow planters in South Carolina to co-sign his promissory notes, that is, to pledge that they would pay off the loans should he default. Langdon Cheves, Nathaniel Heyward, and William C. Heyward agreed to co-sign a $20,000 note drawn on the Bank of Charleston, while George McDuffie, Wade Hampton, and James Hammond together guaranteed another infusion of cash into Hamilton's nearly empty pockets. His friends had little reason to fear he would not repay, Hamilton assured them. Sanguine about his chance for success in Europe, Hamilton fully expected to "close a negociation for a Commission *which will wipe off all my losses at a blow.*" He followed a similar pattern of providing upbeat assessments to his superiors in the Lamar administration as his new European mission got under way.[35]

Leaving New York in early May 1840, Hamilton began nearly a year and a half abroad in very high spirits. Naturally disappointed in having not yet obtained the loan, Hamilton took satisfaction in his increased stature as a diplomat. Officials in Texas, the United States, and several

34. Henry Clay to the Duke of Broglie, 18 April 1840, Albert T. Burnley Papers, TSLAC; Henry Clay to Albert Burnley, 18 April 1840, *Clay Papers*, ed. Hopkins and Hargreaves, 9:407; JH to Daniel Webster, 29 April 1840, *Papers of Daniel Webster*, ed. Wiltse and Moser, 1:5:32–3.

35. See JH to Langdon Cheves, 26 February 1840 (quotation), and the agreement among Langdon Cheves, Nathaniel Heyward, and William C. Heyward to endorse Hamilton's note, dated 25 March 1840, Langdon Cheves I Papers, SCHS. See also JH to James Henry Hammond, 5 April 1840, photocopy in JHP, SHC; and Bleser, ed., *Secret and Sacred*, 55, 86, 89–90.

European countries relied on his information and advice. Daniel Webster described Hamilton as "a very intelligent man . . . & better qualified than any Gentleman I know, to communicate accurate & full information, respecting Texas, & its Government." Surely, the Texas envoy thought, he would succeed.[36]

After a stop in England, where he found the government unwilling to proceed with negotiations, Hamilton traveled to the Continent, where he fully expected to land the loan. In mid-July Hamilton arrived in the Hague hoping to arrange diplomatic recognition and a trade treaty in short order. He considered those goals merely "preliminary" to his main purpose: to obtain in "that stupendous emporium of Mud & Cash— Amsterdam," as he again put it in a proprietary way, "my Loan." As in his dealings with the French, Hamilton made extravagant pledges in Holland. To the foreign minister, Verstolk van Soelen, he outlined a grand vision of Dutch-Texan trade under normalized relations. Ships from Holland, Hamilton promised, would carry Texas cotton to the world, and the Dutch colony of Java would enjoy "almost a monopoly" in supplying Texans with coffee. In considering the proposal, the Dutch foreign minister proceeded cautiously—too slowly for Hamilton, who described him as "one of the kindest & most gentlemanly old men in the world but certainly the *slowest*." Although intrigued by the commercial advantages Hamilton offered, Verstolk van Soelen hesitated until he knew what the British would do. If London did not recognize Texas, the Hague seemed little disposed to do so either. Still, for the rest of the summer, as he met with Dutch bankers and government officials, Hamilton continually entreated Verstolk van Soelen to sit down and hammer out an agreement.[37]

While awaiting a decision from Verstolk van Soelen, Hamilton took time to enjoy Holland. He considered the Hague, his base of operations during the summer of 1840, "one of the most agreeable places in Eu-

36. Daniel Webster to Samuel Loyd, 8 May 1840, *Papers of Daniel Webster*, ed. Wiltse and Moser, 1:5:33–4.

37. JH to Franklin Harper Elmore, 3 June, 30 June, and 20 July 1840, Franklin Harper Elmore Papers, LC; JH to Martin Van Buren, 4 August 1840, MVBP, LC (first quotation); JH to Verstolk van Soelen, 15 July 1840, reprinted in Chase, *Negociations*, 187 (second quotation); JH to Andrew Stevenson, 4 September 1840, Andrew Stevenson Papers, LC (third quotation); and JH to Verstolk van Soelen, 19 and 24 July; [9], 13, 29 August; and 1 September 1840, reprinted in Chase, *Negociations*, 188–93.

rope." The city's parks, bathed in brilliant sunshine during those summer days, delighted him. Although he liked the Dutch people, he preferred socializing with other diplomats; they, he noted, "have very little else to do but to feast & make merry." Hamilton confided to Andrew Stevenson, his former House colleague then serving as U.S. minister to Britain, that he would always remember his two-month sojourn in Holland as "'one of the green spots in the desert of life.'"[38]

Finally, in mid-September, Verstolk van Soelen signaled his readiness to deal, and the pace of diplomacy quickened. Hamilton's persistence certainly played a role in bringing the Dutch to the negotiating table, but, unknown to the Texas diplomat, he had an ally in Britain's foreign minister. At the end of August, in a conversation with Holland's ambassador to England, Lord Palmerston spoke favorably of Texas and gave the impression he soon would extend it recognition. When this intelligence reached Verstolk van Soelen, it tipped the balance in favor of Hamilton's mission. Within days, Hamilton and the foreign minister worked out the final details of an agreement establishing diplomatic and commercial relations, which they signed on September 18.[39]

Two days before the formal treaty signing, King William I of the Netherlands received James Hamilton as the representative of the Republic of Texas. Hamilton's audience with the monarch rather flummoxed the South Carolina aristocrat. William addressed Hamilton in French, which he did not speak. Language, though, was only one reason for Hamilton's dazed state. "To tell you the truth," he confided to Verstolk van Soelen, "that as it was the first time I was ever in the presence of Royalty I felt so much embarrassed that I scarcely was sensible of the precise import even of the few words the King said in english." Still, Hamilton retained enough composure to perform the diplomatic duties the occasion required. He graciously thanked William on behalf of President Lamar for the initiation of diplomatic relations between their two countries.[40]

That summer, while pursuing an agreement with the Dutch, Hamil-

38. JH to Andrew Stevenson, 24 July and 4 September 1840, Andrew Stevenson Papers, LC.

39. Chase, *Negotiations*, 60; and JH to Andrew Stevenson, 24 July 1840, Andrew Stevenson Papers, LC.

40. JH to Verstolk van Soelen, 17 September 1840, and "Adresse de Hamilton au Roi des Pays-Bas," 16 September 1840, reprinted in Chase, *Negociations*, 195–6.

ton also sent diplomatic feelers to the government of Belgium, a potentially important customer for Texas sugar, through its minister in
London. At first, Hamilton's contacts with their London minister, Syl-
vain Van de Weyer, perplexed the Belgians, because they had conducted
preliminary negotiations the previous year with Henderson in Paris.
Since that time, Henderson's contact in Paris had been awaiting the arrival of a Texas representative to continue their talks. Hamilton, though,
concerned himself not a bit with this diplomatic nicety. He was not interested in spending time in Paris; he wished to be in close proximity to the
bankers of England and the Low Countries, who seemed the most likely
sources for "his" loan. In early September, Hamilton met with the Belgian foreign minister, Joseph Lebeau, in Brussels, and convinced him
to transfer the negotiations to London. Hamilton's charms persuaded
Lebeau, who described Hamilton as "this General whose pleasing demeanor predisposes one in his favor."[41]

Having concluded the Dutch treaty and arranged to continue his Belgian talks in London, Hamilton repaired to the British capital in late
September for discussions not only with Van de Weyer but more importantly with Lord Palmerston. Upon arriving in London in late September, Hamilton immediately wrote Palmerston to request a meeting, but
the foreign minister, occupied with more weighty matters than an upstart
American republic, took nearly two weeks to reply. While awaiting
Palmerston's response, Hamilton pursued his negotiations with the Belgian Van de Weyer.[42]

In the evenings, Hamilton found time for more relaxing pursuits. U.S.
Minister Andrew Stevenson and his wife entertained the Texas diplomat
on several occasions. Hamilton also passed time at the Travellers Club,
one of the most exclusive gentlemen's clubs in the fashionable Pall Mall
area of west London. Housed in an ornate, Italian-style palazzo within
walking distance of government offices, the Travellers Club provided
Hamilton a place to catch up on the latest news, take dinner, and amuse
himself at cards. Since the club's membership included only those who

41. J. Pinckney Henderson to David Burnet, 5 August 1839, *TDC* III, 1267; Dubois de
Saligny to Thiers, 30 October 1840, *French Legation*, ed. Barker, 168; and Lebeau quoted in
Chase, *Negociations*, 63 (translation in *Texan Statecraft, 1836–1845*, by Joseph William Schmitz
[San Antonio: Naylor, 1941], 145).

42. JH to Palmerston, 25 September 1840, and JH to Palmerston, 12 October 1840, both
in FO 75 (Texas), vol. 1, LC.

had journeyed outside the British isles at least five hundred miles from London, Hamilton could also exchange stories with other well-traveled men. Given his debts, Hamilton might well have found a less expensive way of spending his free time. But he certainly kept up appearances appropriate for a gentleman and a diplomat.[43]

Soon after Palmerston acknowledged Hamilton's note, the two met to discuss the question of formal negotiations. Hamilton laid out the basic case for Britain's recognition of Texas, even though, as he wrote in terms designed to flatter his British counterpart, "Your Lordship is so well acquainted with the foreign relations of the powers of the new, as well as old world, that I deem it almost unnecessary." Texas deserved recognition, Hamilton argued, because it had achieved de facto independence, established a government, and formed civil and social institutions. Moreover, with its "intelligent & warlike population," Texas had "the undoubted means of maintaining" its independence. Hamilton also pointed out that other countries already had granted Texas recognition.[44]

Although Hamilton outlined a compelling case, it still might not have induced Palmerston, plagued with pressing matters such as the Opium War in China, to move as quickly as the Texas diplomat wished. So Hamilton upped the ante. In a document he presented to Palmerston on October 16, Hamilton sought to impress upon the foreign minister the full importance and urgency of Texas relations for Britain. He first emphasized the benefits to England of full and friendly relations with Texas. The Republic, he observed, would be a major cotton supplier to Great Britain, so that Manchester's mills could spin on should the British go to war with the United States and lose its supply of southern cotton. Also, he proposed very low duties for British goods exported to Texas. In addition, British recognition would guarantee peace to Mexico and payment by Texas of a portion of the Mexican debt. Moreover, he added, British mediation would result in a Mexico-Texas border that would "repress the spirit of future conquest on the part of the Anglo-American race." That last item contained the germ of a threat, one Hamilton made explicit in the final points of his document. Should Palmerston fail to conclude an agreement with him, Hamilton predicted, within sixty days the Texas

43. Alison Adburgham, *Silver Fork Society: Fashionable Life and Literature from 1814 to 1840* (London: Constable, 1983), 109–10; and Stella Magetson, *Victorian High Society* (New York: Holmes & Meier, 1980), 103–6.

44. JH to Palmerston, 14 October 1840, FO 75 (Texas), vol. 1, LC.

navy would blockade Mexican ports and "forthwith join the Federalists, revolutionize the northern provinces of Mexico & make such additions to her Territory as the laws of war would justify." Certainly Hamilton could not have expected Palmerston to believe the tiny Texas navy could conquer Mexico. Still, Hamilton made it plain that, if Britain did not recognize Texas, the Republic would cause Palmerston's government more than a few headaches.[45]

Hamilton's letter was no mere negotiating tactic. Some Texans wanted to pursue precisely the hostile course Hamilton outlined to Palmerston. Hamilton had repeatedly urged the Lamar government to quell its martial impulses toward Mexico for the loan's sake. But Palmerston's inaction on recognition, Hamilton believed, necessitated a more aggressive stance.[46]

Hamilton's increased pressure on Palmerston reflected more than his desire to close a deal with the British for the Republic's sake; it also demonstrated his mounting desperation to receive the commission on the loan he believed would follow British recognition. His already precarious personal finances stood on the very edge of ruin. Even the French chargé d'affaires in Austin knew of Hamilton's predicament. "General Hamilton has advanced enormous sums of money and finds himself financially embarrassed," wrote Dubois de Saligny to his superiors in Paris. "He has no chance of being reimbursed for a long while to come unless he succeeds in negotiating the loan on which he will receive a sizable commission." Dubois de Saligny probably was not aware that the large personal loans tiding Hamilton over would soon come due; in fact, he owed three friends $20,000 on New Year's Day, 1841, only ten weeks away. Moreover, while negotiating in the Netherlands two months before, word reached Hamilton of the failure of his Charleston mercantile house. But he had little time now to mourn shattered dreams. He simply had to keep pushing to bring his negotiations to a diplomatically successful and, he hoped against hope, personally lucrative conclusion.[47]

45. JH to Palmerston, 14 October 1840, quoted in Ephraim Douglass Adams, *British Interests and Activities in Texas, 1838–1846* (1910; reprint, Gloucester, Mass.: Peter Smith, 1963), 53.

46. Justin H. Smith, *The Annexation of Texas* (1911; reprint, New York: Barnes & Noble, 1941), 37, 49–50; Schmitz, *Texan Statecraft*, 128; and Dubois de Saligny to Thiers, 26 October 1840, *French Legation*, ed. Barker, 164.

47. Dubois de Saligny to Thiers, 30 October 1840, *French Legation*, ed. Barker, 168 (quotation); Agreement among Langdon Cheves, Nathaniel Heyward, and William C. Heyward

Palmerston notified Hamilton on October 18 of his willingness to enter into formal negotiations. Hamilton's veiled threats probably helped to speed the talks, but Hamilton had not bullied Palmerston into anything. Ever since Henderson's meeting with him in 1837, Palmerston had looked favorably on the infant republic. Most important, he wished that commercial relations between the two countries be "placed under the security of a treaty."[48]

In early November, their talks produced agreement on the basic issues of recognition, commercial relations, and British mediation between Texas and Mexico. By the middle of the month, with the assent of the British Cabinet, the two principals proceeded to define a new, more formal phase of Anglo-Texan relations in three treaties. As Hamilton exuberantly told Andrew Stevenson, establishing diplomatic relations between the world's greatest power and his own frontier republic was "the greatest triumph in my public Life," second only, of course, to achieving passage of the Nullification Ordinance. In the first of the three treaties, Texas and Great Britain guaranteed each other most-favored-nation trading status. The second treaty bound Texas to assume one million pounds sterling of Mexico's foreign debt if Great Britain successfully negotiated a peace treaty between the two North American nations. Before making that deal, Hamilton discussed with the British holders of Mexican bonds an arrangement by which they would receive, instead of a cash payment from Texas, parcels of land between the Nueces and Rio Grande for colonization by Englishmen. As Hamilton explained to the Texas secretary of state, "so far from costing Texas a Farthing," the second treaty "will be the source of wealth, population, and strength to her."[49]

One more treaty, which Palmerston considered the linchpin of the new relationship, completed the trio: a pact providing for the suppression of the African slave trade. Under its terms, Great Britain gained lim-

dated 25 March 1840 and especially Hamilton's promise to pay on 1 January 1841 written on the reverse, Langdon Cheves I Papers, SCHS; and Glenn, "James Hamilton," 317.

48. Palmerston to JH (draft), 18 October 1840, FO 75 (Texas), vol. 1, LC.

49. See JH to Mirabeau B. Lamar, 6 November 1840, and Palmerston to JH, 5 November 1840, *Austin City Gazette*, 6 January 1841; JH to Andrew Stevenson, 7 November 1840, Andrew Stevenson Papers, LC (first quotation); mediation treaty (draft) in Public Record Office, FO 75 (Texas), vol. 1., 117–23; and JH to Abner Lipscomb, 3 December 1840, TDC III, 918 (second quotation).

ited rights to search Texan vessels to ensure they did not transport slaves. The treaty involved great delicacy because it touched on two areas close to the hearts of Texans: slavery and the rights of the country's vessels on the high seas. Hamilton knew that Texas slaveholders would not receive this treaty well, even though their own national constitution condemned the international slave trade. For years, southern slaveholders and defenders of American maritime rights had resisted British efforts to conclude a similar treaty with the United States. In the treaty's defense, Hamilton could point to a provision that required the British to obtain a warrant from the president of Texas before they could legally board and search a ship flying the Republic's colors. Still, Hamilton never had authority to negotiate such a treaty, and the Lamar administration certainly did not expect it. But Palmerston insisted on the treaty as a prerequisite for the other two, and without British recognition the time and treasure Hamilton had expended on the loan would become a waste.[50]

So he gambled. In early December, Hamilton sent the treaties on commercial relations and the Mexican debt, along with the Dutch-Texan accord, back home for ratification in the care of an Englishman, Arthur Ikin, financially interested in sending colonists to Texas. In a letter accompanying the treaties, Hamilton celebrated the establishment of relations with the British but pointedly neglected to mention the existence of the slave-trade accord. Instead, recognizing that treaty's sensitive nature, he delegated to Albert Burnley the task of taking it to Texas. Since Ikin left England a few weeks before Burnley, Hamilton apparently planned for Congress to commit to the relationship with Britain by ratifying the first two treaties before its members knew about the third. Then, when the slaveholder Burnley appeared with the slave-trade treaty, he would be able to allay any concerns legislators might have about it.[51]

Upon Ikin's arrival in Texas in late December, Congress exuberantly ratified the commercial and Mexican debt treaties. Finally recognized by Britain, as it seemed, Texas stood ready to reap the benefits of formal relations with the world's greatest power—including finalizing the long-promised loan. Hopes for an immediate loan plummeted when Burnley

50. Adams, *British Interests*, 58–9; Schmitz, *Texan Statecraft*, 148; and Chase, *Negociations*, 70.

51. On Ikin, see introduction by James M. Day to Arthur Ikin, *Texas: Its History, Topography, Agriculture, Commerce, and General Statistics* (1841; reprint, Waco: Texian Press, 1964).

arrived. Unable to depart from England until early January 1841 and then delayed by illness and by impassably muddy roads in the southern United States, Burnley arrived in Austin in the latter half of February—after the adjournment of Congress. Because the British insisted on ratification of the slave-trade treaty as the price of recognition, full diplomatic relations would have to await the next meeting of Congress in late 1841.[52]

Soon after signing the treaties with Palmerston, Hamilton again headed across the Channel to Holland. Having established official ties with the British and Dutch, Hamilton believed he had fulfilled all the preconditions laid down by the Amsterdam bankers. Surely now he could strike a deal with them. Instead, he encountered reports of deteriorating American credit. His Dutch contacts insisted on the impossibility of placing Texas bonds on the market at that moment. Returning to England, he heard similar dismal explanations from British bankers.[53]

Hamilton then traveled to Paris in early 1841 to renew his efforts with French bankers. But as Hamilton soon discovered, the good will for Texas his charms and bribes had earlier engendered among members of the French government meant little to the Paris bond market. As in Amsterdam and London, the lingering depression caused by the Panic of 1837 soured French investors on risky American securities. "I assure you," Hamilton wrote officials in Texas, "American credits are totally prostrate." Since Europeans drew little distinction between American states and Texas, Hamilton knew the bonds of his financially strapped republic would require a guarantee from the French government. Not only would official backing increase the confidence of potential investors, it likely would reduce by thousands of dollars the interest Texas would pay over the life of the loan. Although Albert Burnley believed a loan deal with the French unlikely, Hamilton received assurances from various government officials, including King Louis Philippe himself. Despite some misgivings, the Paris banking house of Lafitte & Company gave credence to the rumors of government backing and agreed to sell 37 million francs', or 7 million dollars', worth of Texas bonds on the European

52. James Mayfield to JH, 12 February 1841, *TDC* III, 930–1; Albert Burnley to James H. Starr, 25 January 1841, Treasury Papers, TSLAC; and Albert Burnley to James Mayfield, 21 February 1841, *TDC* III, 932.

53. JH, "To the People of Texas," *Telegraph and Texas Register*, 16 February 1842 (typed copy in JHP, CAH, 3).

market. In return, Hamilton pledged that Texas would set aside land to be sold to European emigrants and that the proceeds from the sales would be placed in a sinking fund for repayment of the loan.[54]

With a burst of fanfare, Hamilton announced his deal to the government in Austin and also to a wider public through New York newspapers. When news of the loan reached them in late April, excited Texans began mentally spending the money.[55]

As the final details of the loan fell into place—after months of nearly constant travel and transatlantic dickering—Hamilton looked forward to the personal financial relief that now seemed within his grasp. "One of the most agreeable circumstances connected with this event," Hamilton wrote his creditor Langdon Cheves after signing the Lafitte deal, "is that it will soon enable me to relieve you from all pecuniary responsibility on my account which you incurred with a kindness which I assure you I can never forget." James Hammond, who had endorsed a Hamilton note for $12,500 the previous year, welcomed the news of his friend's success with the French loan. "For this he gets $250,000. . . . He will now pay off I trust." Hamilton requested his creditors to make short-term arrangements to renew his notes until the first installment of the loan became available, which he believed would be in July. He fully expected to be a debtor for only a little while longer.[56]

Events soon dashed his hopes. Disturbing signs of financial instability appeared in France. The Chamber of Deputies refused to guarantee the bonds of a French railroad company, and the government itself sought a loan. Given those circumstances, the French finance minister informed Hamilton that his government could not formally back the Texas bonds. He did agree, however, to disseminate positive information about the

54. [?] to Franklin Harper Elmore, 3 January 1840 [sic; actual year 1841], Franklin Harper Elmore Papers, LC; JH to David G. Burnet, 14 April 1841, Lamar Papers, ed. Gulick, 3:508–9 (quotation); Albert Burnley to David G. Burnet, TDC III, 934; JH to Langdon Cheves, 15 March 1841, Langdon Cheves Papers I, SCHS; Cornelia English Crook, Henry Castro: A Study of Early Colonization in Texas (San Antonio: St. Mary's University Press, 1988), 15, passim; clipping from New Orleans Bee, 7 April 1841, Lamar Papers, ed. Gulick, 5:467; Austin City Gazette, 21 April 1841; and JH to James Starr, 7 March 1841, Treasury Papers of the Republic of Texas, TSLAC.

55. See Austin City Gazette, 21 April, 12 May, and 30 June 1841.

56. JH to Langdon Cheves, 15 March 1841, Langdon Cheves Papers I, SCHS (first quotation); A.G. Rose to Langdon Cheves, 9 February 1841, Langdon Cheves I Papers, SCHS; and Bleser, Secret and Sacred, 55 (second quotation), 86.

bonds. Even this promise of a "moral" guarantee from the French proved bankrupt. In May, a newspaper with close ties to the government disparaged the Texas loan, and within days Lafitte & Company took it "off book." As the summer dragged on, it dawned on Hamilton that these difficulties were not merely temporary setbacks. The loan had indeed slipped through his hands.[57]

Deeply disappointed by the turn of events in France, a persistent Hamilton returned to London in August with a new strategy to gain the support of the British government for the loan. His hopes rested on the change of government that summer that swept Lord Melbourne's Whigs from power and installed a Tory administration under Sir Robert Peel. The Conservatives, Hamilton believed, might be "less precise" than their predecessors about the fact that Texas had yet to ratify the slave-trade treaty. Perhaps, he hoped, they would agree to a loan deal before ratification.[58]

Hamilton met with the newly appointed foreign minister, Lord Aberdeen, in early September. In a bold step masking desperation, Hamilton proposed that the British government back the loan in exchange for ratification of the slave-trade treaty by Texas and a few trade concessions. In effect, Hamilton had turned Palmerston's condition for formal recognition on its head and hoped that Aberdeen would go along. Although Hamilton reportedly made favorable impressions on both Aberdeen and Peel himself, the diplomat's charm proved insufficient to cinch the deal. A key Aberdeen advisor, Lord Ripon, chairman of the Board of Trade, expressed little enthusiasm for Hamilton's plan.[59]

While Hamilton's proposals received a cool reception in one part of the government, he presented the Chancellor of the Exchequer with an eleven-page memorandum touting the advantages Texas offered British industry. Earlier, he had promised the Dutch and the French virtual trade monopolies with Texas. Now the Texas diplomat held out to the British even more desirable privileges. "In fact," Hamilton observed, while the concessions he offered the British "do not surrender a jot of

57. JH, "To the People of Texas," 6–7; JH to David G. Burnet, 14 April 1841, *Lamar Papers*, ed. Gulick, 3:508; JH to James H. Starr, 18 May 1841, Treasury Papers of the Republic, TSLAC; and Chase, *Negociations*, 80–2.

58. Arthur Ikin to Mayfield, 18 May 1841, *TDC* III, 937.

59. Wilbur Devereux Jones, *Lord Aberdeen and the Americas* (Athens: University of Georgia Press, 1958), 8.

the Sovereignty of Texas, they nevertheless give to England all the benefits of a Colony without the Expence of its Civil Government, or a responsibility for its national Defence." For a man who considered himself a son of the American Revolution, his willingness to place Texas under British commercial suzerainty constituted an act of self-betrayal.[60]

Like a huckster making an offer too good to be true, Hamilton pressed Aberdeen for a quick decision. He claimed he needed to resolve the issues between Texas and Great Britain before his rapidly approaching departure for America. Hamilton told Aberdeen that, if the British rejected his plan, he would offer the Belgians a similarly generous deal. Still, Hamilton frankly acknowledged that he would rather work with the British than with the small, recently independent Belgium. As he put it bluntly to Aberdeen, "on the stock exchange your Guarantee would be worth from 15 to 20 percent more than that of Belgium." Though Aberdeen considered Hamilton an amiable fellow, he turned down the risky Texan deal. Aberdeen explained that the short time available to study Hamilton's "novel" proposal simply ruled out a favorable reply. Hamilton's attempt to pressure the British for a fast answer gave Aberdeen an easy way to turn him down.[61]

Only the Belgian option now remained. During talks in October following his retreat from England, Hamilton found even the Belgians unwilling to commit. But he charmed them enough to interest them. The government agreed to consider guaranteeing a seven-million-dollar loan in exchange for special commercial considerations and rights to settle Belgian colonists in Texas. A Belgian diplomat, Major Pirson, would accompany Hamilton to Texas and report back on the Republic's political and financial stability. Hamilton soon steamed across the Atlantic to Havana and then on to New Orleans, where he disembarked in mid-January 1842.[62]

Even amid the busyness of the slave market, counting houses, and cotton-heavy wharves, New Orleans took notice of Hamilton's arrival. Businessmen in a city so close to Texas naturally wondered whether Hamilton had succeeded with the loan, and rumors abounded that he

60. JH to [Aberdeen], 27 September 1841, FO 75 (Texas), vol. 2, LC ; and JH to Aberdeen, undated [September/October 1841], ibid, 42 (quotation).

61. JH to Aberdeen, 4 October 1841, ibid., 71–2 (first quotation from 72); and Aberdeen to JH, 4 October 1841, ibid., 73–4 (second quotation).

62. Chase, *Negociations*, 86–90; and Winkler, ed., *Secret Journals*, 222–3.

had. But Hamilton offered little intelligence about his mission beyond informing the *New Orleans Bee* that he had signed with Lord Aberdeen "a protocol strongly indicative of . . . friendly feelings" between Texas and Britain. Now he headed to Texas, as the paper told its readers, "to obtain the confirmation of its government, of some important international and financial measures he has arranged in Europe." Whether the important measures included the loan or somehow involved Belgium, as indicated by Hamilton's Belgian traveling companion, remained something of a mystery to Texas watchers in New Orleans.[63]

While in the Crescent City, Hamilton gleaned information about Texas politics from various sources. He already knew of Sam Houston's accession to the presidency the previous month, and he knew that boded ill for him. Not only did Houston personally dislike Hamilton, but the president had won election largely by criticizing the Lamar government's spendthrift ways and its unrealistic hopes for the illusory loan. As Hamilton waited to leave New Orleans on the last leg of his journey, the news from Texas confirmed his foreboding. Houston's December inaugural address drew attention to the deplorable condition of the national treasury and alluded to the utter failure of Hamilton's mission. "The nation is not only without money, but without credit," Houston declared. More disturbing than Houston's predictable sentiments was unconfirmed word that the new Texas Congress had repealed the law authorizing both the loan and Hamilton's mission.[64]

As he left New Orleans for Galveston in late January, Hamilton had a great deal of planning to do during the day-and-a-half steamer trip across the Gulf of Mexico. Somehow he had to find a way to convince Houston to approve his Belgian strategy. If he failed, his three years of international travel and negotiations would be for naught. More sobering still, his house of personal IOUs would come crashing down.

Upon reaching the Republic, Hamilton prepared to forge ahead into potentially hostile territory to persuade the president and Congress to approve his Belgian proposal. He realized just how difficult a struggle lay before him when he received confirmation of the loan law's repeal. Hamilton then began implementing a plan to carry the day for his pro-

---

63. Dubois de Saligny to Guizot, 22 January 1842, *French Legation*, ed. Barker, 279; and *New Orleans Bee*, 20 January 1842 (quotation).

64. *New Orleans Bee*, 10 January 1842.

posal. He dispatched a note to Sam Houston, asking that he delay the adjournment of Congress until Hamilton arrived in Austin to explain his proposal personally. In Galveston and Houston, he recruited supporters from among Lamar associates, and at least one, former war secretary Albert Sidney Johnston, accompanied him to Austin. He also instructed his old loan partner, Albert Burnley, then in the capital, to "[s]tand by your post, and keep the forces together until we come up." Then Hamilton hurried on to Austin.[65]

Arriving on February 1, Hamilton immediately met with Houston and Secretary of State Anson Jones to outline the Belgian proposal. With his trademark enthusiasm, Hamilton described the plan, fully drafted legislation for which he pulled from his pocket. He promised his scheme would bring Texas financial security and a steady supply of hardworking European immigrants. With Major Pirson by his side to confirm the Belgians' seriousness, Hamilton insisted that this time the loan would succeed. Cordial but noncommittal, Houston and Jones listened attentively. Following the conference, Houston forwarded Hamilton's proposal to Congress with no recommendation. Without the president's endorsement, it stood little chance in a Congress dominated by loan skeptics unwilling to delay adjournment further. Within three days of Hamilton's meeting with Houston, a Senate committee issued an unfavorable report on the initiative and the full Senate formally killed it. Suddenly, after more than three years of chasing the loan, Hamilton's quest came to an abrupt halt.[66]

More stunning news soon reached him. The word around the capital was that Hamilton had been fired from his diplomatic post before his arrival in Austin. Neither Houston nor Jones had mentioned this to Hamilton during their meeting. On Houston's orders, Jones had sent Hamilton a letter on January 26 notifying him of his dismissal, but the letter missed Hamilton in transit. When they met with Hamilton about

65. Schmitz, *Texan Statecraft*, 163; Sam Houston to Margaret Houston, 30 and 31 January 1842, *The Personal Correspondence of Sam Houston*, vol. 1, *1839–1845*, ed. Madge Thornall Roberts (Denton: University of North Texas Press, 1996), 201; Albert Sidney Johnston to JH, 11 March 1842, copy in JHP, SHC; and JH to Albert Burney, quoted in Sam Houston to Margaret Houston, 31 January 1842, *Personal Correspondence*, ed. Roberts, 206. Perhaps trying to get on Houston's good side, Burnley had dispatched Hamilton's note to the president.

66. Herbert Gambrell, *Anson Jones: The Last President of Texas*, 2nd ed. (Austin: University of Texas Press, 1964), 234–5; Sam Houston, Message to the Texan Congress, 2 February 1842, *Writings of Sam Houston*, ed. Williams and Barker, 2:471–2; Winkler, ed., *Secret Journals*, 222–4.

the Belgian plan, Houston and Jones must have known that he had not received the letter. Yet they said nothing, and let him present his Belgian plan as though he were still an official representative of Texas.[67]

Hamilton also discovered the extent to which his reputation had suffered since his last visit to Texas. Once a trusted advisor to President Lamar, his influence had evaporated. Critics accused him of having misrepresented the loan as a done deal when there had been no actual payments. They charged, too, that he negotiated unfavorable loan terms that would saddle the Republic with exorbitant interest payments. Even more malicious reports questioning his personal integrity circulated. Some detractors, for instance, whispered that Hamilton had pocketed an outrageously high profit when he sold the *Zavala* to the government. But most damning of all, rumors swirled that Hamilton was in cahoots with British abolitionists. The Land and Emigration Board involved in some of his loan negotiations, it was claimed, aimed to destroy slavery in Texas by flooding the Republic with anti-slavery Europeans.[68]

Angered by his dismissal, by the lack of notification, and by the gossip about him, Hamilton stormed into Houston's office to confront the president. Hamilton came not as a subordinate, but as a gentleman seeking to defend his honor. Accompanied by Albert Sidney Johnston, a potential presidential challenger to Houston, Hamilton demanded an explanation. Hamilton claimed particularly to object to being prevented from completing his diplomatic mission. He deserved the chance to return to Europe, he protested, so that he might formally exchange the treaties he had negotiated with the British and the Dutch.[69]

When Houston replied that Hamilton should write a letter to Anson Jones to obtain details of his dismissal, Hamilton cut through the semblance of diplomatic protocol. Barely controlling his temper, the scorned minister informed the president that he wanted to know what scoundrel had been spreading rumors about him so that, face-to-face, "I may seek and obtain redress for the outrage & injustice." Rather than take Hamilton's bait, Houston coolly sent for Jones. When the secretary of state

---

67. Anson Jones to JH, 26 January 1842, copy in Public Debt Papers, reel 158, TSLAC; and Sam Houston to Margaret Houston, 30 and 31 January 1842, *Personal Correspondence*, ed. Roberts, 203, 206–7.

68. JH, "To the People of Texas," 19–27.

69. Charles P. Roland, *Albert Sidney Johnston: Soldier of Three Republics* (Austin: University of Texas Press, 1964), 106.

arrived, he informed Hamilton that no one in the government was spreading bad reports about him. Rather, in letting Hamilton go, the administration simply complied with Hamilton's well-known wish to spend more time with his family. His verbal assault effectively flanked, Hamilton responded that Jones knew that his longing for home was coupled with a desire to complete his diplomatic mission. Having established, however, that neither Houston nor Jones was spreading malicious rumors about him, Hamilton announced that he could leave their presence satisfied. If Hamilton entered Houston's office with thoughts of a duel, he retreated with his honor, at least in his own mind, fully intact.[70]

So ended, whimper-like, James Hamilton's career as a diplomat. He planned to leave Texas for Charleston, where new challenges as great as the loan lay before him. The time had come to turn his attention back to family and personal finances. He had risked a great deal on Texas—sometimes selflessly, sometimes selfishly—but that seemed all over now. True, he still had private interests in the Republic. He co-owned a coastal plantation with Albert Burnley and continued to represent his fellow investors in the South Carolina Land Company, which still needed to claim its holdings officially. For now, though, he prepared to head home.

Before he steamed away from Galveston, he attempted to restore his damaged reputation. In a public letter that appeared in an anti-Houston newspaper, Hamilton detailed his years of service to Texas and answered his critics in plain, blunt language. He argued that the interest rate he negotiated for the loan was quite favorable, considering the poor state of all American securities. He boasted that without him Texas would have never received its only par loan, the one he negotiated with Nicholas Biddle. As for the failure of the European loan project, he blamed the French government. He even reprinted his official correspondence with French ministers to demonstrate that they had failed to honor their promises of a loan guarantee. He also denied the most serious charge against him, that abolitionists dominated the emigration board with which he had cooperated. "The whole force of their panacea was," he admitted, "the very harmless recipe of making free labor cheaper than slave; for which I believe every person in the world would thank them, if

70. See typed copy of notes on the meeting apparently made by JH and endorsed by Johnston, JHP, SHC; and Sam Houston to Margaret Houston, 31 January 1842, *Personal Correspondence*, ed. Roberts, 207.

they could practically prove their hypothesis." Misty-eyed philanthropists rather than abolitionists, these associates of Hamilton's had recently provided one hundred pounds at his request to keep the Texas minister in Paris "from the absolute humiliation of want."[71]

To charges that he had reaped a windfall from the *Zavala* sale, Hamilton pointed out that not a cent had yet been paid on the bonds. Doubting he would ever receive the money, he offered to give his bonds and a 15 percent cash bonus to anyone who would pay the specie due him. "If this offer is not accepted in 60 days," he concluded, "I shall expect every backbiter, from the Sabine to the Rio Grande, forever after to hold his peace, and allow me to pocket my loss with what philosophy I can."[72]

Hamilton's public letter sent ripples from Austin to Paris. Its leaking of diplomatic correspondence shocked Dubois de Saligny, who was understandably embarrassed for his government. But the French chargé was not half as upset as Houston. "His appeal to the people was in wretched bad taste!!!" complained the president.[73]

His letter published, Hamilton boarded a steamer for New Orleans as the first stop on his long way home. Still, the repercussions of Hamilton's diplomacy continued to be felt even after his departure for home. In March, Mexican president Santa Anna made public a letter Hamilton had written when he still represented Texas. While aboard ship from Havana to New Orleans in mid-January, Hamilton had written to remind Santa Anna of the five-million-dollar indemnity Texas was prepared to offer Mexico. The letter practically dangled before the Mexican president $200,000 of that sum as a bribe. Santa Anna's reply to Hamilton, published in Mexican and American newspapers, rejected the offer as an insult to his honor.[74]

Unwilling to give the Mexican the last word, Hamilton took on Santa Anna in a public letter of his own. After putting the five-million-dollar indemnity in the context of the Texas pact with Britain, he explained that the additional $200,000 covered the cost of running the boundary line,

71. JH, "To the People of Texas," 25–7.

72. Ibid., 24–5.

73. Dubois de Saligny to Guizot, 9 March 1842, *French Legation*, ed. Barker, 292–3; Houston to Daingerfield, 27 February 1842, *Writings of Sam Houston*, ed. Williams and Barker, 2:486 (quotation); and JH to Anson Jones, 18 February 1842, *TDC* III, 944.

74. *NR* 62 (26 March 1842): 50.

legation expenses, and what Hamilton termed "secret service." His pen dripping contempt, Hamilton sarcastically scribbled:

> You are too disciplined a veteran in the politics of your own country not to know the necessity and value of this last item. Yet you have thought proper, it appears, to pay yourself the compliment of supposing that I designed that this money should be insinuated as a *bribe* to yourself. I assure your excellency that I am too well aware of the spotless integrity of Don Antonio Lopez de Santa Anna, president of the republic of Mexico, to have hazarded such an experiment on the virgin purity of your excellency's honor.

Defending the Texas Revolution, Hamilton dared the Mexican president to try to retake Texas from the Anglo-Americans who ruled it. And, "when you do come," he added with typical flourish, "I hope that I may hear the neighing of your war steed on the banks of the Rio Bravo."[75]

Once again, a Hamilton letter designed to defend his activities angered officials in various governments, and not just in Mexico. Houston, naturally, was incensed that this former diplomat was stirring up trouble for his government. The letter also infuriated Richard Pakenham, Britain's minister to Mexico, who had delivered it to Santa Anna without knowing its contents. But back in South Carolina, publication of the letter boosted Hamilton's personal stock. James Hammond spoke for many when he praised it as a "most triumphant" missive. What South Carolinians thought, indeed, was in the end what mattered most to Hamilton, and it was to them he returned in the late winter of 1842, his years of long, fruitless labor for Texas behind him.[76]

75. Ibid., 67–8.
76. Adams, *British Interests*, 80; and Bleser, *Secret and Sacred*, 90 (quotation).

CHAPTER 8

Frustrated Hopes
1842–1848

AFTER THREE YEARS OF ALMOST CONSTANT travel and long absences from his family, plantations, and business, James Hamilton returned home with the coming of spring in 1842. He had been apart from loved ones during important times—the death of a son, the birth of a grandson, the transformation of his boys into young men. He had even been in France dickering about the Texas loan rather than in Charleston giving away his only daughter in marriage a year before. While his family learned to get along without him, his business failed in his absence, largely because of his ill-advised cotton speculations in 1839. He returned home, then, to a place that felt very different from that he had left behind—a family somehow less familiar, and business debts weighing him down. Hamilton might have hoped to embark on a time of rebuilding relationships and recovering a lost fortune. It was not to be. He had gambled on the Republic of Texas and lost. That failure cast a longer shadow across his future than he knew when he again saw the familiar outline of St. Philip's Church against the sky that March. Even though he was back home in Charleston, Texas continued alternately to haunt and to entice James Hamilton for the remainder of the decade, and indeed for the rest of his days.[1]

Soon after his return to South Carolina, events in Texas beckoned his thoughts back to the Lone Star Republic. Word arrived that Mexican forces, having taken San Antonio and Victoria, were poised for a full-

1. Jacob Schirmer Diary, 31 March 1841, SCHS; and JH to Langdon Cheves, 26 February 1840, Langdon Cheves I Papers, SCHS.

scale invasion. Part of him wished the Mexicans well: their success would embarrass Houston and give Hamilton just the opportunity he needed to redeem his reputation in Texas. Throughout the South, groups of volunteers with a shared dream of martial glory began organizing to expel the Mexican army from Texas, and Hamilton longed to lead them into battle. With Houston's "Star . . . in the wane your humble servant will unfurl his banner to the breeze [and] go with many of the 'keenest spirits' of the So[uth] & West to the rescue." Still, he knew his return to the Republic must be timed carefully. As Hamilton explained to Albert Sidney Johnston, who supplied him with frontline information, a quick victory for the Texans would be credited to Houston, and Hamilton could not bear to be present under those circumstances. "To render me useful I must come in the hour of disaster, and with the means of rolling back the tide of War. I have therefore concluded to wait the next advices—when I shall decide upon my course." In the meantime, he took it upon himself to order a battery of large cannons, called Paixhan guns, from a New York arms supplier to be used in the defense of Galveston.[2]

Even as he imagined becoming the savior of Texas, Hamilton entertained grander dreams. Should he return to Texas at the head of an army, he confided to a friend, "I trust in God . . . we may not stop short of Mexico." The realization of his vision of a Greater Texas, which he had outlined in his triumphant 1839 speech in the Republic's capitol, seemed within grasp—with Hamilton himself playing the leading role. Hamilton conceded he probably could not conquer Mexico immediately, but, as he wrote Johnston in late March, "I think you, Burnley & myself can take Mexico in one year from this day of our Lord." The adventure would require money as well as more time, and Hamilton volunteered to raise the necessary funds in Europe. He even proposed fomenting "a Revolution in Texas if the constituted authorities should not" approve his Mexican plans.[3]

2. Albert Sidney Johnston to JH, 11 March 1842, copy in JHP, SHC; *NR* 62 (2 April 1842): 66–7; Joseph Milton Nance, *Attack and Counter-Attack: The Texas-Mexican Frontier, 1842* (Austin: University of Texas Press, 1964); JH to Pierce Butler, 25 March 1842, Wister Family Papers, Butler Section, HSP (first and second quotations); JH to Albert Sidney Johnston, 27 March 1842, JHP, SHC (third quotation); and James Love to Albert Sidney Johnston, 9 April 1842, JHP, SHC.

3. JH to Pierce Butler, 25 March 1842, Wister Family Papers, Butler Section, HSP (first quotation); and JH to Albert Sidney Johnston, 27 March 1842, JHP, SHC (second quotation).

Reality soon shattered his dreams of conquest. During April, reports from Texas convinced Hamilton that there would be no large-scale Mexican invasion. In a speech to a meeting of potential Texas soldiers in the southwest Georgia town of Palmyra, Hamilton reassessed the Republic's strategic situation. Whereas only weeks before he had believed the Mexicans practically in Austin, now he dismissed the conquest of Texas as an absurdity. Given Santa Anna's last tangle with the Texans, there was no way he would try a land invasion, Hamilton said. Although he still considered a naval attack on Galveston quite possible, Hamilton deflated the hopes of his Georgia audience for a heroic land war. After hearing Hamilton out, those present "resolved that the aspect of affairs had changed and there seemed now no necessity for Troops." Instead, they donated $300 for the Republic's defense.[4]

Later that summer, convinced that Texas again faced military ruin, Hamilton sought to be its savior. In England on business, he learned that two ships newly built there on orders of Mexican agents were set to join the Mexican navy. In all likelihood, he believed, they would be used to attack the Texas coast. The *Guadeloupe* embarked in June before Hamilton's arrival, but he managed to dash off a complaint to customs officials about the *Montezuma* before its scheduled July departure. The customs office agreed that the ships violated Britain's neutrality laws, and it ordered the detention of the *Montezuma* pending an investigation. Several weeks later, however, the government allowed the ship to leave port.[5]

Hamilton's intrusion into official matters upset the new Texas minister to Britain, Ashbel Smith, not to mention Lord Aberdeen's government. He continued his efforts on behalf of Texas when he returned home that fall. In Washington, he outlined to President Tyler and the Mexican minister an elaborate plan by which Mexico would cede Texas to the United States to satisfy American claims on Mexico and then the United States would cede it to the government of the Republic. Hamilton's continued meddling in Texas affairs flabbergasted Sam Houston. "How the poor soul ever conceived that he had any Diplomatic tact, I never could conceive," the Texas president wrote, "unless it was, that he

4. *Western Georgian* [n.p.; story dated 23 April 1842], clipping in JHP, SHC.

5. JH to Albert Sidney Johnston, 27 November 1842, JHP, SHC; Pierce, "Service of James Hamilton," 103–8; Nance, *Attack and Counter-Attack*, 127–9; Adams, *British Interests*, 89–90.

ascertained that he was destitute of all sincerity, and supposes this the highest qualification for a negociator."[6]

As it turned out, Mexico never launched its full-scale invasion of Texas, and its failure to do so left Hamilton without a military option for restoring his reputation. Indeed, only a bill for the Paixhan guns, which Galveston refused, remained to remind him of the episode.[7]

As Hamilton's hopes of restoring his public image by saving Texas disappeared, a new personal financial crisis arose, one with a lasting negative impact on his reputation. Before going abroad in 1840, Hamilton had contracted with the James River and Kanawha Company, a Virginia canal-building enterprise, to sell its bonds on the European market. That summer, he had placed some of the bonds with an Amsterdam banking house and received approximately $50,000 for them. Then, acting with poor judgment, he did something that he would regret for the rest of his life. Rather than remitting the money to the company, he used it to finance his diplomatic mission. At the time, he reasoned that the commission on the Texas loan, which he expected to close shortly, would allow him to reimburse the canal company. But events did not work out as he hoped.[8]

In February 1842, just as Hamilton returned to North America, word leaked out about his diversion of funds. Embarrassed by coverage in several newspapers, Hamilton informed the company's directors by mail about his dealings. He also gave the company a lien on his property in Alabama, Mississippi, Georgia, and South Carolina, for which he claimed a value of $85,750. In June, Hamilton traveled to Richmond to provide a full account of his actions to the company's board of directors and pledged to repay the money. They accepted his explanation and cleared him of malfeasance. Hamilton then substituted for his earlier lien an as-

6. Elizabeth Silverthorne, *Ashbel Smith of Texas: Pioneer, Patriot, Statesman, 1805–1886* (College Station: Texas A&M University Press, 1982), 79; and Sam Houston to Ashbel Smith, 9 December 1842, *Writings of Sam Houston*, ed. Williams and Barker (Austin: University of Texas Press, 1941), 3:223 (quotation).

7. W. Kemble to JH, 6 November 1842, and JH to Albert Sidney Johnston, 27 November 1842, both in JHP, SHC.

8. *Journal of the Virginia House of Delegates*, 1841, *State Records*, reel 599, 12; Answer of James Hamilton, 10 July 1856, in *James River and Kanawha Co. v. Hamilton et al.*, RG 21; and Statement of Thomas H. Ellis, President of the James River and Kanawha Co. (hereinafter cited as Ellis statement), 30 May 1856, 12, Ballinger Papers, CAH.

signment to the company of "all my right, title, and interest, in my claims on the Texian Government." He estimated these claims, including his salary and expenses as Texas loan commissioner and diplomat, to be worth $60,000. Just as soon as the Republic reimbursed him, he assured the board members, the James River and Kanawha Company would get its money back.[9]

The consequences of his failure to obtain the Texas loan went well beyond his indebtedness to the canal company. The failure of James Hamilton and Son, his Charleston merchant house, had left him with staggering debts, and he also owed numerous friends for funds he had borrowed to finance his European travels over the previous three years. Without benefit of the commission on the illusory Texas loan, Hamilton somehow had to repay hundreds of thousands of dollars. Lowcountry Carolinians knew Hamilton's personal financial situation well. When some of Hamilton's fellow planters and banking friends proposed an arrangement to raise $25,000 to get him on his feet, his former law partner James Petigru reportedly replied, "What? $25,000 to set Hamilton on his legs? Why it would not be enough to help him to sit up!"[10]

Friends and acquaintances were so familiar with Hamilton's insolvency because it touched many of them. Leading men in South Carolina and Georgia who had co-signed Hamilton's notes or loaned him money thinking that he would surely reel in the big Texas loan came up short when bank officials knocked on their doors to collect on delinquent paper. Wade Hampton, James Hammond, Pierce Butler, and others each owed thousands, even tens of thousands of dollars, because of their reliance on Hamilton's sanguine promises. Some faced ruin as a result. Even Hamilton's widowed sister, Elizabeth Lynch Prioleau, eventually lost her Charleston house because her husband had endorsed a Hamilton note. Petigru suffered more than any other person enmeshed in Hamilton's network of indebtedness. Not only had the eminent lawyer co-signed

9. "An Explanatory Statement of the President and Directors of the James River and Kanawha Company, in relation to the Agency of Gen. James Hamilton," 23 February 1842, in RG 21, box 214, case 1173, folder 1 of 2; Ellis statement, 16; *Journal of the Virginia House of Delegates, 1841–42, State Records,* reel 599, 232.

10. The precise amount of Hamilton's indebtedness in 1842 is impossible to determine from extant records, but James Hammond estimated Hamilton's liabilities circa 1840 at $700,000. See Bleser, ed., *Secret and Sacred,* 86; Crane, "Two Women," 209 n. 23; and Carson, ed., *Petigru,* 220 (quotation).

notes for his old nullification nemesis—the Bank of Charleston held $25,000 of such paper as early as 1838—he had also unwisely invested in various land speculations concocted by Hamilton. As notes became due and land bubbles burst, Petigru, a man of relatively modest wealth, found himself in a hole of debt well over $100,000 deep.[11]

The sort of credit and debt relationships that tied Hamilton to Petigru, Hampton, and the others was a common feature of the antebellum southern economy. Southern gentlemen often wrote off bad loans made to friends as gifts. Petigru, for instance, accepted his losses as evidence of his regard for his old friend and as testimony to his own sense of honor. (Fortunately for Petigru, he worked out favorable plans for repaying at least two of the banks that held notes he had co-signed for Hamilton.) Others grumbled, however, when confronted by the enormity of the obligations they incurred because of Hamilton, who certainly strained relationships of honor to the breaking point with his recklessness and bad promises.[12]

Southern planters referred to their financial woes as "embarrassments" for good reason. Given the nature of their credit relationships, they experienced debt as a personal failing when they owed so much to friends and family. Hamilton avoided friends to whom he owed money when he saw them on the street rather than be forced to offer "painful & mortifying" explanations about his delinquency in meeting his obligations to them. Debt affected his self-image, for it hampered his ability to act in the world as the free and independent man of republican ideology. When he bowed out of active participation in an important political question in the 1840s, he blamed it on his financial situation. "A man in debt," he explained, "is but half a man." Despite feelings of impotence, Hamilton sought to pay some of his debts because, as he proclaimed on more than one occasion, the Anglo-Saxons, his "race," were a debt-paying people.[13]

11. Bleser, ed., *Secret and Sacred*, 87; Charles K. Prioleau to Petigru, 11 and 13 July 1853, *Petigru*, ed. Carson, 220–1; Pease and Pease, *Petigru*, 92; List of assets and liabilities, 30 June 1842, James Louis Petigru Papers, LC.

12. Greenberg, *Honor and Slavery*, 78–80; Henry W. Conner to James L. Petigru, 1 July 1842, and James Rose to James L. Petigru, 19 July 1842, both in James Louis Petigru Papers, LC.

13. JH to Langdon Cheves, 3 January 1843, Langdon Cheves I Papers, SCHS (first quotation); JH to Hammond, 4 October 1844, copy in JHP, SHC (second quotation); *Telegraph and Texas Register*, 27 March 1839, and *NR* 63 (8 October 1842): 90.

In keeping with his racial self-definition, Hamilton attempted to make good on what he owed his creditors. His purse devoid of cash, he offered other things of value. He arranged to pay back Langdon Cheves by processing that neighbor's rice at Pennyworth's state-of-the-art mill, and he partially repaid Petigru by giving him a house, albeit still mortgaged, on Sullivan's Island. To cover his $10,000 debt to Pierce Butler of Georgia, Hamilton assigned the bonds with which the Republic of Texas had paid him for the warship *Zavala*. Still, Hamilton could not make arrangements for all of his creditors.[14]

Not all of those Hamilton owed demonstrated the patience and flexibility of Cheves or Petigru. To a few, their relationship with Hamilton was clearly business, not a matter of honor. His partner in the ill-fated *Pulaski* shipping enterprise, Gazaway Buggs Lamar, prosecuted Hamilton for years over a lapsed $10,000 promissory note that Lamar had been forced to pay. Lamar, cousin of the Texas president Hamilton had served abroad, won a judgment against Hamilton in a Savannah court in the spring of 1842. Unable to pay it, Hamilton delayed complying with the decision until he finally placed himself under Georgia's Honest Debtor Act in 1848 and essentially declared himself bankrupt. Irate, Lamar sued Hamilton again, this time claiming that his debtor had fraudulently covered up assets that should have been used to satisfy the original judgment. Fortunately for the old general, a Chatham County jury cleared him of fraud. Angry that Hamilton had again slipped through his grasp, Lamar pressed legal actions against the Carolinian well into the 1850s.[15]

In order to protect the family property, particularly Rice Hope and Pennyworth, from creditors such as Lamar, Hamilton cooperated in a suit his wife brought against him for misuse of the property in her trust estate. This legal maneuver stemmed from a postnuptial agreement that James and Elizabeth had entered into in 1819 under which her property, which then consisted mainly of the couple's Charleston house, bank stock, and other paper investments, was placed in a trust. Although James and Elizabeth each received a "life estate" in the property, meaning that both could benefit from it, the property clearly belonged to Elizabeth.

14. JH to Cheves, 3 January 1843, Langdon Cheves I Papers, SCHS; Thomas Gadsden to James L. Petigru, 19 April 1844, James Louis Petigru Papers, LC; and copy of legal document dated 10 April 1842, Wister Family Papers, Butler Section, HSP.

15. Petition of Gazaway B. Lamar in *G. B. Lamar* v. *Hamilton*, RG 21, box 214, case 1173, 2 of 2.

James, who served as one of the four trustees, was given the right to control the property, with one proviso. He could not legally make any changes in the estate, such as selling any part of it, without the approval of a majority of the trustees. In the case of *Hamilton* v. *Hamilton*, which began in 1842, Elizabeth sued her husband for having violated that proviso in 1824, when he had sold part of her property in order to raise funds to purchase Rice Hope, Pennyworth, and the slaves who lived there. The suit correctly charged that Hamilton had acted without the approval of the other trustees and, further, that he had placed the plantations in his own and not his wife's name, although Elizabeth claimed no malicious intent on her husband's part.[16]

Elizabeth brought the suit to shield her property from her husband's creditors. Over the years, Hamilton had heavily mortgaged his wife's land and slaves to cover his personal as well as business debts, all the while representing his wife's properties as his own. For instance, Rice Hope, valued at $40,000, was encumbered with five mortgages totaling just under $50,000. Holders of these liens might have gone after the property in court, hence the Hamiltons' shared interest in having the plantations declared to be Elizabeth's. During 1842, while discovery proceeded in the case, the court gave the couple temporary relief by forbidding the husband's creditors from foreclosing on these mortgages.[17]

The following February, the chancellor of the equity court ruled in Mrs. Hamilton's favor by recognizing that the marriage settlement covered Rice Hope, Pennyworth, and their labor force. He ordered the creation of a new trust for Elizabeth, one in which James would have no rights or interest. Technically, James Hamilton lost the case, yet, by clearly designating the plantations and slaves as his wife's protected property, the court's decision served his interest by preventing the wholesale loss of the family lands and chattel to creditors. On the heels of the decision, Hamilton moved to preserve any assets that might be deemed his rather than his wife's. He did so by assigning to Elizabeth's new trustees all of his claims to Rice Hope and Pennyworth, to a group of 103 slaves, and to all furnishings and goods in the houses he occupied in Charleston, on Pennyworth, and upon an Alabama plantation that even then he was settling.[18]

16. On *Hamilton* v. *Hamilton*, see Crane, "Two Women."

17. Appellate brief in *Hamilton* v. *Hamilton*, South Carolina Pamphlets, 1840–1859, vol. 12, no. 11, pp. 1, 10, Duke.

18. See indenture of JH to Henry Cruger, 20 March 1843, copy in JHP, SHC.

Although the court's ruling on the case's essential question pleased both of the Hamiltons, another part of the decision went against them. The chancellor validated the existing mortgages on the properties because Hamilton had failed to inform his creditors that the liens were on trust property. In order to satisfy the legitimate mortgage creditors, the court ordered the public auction of Rice Hope in early 1844.

Hamilton attempted to turn this adverse legal holding in his favor. Before the sale, Hamilton approached Henry Gourdin, president of the Bank of Charleston, which held two mortgages on the plantation, and intrigued to keep the property in the family. In exchange for Hamilton's assurances that the bank would eventually be paid out of Rice Hope's revenues if the family owned it, Gourdin acted as his agent in dissuading others from bidding on the property. These arrangements enabled the bank to buy Rice Hope for $11,000, about one-fourth of its value. Gourdin then extended sufficient credit to Lynch and Dan Hamilton to permit them to purchase the plantation from the bank. This sweetheart deal did not last, however. Holders of two Rice Hope mortgages who had not been privy to the plan to help Hamilton and whose claims had not been satisfied by the low-bid sale successfully sued to overturn the transaction. As a result, in a new sale in 1846, Lynch and Dan were forced to pay over $55,000 to keep Rice Hope—literally a high price to pay, but they kept their father's lowcountry empire in the family for a time.

While courts decided the fate of Rice Hope, Hamilton expanded his plantation empire outside South Carolina. One of his new cotton plantations was in southwest Georgia. Technically owned by his wife's trust estate and managed by Oliver Perry Hamilton for most of the 1840s, the plantation provided income to meet family expenses as well as to service Hamilton's personal debts. While Oliver ran the Georgia place, Hamilton moved with his wife and younger children to a six-thousand-acre cotton plantation in Russell County, Alabama, around the spring of 1843. Located at the Oswichee Bend of the Chattahoochee River in the southeastern part of the state, the plantation was owned by a partnership, known as the Oswichee Company, that included Hamilton, Petigru, and several others. The partners dreamed that this dark, rich soil so recently wrested from the Creek Nation would yield vast profits, but start-up costs and poor management had the company awash in at least $65,000 worth of red ink by 1842. Hamilton took personal charge of the plantation and its three hundred slaves in order to make the enterprise profit-able. "I have obtained the most valuable concessions from my copartners, on the express condition that I should reside on the Estate." Presumably the concessions included allowing Hamilton to keep a larger share of the plantation's profits to apply to his own debts, and he migrated to Ala-bama with the highest hopes.[19]

While Hamilton saw the Oswichee Bend plantation as a means of re-covering his fortune, his wife took a very different view of the rough-hewn, isolated world of which she found herself the mistress. Sweltering in the Alabama heat, she longed for Atlantic sea breezes. She missed her older children, their spouses, and her grandchildren, who remained be-hind in South Carolina. Her loneliness weighed on her most heavily when her husband left her behind during his frequent travels. And, of course, rural Alabama lacked the refinement of Charleston or Savannah. Although she had her piano shipped to Oswichee Bend, that hardly com-pensated for the more sophisticated urban society she had been forced to forsake.[20]

More distressed her, though, than the crude society or the heat or the great distance that separated her from kin. Society defined Elizabeth by her husband's rank, a fact that proved problematic for the wife of the ill-starred James Hamilton. Hailed as "the Duchess" when her husband ruled as one of Carolina's oligarchs, by the early 1840s she was simply the wife of a heavily indebted man of dubious reputation. And Elizabeth knew it. She eschewed "fine dressing," she told a daughter-in-law, not only because the latest fashions were unnecessary in rural Alabama, but more tellingly because "it seems now entirely out of my station." "This want of money in our pockets makes very cramped arrangements," she complained, but, with resignation added, "I suppose we will become more & more accustomed to it." She could do precious little about her situation.[21]

19. JH to Francis Porteus Corbin, 30 March 1843, Francis Porteus Corbin Papers, Duke; Pease and Pease, *Petigru*, 92; Debt settlement, originally dated 9 April 1846 (copy dated 27 April 1853), Ballinger Papers, CAH; JH to Albert Sidney Johnston, 27 November 1842, JHP, SHC (quotation); and JH to James Henry Hammond, 4 October 1844, copy in JHP, SHC.

20. Elizabeth Hamilton to Rebecca Middleton Hamilton, 18 May 1845 and 14 November 1845, JHP, SHC.

21. Alfred Huger to [John S. Preston], 27 November 1857, Alfred Huger Letterpress Book, 187, Duke ("Duchess" reference); and Elizabeth Hamilton to Rebecca Middleton Hamilton, 12 October 1844, JHP, SHC (quotations).

She resented not only the family's descent toward destitution but also her subjection to the whims and authority of the unreliable husband responsible for their social slippage. "The Gen. has not yet returned," she observed during one of his many travels in the 1840s, "and we count so little on his punctuality, that we calculate on no particular time." Despite his lack of dependability, Hamilton insisted on exercising patriarchal prerogatives and directing his family members' lives. On one occasion, Elizabeth became quite exasperated when, in one letter, Hamilton instructed their married daughter to spend the winter up North, then in a subsequent one exhorted her by all means to return to South Carolina. "This love of making plans at a distance in which our good old Gentleman delights, puts those under his direction in great perplexity," she complained. In 1844, Elizabeth herself experienced great inconvenience because of her husband's bare pockets and poor planning. While visiting relatives on Long Island, as she often did during the summer and early fall while her husband traveled on business, Elizabeth became stranded because James had sent no money to pay her passage home. She had no idea when she might return South or even where precisely she was to go: "I have no necessity or wish to pay a visit of more than a few days in Charleston—therefore there need be no detention there—except by some plans or movements of the Gen's. I will write to Dan when I get to Charleston, and can find out what his Father means me to do." Elizabeth mainly kept her criticisms of James confined to the circle of other Hamilton women and simply endured. Later in the decade, however, she acted to ameliorate her situation. Tired of the "solitudes of the Chattahoochee," she moved to Savannah to be closer to family and friends.[22]

Alabama and Georgia were not the only places Hamilton sought to restore his fortunes. Long captivated by the very idea of Texas and a veteran of its political life, Hamilton quite naturally became interested in developing plantations there. His South Carolina Land Company investment had not panned out by the early 1840s, but he forged ahead with other land deals in the Republic. Hamilton and his Texas loan partner, Albert Burnley, bought a plantation, which they operated with slaves

22. Elizabeth Hamilton to Rebecca Middleton Hamilton, 18 May 1845, JHP, SHC (first quotation); Elizabeth Hamilton to Rebecca Middleton Hamilton, 12 October 1844, JHP, SHC (second and third quotations); JH to John C. Calhoun, 2 August 1846, *Calhoun Papers*, ed. Wilson, 23:386 (fourth quotation). Elizabeth probably moved to Savannah in 1848; see petition of Gazaway B. Lamar, RG 21, box 214, case 1173, folder 2 of 2, 27–28.

hired from the Virginian Beverly Tucker. Burnley actually managed the place, which sustained heavy losses, all of which the Kentuckian underwrote. At the same time, Burnley owed Hamilton for advancing him money during their European mission. In early 1845, the two agreed to call themselves even. Hamilton released any claim on the plantation, while Burnley conveyed to Hamilton his claims on the Texas government for expenses Burnley incurred while its agent.[23]

While still associated with Burnley in that plantation, Hamilton became involved in a longer-lasting and more promising real estate venture, one that began under suspicious circumstances. In 1842, Abner Jackson, Hamilton's partner in a South Carolina plantation in the late 1830s, relocated some slaves from Hamilton's southwest Georgia property to Texas. Although publicly Hamilton denied knowing anything about his partner's plans, Jackson acted in Hamilton's best interests and, in all likelihood, with his approbation. Taking the slaves to Texas, after all, put them beyond Hamilton's creditors in the United States. Even while claiming not to have anything to do with the removal of the slaves, Hamilton urged his friend, Albert Sidney Johnston, to assist Jackson in selecting good real estate on which to place the bondsmen. Soon, Jackson bought 3,275 acres of prime sugar lands on either side of Oyster Creek in coastal Brazoria County. There he constructed a two-story brick residence and slave cabins. In 1844, Hamilton became involved in this agricultural enterprise, but in a way that protected the property from the Carolinian's creditors should Texas join the Union. Jackson sold a one-half interest to two close associates of Hamilton's—Henry R.W. Hill, Hamilton's New Orleans factor, and Lynch Hamilton, who acted as a trustee for the estate of Elizabeth Hamilton. With the property officially in the names of Hill and his wife's estate, Hamilton became Jackson's acting partner.[24]

The plantation promised excellent returns. Its name, Retrieve, re-

23. Agreement of JH and Albert Burnley, 6 January 1845, and JH to Albert Burnley, 26 February 1846, Albert T. Burnley Papers, TSLAC.

24. Charleston Mortgage Book, 3Y, 365 [1838] and 3Z, 352 [20 February 1838], SCDAH; Tyler et al., eds., *New Handbook of Texas*, 3:892, 2:85; JH to Albert Sidney Johnston, 4 March 1842, copy in JHP, SHC; JH to Abner Jackson, 4 March 1842, copy in JHP, SHC; Abner J. Strobel, *The Old Plantations and Their Owners of Brazoria, County, Texas*, rev. ed. (Houston: Union National Bank, 1930), 32, 39; and Declaration of Trust and Trust Deed of Henry R. W. Hill, 15 April 1848 (copy dated 27 April 1853), Ballinger Papers, CAH.

flected the partners' belief that it would help them retrieve their fortunes. David McCord raved about the place while on a business visit to Texas for his father-in-law, Langdon Cheves. Describing Retrieve as "decidedly the best place I have seen in Texas," McCord declared with wonder, "I have never in my life seen such lands. There seems to be no bottom to the good soil. . . . It is close to good navigation and thus to markets." Hamilton's enthusiasm exceeded McCord's. But when Retrieve's first crops of cane produced "more sap than sugar," even Hamilton realized that wringing profits from the Texas soil would not be so easy a task as he imagined.[25]

Only politics could distract Hamilton from his debts and uncooperative crops. But American politics of the early 1840s presented him with a conundrum. He confessed "some difficulty 'in defining my own position' & ascertaining my own 'whereabouts'" in the competition between Whigs and Democrats that dominated the national scene. Whiggish on financial issues like the Bank, he also supported Democratic states' rights and free trade doctrines. His fence-sitting stemmed in large part from South Carolina's "no-party" ideology, best exemplified by John C. Calhoun, which reflected an unwillingness to commit to political partners who might require compromise on issues related to slavery. Moreover, for much of the period from 1838 to early 1842, crucial years in the solidification of loyalties in the country's "second party system," Hamilton sojourned in Europe or Texas, far from America's partisan fray.[26]

In addition to Hamilton's inability, as he put it, to "fix my own longitude & latitude," his "intense occupations in the endeavour to retrieve my affairs" left him little time for politics. Forced to take leave of South Carolina and the political landscape he knew best, he felt constrained to stay put on his Alabama plantation and generate income to pay off creditors. Even if cotton planting left time for politicking, the isolated Oswichee Bend of the Chattahoochee River promised little as a staging area for a Hamiltonian political comeback.[27]

25. David McCord to Langdon Cheves, 17 February 1845, Langdon Cheves I Papers, SCHS (first quotation); and Appellate brief in *Albertus C. Spain, Committee of Mary M. McRa, Complainant and Appellant* v. *Robert J. Brent, Adm'r of James Hamilton and al.*, in RG 21, box 215, case 1174, file 1 of 2, 19 (second quotation).

26. JH to John C. Calhoun, 26 October 1842, *Calhoun Papers*, ed. Wilson, 16:511 (quotation); JH to Martin Van Buren, 4 August 1840, MVBP, LC.

27. JH to John C. Calhoun, 26 October 1842, *Calhoun Papers*, ed. Wilson, 16:511.

With the approach of the 1844 presidential election, however, Hamilton could not resist the spell of politics. The prospect of a political campaign quickened his long-suppressed instinct for the management of free men, but even more important, the outcome of the race mattered to him. The right leadership could show the country the way to a sounder currency and an expanding economy, which in turn might ease his indebtedness. Perhaps, too, he imagined claiming his share of spoils in a new administration and returning to a position of power.

After briefly backing Calhoun for the White House before the senator withdrew from the race, Hamilton concluded by early March 1844 that "Mr. Clay's election is about as probable as any human event . . . can well be," and he prepared to support the Kentucky Whig. He saw in Clay a man not unlike himself—a gentleman who appreciated the benefits healthy commerce and a well-regulated banking system brought to a slave economy. Hamilton expressed confidence that Clay could calm the agitation over slavery, and he convinced himself that Clay would return tariff policy to the principles of the Kentuckian's own 1833 compromise. He praised Clay as a man of "gifted sagacity" and rare "moral courage," for whom "a vista of renown will be opened . . . which has awaited the administration of no previous President, since that of the 'Father of our country.' "[28]

Hamilton even made a speech or two on Clay's behalf early that spring—and thereby became involved in a public controversy with Andrew Jackson. Word reached the Hermitage that Hamilton claimed to have a letter from the former president in which Old Hickory recanted his accusation of Clay's complicity in a corrupt bargain with John Quincy Adams twenty years before. Jackson, "greatly afflicted and debilitated, so that I can scarcely wield my pen," published a notice in Nashville, soon widely reprinted, flatly denying the existence of such a letter. Moreover, Jackson virtually challenged Hamilton to produce it. If Hamilton had, in fact, made the claim as charged, he faced a sticky situation; there was no such letter. Hamilton issued a public response acknowledging the falsity of the reports about the existence of a letter, just as Jackson had said. He blamed all the fuss on a misunderstanding. As Hamilton explained it, he himself had never believed the "corrupt bargain" allegation, and perhaps

28. JH to [Muscogee Clay Club of Columbus, Georgia], 4 March 1844, printed in *Hillsborough Recorder*, 28 March 1844.

his opposition to exploiting the issue in 1828 had through time been transformed into this nonsense about a letter in 1844. Hamilton's claim that comments made sixteen years before somehow accounted for the new rumors rang as untrue in 1844 as today. Most likely, in an effort to win Clay the votes of nominal Democrats like himself, Hamilton had denied the corrupt bargain charges on the stump that very spring. One can imagine that in a moment of heated oratory Hamilton alluded to conclusive proof of Clay's innocence—maybe even in the form of a letter from Old Hickory himself.[29]

Hamilton's "explanation" closed the matter as far as he was concerned. He was ready to move on to an issue more pressing than the defense of Clay. In the remainder of his reply to Jackson, Hamilton expressed gratitude that he and his old chief were now finally reconciled after their "painful separation" over nullification. "I thank God before we die," Hamilton wrote, "that we are both again on the same side of a great American question." The "question" to which he alluded dominated his thinking about public affairs by late May, when his correspondence with Jackson appeared in the press. It also made his defense of Clay moot, for the "question" had caused him to rethink his support for the Kentuckian.[30]

That question was Texas annexation, which had strong backing both in the Republic and the southern states, and was heating up as a political issue during this campaign season. Southern politicians wanted another slaveholding state to bolster pro-slavery forces in Congress, and President Tyler hoped his own advocacy of annexation might be just the thing to restore his political fortunes and sweep him back into the White House. Abel Upshur, Tyler's secretary of state, concluded negotiations for a secret treaty of annexation with Texas early in 1844, but then died, along with naval secretary and former Texas loan commissioner Thomas Gilmer, in an explosion aboard the USS *Princeton* that February. Determined to carry the treaty, Tyler appointed John C. Calhoun as Upshur's successor. The former presidential candidate accepted the job primarily to shepherd the treaty through Congress and realize his dream of strengthening slavery through annexation.

29. Andrew Jackson to John Tyler, 27 February 1844, printed in *Savannah Daily Georgian*, 19 March 1844.
30. *NR* 66 (15 June 1844): 247.

Hamilton's own views on annexation had evolved since Texas declared its independence eight years before. In 1836, he cared little whether Texas were annexed or remained independent; he simply wished it free of Mexico and open to American land speculators and settlers. Once he began negotiating the five-million-dollar loan, Hamilton insisted on independence because Europeans had little incentive to help Texas if it were only to be absorbed by the United States. By 1844, however, he firmly favored annexation, and here again concerns about slavery figured most prominently. He feared that a large influx of non-slaveholders and closer British-Texan ties would put the Republic on the path to emancipation. Of course, as recently as 1842, he had supported European emigration to Texas because European bankers and government officials conditioned the loan on the settlement of some of the Old World's surplus population in the Republic. Back then, Hamilton would have done just about anything to close the deal for the loan and obtain the commission he so desperately needed. In 1844, by contrast, the loan was a dead issue. Moreover, now Hamilton operated a plantation in Brazoria County, which he had stocked with mortgaged slaves from his Georgia place. Threats to slavery in Texas—even the hint of a threat—imperiled his economic future and his ability to some day emerge from indebtedness. He considered the annexation of Texas, with slavery intact, crucial.

Hamilton made his new stance public in early April 1844. A few weeks earlier, the public prints began circulating a letter written by Tyler's former secretary of state, Daniel Webster, in which he came out strongly against the annexation of Texas and indeed the admission of any new slave state. Learning of Webster's pronouncement while en route to Alabama from a brief visit to his Brazoria plantation, Hamilton composed a public letter to George McDuffie, by then a U.S. senator, urging him to oppose Webster. With images of his Texas slaves fresh in his mind, Hamilton excoriated the Massachusetts senator's proposal in intemperate language he would later regret.

> I ask, my friend, as men can we stand this? Even if we have a craven willingness to remain in the house of our fathers, insulted and reviled as long [as] we are permitted to abide, what security have we that we shall not at last be kicked ignomiously [sic] out of doors and sink to the level of our own slaves? With all possible moderation allow me to ask, if this is the ground on which Texas is to be excluded from the confederacy; have we

any other alternative but ANNEXATION OR DISUNION? . . . if slaveholders are not fit to be admitted into the Union, *we are not fit to be there.*

Hamilton's hotheaded rhetoric prompted southern Whig journals to
question his judgment in unflattering terms. The *Richmond Whig* characterized Hamilton as a "fidgetty, unsettled and unstable gentleman," while
a New Orleans paper accused him of being a foreigner—a Texan—bent
on stirring up disunion in the United States.[31]

In the latter part of April, events moved rapidly on the annexation
front, with important consequences for Hamilton's presidential choice.
On the 22nd, to the delight of southern expansionists, President Tyler
submitted the Texas annexation treaty to the Senate. A few days later,
annexationists cheered again with the publication of Secretary of State
Calhoun's letter to Richard Pakenham, Britain's minister to Washington
and Hamilton's former diplomatic contact in Mexico, in which Calhoun
took the British to task for their supposed abolitionist designs on Texas.
Implicitly, Calhoun's letter to Pakenham rested on the theory Hamilton
endorsed, that the United States should annex Texas quickly before slavery disappeared there. By a strange coincidence, the very day the Pakenham letter appeared in print, two other prominent Americans used the
columns of Washington newspapers to make public their views on Texas.
Much to the consternation of southerners eager to grab the Republic,
both Henry Clay and Martin Van Buren announced their opposition to
immediate annexation. These public notices from the likely standard-
bearers of the major parties influenced many Whigs and Democrats on
Capitol Hill to oppose the treaty and thus sealed its fate.

Hamilton might have expected an anti-annexation announcement
from New Yorker Van Buren, but Clay's anti-annexation "Raleigh letter"
surprised and disappointed the new Texas planter. Not only did Clay's
Texas policy damage Hamilton's faith in the Whig candidate's reliability
on matters related to slavery, it also promised to hit him in the pocketbook. "Clay's brochure against Texas has been a sad thing to me personally," Hamilton wrote revealingly to James Hammond, "as in the Union
I have enough there to redeem all my affairs." Although he still held Clay
in high personal regard, the Raleigh letter forced Hamilton to reassess

31. Robert V. Remini, *Daniel Webster: The Man and His Times* (New York: W. W. Norton,
1997), 591–2; and *NR* 66 (27 April 1844): 132–3 (quotations).

the Kentuckian's "moral courage" purely from the perspective of a debtor and Texas slaveholder. Rather rapidly, Hamilton's brief rapprochement with official Whiggery came to a close. Annexation, not the promotion of Henry Clay, consumed Hamilton's public energies and guided his actions over the next several months.[32]

Hamilton imagined with horror that the British would "abolitionize" Texas before the United States could stop them. Texas, he told a Savannah audience in May, was "rapidly filling with a population totally alien in habits, sentiments, and feeling to the people of the United States" because of land grants to foreign speculators. Failing to acknowledge his own earlier encouragement of such land grants, Hamilton prophesied that soon "every public officer, under the rank luxuriance of the principle of universal suffrage, will be elected . . . by a population in direct hostility to the U. States, speaking as many languages as rendered Bable [sic] melodious, and fit subjects on which European fanaticism may operate with rabid virulence." The South, he believed, should unite behind annexation and free itself from party divisions.[33]

As Hamilton publicly took up the annexation cause, critics such as the Whiggish *Charleston Courier* attributed his campaign to personal financial interest. Texas, it was known, owed Hamilton for his salary and expenses as its roving European representative, but the financially strapped Republic was in no position to pay. Under Tyler's annexation treaty, the United States government would assume up to ten million dollars of Texas's debt, and then Hamilton could presumably present his claims to the federal treasury for payment. Although his personal debts did not constitute Hamilton's sole motive—he truly harbored concerns about the loss of slavery in Texas—the *Courier* was largely right. Hamilton responded to such criticisms by arguing that the treaty actually worked against his financial interests. If Texas remained independent, he said, that country had an obligation to pay him in full eventually. Tyler's treaty, by contrast, implied a scaling down of the Republic's debt and only partial payment to its creditors.[34]

32. JH to James Henry Hammond, 10 July 1844, James Henry Hammond Papers, LC (quotation).

33. *NR* 66 (20 July 1844): 326–7; *Charleston Mercury*, 20 May 1844; and *Savannah Republican*, 17 May 1844.

34. The treaty specifically provided for full payment to only one creditor, Frederick Dawson, who had fronted money for the Texas navy. Others would be subject to the decisions of a

Instead of dwelling on the particulars of the defeated treaty, Hamilton hammered away that spring at the necessity for southern unity. He force-fully contended that anti-annexation sentiment constituted only part of a broader threat to the security of southern slaveholders. At a public meet-ing near his Alabama home, Hamilton led neighboring planters in adopt-ing highly sectionalist, pro-slavery resolutions. Asserting slavery as a positive good, Hamilton's resolutions declared that the peculiar institu-tion had civilized and christianized millions, "many of whom would oth-erwise have now been [in] a state of Cannibal barbarity" but now are "the best fed, best clothed, least tasked, and most contented field laborers in the world"—with the exception, of course, of white American farmers.[35]

The Russell County resolutions also laid out a plan of protest that clearly bore the mark of the organizer of the nullification movement. They called for an October convention in Richmond where delegates from throughout the South could devise a common response to northern insults. Carefully distancing themselves from disunionism, Hamilton and his neighbors argued that their approach would strengthen the federal bonds by making the South's position clear to the North. Hamilton's plan even proposed a convention of all the states if necessary to prevent the dissolution of the Union, which, he maintained, through "irresolu-tion and apathy is rapidly approaching."[36]

The published resolutions caused quite a stir. With James Hamilton's name attached to them, it appeared that a constitutional crisis like that of 1832–33 might be in the offing. Moderates reacted accordingly. Virginia Whigs denounced the choice of their capital as the site for what they termed another Hartford Convention, and even Thomas Ritchie, the an-nexationist editor of the Democratic *Richmond Enquirer*, opposed a con-vention he considered potentially harmful to the Union.[37]

As it turned out, nothing came of Hamilton's Russell County resolu-tions because the prospects for annexation brightened following the na-tional Democratic nominating convention. Expansionists defeated Van

special commission. See Treaty of Annexation, especially Articles V and VI, in *Documents of Texas History*, 2nd ed., ed. Ernest Wallace, David M. Vigness, and George B. Ward (Austin: State House Press, 1994), 143–4. For Hamilton's belief that he would receive only partial pay-ment, see *NR* 66 (20 July 1844): 326.

35. *NR* 66 (13 July 1844): 312–3 (quotation, 312).
36. Ibid., 313.
37. *NR* 66 (10 August 1844): 391.

Buren and anointed one of their own, James Polk, as the Democratic standard-bearer. A former U.S. House Speaker and Tennessee governor, Polk pleased both southern and northern expansionists with his support of the "re-annexation" of Texas and the "re-occupation" of the Oregon country.

Although Hamilton had sought annexation "totally irrespective of men and the pending presidential election," he altered his strategy and became a Polk supporter that summer. Polk's election, he was convinced, would result in the admission of Texas and the swift payment of his claims against the Republic.[38]

Extreme annexationists in South Carolina had other ideas. At a July public dinner in Bluffton, Congressman Robert Barnwell Rhett proclaimed before a cheering crowd that South Carolina should secede were Texas not annexed to the Union. Of course, Hamilton's April tirade against Webster and his Russell County resolutions had certainly implied secession. But by late July, he feared that Rhett's "Bluffton Movement" might very well derail annexation by destroying Polk's chances to gain the White House. The hotheaded Nullifier of a dozen years earlier came before the public in 1844 as the very soul of moderation. He openly, albeit politely, opposed the separate state action advocated at Bluffton, and he even backed away from the idea of a southern convention embodied in his own Russell County resolutions. Hamilton realized that his sudden embrace of Polk and ordinary party politics must have appeared almost traitorous to his onetime lieutenants such as Rhett. Indeed, the *Charleston Mercury*, edited by Rhett's brother-in-law, singled out Hamilton for rebuke. To protect his states' rights credentials, Hamilton issued a statement declaring his solemn wish that South Carolina had nullified the high tariff of 1842 two years before. That moment had passed, however. Now was the time to work with the national Democrats, and he pointed out that Calhoun concurred with his views. Privately, he assured friends well into the fall that, in contrast to his public position, he remained committed to the idea of a southern convention. He even left open the possibility that he might support the separate secession of the Palmetto State if all else failed.[39]

38. *NR* 66 (13 July 1844): 313.

39. *Charleston Mercury*, 23 August 1844; Letter of James Hamilton, 8 August 1844, *NR* 66 (24 August 1844): 420–1; Glenn, "James Hamilton," 380; and JH to James Henry Hammond, 4 October 1844, copy in JHP, SHC.

By taking such contradictory positions, Hamilton seemed to exemplify Sam Houston's description of him as one "destitute of sincerity." But it was not so much a case of lack of sincerity as a conflict within himself. His heart may very well have been with the Bluffton agitators, but his pocketbook ruled his public course. "If Texas is annexed," he believed, "I shall be relieved of every embarrassment I have in the world." Polk's election, not a blustering threat of secession, was the surest way to accomplish the annexation he deemed so crucial to his financial recovery.[40]

As Hamilton publicly attempted to extinguish the secessionist fires his words had helped set, he campaigned for Polk throughout the late summer and fall. Valuable to the campaign as an expert on Texas who could assure southerners of Polk's reliability on annexation, Hamilton concentrated his efforts on Georgia so that he could remain close to his Alabama plantation and also check in on his operations in Baker and Lee Counties while politicking. He spoke on behalf of the Democratic candidate at Macon and Columbus, but demands back at Oswichee Bend forced him to decline invitations to party gatherings in the north Georgia town of Marietta as well as in Nashville, Tennessee. He very much hoped to debate Senator John Berrien in Savannah in October and "floor him before *his own people*," but the Georgia Whig went on a New England speaking tour instead. Although Hamilton confined his personal campaigning to Georgia, his strategic thinking about the race encompassed the whole country. After a business trip to New York late that summer, he offered Polk advice on how to win the doubtful electoral votes of the Empire State.[41]

Hamilton relished once again being active in a political campaign. To receive the acclaim of crowds and to be accorded respect for his expertise helped him forget, even for just a moment, his troubles. His sense of worth returned. By the end of the campaign, he had convinced himself that his efforts had largely made Polk president. He expected a reward.

40. JH to John C. Calhoun, 18 February 1845, *Calhoun Papers*, ed. Wilson, 21:313.
41. *Nashville Union*, quoted in *Charleston Mercury*, 22 November 1844; JH to the Marietta Committee of Invitation, 16 September 1844, in *Charleston Mercury*, 26 October 1844; JH to J. J. B. Southall, 10 September 1844, reprinted from *Nashville Union* in *Charleston Mercury*, 22 November 1844; JH to James K. Polk, 13 October 1844, *Correspondence of James K. Polk*, ed. Herbert Weaver, vol. 8, ed. Wayne Cutler (Knoxville: University of Tennessee Press, 1993), 180 (quotation); and JH to James K. Polk, 8 September 1844, ibid., 29–30.

Even before Polk's victory was assured, Hamilton began maneuvering for an appointment in the new administration. Hamilton hoped that the new president would retain Calhoun at the State Department and that Calhoun would use his influence to place Hamilton in a suitable diplomatic post.

As he peppered Calhoun with letters suggesting his availability for a post in the next administration, Hamilton also offered his services in assisting Tyler to achieve one final foreign policy coup. Hoping to admit Texas on their watch, Tyler and Calhoun decided to send an envoy to negotiate annexation with Republic authorities. Their appointment of Andrew Jackson's nephew, Andrew J. Donelson, pleased Hamilton, but he offered to take Donelson's place should the Tennessean decline to go. To Calhoun, Hamilton declared, "without mock modesty," that he could obtain by the first of the year a better annexation treaty than the one defeated in the spring of 1844. In his view, that earlier treaty suffered from a fundamental flaw in that it scaled down the debt owed by Texas to creditors like himself. His hopes to negotiate a better deal disappeared when Donelson accepted the mission. Hamilton then concentrated on procuring a post in the incoming administration.[42]

Specifically, Hamilton longed to return to the scene of his greatest diplomatic triumph, the recognition of Texas by Great Britain, and thus lobbied to be Polk's minister to the Court of St. James. Hamilton's stated goal in going to London was to negotiate with the British a reciprocal free trade treaty in order to nullify—by treaty rather than state convention this time—the Whigs' protectionist 1842 tariff. To deliver the South permanently from high tariffs would be as great an accomplishment for Hamilton as leading the Nullifiers or coming to terms with Lord Palmerston. Polk had several others in mind for the post, including Calhoun, to whom Polk offered the job after deciding not to retain him as secretary of state. In letters that always deferred to Calhoun's greater qualifications for the post, Hamilton asked that Calhoun recommend him to Polk should Calhoun not wish to go abroad. Tell Polk, Hamilton said, that "you consider me . . . better qualified for the duties of this office than any other man you know South of the Potomac & that no other individual but one of the South Side of that fearful line should occupy it at this crisis of anxiety and peril." After declining the British Mission,

42. JH to John C. Calhoun, 4 October 1844, *Calhoun Papers*, ed. Wilson, 20:29.

Calhoun put in a good word for Hamilton, who traveled to Washington in early 1845 hoping to secure his share of the spoils. Careful never to ask for the position directly, Hamilton held friendly meetings with the new secretary of state, James Buchanan, and the president himself. Polk knew what Hamilton wanted and soon informed him that he could not grant his wish. The fact that Hamilton had served Texas as minister to England made his representing the United States in the same capacity rather awkward, and on these grounds Polk passed over him.[43]

While Hamilton sought an appointment, he also prepared for the annexation of Texas made inevitable by Polk's election. Just days before the Tennessean took office, the United States Congress passed a joint resolution that extended terms of annexation to the Lone Star Republic. It was a moment of great triumph for the outgoing administration of President Tyler and Secretary of State Calhoun as well as for the incoming southern Democrat. For Hamilton, too, annexation proved a great moment, for now he could turn his attention to the money Texas owed him.

Hamilton was one of the leading individual creditors of Texas. According to his account, the state owed him about $60,000 for his salary and expenses as a diplomat. Moreover, he wanted Texas to make good on the bonds issued in payment for the *Zavala* back in 1839. He estimated the par value of these bonds, which he had assigned to Pierce Butler to cover a personal debt, at $50,000. In addition, touting his influence with politicians in Texas, Hamilton soon after annexation contracted to be the attorney for several other creditors. Altogether, Hamilton represented individuals and institutions holding over half of the old Republic's paper debt. The trustees of the defunct Pennsylvania Bank of the United States, who owned more than one million dollars in Texas bonds, constituted his single largest client. They offered Hamilton a 10 percent commission on the amount he could obtain from Texas for the bonds. Also, Hamilton acted as the agent for the estate of James Holford, the English merchant who had advanced half the purchase price of the *Zavala*. All told, Hamilton expected to receive reimbursements and commissions totaling approximately $210,000.[44]

43. See JH to John C. Calhoun, 4 October 1844, 24 November 1844, 27 December 1844, *Calhoun Papers*, ed. Wilson, 20:29–30, 364–5, 641; and 12, 18, 24, and 28 February 1845 and 5 May 1845, ibid., 21:283–5, 313–4 (quotation, 313), 351, 387, 535.

44. Hamilton Holman, *Prologue to Conflict: The Crisis and Compromise of 1850* (Lexington: University of Kentucky Press, 1964), 66. On Hamilton's agreement with the B.U.S. trustees, see T. S. Taylor to JH, 16 October 1845, attached to Ellis statement as Exhibit F, 26; Ellis

Obtaining payment, Hamilton knew, would be fraught with difficulty. First, the joint resolution of annexation, unlike the treaty of the previous spring, failed to provide federal funds to retire the Texas debt. In fact, the resolution clearly stated that "in no event" were the Republic's debts "to become a charge upon the Government of the United States." Therefore, the state itself became solely responsible for repaying the Republic's creditors. This led to a second concern, precisely where Texas would get the money. As an independent country, Texas could fund its debt with tariff revenue. But after annexation, the state no longer enjoyed that reliable source of funds. That left only the proceeds from the sale of the state's public lands as a source of income to pay creditors. That worried Hamilton because he knew from personal experience of the confusion attending land claims in Texas. For years, he and his South Carolina Land Company partners had realized nothing from their Texas investment because of the near impossibility of straightening out overlapping claims. Just two months before annexation, Hamilton made another fruitless journey to Texas in hopes of locating the company's land. Returning from that trip, he learned that the joint resolution shifted Texas bondholders' hopes for payment from customs revenue to the "utter[ly] unava[i]ling & unavailable resource" of the state's public lands.[45]

Given the state's poor finances, Hamilton devised plans to throw the Texas debt issue back to Congress and more ample federal coffers. He prepared a memorial outlining "a case so just & irresistible" to convince Congress to authorize payment to the creditors out of customs revenue collected in Texas, but events intervened to frustrate his efforts. President Polk provoked war with Mexico in early 1846, and Hamilton put off his petition until the cessation of hostilities.[46]

Hamilton opposed "the accursed war" because it interrupted his efforts at reimbursement from Texas, but it also stimulated his martialism.

statement, 26–8; and *Spain v. Hamilton's Administrator*, in *Cases Argued and Adjudged in the Supreme Court of the United States*, by John William Wallace, vol. 1 (Washington: W. H. & O. H. Morrison, 1866), 605–9, 614. For Hamilton's total claim against Texas, see Ellis statement, exhibit B, 16; and JH to Albert Burnley, 26 February 1846, Albert T. Burnley Papers, TSLAC.

45. "The Resolution Annexing Texas to the United States," in *Texas History*, ed. Wallace, Vigness, and Ward, 146–7; and JH to John C. Calhoun, 18 February 1845, *Calhoun Papers*, ed. Wilson, 21:314 (quotation).

46. JH to John C. Calhoun, 21 June 1846, *Calhoun Papers*, ed. Wilson, 23:188 (quotation); JH to John C. Calhoun, 25 May 1846, ibid., 136; and JH to John C. Calhoun, 19 April 1848, John C. Calhoun Papers, Clemson.

On a visit to Polk early in the administration, the president, as Hamilton perceived it, offered him a military commission should war with Mexico break out. "I thought I should be able to resist the temptation," Hamilton told the president once war came. "But the Contest is becoming so intensely interesting that notwithstanding my large private & domestic engagements, I can resist it no longer." As a veteran of the War of 1812 and former commander-in-chief of South Carolina, Hamilton boldly informed Polk that "I will take nothing short of the rank of Major General." All that he asked "in the case of my appointment will be the command of the advance division on its route to the Capital of Mexico." Hamilton could almost taste the military glory long denied him. Although solicitous of the sixty-year-old volunteer, the president rejected his request. So died Hamilton's hopes that he might have real combat command experience to go with his nullification-era title of "General" Hamilton.[47]

Denied by Polk the opportunity to serve his country as either a diplomat or a soldier, Hamilton largely withdrew from active participation in national politics. Briefly, he sought to promote Calhoun's candidacy for president in 1848, but that effort fizzled. And, although he liked Democratic presidential nominee Lewis Cass, whom Hamilton knew from his days as a Texas diplomat and Cass's as U.S. minister to France, Hamilton did not work for his election. After all, he believed he "had made one President" in 1828 "& contributed largely to making another" in 1844, yet never had he enjoyed commensurate rewards or influence. Now sixty-two, juggling debts, seeking to manage frustratingly unprofitable plantations, and hounded by creditors in the courts, Hamilton could spend time more productively than worrying about a presidential campaign that would not materially affect him. Instead, with the war over, he turned his energies with renewed vigor to something that, he prayed, would finally provide him with relief from his many troubles. Finally, he could pursue his claims against Texas.[48]

47. JH to John C. Calhoun, 7 February 1847, John C. Calhoun Papers, Clemson (first quotation); JH to James K. Polk, 19 March 1847, James K. Polk Papers, LC (other quotations); JH to Polk, 22 March 1847, LC; and James K. Polk to JH, 12 April 1847, James K. Polk Papers, LC.
48. JH to John C. Calhoun, 19 April 1848, John C. Calhoun Papers, Clemson.

CHAPTER 9

"Fortunes Greatly Impaired but a Spirit Unsubdued"
1849–1857

As the 1840s ended, enormous financial challenges confronted James Hamilton while his sources of income slowly disappeared. A forced sale took his beloved Pennyworth Island, while he also lost the Oswichee Bend plantation, which for some time his son Oliver had managed during Hamilton's frequent business and lobbying trips to Texas and Washington. Even with the relatively high cotton prices of the late 1840s, the Alabama plantation failed to generate sufficient income to pay the debts of its owner, the Oswichee Company. As early as 1846, Hamilton began shifting capital and labor—including thirty-two slaves mortgaged to European merchants—from Oswichee Bend to his Retrieve plantation in Texas. He then dispatched Oliver and Lynch to oversee Retrieve.[1]

Retrieve became Hamilton's best hope for recovering his lost fortunes, as he gambled that Texas sugar cane would yield more wealth than Alabama cotton or Carolina rice. Technically, Elizabeth Hamilton's trust estate, not Hamilton himself, shared the ownership of Retrieve with Abner Jackson (until he sold out in 1848) and Henry Hill, Hamilton's New Orleans factor. Hamilton's role at Retrieve varied over time from being Hill's designated manager to serving as attorney for Lynch, Elizabeth's trustee. Nor did Hamilton own outright any of the 130 slaves who

1. Debt settlement between JH, acting on behalf of the Oswichee Company, and Hope & Company and Solomon Heine, 9 April 1846 (copy dated 27 April 1853), Ballinger Papers, CAH.

worked the plantation by 1850; the slaves comprised at least six different groups owned by or mortgaged to various individuals or banks.[2]

Although Hamilton received income from Retrieve, by the late 1840s it had failed to yield riches enough to retire his debts. A more promising way to personal debt relief appeared with the end of the war with Mexico. Peace brought new opportunities for Texas creditors like Hamilton to receive their long-promised payments.

Under the Treaty of Guadalupe Hidalgo, the United States acquired a vast region between Texas and the Pacific, including California—long coveted by Americans and once described by Hamilton's friend Waddy Thompson as "the richest, the most beautiful and the healthiest country in the world"—and the mineral-rich remainder, New Mexico, which featured the important trading center of Santa Fe. Two questions immediately arose regarding these new United States territories. First, would slavery be permitted there? Already proponents and opponents of slavery extension had argued over that in the Wilmot Proviso debates. Now a new president and Congress would try their skills at crafting an answer. The second question asked: Where precisely was the eastern boundary of New Mexico?[3]

The Texas debt issue became entangled with answering the second question especially. Any adjustment in the eastern border of New Mexico obviously affected Texas. Contending that New Mexico encompassed only land west of the Rio Grande, Texans claimed a huge tract east of that river, including Santa Fe. New Mexicans and federal authorities disputed this expansive definition of Texas. The resolution of the border dispute, it soon appeared, might involve a deal by which Texas would relinquish its claims to New Mexican soil for a price: federal assumption of the old Republic's debt.[4]

Hamilton enthusiastically supported linking the boundary dispute to the Texas public debt. Doing so meant getting powerful forces in the fed-

2. U.S. Census, 1850, Texas Slave Schedule, Brazoria County. See list of slaves dated 11 March 1852 as well as the Declaration of Trust, 27 April 1853, Ballinger Papers, CAH.

3. Waddy Thompson to Daniel Webster, 29 April 1842, *The Papers of Daniel Webster*, ser. 1, *Diplomatic Papers*, vol. 1, *1841–1843*, ed. Charles M. Wiltse and Harold D. Moser (Hanover: University Press of New England, 1983), 420.

4. Mark J. Stegmaier, *Texas, New Mexico, and the Compromise of 1850: Boundary Dispute and Sectional Crisis* (Kent: Kent State University Press, 1996), chapter 2.

eral government interested in settling the debt issue. On the day after Christmas 1849—which Hamilton spent in Texas, far away from his family—he laid the groundwork for a land-for-debt swap by urging key state legislators to support such a measure.[5]

The money Hamilton hoped to receive once assumption occurred would not have made him a rich man, simply a less indebted one. "The payment of the Debt of Texas," he wrote, "will enable me . . . to do a partial if not a total & plenary justice to all my Creditors." By 1850, Hamilton had already pledged most of any potential Texas windfall to his major creditors, including the James River and Kanawha Company and a New Orleans factorage firm. His debt to the canal company, stemming from his misuse of the proceeds of its bond sales back in 1841, amounted to over $77,000 with interest by late 1849. He also owed approximately $55,000 to his New Orleans factor for expenses related to Retrieve. Moreover, other creditors sought payment from Hamilton. After a series of legal maneuvers in Georgia courts relating to his debt to G. B. Lamar, Hamilton placed himself under the provisions of that state's "Honest Debtor Law." In essence, Hamilton declared bankruptcy in Georgia, and a Chatham County judge appointed trustees to give Lamar some of Hamilton's possessions as well as proceeds from a sheriff's sale of certain Hamilton property in that state. Hamilton also owed smaller amounts to various friends and acquaintances, many of whom had given up hope of repayment.[6]

Although by the end of 1849 only Lamar had taken legal action against Hamilton, other creditors believed the worst of their old friend. When the severity of Hamilton's difficulties became widely known in 1842, James Hammond could not "believe that he ever intended to deceive or defraud any one." Instead, he chalked up Hamilton's problems to his being "so visionary, so sanguine. So reckless." By 1850, however, Hammond considered his onetime mentor "a swindler and notoriously one now. He has recently swindled me out of $2100 after heretofore swindled me out of $18,000." Hamilton knew his indebtedness had frayed further an already tattered reputation. His inability to repay

5. JH to Benjamin Cromwell Franklin and William E. Crump, 26 December 1849, Benjamin Cromwell Franklin Papers, CAH.

6. JH to James Henry Hammond, 31 March 1850, JHP, SHC (quotation); and Ellis statement, Exhibits C and D, 17–23, Ballinger Papers, CAH.

friends left Hamilton "so humiliated & mortified that I can not venture to describe the torture of my own feelings."[7]

Desperate to restore his good name, Hamilton believed the federal government's assumption of the Texas debt the most likely means to that end. From late 1849 through most of 1850, Hamilton worked tirelessly with influential men in Austin, Washington, and New York to make assumption a reality. Ironically, his efforts to erase his personal debts and redeem his reputation actually produced quite the opposite result. By aligning himself with bondholding eastern bankers and moderate politicians, Hamilton earned the hostility of those whose opinions mattered most to him—his old friends and allies in the Palmetto State.

During 1849, southern congressional Democrats, especially South Carolinians, staked out a position on the Mexican Cession very different from Hamilton's. While Hamilton focused on the Texas–New Mexico border, the possible "loss" of California to the free states most angered Carolinians. Insulted by the exclusion of slaveholders from the Mexican Cession, southern rights Democrats objected to the one-state advantage free states would enjoy in the Senate with slavery banned in California. Concerned southerners huddled on Capitol Hill before Zachary Taylor's inauguration to plot a strategy. Calhoun, gaunt and frail from tuberculosis, once again essayed to form a united southern front to head off any plans for a free California. As a pan-southern effort, it failed. Calhoun's Southern Address of January 1849, which denounced northern designs on slavery, attracted the signatures of only 48 of the 121 southerners in Congress. Still, Hamilton's old friends in the South Carolina delegation firmly backed it. Southern agitation continued as Calhoun convinced Mississippians to propose a southern convention to meet in Nashville in June 1850.[8]

Once Taylor took office, the slaveholding president sent surprising signals of a decidedly northern tilt to his intended territorial policies. Early in his term, he virtually promised a Pennsylvania audience that he would halt slavery's spread and floored a leading southern Whig by flatly stating he would not veto the Wilmot Proviso. In another unexpected

7. Bleser, ed., *Secret and Sacred*, 87 (first and second quotations) and 199 (third quotation); JH to James Henry Hammond, 31 March 1850, JHP, SHC (fourth quotation). See also JH to Thomas Middleton, 9 June 1849, Thomas Middleton section of Cheves-Middleton Papers, SCHS.

8. Stegmaier, *Compromise of 1850*, 43; and Freehling, *Road to Disunion*, 480–2.

move, Taylor dispatched Hamilton's old friend, former Georgia Whig congressman Thomas Butler King, to the West Coast to urge Californians to bypass the territorial stage altogether and apply for immediate admission to the Union. In December 1849, Taylor announced California's request for statehood and informed Congress that New Mexico would quickly follow suit. Because the Treaty of Guadalupe Hidalgo stipulated that Mexico's anti-slavery laws still applied in both areas until Congress legally organized them, swift admission meant that California and New Mexico would be free states. Southern Whigs, who had vouched for Taylor's reliability on slavery in 1848, felt betrayed. More radical southerners looked toward June's convention in Nashville to lay the groundwork for secession.[9]

Hamilton, however, considered the Union worth preserving. Indeed, he foresaw further national expansion that would bolster the South. He hatched a scheme with Joel Poinsett and James Robb, a New Orleans banker, to give the country another slave state by arranging the purchase of Cuba from Spain. Of course, an independent South might be able to buy—or wrest—Cuba from Spain just as easily as the United States. Federal assumption of the Texas debt, however, would take place only if the Union remained intact. More than anything else, that crucial fact made a sectional moderate out of the former chief Nullifier during the ensuing months of wrangling over the Mexican Cession.[10]

When Hamilton arrived in Washington in early February 1850 to press his case for assumption, discussions in boardinghouses and committee rooms already centered on congressional alternatives to Taylor's plans. Proposals with any chance of garnering majorities followed the main contours laid down in late January by Henry Clay.[11]

Clay's plan demonstrated his desire to go beyond issues of the Mexican Cession to produce a more comprehensive sectional settlement. Like Taylor, the senator called for the admission of California as a free state but suggested that the remainder of the Mexican Cession be organized without "any restriction or condition on the subject of slavery." Bowing to the oft-expressed complaints of abolitionists over the existence of slave

9. Michael F. Holt, *The Rise and Fall of the American Whig Party: Jacksonian Politics and the Onset of the Civil War* (New York: Oxford University Press, 1999), 444.

10. Glenn, "James Hamilton," 398; and JH to James Henry Hammond, 31 March 1850, JH, SHC; and Stegmaier, *Compromise of 1850,* 101.

11. *Washington Republic,* 8 February 1850; and Remini, *Henry Clay,* 714–5.

pens in the very shadow of the Capitol, he also called for ending the slave trade in the District of Columbia. A companion resolution pitched at southerners reaffirmed the right of District residents to own slaves, and he also asked Congress to pledge that it would not interfere in the inter-state slave trade. In the clearest bid for southern support, he proposed easing the recovery of fugitive slaves in the North by southern masters.[12]

A bipartisan group of Union-minded politicians, including most northern Democrats and southern Whigs, applauded Clay's approach. Hamilton also liked the Kentuckian's proposals, especially one on Texas. The Great Compromiser included resolutions calling for federal as-sumption of the Texas debt in exchange for the state's relinquishing of claims to the disputed New Mexican territory. Moreover, Clay suggested the federal treasury compensate the Texas bondholders directly. This de-lighted creditors fearful that the Texas legislature might very well accept a large sum from the federal government but pay off its debtors at a scaled-down rate.[13]

Clay's resolutions threw a strange combination of fellows into the same political bed. Northern anti-slavery Whigs naturally detested the fugitive slave act; they also opposed the debt-assumption plan and feared that slavery might take root in New Mexico under Clay's formulation. Deep South Democrats, meanwhile, blasted the California and Texas proposals as dishonorable and injurious to their region. Why should their property be excluded from California, and why should so much of northwestern Texas—where slaves already toiled—be handed over to a potentially free-soil New Mexico? They bristled, too, at the ten-million-dollar "bribe" being offered to Texas to part with its land. The precedent such a transaction would set for the transformation of slave into free ter-ritory alarmed pro-slavery spokesmen.

Hamilton perceived the situation rather differently than did his south-ern friends. He already supported the notion that Texas should exchange some of its claims to New Mexico for debt relief. Surely a final boundary more favorable to Texas than in Clay's plan would emerge through nego-tiations. In any event, he believed the disputed land wholly unsuited to slave-based agriculture. As for California, its imminent status as a free

12. David M. Potter, *The Impending Crisis, 1848–1861* (New York: Harper & Row, 1976), 99.

13. Holt, *Whig Party*, 480 and 1064, fn. 67; and Stegmaier, *Compromise of 1850*, 101.

state appeared a fait accompli; why waste good oratory on it? To allay southerners' concerns about the sectional unbalance caused by California's admission, Hamilton supported the resolutions of Senator John Bell to divide Texas into three slave states. The Tennessee Whig's plan would compensate the South not only for the "loss" of California, but also for an additional free state (possibly New Mexico) that might later join the Union.[14]

Hamilton began lining up support for Clay's compromise measures. On February 11, he convened a group of Texas bondholders at Washington's National Hotel to plot a course of action. The secret meeting of powerful, well-connected men produced a petition requesting Congress pay the public debt of Texas as part of any settlement. A few days later, commenting that the petition's pro-assumption argument "is better than the one which I offered," Clay presented it to the Senate.[15]

Although Hamilton touted these compromise measures as perfectly consistent with demands for justice to the South, his nullification-era allies back home hardly agreed. They perceived principles other than concern for southern interests as underlying their former leader's lobbying campaign. James Hammond, who preferred secession to accommodating the North, confided to his diary that Hamilton was "now moving heaven and earth to get the U.S. Govt. to assume the debts of Texas, and his very scheme is that of Bell, Clay & Co, to make it part of the Compromise at Washington. In other words to sell the South to get his Texas claims." Hamilton's pro-compromise efforts won no support from his home state representatives. During the months of struggle over the Texas–New Mexico border, California statehood, and related issues, not a single South Carolina member of the House or Senate cast a vote with the pro-compromise bloc.[16]

Hamilton's pains on behalf of the bondholders obviously ran counter to the wishes of his old friend Senator Calhoun, now gravely ill with advanced tuberculosis. Despite their political differences, the two men kept up cordial relations, and Hamilton visited the feeble man almost every evening before leaving town in late March. Mercenary considerations in-

14. JH to James Henry Hammond, 31 March 1850, JHP, SHC; and Stegmaier, *Compromise of 1850*, 105–8.

15. *Cong. Globe*, 31st Cong., 1st sess. (1850), 353.

16. Bleser, ed., *Secret and Sacred*, 199 (quotation); and Stegmaier, *Compromise of 1850*, 328, 344–5.

fluenced the Texas lobbyist's close attention to Calhoun; he hoped to soften the older man's rigid opposition to compromise. But Hamilton also genuinely felt for the man to whom he had been linked for nearly thirty years. Calhoun reciprocated those friendly feelings. When Calhoun made what many believed would be his final speech in the chamber he had so long dominated, he chose Hamilton to escort him onto the Senate floor.[17]

That March 4 speech sounded themes long familiar to Calhoun watchers. As Virginia's James Mason read the text to the unusually attentive listeners—Calhoun too ill to speak at length—the "cast iron man" sat and stared straight ahead as though peering into a dreaded future. Calhoun's dreary warning of inevitable disunion should the North prevent the expansion of slavery into all of the Mexican Cession reflected none of Hamilton's pragmatic, compromising influence. Apparently, Hamilton's long evenings with Calhoun had produced no political effect.[18]

Three days later, Hamilton listened in the same chamber as Daniel Webster delivered a speech he much preferred to Calhoun's. A vast throng filled the galleries hoping to glimpse "Black Dan" and hear his soliloquy in the great national drama being played out in Congress. Taking advantage of his privilege as a former congressman, Hamilton avoided the crowded public spaces and sat downstairs near the action. Webster's support for compromise earned the silver-tongued orator the wrath of anti-slavery men but the gratitude of Hamilton and other moderates. Even Calhoun "expressed much gratification at" Webster's conciliatory words to the South.[19]

While Webster's words inspired Hamilton's optimism about a settlement favorable to his vision of southern interests, South Carolinians proceeded with preparations to protect "southern rights" at the upcoming Nashville Convention. Voters in Hamilton's old congressional district, unaware of his pro-compromise position, nominated him to represent

17. Charles M. Wiltse, *Sectionalist: 1840–1850*, vol. 3 of *John C. Calhoun* (Indianapolis: Bobbs-Merrill, 1951), 460, 474; and JH to William Seabrook, 3 April 1850, *Charleston Courier*, 8 April 1850.

18. "Speech on the Admission of California—and the General State of the Union," in *Union and Liberty: The Political Philosophy of John C. Calhoun*, ed. Ross M. Lance (Indianapolis: Liberty Fund, 1992), 573–601.

19. Waddy Thompson to Daniel Webster, 2 March 1850, *Papers of Daniel Webster*, ed. Wiltse and Moser, 1:7:20; and *Charleston Courier*, 11 March 1850 (quotation).

them at Nashville: "[N]o matter where the General may be at the moment, or in what engaged, he will be ready to take his seat. There is 'a place in the picture,' which none can fill so well as himself." Reading of the nomination while still in Washington, Hamilton used the columns of the *Charleston Courier* to refuse the honor because of "private engagements of an imperative character." He then shared with lowcountry readers his analysis of recent developments in the capital. Neglecting to mention Calhoun's speech, Hamilton lavished praise on Webster for his "moral courage" in striking a "great blow" for sectional compromise. He assured his former neighbors that "we have every reason to hope that a pacification will soon be established between the two great sections of the Confederacy, on terms of safety and honor to the South, and in which the North will not be called upon to surrender a single right or interest which she can fairly claim." Their convention plans, he implied, would be unnecessary.[20]

Hamilton left the capital in late March destined for Austin, where he hoped to persuade politicians to accept Senator Bell's plan of dividing Texas into three states. This crucial mission required the postponement of congressional arm-twisting for a time. Still, he parted from South Carolina's gravely ill senator with genuine sorrow. "I left Mr Calhoun in very precarious health indeed it did not appear possible for him to live five Days when I took leave of him," Hamilton reported to Hammond. On the morning of March 31, while in Savannah to see his family before pushing on to Texas, he received the expected but still shocking word: Calhoun was gone.[21]

As the reality of this news took hold, rumors of new developments in Washington aroused the Carolinian "from the stupor into which I have been thrown" by Calhoun's demise. Like most southern supporters of compromise, Hamilton preferred a comprehensive bill that wedded California statehood to the provisions such as Texas debt relief and Bell's partition plan that he considered concessions to the South. Were those issues not legislatively linked, he feared the northern congressional majority would admit California as a free state and kill the other proposals. Word that Illinois Democrat Stephen Douglas backed a Senate plan to

20. *Charleston Courier*, 27 February 1850 (first quotation) and 15 March 1850 (other quotations).

21. JH to James Henry Hammond, 31 March 1850, JHP, SHC.

handle the issues separately alarmed him. "If the occasion of the admission of California is not embraced we shall never get another Slave State into the Union," he wrote to Senator Bell two days after learning of Calhoun's death.[22]

After Hamilton completed his letter to Bell, he received an important-looking message from South Carolina's governor, William Seabrook. As Hamilton opened it and read, surprise and elation overcame him. Unexpectedly, Seabrook was offering to appoint him as Calhoun's successor. Instantly, Hamilton's long string of misfortunes had seemingly ended. No longer would he simply be a lobbyist for the compromise measures; now he could shape them as a senator. Hamilton knew he hardly seemed the logical replacement for Calhoun; other Carolinians enjoyed greater prominence than he in 1850. Perhaps Hamilton suspected that Seabrook himself aspired to fill the seat once his gubernatorial term ended and that the governor imagined it would be far easier to displace him than a better-known man.[23]

Whatever Seabrook's motivations, Hamilton knew what he must do. In an excessively obsequious response to the governor laden with disavowals of his worthiness for the office, Hamilton accepted the appointment. His letter misleadingly presented himself as Calhoun's political soul mate. He and Calhoun, Hamilton averred, had "been united in entire sympathy and accord on every public question" for decades. Moreover, he carried "the instructions of [Calhoun's] last moments and sick bed." "I cannot believe that occupying his seat there will be a single vote I may be called upon to give," wrote the senator-designate, "that will be at variance with that which he would have given if his valuable life had been spared." Hamilton followed this brazen untruth with a proviso that he would only hold the position for the current session of Congress. Sealing the letter, Hamilton dispatched it to Seabrook on the April 3 mail steamer.[24]

Meanwhile, after offering the post to Hamilton, Seabrook hastened

22. JH to John Bell, 2 April 1850, JHP, SHC (quotations); and Stegmaier, *Compromise of 1850*, 104–5.

23. William Gilmore Simms to James Henry Hammond, 10 April 1850, James Henry Hammond Papers, LC; JH to James Henry Hammond, 19 April 1850, quoted in *Love of Order: South Carolina's First Secession Crisis*, by John Barnwell (Chapel Hill: University of North Carolina Press, 1982), 219 n. 57.

24. JH to William Seabrook, 3 April 1850, printed in *Charleston Courier*, 8 April 1850.

from his Edisto Island home to Charleston to render tribute to Calhoun at an April 2 public meeting. Eulogizing the fallen leader, the governor dropped hints about his choice of an heir to Calhoun's mantle. The post, Seabrook said, required someone with the combined talents of a commander-in-chief, a tactician, a statesman, and finally, a manager. Audience members could barely believe their ears as they pieced together Seabrook's clues. William Gilmore Simms breathlessly reported to Hammond that "the public mind is persuaded he refers to James Hamilton! The report tonight is that the appointment *has* been made, and has been accepted. The indignation of the community is immense. They will not stomach it here: and Seabrook has been told of it!"[25]

Clearly, Seabrook had badly miscalculated. Although the governor's plans to take the Senate seat himself in a few months depended on Hamilton's being somewhat unpopular, the former Nullifier apparently had sunk lower in public estimations than Seabrook realized. Younger Carolinians who had not cheered the conquering Nullifier in the early 1830s tended to be especially dismissive of the senator-designate. In 1845, Francis Pickens had contended that Hamilton's "name is laughed at in Charleston by all the gentlemen of standing." Although that statement was not literally true—such "gentlemen" as Langdon Cheves, Governor Seabrook, and even the late Calhoun proved exceptions to that rule— many lowcountry leaders were becoming convinced that Hamilton was "so utterly prostrated and pressed in his private affairs that he cannot act" with the political independence he once had. Hamilton's support for the compromise measures, news of which spread quickly around town following the governor's April 2 speech, confirmed for many Pickens's appraisal of the man. Hamilton wished to be senator, they believed, not to defend the rights of the South but to line his pockets by supporting policies most Charlestonians considered detrimental to southern rights and honor.[26]

As prominent men argued against Hamilton's appointment "in the

25. Henry W. Conner to James Henry Hammond, 3 April 1850; and William Gilmore Simms to James Henry Hammond, 4 April 1850 (block quotation), James Henry Hammond Papers, LC.

26. Francis Pickens to John C. Calhoun, 23 May 1845, *Calhoun Papers*, ed. Wilson, 21:571–2 (quotations); Francis Pickens to John Edward Colhoun, 7 May 1845, ibid., 541; *Charleston Mercury*, 4 April 1850; and Joseph A. Scoville to James Henry Hammond, 18 April 1850, James Henry Hammond Papers, LC.

strongest terms," Seabrook feared for his political life. Yet he could not withdraw the appointment without great embarrassment. Fortunately for the governor, the anti-Hamilton crowd provided him a way out of the crisis. Hamilton, they suggested, did not qualify as a citizen of South Carolina and therefore could not constitutionally represent the state.[27]

Hamilton's enemies made a very good point. Although often identified in public prints as "General Hamilton of South Carolina," he no longer owned property in the state nor did he spend much time there. Over the previous decade, he had arguably been a resident of several states other than South Carolina. Alabama and Texas could both make good claims to him, though perhaps Georgia's was best. In 1845, Hamilton himself had regarded Georgia "somewhat as my Domicile," because of Pennyworth and his plantations in the southwestern part of the state. In 1850, Savannah served as the base of operations in Hamilton's peripatetic life. At the time of the appointment controversy, he could only assert South Carolina residency based on having spent part of the previous summer at the Beaufort District home of his married daughter. His opponents argued that visit qualified as a "temporary resort for health," not evidence of permanent residence. Having gathered advice from various friends, Seabrook wrote Hamilton on April 4 to express his doubts as to whether Hamilton qualified as a South Carolinian. The governor left it up to Hamilton to take the next step.[28]

Two days later, Hamilton arrived in Charleston to find public opinion, that creature he had tamed years before, now snarling at him menacingly. The fierce opposition to his appointment rendered resistance unseemly. Hamilton met with the governor, and, to Seabrook's great relief, informed him of his decision to decline the appointment. The two exchanged letters, carefully worded to avoid further public embarrassment to either man, which local newspapers published. In his note, Hamilton refused to concede he belonged to any state except South Carolina, but he yielded to Seabrook's doubts about the matter. Seabrook mentioned nothing of the uproar in Charleston over Hamilton's financial interest in the congressional compromise. Instead, praising the bond-

27. Henry W. Conner to James Henry Hammond, 4 April 1850, James Henry Hammond Papers, LC.

28. JH to J. McPherson Berrien, 16 February 1845, JHP, SHC; William H. Perronneau to Whitemarsh Seabrook, 18 April 1850; and I. W. Hayne to Whitemarsh Seabrook, 18 April 1850, Whitemarsh Seabrook Papers, LC.

holders' lobbyist for his "past services in the noble cause of State rights," Seabrook lauded Hamilton's "rigid adherence to the dictates of a high sense of honor" in declining the appointment.[29]

With the Senate seat pulled from beneath him, Hamilton decided to head north rather than continue his journey to Texas. Perhaps the word he had received earlier about Douglas's intentions caused his change in plans. He soon traveled to Philadelphia to request a $5,000 loan from his wealthy friend Pierce Butler, who agreed. The old general believed federal assumption of the Texas debt would shortly be concluded and that then he could repay his friend out of the commission that the B.U.S. trustees owed him. For good measure, he again assigned Butler his interest in the *Zavala* bonds as collateral for the loan.[30]

Returning to Washington, he continued lobbying. By now, Clay's compromise measures had been combined into a single large bill, known as the Omnibus. That July, the unexpected death of compromise opponent President Taylor increased the possibility of its passage by placing pro-Omnibus Millard Fillmore in the White House.

As the Omnibus's chances improved, southern rights men vented their anger on Hamilton's lobbying efforts. South Carolina congressman Daniel Wallace publicly scorned the "lobby members, . . . who throng the purlieus of the Capitol, ready to grasp the promised spoils." Hamilton responded with good humor to this veiled attack on himself. He attributed Wallace's heated rhetoric to that "occasional inflammation" peculiar to those who inhabit southern climes. "As no one has probably suffered more under the fever than myself," Hamilton wrote, "there can be none more ready to forgive it in others." Denying that any "Texan bondholder had solicited a single member of Congress to support Mr. Clay's compromise," Hamilton argued for the justice of the assumption provisions under discussion in Congress. The United States, he insisted, was morally obligated to pay those creditors to whom Texas tariff revenue had been pledged because the federal government now controlled the former Republic's customs houses.[31]

29. A series of letters between Seabrook and Hamilton, dated 1 April through 6 April 1850, appears in both the *Charleston Mercury* and the *Charleston Courier*, 8 April 1850. Quotations from Seabrook to JH, 6 April 1850.

30. See copy of JH to Trustees of the late Bank of the U.S., 19 June 1850, included in F. B. Cutting to William S. Wetmore, 31 May 1856, RG 21, box 215, case 1174, file 1 of 2; and copy of Hamilton's assignment of the *Zavala* bonds, 17 June 1850, in ibid., box 216, case 1186.

31. *Texas State Gazette*, 27 July 1850.

To the dismay of Hamilton and other compromise advocates—and to the great delight of northern anti-slavery men and hard-line southern rights supporters—Congress destroyed the Omnibus in late July. A parliamentary blunder by pro-compromise senator James Pearce of Maryland led to the stripping of every provision until only a bill organizing the Utah Territory remained. Pearce then compensated for that error by crafting a bill on the boundary issue that included debt-settlement provisions favorable to the bondholders. Hamilton enthusiastically supported this Texas Boundary Bill and lined up support among moderates. Because Pearce's bill gave more of the disputed territory to Texas than had the Omnibus, Texas senators Sam Houston and Thomas Rusk also endorsed it.[32]

In the Lone Star State itself, however, opposition to any measure requiring the surrender of Texas soil reached the boiling point during the summer of 1850. Governor Peter Bell, egged on by "ultra" southern-rights advocates, proposed sending troops into the disputed region to defend the state's right to what his allies considered Santa Fe County, Texas. In this militant atmosphere, the state legislature took up the question of whether to re-elect Rusk to the Senate. Rusk's support for the Pearce bill made him quite vulnerable.

Considering Rusk's re-election vital to the eventual success of the compromise, Hamilton pleaded the senator's case with an important Laredo legislator, native South Carolinian and Hamilton's namesake Hamilton Prioleau Bee, son of Barnard Bee. Appealing to Bee's sense of Carolina pride, Hamilton urged him to support Rusk, also a former Palmetto State resident. But Representative Bee now led the "ultra" faction. He cast his vote for Louis Wigfall, who, as Bee defiantly informed Hamilton, was a native Carolinian more devoted to southern rights than was Rusk. As it turned out, by the time of the election, moderation had largely snuffed out the flames of southern rights in Texas. Bee stood in a distinct minority, and Rusk won his race handily.[33]

Die-hard Texas opponents of the Boundary Bill traced Rusk's victory to one cause, the influence of "men like Gen. HAMILTON who have speculated deeply in Texas bonds." An anti-compromise Texas newspaper blasted Hamilton's role in the state's business:

32. Stegmaier, *Compromise of 1850*, 204.
33. Ibid., 249–59.

For motives of a mercenary character, he has renounced the principles of his life, and consented to pander to abolitionism. If Mr. Pearce's bill, or any other bill selling the public lands of Texas, is sanctioned by our people, the consequence will be that Gen. Hamilton and others will be made immensely rich men. The rebuke of Mr. BEE is, therefore, well-timed and well-directed, and the more to be applauded as it shows that this gentleman does not hesitate a moment to do his duty, even at the sacrifice of the strongest ties of friendship. We see the motive of Gen. HAMILTON's praise of Gen. RUSK, and although we do not even suspect the latter of impure intentions, his course in reference to the sale of our public domain, we do not think at all creditable to his understanding.[34]

The editorial writer wildly overstated Hamilton's role in the cooling of southern rights sentiment that led to Rusk's victory; President Fillmore's firmness in preparing to defend New Mexico from an attack by Texas troops proved far more important. Most Texas legislators could not stomach real conflict with the U.S. Army. Moreover, they realized their state could ill afford the cost of such a foolhardy military adventure. Still, Hamilton's public activities on behalf of the bondholders made him a convenient target for militant Texans.[35]

The attacks of southern rights men in Texas amounted to minor annoyances for Hamilton once the Boundary Bill became law in early September. James L. Petigru observed that the new law put his old friend "in very good spirits, as well he may be, for the Texan Boundary Bill will put money in his pocket, to which, the said pocket is little accustomed." The successful lobbyist's prospects continued to brighten. Washington banker William Corcoran wanted the government to appoint his institution, Corcoran & Riggs, as the agent to administer the ten-million-dollar payment to Texas called for in the Boundary Bill. Hamilton made a deal with Corcoran. In exchange for a $25,000 loan, Hamilton agreed to help Corcoran procure the Texas agency. Just two days after Hamilton and Corcoran shook hands on their deal, Senator Rusk wrote Corcoran's bank for advice on the appointment of an agent. Rusk's letter constituted a quasi-official query about Corcoran's willingness to handle the payment, and almost certainly, Rusk acted at the behest of Hamilton. Rusk

34. *Texas Republican*, 7 September 1850.
35. Stegmaier, *Compromise of 1850*, 247–52.

also did Hamilton's bidding by putting in a good word for Corcoran with Treasury Secretary Thomas Corwin.[36]

Despite the apparent improvement of Hamilton's prospects with the adoption of the Boundary Act, fresh problems arose to bedevil him. First, new financial and legal concerns exacerbated his already precarious personal economic situation. Second, his reputation in South Carolina further declined as he publicly opposed the state's radical response to the compromise measures. Compounding these problems was the fact that the Boundary Act failed to bring the old Texas creditor the quick relief he needed.

Hamilton's newest pecuniary difficulty emerged during his lobbying campaign but stemmed from indiscreet acts he committed some years before. From the late 1830s through 1846, Hamilton had served as the trustee for the estate of Mary Martha McRa, a wealthy South Carolina woman separated from her husband. For several years, Hamilton paid McRa dividends on her funds he invested in Bank of Charleston stock. Beginning in 1840, under an agreement with McRa's son, Hamilton deposited the dividends in her account with a Charleston factor. Before long, according to his accusers, Hamilton began diverting her money to his own use. Then, in 1846, while McRa's legal affairs were rather unsettled following her being declared insane, Hamilton sold her bank stock for over $37,000 and used most of the proceeds to purchase twenty-five slaves, thereafter known as the Lundy gang, whom he settled at Retrieve. By 1850, the total principal and interest Hamilton owed McRa's estate approximated $50,000.[37]

In February 1850, as Hamilton met with the other Texas bondholders at the National Hotel, Albertus Spain, Mrs. McRa's lawyer, arrived in Washington to file a lawsuit against the unscrupulous trustee in a District of Columbia court. Having his misdeeds revealed in the midst of the congressional session was bad enough; but Hamilton faced the further embarrassment of imposing on Carolina friends in Washington, including

36. James L. Petigru to Susan Petigru King, 12 September 1850, *Petigru*, ed. Carson, 284 (quotation); Thomas Rusk to Corcoran & Riggs, 23 September 1850, and Thomas Corwin to Thomas Rusk, 1 October 1850, Thomas Jefferson Rusk Papers, CAH.

37. Appellate brief, *Albertus C. Spain, Committee of Mary M. McRa, Complainant and Appellant* v. *Robert J. Brent, Adm'r of James Hamilton and al.*, 1–2, in RG 21, box 215, case 1174, file 1 of 2; JH to Mary Martha McRa, 13 June 1835; and J. Hamilton Son & Co. to Mary M. McRa, 11 July 1842, Richard Singleton Papers, Duke.

Senator A. P. Butler and Congressman Isaac Holmes, to sign his bail bond. Butler and Holmes, opponents of the Texas debt-assumption plan, thus became privy to the messy finances that they claimed accounted for Hamilton's support for the compromise.[38]

The bail bond's conditions forced Hamilton to turn property over to McRa's lawyer. Threatened with arrest, Hamilton executed an order to his son Oliver, manager of Retrieve, to deliver the Lundy gang to Albertus Spain by late April. Moreover, Hamilton signed over to McRa's estate all of his personal "claims on the Texas government" as well as any commissions due him for prosecuting the claims of others against the Lone Star State.[39]

Mary Martha McRa thus joined a growing list of individuals and institutions—including the James River and Kanawha Company, Pierce Butler, G. B. Lamar, the estate of James Holford, New Orleans banker James Robb, and factor Henry Hill—to whom Hamilton had pledged his Texas claims as either security for loans or as repayment for debts. To some, he assigned only certain bonds, while to others he surrendered all of his claims, including those for his diplomatic expenses. Moreover, he continued to use these claims as collateral in other transactions. For instance, he later sold to Henry Hill for $33,000 his rights to the commission owed him by the trustees of the Bank of the United States as well as his personal diplomatic claims against Texas.[40]

Soon, the various assignees of Hamilton's Texas claims began arguing among themselves about who had the best rights to the funds. By the mid-fifties, his creditors were hopelessly entangled in a web of lawsuits. In order to prevent others from collecting on the claims, for instance, Albertus Spain sued G. B. Lamar and the Virginia canal company and entered injunctions to prevent several others, including the B.U.S. trustees and Corcoran & Riggs, from collecting on several Hamilton claims that the federal government was prepared to pay off. In 1856, Pierce Butler, who pursued his own injunctions against other Hamilton creditors, characterized the lawsuits surrounding his friend's Texas claims as "a regular Kilkenny fight all around": "First, all parties will make common

38. *Washington Republic*, 12 February 1850.

39. Complainant's Exhibit "A," 12 February 1850, appellate brief in *Albertus C. Spain, Committee of Mary M. McRa, Complainant and Appellant v. Robert J. Brent, Adm'r of James Hamilton and al.*, in RG 21, box 215, case 1174, file 1 of 2.

40. Declaration of conveyance, 27 May 1853, RG 21, box 215, case 1174, file 2 of 2.

cause against A. C. Spain's claim: if that shall be broke down, we shall then fall to among ourselves, and it will be 'the hardest feud off.' Of course there will be an appeal to the Supreme Court, & two years will not more than end it."[41]

The various lawsuits actually worked to Hamilton's advantage. With his creditors slugging it out in court, none could collect from him. He helped himself, too, by dragging his feet in the performance of his duties. For instance, he failed to turn over the Lundy slaves to McRa's lawyer as promised, and several years later he claimed not to know their true owner. In the meantime, the slaves remained at Retrieve to keep producing their master's main source of revenue.[42]

Amid the maelstrom of legal proceedings, protecting Retrieve became Hamilton's top priority. He believed the plantation could save him if properly capitalized. In 1852, he found himself in need of a new partner at Retrieve and begged the wealthy Pierce Butler to join him in the enterprise. He promised Butler a net annual yield of $20,000 on an initial $100,000 investment in the sugar plantation. "No Hotel you can build in Philadelphia can do half so much on the same amt of capital," Hamilton assured him. If circumstances prevented Butler from buying into the plantation, Hamilton entreated him to at least purchase a gang of slaves who worked on the place, a gang that Hamilton was then renting from the brother of his son-in-law. The owner, William Middleton, found himself forced to sell the slaves as a result of "some youthful extravagance," and Hamilton feared the new buyer would remove them from Retrieve. Despite Butler's apparent wealth, however, he lacked the cash and credit to purchase either the plantation or the slaves. Again, Hamilton's friend Henry Hill came to his rescue. Hill, who had already loaned Hamilton tens of thousands of dollars and earlier complained of having "been nearly ruined by the Genl," bought the Middleton slaves so they could remain at Retrieve.[43]

41. Pierce Butler to JH, 24 June 1856, Pierce Butler Letterpress Book, 2:250–3, Wister Family Papers, Butler Section, HSP.

42. Statement of Abner Jackson, 10 February 1855, and JH to J. M. Bass, 27 January 1856, Ballinger Papers, CAH.

43. JH to Pierce Butler, 14 September 1852 (first quotation); JH to Pierce Butler, 21 December 1852 (second quotation); JH to Pierce Butler, 8 January 1853; and Pierce Butler to JH, 14 January 1853, Pierce Butler Letterpress Book, 2:258–60, all in Wister Family Papers, Butler Section, HSP; Henry R. W. Hill to John Jordan Crittenden, 2 November 1851, John Jordan Crittenden Papers, LC (last quotation).

Despite Hill's assistance on that occasion, Retrieve failed to be Hamilton's salvation. With Hill's death in September 1853, Hamilton lost his major line of credit; Hill's executor refused to be as generous to Hamilton as the factor himself had been. Then in late 1854, bad weather destroyed a crop Hamilton estimated would have yielded 900 hogsheads of sugar. Losses reached the point that in February 1855 Hill's executor and Lynch Hamilton, trustee for his mother's trust estate, were forced to sell Retrieve and everything on it, down to a 25-cent pair of cart wheels. Legal complications with the sale, however, arose. As those were sorted out, the slaves continued working on Retrieve under the direction of Hamilton's former partner, Abner Jackson, who acted as the agent of Hill's estate in managing the plantation. Meanwhile, Hamilton prayed that the legal questions surrounding the sale would result in its being set aside and in his wife's trust estate regaining control of half of the plantation. The legal system once again provided Hamilton temporary relief and buoyed his hope, the only commodity he seemed to have in abundance.[44]

As Hamilton's legal and financial problems worsened, his political distance from old Carolina allies increased. He celebrated the passage of the Texas Boundary Bill and the rest of the Compromise of 1850, but southern rights extremists in South Carolina responded by contemplating radical action, including secession. Like other Carolina "ultras," Governor Seabrook recognized that his own state could not take the first step in that direction. South Carolina's lone stand during the nullification controversy had taught that lesson well. But as soon as two other states gave evidence of their willingness to adopt "determined resistance," Seabrook pledged South Carolina would follow. The second, smaller meeting of the Nashville Convention in November 1850, which radicals dominated, hatched a plan of resistance. The convention implored southerners to elect delegates to a new southern congress, which most observers considered a precursor to cooperative secession. The following month, South Carolina lawmakers endorsed the Nashville Convention's call. The legislature approved elections for not only a southern congress, but also for a state convention. Patterned after Hamilton's Nullification Convention,

44. JH to Pierce Butler, 12 November 1854, Wister Family Papers, Butler Section, HSP; Account of property sale on the Retrieve Plantation, 8 and 9 February 1855, Ballinger Papers, CAH; JH to John M. Bass, 14 February 1856; and John M. Bass to Abner Jackson, 30 May 1854, Ballinger Papers, CAH.

this conclave would meet after the special congress, presumably to approve the dissolution of the Union.[45]

Even as old Carolina allies advocated secession either separately or in concert with other states, Hamilton counseled calm. As the Nashville meeting convened, he took up his pen at Retrieve to oppose secession. Hamilton's letter to the people of South Carolina combined several different and sometimes conflicting arguments to make its point. Most tellingly, he declared that nothing in the compromise measures warranted secession. Hamilton claimed that "the admission of Texas furnished a far greater provocation to the North to secede, than the admission of California does to the South." Southerners could only blame themselves for the fact that the Golden State was free; they had failed to match the enterprise of northerners in immigrating to the region. He gently chided southern legislators for having failed to act on his suggestion to "several distinguished men in two or three of the Southern States" to provide bounties for slaveholders to settle in California. Then, implying the shortsightedness of such a plan, he argued that southerners should be relieved that California did not permit slavery. He proclaimed that a slave state of California would have attracted so many slaveholding masters as to have drained the South of its black labor force. Hamilton also dismissed southern anger over the cession of Texas claims to New Mexico. The territory Texas relinquished, he argued, consisted of lands as barren as the "Arctic coasts." Southern slaveholders, in short, had surrendered nothing of any real value in the Boundary Bill. Hamilton further warned that in the battle for northern public opinion South Carolina's secession would simply play into the hands of the state's abolitionist and free soil enemies while harming true friends of the South, including President Fillmore and Senators Henry Clay and Daniel Webster.[46]

As South Carolina's leaders ignored their former governor's unwelcome advice and moved ahead with their convention plans, Hamilton sought some way for them to retreat gracefully. Convinced that ordinary Carolina voters opposed secession, he suggested a plebiscite on the issue so that its results could guide the convention. The state's leaders were as

45. William Seabrook to [Henry W. Collier], 20 September 1850, William Seabrook Papers, LC.

46. Hamilton's letter, dated 11 November 1850, appears in *Texas State Gazette*, 15 March 1851.

unwilling to call for such a vote in 1851 as Governor Hamilton would have been in 1831, and Hamilton's suggestion never received serious consideration.[47]

Instead, the convention met as scheduled in early 1852. By then, however, enthusiasm for immediate secession had waned considerably throughout the South. Most white southerners now accepted the Compromise, provided the federal government faithfully enforced the Fugitive Slave Act, and few South Carolina leaders wished to secede alone. Hamilton did not participate in the 1852 state convention, given all his activities that had rendered him "exceedingly unpopular in" his native state.[48]

The citizens of St. Peter's Parish did, however, tap Hamilton's thirty-five-year-old son, Daniel Heyward, to represent them. Dan, trained as a physician in Philadelphia but long a planter in the parish, was the only grown Hamilton son to be financially independent of his father. Whether working in the elder Hamilton's factorage business, assisting in his diplomatic missions, or overseeing his far-flung plantations, Dan's adult brothers had always subordinated their interests to their father's. By contrast, Dan early established his own identity by marrying the wealthy Rebecca Middleton and settling down as a respectable lowcountry planter. Still, he was his father's son. At the convention, Dan voted as James Hamilton himself would have that year and showed the contrast between the Hamiltons' position in 1852 and the chief nullifier's stand in 1832. Joining a tiny minority of cooperationists and Unionists, Dan even opposed a resolution that declared South Carolina's theoretical right to secede.[49]

As a result of Hamilton's support for the Boundary Bill and his opposition to secession, public regard for him in South Carolina sank to new lows. An official toast at the 1852 Independence Day celebration in Walterborough proclaimed "Gen. James Hamilton, formerly of South Carolina, now of Texas; once styled the 'Bayard of the South, without fear and without reproach,' now with impious hands assist[s] at the burial of State Rights and State Sovereignty, by his active participation and indecent

47. JH to Armistead Burt, 11 September 1851, Armistead Burt Papers, Duke.
48. *Charleston Mercury*, 7 April 1850.
49. The convention passed the resolution 136 to 19. *Journals of the Conventions of the People of South Carolina, Held in 1832, 1833, and 1852* (Columbia: R. W. Gibes, 1860), 150–3.

haste in the dismemberment of the fairest portion of the South."[50] That the citizens of the town where Hamilton had pronounced his pioneering endorsement of nullification expressed these sentiments provides a poignant measure of his fall in public esteem.

Winning approval of the Compromise and even enduring the slights of Carolina secessionists proved easier than actually receiving payment under the Boundary Act. That law required that Texas creditors file releases of any claims against the federal government related to the Texas debt before they could receive payment. Questions arose regarding precisely which of the various classes of creditors the act covered and whether *all* creditors had to sign releases before *any* creditor could receive payment. According to the law, the president would decide those matters.

Hamilton led the faction of bondholders slated to receive full payment; arrayed against them was a group of speculative investors who had bought bonds at a small fraction of their face value. The speculators refused to sign releases against the federal government until they received a promise of par payment for their bonds. Unfortunately for Hamilton, the speculators included much more powerful men than he, most notably his onetime benefactor, William Corcoran.

Hamilton organized his band of bondholders to pressure the Fillmore administration to render a decision favorable to their interests. Over the course of five months in 1851, Hamilton pleaded their case in personal meetings with Fillmore and other officials. He sought to ensure that the federal government rather than Texas determined how payments would be made to the creditors. Many Texans, he knew, blamed the state's large debts on the creditors; as one of the state's leading newspapers charged, bondholders had stimulated the Republic "to incur expenses and contract debt upon ruinous terms, themselves the operators and beneficiaries of the scheme." Texas officials, Hamilton believed with good reason, were likely to throw as many roadblocks as possible into the path of the creditors. So, ironically, the popularizer of nullification insisted that, because the Boundary Act was a federal law, only federal authorities could interpret it. Fillmore agreed with Hamilton on that point, but his decision on the main issue greatly displeased the chief bondholder lobbyist. Before

50. *Charleston Mercury*, 9 July 1852.

any creditor received payment, the president ruled, each of the nearly sixteen hundred creditors needed to sign a release.[51]

Once Franklin Pierce's election to the presidency appeared secure in the autumn of 1852, Hamilton sought to enlist the New Hampshire Democrat's aid in reversing Fillmore's decision. Introducing himself by letter, Hamilton proudly pointed to his personal contributions to Pierce's beloved Democratic Party. "I led with [Robert Hayne and George McDuffie] the triumphant opposition" to the administration of John Quincy Adams, he noted, and "contributed as much as any other man in the U.S." to Andrew Jackson's 1828 victory. Hamilton apologized for not taking an active role in the canvass for Pierce, explaining that his Texas petitions before Congress meant "I . . . cannot afford to make enemies." He assured Pierce that privately he was attempting to win support for the candidate from old Nullifiers, some of whom were leaning to former Georgia governor and states' rights idol George Troup from "a mistaken & perverse adhesion what they might deem the consistency of public principle." In a postscript, Hamilton revealed the real purpose of his letter. "I take the liberty to enclose you one of my memorials to Congress, the subject of which is quite likely to come before you after the 4th March." Ultimately, however, Hamilton's pleas failed to persuade Pierce to overrule Fillmore.[52]

Not until 1855 did Congress approve what Hamilton considered a satisfactory if not ideal solution to the Texas debt issue. All of the Texas debt would be scaled to 76 cents on the dollar and paid out of a special congressional appropriation. This meant that speculators such as Corcoran made killings on bonds bought for 20 or 30 cents on the dollar, while Hamilton's contingent of par value creditors failed to receive full payment. Still, after waiting five years since the passage of the Boundary Act and many more than that since the original debts were contracted, a 76 percent payment beat none at all.[53]

51. *Texas State Gazette*, 7 December 1850 and 2 August 1851 (quotation); JH to Thomas Corwin, 9 May and 5 September 1851, Thomas Corwin Papers, LC.

52. JH to Franklin Pierce, 18 October 1852, Franklin Pierce Papers, LC (quotations); "Memorial of James Hamilton, for Himself and Others, Creditors of the State of Texas, to the President of the U. States" (Washington: C. Alexander, 1853); JH to Franklin Pierce, 7 March 1853, JHP, SHC; and JH to Pierce Butler, 20 September 1853, Wister Family Papers, Butler Section, HSP.

53. *Cong. Globe*, 33rd Cong., 2nd sess. (1855), 383, Appendix; and *Texas State Gazette*, 22 March 1856.

While lobbying two presidents about the bonds, Hamilton also sought to extract payment from the Texas legislature for his ministerial salary and other diplomatic expenses. During the winters of the early 1850s, Hamilton could be found buttonholing legislators in the Texas capitol and imploring them to approve his various petitions for reimbursement.[54]

He succeeded, but only in part. In early February 1852, as the South Carolina convention met, Hamilton was in Texas receiving $10,000 from the state for a year's salary and expenses as the former Republic's diplomatic agent. Not content, Hamilton pressed to be compensated for the other expenses he had incurred on behalf of the Republic. For instance, he wanted reimbursement for the $30,000 in bribes he had paid to French officials—money he had obtained from the sale of the James River and Kanawha Company's bonds. Understandably, Hamilton lacked full documentation for this large "secret service" expenditure; none of the greasy-palmed recipients had signed receipts with their full names acknowledging the purpose of the payments. Without such documentation, the legislature repeatedly refused to reimburse Hamilton for this and many other legitimate claims. Texas did, however, eventually acknowledge a much smaller debt of $6,141.66 to its onetime spokesman in Europe.[55]

Disappointed with the Texans' chariness, Hamilton held out hope that they would change their minds. In the meantime, he treated his own creditors with even less consideration than the state had extended to him. He did request that the Texas comptroller pay the James River Company "whatever sum . . . Texas should allow either in the shape of principal or interest on the adjustment of my open" account for diplomatic services. But, significantly, he failed to use the $10,000 he received from Texas to provide even partial payment to any creditor to whom he had pledged his Texas claims.[56]

54. Hamilton petitions to Texas legislature, 21 December 1851, 17 January 1852, and 16 December 1853, TSLAC.
55. Certificate #3362, 2nd class, and Certificate #2763, 2nd class, Public Debt Papers, reel 158, TSLAC. Also see M. D. K. Taylor to D. C. Dickson, 4 January 1854, and JH to James B. Shaw, 8 August 1854, Public Debt Papers, reel 158, TSLAC. For the "secret service" bribes, see Hamilton Prioleau Bee to Samuel Prioleau Hamilton, 6 September 1887, and Ashbel Smith to Samuel Prioleau Hamilton, 29 March 188[5?], JHP, SHC.
56. JH to James B. Shaw, September 1852, copy made by Texas Auditor's office, 29 August 1854, Public Debt Papers, reel 158, TSLAC.

Wandering Austin's legislative halls in the 1850s, Hamilton also tried to enlist the state's support for railroad development. His rail schemes changed over time but always involved the Texas debt. After passage of the 1855 federal law settling the debt on a 76 percent scale, he urged the Texas creditors to deposit one-third of their payments into a special account whose funds the state comptroller would invest in the construction of railroad lines from the coast into the interior.[57]

Rail construction would be crucial in developing areas of central and west Texas for which Hamilton held land scrip. Claiming to have "removed to Texas and settled permanently for the residue of my life, in the valley of the Leon," he wrote a circular letter inviting others to join him in farming the fertile lands north of Austin. In truth, Hamilton had not taken up residence in a frontier cabin on the Texas plains. Instead, his hopes for Texas land development fizzled, and in 1855, both he and his wife moved to Bluffton, South Carolina, to live with their daughter and her family. For the first time in more than a decade, he was again a more or less permanent resident of South Carolina.[58]

Through all his troubles in the 1850s, Hamilton maintained an optimistic public front. Yet, during rare moments of deep reflection, shared only with his wife, he revealed severe anxieties. He experienced one such moment in March 1850 as he traveled south from Washington during the Texas boundary debate. As the capital city receded in the distance and the miles home shortened, thoughts of Texas bonds, congressional arm-twisting, and even of the latest lawsuit against him gave way to family concerns. A year before, twelve-year-old Arthur St. Clair Hamilton, his youngest child, had died. Memories of that son and of Hamilton's oldest son, dead fourteen years by then, filled his mind. Steaming down North Carolina's Cape Fear River towards Wilmington, he took up his pen on the first anniversary of Arthur's death to assure Elizabeth she did not grieve alone. "I have had a dreadful day of depression on the Rail Road & in this Boat on dwelling on the loss of our darling Child," he confided. "Alas how vividly have his last moments come back to my memory with a weight of sorrow I can neither surmount or describe."

Mingled with Hamilton's grief and his concern for Elizabeth's feel-

57. *Texas State Gazette*, 22 March and 19 April 1856.

58. "Gen. Hamilton's Circular, Descriptive of the Table Lands of the Leon," 1 January 1855, JHP, SHC; and Petition # 0010 003 ND00 0390800, n.d. [indexed c. 1855], General Assembly Papers, SCDAH.

ings was a frank admission. Arthur's death was, Hamilton believed, "a dreadful blow of Almighty God which . . . I deserved . . . for my Sins & hardness of heart." Such divine chastisement Hamilton could "almost bear under a sense of Gods justice," but he found it "almost too much to stand when I think that you innocent unsinful & pious have been a far greater sufferer in this calamity than myself." His own failings, he realized, affected others besides himself.

Hoping to cheer his wife on the melancholic anniversary, James expressed his belief that their boy was now "happy beyond all human utterance & that he has joined in blessed companionship his dear & never to be forgotten Brother & his other Relatives in a world where I am sure My Dear Elizabeth it will be your happy allotment to join them." Conscious of his own shortcomings, Hamilton could only pray that he, too, would one day be reunited with his family in that better world.[59]

Buffeted by personal, political, and financial defeats over more than a decade, Hamilton needed assurance of a better world beyond the grave to keep him going. Like so many others in mid-nineteenth-century America, Hamilton found peace of mind in communion with the spirit world. By the early 1850s he knew of Catherine and Margaret Fox, two young sisters from upstate New York who claimed to communicate with the dead through a kind of ghostly Morse code. The phenomenon of spiritual "rappings" spread from the Fox home near Rochester in 1848 to parlors and public halls in much of the East and the Old Northwest by the 1850s. Along the way, the spirits added table tipping, ghostly scribblings, haunted music, and similar means of communication to their repertoires. They wowed large audiences in New York, Boston, and other cities, courtesy of mediums such as the Fox girls and promoters such as P. T. Barnum. More genteel folks "investigated" spiritual happenings in private séances. Although from the very beginning the Fox sisters and other mediums had their critics, thousands of Americans believed in, indeed, relied upon, communication across the veil separating this world from the next.

As a southerner and a member of an orthodox Protestant denomination, Hamilton's interest in spiritualism bordered on the unusual. Many southerners considered this subject yet another "ism" that gulled weakminded Yankees and threatened the social order. But by the early 1850s

59. JH to Elizabeth Hamilton, 19 March 1850, JHP, SHC (microfilm).

Hamilton was politically out of step with the southern rights men who denounced spiritualism. And, although nominally an Episcopalian, Hamilton by this time dabbled in Swedenborgianism, a more esoteric religion that placed great faith in communication with the dead.[60]

For Hamilton, spiritualism offered solace, even absolution for his sins of paternal omission. In nighttime communion with his dead sons—five of his eleven progeny eventually predeceased him—he received assurance that, despite his failings as a father, they still loved him. They existed quite happily in their world, unburdened by the cares of debt, crop loss, and diminished reputation that constantly dogged their father in his world.[61]

Spiritualism also played a politically therapeutic role in Hamilton's life, as suggested by his participation in séances mediated by Catherine and Margaret Fox when they visited Washington in February 1853. In the national capital on Texas business, he attended the Foxes' functions in the company of colleagues such as Waddy Thompson, the former South Carolina congressman, and Nathaniel Tallmadge, an ex-U.S. senator from New York. During one of these events, the sisters conjured up the spirit of John C. Calhoun for their guests. On previous occasions Calhoun had rung bells and played a guitar to prove his presence; this time he honored a request to beat time to "Hail Columbia." At a subsequent gathering in Hamilton's absence, Tallmadge asked Calhoun's ghost to write a sentence in his own hand. In the darkened room, participants heard the scratching of pencil on paper. When the lights went on, before Tallmadge was a piece of paper bearing the words: "I'm with you still." To confirm the handwriting's authenticity, Tallmadge took it to Hamilton, Thompson, and other former colleagues of Calhoun. Each acknowledged it to be that of the dead senator. Hamilton further attested to its genuineness by pointing out that Calhoun had always used the contraction "I'm" for "I am." Clearly, Hamilton believed—perhaps even needed to believe—that he could communicate with the dead Calhoun.

60. Robert W. Delp, "The Southern Press and the Rise of American Spiritualism, 1847–1860," *Journal of American Culture* 7, no. 3 (1984): 91; [Lewis Cruger], *A Brief Notice of the Death and Character of Gov. Hamilton, of South Carolina* (Washington: Henry Polkinhorn, 1857), 9, in JHP, SHC; and Richard Kenneth Silver, "The Spiritual Kingdom in America: The Influence of Emanuel Swedenborg on American Society and Culture: 1815–1860" (Ph.D. diss., Stanford University, 1983).

61. [Cruger], *A Brief Notice*, 9–10.

After his experience with the Fox sisters, he claimed to hold sometimes "nightly communion" with the "mighty and cherished spirit" of Calhoun.[62]

Séances with the likes of Calhoun (and Clay and Webster after their deaths in 1852) renewed a sense of political relevance for Hamilton and his spiritualist friends. No member of his circle of Washington spiritualists had held political office for years; each had fallen out of favor with their constituencies. That was certainly the case with Hamilton. Thompson, for his part, had rendered himself unelectable in the Palmetto State by embracing the national Whig program, while Tallmadge's indecision about his party affiliation made him suspect in a political world that prized partisan loyalty. On their frequent visits to Washington, these men looked on with more than a little envy as others wielded the power they felt should have been theirs. Spiritualism served as partial antidote to their political powerlessness. As the ghost of Henry Clay told a former judge and Tallmadge associate, "you will do more good with spiritualism, than I ever did in politics. Go on."[63] That sort of affirmation washed the dusty shame of the political wilderness from Hamilton and his spiritualist confreres.

Although communicating with the dead brought Hamilton some relief from the pressures he experienced in the world of the living, it hardly eliminated them. The reality of lawsuits and debts remained. His best hope lay with making Retrieve more profitable. For years, he had envisioned rendering the plantation more accessible to markets by connecting the property with Galveston Bay by a series of canals. Little had come of these plans. Then, in 1856, both the state and the county appropriated funds to clear obstructions from Oyster Creek, which ran through Retrieve. Such improvements would have made it possible to

62. Eliab Wilkinson Capron, *Modern Spiritualism: Its Facts and Fanaticisms, Its Consistencies and Contradictions* (1855; reprint, New York: Arno Press, 1976), 337; John W. Edmonds and George T. Dexter, *Spiritualism*, vol. 1 (New York: Partridge & Brittan, 1853), 428–31 (first and second quotations); and [Cruger], "A Brief Notice," 10 (last quotation).

63. Henry T. Thompson, *Waddy Thompson*; Robert Tinkler, "Jacksonian Politics in the Greenville-Pendleton Congressional District" (master's thesis, University of North Carolina at Chapel Hill, 1992), 1–6, 34–40; A. Leah Underhill, *The Missing Link in Modern Spiritualism* (1885; reprint, New York: Arno Press, 1976), 362–3; entry for 14 October 1845, Diary, James K. Polk Papers, LC; Edmonds and Dexter, *Spiritualism*, 48 (quotation); Delp, "Southern Press," 90.

ship sugar and molasses directly from his plantation by steamboat down Oyster Creek to the Gulf of Mexico.[64]

Delighted with the government funding, he sought the contract to make the creek navigable. To accomplish that particular internal improvement, Hamilton required additional slave labor. With his credit in New Orleans and South Carolina tapped out, he turned to a New York mercantile firm. Hamilton requested that J. H. Brower and Company, which handled Retrieve's accounts, advance him $7,500 to buy a gang of ten slaves evenly divided between men and women. He intended to use the men in the Oyster Creek project, while putting the women to work in Retrieve's cane fields (these female laborers, he declared, would add $20,000 to the plantation's value). The New York firm agreed to give Hamilton $6,000, provided he come up with the additional $1,500.[65]

Hamilton's search for the necessary money led him to the familiar halls of Congress, which was considering a bill to provide payments to the surviving Revolutionary War officers and their children. Back in 1780, Congress had promised half pay for life to officers who remained in the Continental Army through the end of war. Later Congress voted to give them interest-bearing securities instead. Circumstances had forced many veterans to sell their certificates for well below face value so that they never received the full benefit Congress intended. Now a bill proposed providing pensions to those officers and their children.[66]

Hamilton began lobbying for the bill so that he might, in essence, cash in his dead father's Revolutionary legacy. Although the House passed the bill during the summer of 1856, the Senate essentially killed it by postponing further consideration until the next Congress. Afterward, his New York merchant partners, who had already paid for the slaves in full, demanded that Hamilton "provide us the $1500 which, from your assurances, we so confidently expected from Washington."[67]

64. James L. Smith, "The Lake Jackson Slave Ditch or The Hamilton-Jackson Canal," *Sherd News* (newsletter of the Brazosport Archaeological Society, Lake Jackson, Texas) (March 1999), 1–5.

65. JH to John H. Brower, n.d. [late 1856] (microfilm); J. H. Brower & Company to JH, 29 January 1857 (microfilm) and 12 February 1857, all in JHP, SHC.

66. *Cong. Globe*, 34th Cong., 3rd sess. (1856), 117–8.

67. *Cong. Globe*, 34th Cong., 1st sess. (1856), 1839; JH to Clement C. Clay, 21 [11?] January 1856 [sic; the actual year was 1857], Clement C. Clay Papers, Duke; *Cong. Globe*, 34th Cong., 3rd sess. (1857), 347; and J. H. Brower & Company to JH, 29 January 1857 (microfilm), JHP, SHC (quotation).

Denied proceeds from his father's Revolutionary pension, Hamilton spent the summer of 1857 searching New York, Philadelphia, and Washington for other money-making opportunities. It was an inopportune time, given the financial panic. Still, he convinced his old clients, the trustees of the defunct Bank of the United States, to pay him a commission of $22,000—"far better than a dozen Tickets in the Havanna Lottery"—if he succeeded in settling some of their Texas claims. In July, the trustees advanced their longtime attorney $500, which allowed him to send his daughter some promised funds.[68]

For the most part, though, events that summer wore heavily on the seventy-one-year-old man. Wearying travel in unusually hot weather took its toll, but family concerns burdened him even more. In June, his thirty-five-year-old son Oliver died of a pulmonary disorder. Olly, who had served his father faithfully for years as an overseer on various Hamilton properties, had traveled to Red Sulphur Springs in Virginia in a futile attempt to regain his health. This latest loss in his family—in the previous two years he had also buried sons Lewis and William—brought James Hamilton's own mortality forcefully to his mind. He also now more highly valued his remaining living relatives and especially recognized how much he missed his wife. "If I am alive & well," he wrote Elizabeth from Washington, "nothing shall prevent my embarking, for I am intensely anxious to return home & to your embrace." "I feel greater anxiety to be at home with you than I have ever felt before," he confessed a week later, and "ardently . . . wish to be again by your side."[69]

"I will indulge in no gloomy forebodings," Hamilton assured his wife later that summer, "but trust in God I may live to struggle on and ultimately triumph in my efforts to improve the condition of you & ours & that I may somewhere live to be the prop, stay & comfort of your declining years." Precisely where he would live and how he would support Elizabeth the old general could not say with any certainty. That summer he mulled over two possibilities. First, he sensed a political opportunity. In May, the death of A. P. Butler created an open U.S. Senate seat from South Carolina. With a poor sense of political reality, Hamilton imagined he might receive an appointment from Governor Robert F. W. All-

68. JH to Elizabeth Hamilton, 12 (quotation) and 20 July 1857 (microfilm), JHP, SHC.

69. JH to Pierce Butler, 9 July 1857, Wister Family Papers, Butler Section, HSP; Hamilton genealogical papers (box 3, folder 24), JHP, SHC; JH to Elizabeth Hamilton, 12 July (first quotation) and 19 July (second quotation) 1857, JHP, SHC (microfilm).

ston. "I have not heard from the Gov yet," he wrote his wife from Washington in July. "If I move I mean to do justice to myself & have no child's play about it." With Congress out of session, however, the governor decided to leave the choice to the next legislature. Hamilton would have to wait until the fall for a decision.[70]

Hamilton's second option was to quit South Carolina and, indeed, the South, for good. Leaving his home state would be a momentous decision, but one that long years of political disagreements with Carolina's leaders made understandable. "If I am candidate & am rejected I shall regard it as conclusive that SoC does not want me within her limits," he told Elizabeth. Hamilton would sell his wife's South Carolina rice fields and move her slaves to Texas. As soon as he could "secure an income to you of $4000 clear," he promised her, "we will move to Philadelphia . . . [to] pass the evening of our life." He proposed bringing their youngest child, twenty-six-year-old Harry, with them, and Hamilton would prevail upon his influential friends in the city to set the young man up in business.[71]

As Hamilton turned these plans over in his mind upon his return to Bluffton, he received encouraging word from Hamilton Bee. Elected Speaker of the Texas House the previous year, Bee suggested that the legislature might finally be willing to pay off some of his remaining claims against the state. Bee urged his old family friend to come to Austin that fall and once again plead his case. Hamilton decided to give it one last try.

Hamilton informed his old boss, ex-Texas president Lamar, that the trip would be "my last pilgrimage to the Shrine of the public faith of Texas." If the legislature failed to satisfy his claims on this occasion, Hamilton declared, "I shall submit without a murmur. . . [and] leave off my vocation for the last ten years as Beggar & like Cincinnatus" would endeavor "'to be nobly Poor.'" He requested that Lamar compose a summary of the diplomatic services Hamilton had rendered to the old Republic and publish it to coincide with his arrival in Texas. Later he expressed reservations about Lamar's writing such a piece "as it might look like an affair got up by preconcert." Still, Hamilton provided the former president with information to refresh his memory should he de-

70. JH to Elizabeth Hamilton, 11 August (first quotation) and 12 July (second quotation) 1857, JHP, SHC (microfilm).

71. JH to Elizabeth Hamilton, 12 July 1857, JHP, SHC (microfilm).

cide to do it anyway. Hamilton ended his résumé of Texas service with a reminder that ever since being fired by Sam Houston, "I have been a Petitioner to the Legislature for a justice yet denied with fortunes greatly impaired but a spirit unsubdued."[72]

Hamilton left Bluffton for Texas in late October 1857. He traveled by rail and stagecoach from the lowcountry to Montgomery, then steamed down the Alabama River to Mobile. While on the river, he composed a long letter to the South Carolina legislature laying out the case for his election to the Senate. The issue on which he pinned his candidacy was not the sectional struggle over Bleeding Kansas, with which Butler had been identified. Hamilton mentioned that matter only in passing. Instead, harking back to the political question that had brought him the greatest fame, he proposed to destroy the federal tariff once and for all. Direct taxation, he argued, would more fairly raise revenue and also spur direct trade between the South and Europe. If the North rejected these attempts, then the South should secede. But he played down that eventuality.[73]

Implying that his election would be the key to saving the Union, he shared a story of the last days of the revered Calhoun. Hamilton claimed that on his deathbed Calhoun had urged him to " 'return to the public service of our State, to carry out my principles and unfinished labor. A great crisis will come when her interests and your reputation will demand it.' " Now that crisis had arrived, Hamilton believed, and he called upon Calhoun to hallow his cause.

> August Spirit, at the foot of the throne of the Almighty! Look down from that footstool, where you look undazzled at the glories of your God, and bless the State which in life you served with so much honor. Look down, too, with tenderness on your weak, humble and suffering friend, who believes the crisis has come when he might obey your high commands. He comes ready to peril all of life and honor on the issue, if others will it so. Mighty Spirit! all hail and farewell!

Neglecting to mention his more recent visits with the "august spirit" of Calhoun, Hamilton instead apologized for the "exhibition of vanity

72. JH to Mirabeau Buonaparte Lamar, 4 September and 5 October 1857, *Lamar Papers*, ed. Gulick et al., 4:51, 55–7 (in part 2).

73. Hamilton's letter is printed in *Charleston Mercury*, 24 November 1857, from which quotations referred to below are taken. See also JH to Elizabeth Hamilton, 13 November 1857, JHP, SHC (microfilm).

and self-love" involved in retelling this story. Then the former governor and leader of nullification ended his appeal by acknowledging just how unfamiliar he must be to the state's comparatively young legislators. Indeed, he reckoned they "knew more of the heroes of the Trojan war than of the men of 1832" who had battled Old Hickory and the tariff.

The letter was a marvelously self-indulgent bid for recognition from a state that wished to forget him. Even as he wrote it, Hamilton admitted the "utter hopelessness" of his obtaining the Senate seat. Yet he put his case before the legislature to show that, even with all of his troubles and despite the hostility of so many fellow Carolinians, he stood ready to serve in an office he deserved.[74]

After finishing the letter, he continued down the Alabama River on a journey that was proving too much of a strain. In the nearly two decades since his first trip to Texas, he had traveled this route many times—more than he could count—but something was different on this occasion. The effects of the "debility of old age" and the sense of foreboding he had experienced during the summer returned. "I have scarcely courage to go on," he wrote Elizabeth when he reached Mobile, "& wish to the eternal God who made me [that] circumstance willed me to return." In New Orleans, old friends lifted his spirits with a warm welcome. As he prepared to board a steamer for Galveston, however, melancholy again overcame him. "I have never felt so homesick in my life," he confided to his wife. "God send me courage & you Resolution."[75]

He boarded the steamer *Opelousas* on Saturday morning, November 14, and soon the boat began chugging down the river on its way to the Gulf. He knew the routine. In thirty-six hours or so, they would dock at Galveston. Then would follow a fatiguing overland journey to the capital city lasting at least a day. As he drifted off to sleep that night aboard the *Opelousas*, Hamilton no doubt hoped that the reward awaiting him in Austin would make this troublesome trip worthwhile.

Just after midnight a deafening crash aroused Hamilton from his slumber. As he emerged from his cabin, confusion reigned. Passengers ran to and fro amid a ghostly cloud of steam, from which issued shrieks of terror. Water rapidly rose inside the boat. Although none of the fran-

74. JH to Elizabeth Hamilton, 13 November 1857, JHP, SHC (microfilm) (quotation).

75. JH to Elizabeth Hamilton, 19 July (first quotation), 11 November (second quotation), and 13 November 1857 (last quotation), JHP, SHC (microfilm).

tic passengers knew it then, another ship, the *Galveston*, had rammed the *Opelousas* and cut it nearly in two.[76]

Hamilton made his way to the deck and obtained a life jacket. His arm apparently injured during the accident, he struggled unsuccessfully to strap it on. Seeking assistance from panic-stricken passengers, Hamilton encountered a young mother with her infant child. To the elderly man's plea for help, the young woman replied only that she had no means of saving herself or her baby. The old general, whom Harriet Martineau had considered the model of a southern gentleman, then surrendered his jacket to the woman. With that act of gallantry, he disappeared to fend for himself on a sinking ship in the dark of night.

Several hours later and six hundred miles to the east, as dawn broke over the rice fields of lowcountry Carolina, Elizabeth Hamilton awoke. The day was special, the forty-fourth anniversary of her wedding, yet as on so many occasions during her marriage to James, she greeted the new day alone. For years, politics, business, and financial difficulties had kept her husband away from her. Now she could only hope that James would shortly send word of success in his heretofore fruitless efforts to obtain full payment from the Texas legislature. Then, perhaps, the two of them would find a nice house in Philadelphia and finally settle down for their remaining years as a couple. Her hopes, however, like her husband's on that dark Gulf night, proved in vain.

76. *Charleston Mercury*, 24 November 1857.

The Legatee's Legacy

SOUTH CAROLINA NEVER GRANTED Alfred Huger's wish. Despite his pleas to William Preston and Preston's brother John, a state senator, the home state of his old friend, James Hamilton, failed to mourn the death of the former governor in any official way. No resolutions honoring Hamilton passed the legislature, nor did Governor Robert F. W. Allston issue a proclamation remembering his service to the state.

A few Carolinians, including Huger himself and the ever-loyal friend James Petigru, paid calls on Hamilton's widow. Others sent letters of condolence. In one note of sympathy, William Preston assured Elizabeth Hamilton that a "very wide circle of affectionate and admiring friends will pour forth its sorrow in the death of General Hamilton your illustrious husband." But the outpouring was not as great as Elizabeth thought it should be, nor did she draw much comfort from the well-wishers. Although she appreciated Preston's attempt at kindness, she told him that his words amounted to too little, too late. Preston, she noted, "loved and admired" her husband "only in the height of his popularity & in the dazzling success of his career." If Preston and others had only tendered "some of these encouraging proofs of recollection & just admiration" in her husband's later years when "disappointments, mortifications & neglect surrounded him," then his final days might have been easier.[1]

The disappointments as well as the successes James Hamilton experienced during his adult life sprang from his efforts to live up to his Revolutionary heritage on a public stage. He re-interpreted that heritage over

1. James L. Petigru to Robert F. W. Allston, 30 January 1858, Allston Papers, SCHS; and William C. Preston to Elizabeth Hamilton, 5 December 1857 (first quotation), and Elizabeth Hamilton to [William C. Preston], 22 January 1858 (second quotation), JHP, SHC (microfilm).

time; it appeared in different guises. Whether a neo-Federalist Republican, the chief Nullifier, or a Texas diplomat, he perceived himself as the living political legacy of his Lynch and Hamilton forebears as well as of his Moultrie step-grandfather. He also sought to build a grander version of the Lynch barony. Indeed, Hamilton displayed economic ambitions on a truly imperial scale. He would be a great planter—of rice, cotton, *and* sugar. He would outdo the accomplishments of the Lynches and his own father by taking over the middleman functions of banker and merchant. The southern economy, however, could not provide the sort of return needed to finance his dreams of personal empire, especially following the 1837 panic. Debt latched onto him and would not let go. To rid himself of debt so that he could proudly present himself to the world as the heir of great Carolina planter-politicians, Hamilton was, paradoxically, willing to alienate his closest allies and even, by the late 1850s, to take his Revolutionary birthright in cold, hard cash.

The difficulties Hamilton experienced over his final twenty years embarrassed his planter friends as the rantings of an odd relative might disturb members of a family. To many of his contemporaries, Hamilton became a pathetic figure as his very public problems and his search for funds to relieve them apparently affected his political views and basic judgment. How could southerners claim moral superiority in the intensifying sectional crisis of the 1840s and 1850s when the man they once looked to as the very soul of southern chivalry behaved no better than the average money-grubbing Yankee?

More troubling still, Hamilton's example reminded his fellow planters that their world of wealth and honor rested precariously on the vagaries of an international commodities market they could little influence, let alone control. The truth was sobering: the market had made the planters, and it could also unmake them. When a debt-ridden planter looked into a fancy French mirror he could ill afford, perhaps he saw a bit too much of the latter-day James Hamilton staring back. By ignoring the reflected image, by forgetting Hamilton, perhaps that planter could hold off, at least in his own mind, his personal day of reckoning. More land and more slaves could always solve his problem.

Even though honor-obsessed Carolinians shied away from public laments for Hamilton, others did remember him. Texas paid homage to its onetime minister plenipotentiary soon after the sinking of the *Opelousas*. Both the state's legislature and its supreme court, presided over by a former Carolina Nullifier, interrupted their official proceedings to memorialize him with fine oratory. The following year, Texas even named a county for him in a region he had hoped to develop. Still, the state never paid Hamilton's family the tribute he had most desperately sought on his final voyage to the Lone Star State.[2]

Hamilton's creditors also could not forget him. The lawsuits regarding his tangled debts continued after his death. One case stemming from Mary Martha McRa's claims wound through federal courts and ended up before the United States Supreme Court. In a complex decision, the justices disappointed the guardian of the legally insane woman by ruling that she did not have priority over other Hamilton creditors. Whether a contrary decision would have made a difference is unclear. After all, some of the creditors at the time of the 1863 decision were Confederate citizens who refused to accept the Court's jurisdiction.[3]

Certainly members of his family remembered him and bore his legacy after his death. Several of his sons and grandsons perpetuated the family military tradition in the Confederate army. But they also continued to work the Texas plantation Hamilton had considered his best hope to retrieve his fortunes. During the Civil War, Lynch Hamilton ran Retrieve, which he somehow saved from the auction block. Under Lynch, the plantation provided sugar, molasses, pork, and slaves as taxes-in-kind for the Confederate cause. After the war, Harry relocated from Georgia to help his brother realize their father's dreams on the Texas coast. But neither man ever generated the riches from Retrieve that so long had eluded the elder Hamilton. In 1877, an embittered Harry reported problems with the sugar crop that his father would have found familiar as well as difficulties with worm-eaten cotton and unruly convict laborers hired to replace the slaves. All things considered, this youngest surviving Hamilton son cursed the day eleven years before he had left Savannah for Texas. Eventually, the Hamiltons gave up on Retrieve, which by the early twentieth century became, appropriately enough for a place developed by forced labor, a state prison farm. Inmates called Retrieve "Burnin'

2. *Obituary Addresses on the Occasion of the Death of Gen. James Hamilton, of South Carolina, Delivered in the Supreme Court, Senate and House of Representatives of the State of Texas* (Austin: John Marshall, 1857), JHP, SHC; and "Hamilton County" in *New Handbook of Texas*, ed. Tyler, 3:431.

3. See *Spain v. Hamilton's Administrator*, in *Cases Argued in the Supreme Court, 1863*, by Wallace, 1:604–27.

Hell," an appellation that members of the Hamilton family might have easily applied to the plantation.[4]

Just as the Hamilton heirs tried to make a success, finally, of Retrieve, they also sought to bring closure to other items of their father's unfinished business. In the 1880s, Lynch offered an attorney half of any Texas lands to which he might prove the family had a legitimate claim. Then in the 1920s, some seventy years after James Hamilton's death, one of his grandsons contemplated a lawsuit to squeeze from the state of Texas the money the old diplomat himself never could. There is no record of success in either case.[5]

Other Hamiltons decided to honor James by telling his story to a wide audience. Samuel Prioleau Hamilton, one of Hamilton's Confederate-soldier sons, devoted over a decade to writing a biography of his father. He gathered information, composed multiple drafts, and solicited subscriptions for the intended volume. He even, it seems, interested a major publisher in the project. Yet he never completed the work. Another Hamilton descendant also tried his hand at writing a biography of the planter-politician. Joseph Gregoire de Roulhac Hamilton, grandson of Hamilton's son Dan, could perhaps claim better credentials for doing the job than his great-uncle Prioleau. A professional historian at the University of North Carolina, Roulhac Hamilton established Chapel Hill's Southern Historical Collection. At the Southern, he gathered letters, newspaper clippings, and other materials related to his great-grandfather, from which he made meticulous notes. To learn about his famous relative's activities, he also corresponded with family members and with other historians, especially Yates Snowden of the University of South Carolina. He worked on the project, off and on, for at least twenty-two years. Yet, despite all that effort, he never published a book or an article about James Hamilton. His efforts produced only a short

4. Daniel Heyward Hamilton to Elizabeth Hamilton, 30 November 1861 and 13 October 1862, and extract of special orders from Adjutant and Inspector General's Office, 20 March 1865, JHP, SHC; see receipt for payment to the First Battalion Cavalry, Texas State Troops, dated 24 December 1863, and also a receipt for two Negro men for use by the Confederate States government, dated 10 December 1864, JHP, SHC; Henry Cruger Hamilton to Daniel Heyward Hamilton, Jr., 11 March 1877, JHP, SHC; and "Retrieve Plantation," in *New Handbook of Texas*, ed. Tyler, 5:551–2.

5. Contract of Thomas Lynch Hamilton with Branch T. Masterson 22 July 1881; and Herman T. Hamilton to Joseph Gregoire deRoulhac Hamilton, 5 November 1927, JHP, SHC.

typewritten manuscript now stuffed in a manila file folder in the archive he founded.[6]

Perhaps the Hamilton historians, both amateur and professional, discovered that James Hamilton was not quite the man they had hoped. The financial indiscretions that landed him so deeply in debt, for instance, could not have been welcome news to a son seeking to defend his father's honor. Nor did stories of Hamilton's diversion of funds from a Virginia canal company and from a legally insane woman to his own uses provide a usable past for so strident a critic of Reconstruction corruption as Professor Hamilton. Prioleau and Roulhac Hamilton perhaps came to see James Hamilton as many South Carolinians did in 1857, that embarrassing relative who reminds us of our own flaws.[7]

6. See handwritten drafts of Samuel Prioleau Hamilton's biography of his father on microfilm in JHP, SHC. See also Pat Calhoun to S. P. Hamilton, 29 May 1897, and 1897 subscription lists for the intended book, JHP, SHC. Joseph Gregoire de Roulhac Hamilton's correspondence regarding a biography about his great-grandfather spans from 1907 to 1929 at least. The resulting manuscript is "Among the Present: James Hamilton, Jr., of South Carolina," box 3, folder 35, JHP, SHC.

7. A doctoral student of William Dunning at Columbia University, Roulhac Hamilton contributed to the negative interpretation of Reconstruction associated with the "Dunning School." See, for instance, Joseph Gregoire de Roulhac Hamilton, *Reconstruction in North Carolina* (New York: Columbia University, 1914).

Bibliography

Primary Sources

UNPUBLISHED PAPERS

Center for American History, University of Texas at Austin

William Pitt Ballinger Papers
Hamilton Prioleau Bee Papers
James Hamilton Papers
Madge Williams Hearne Collection
Joel Roberts Poinsett Papers
Thomas Jefferson Rusk Papers
Samuel Swartout Papers

Clemson University, Special Collections

John C. Calhoun Papers

Historical Society of Pennsylvania

Ferdinand Julius Dreer Papers
Simon Gratz Collection
Joel Roberts Poinsett Papers
Wister Family Papers, Butler Section

Library of Congress, Manuscript Division

Nicholas Biddle Papers
Thomas Corwin Papers
John Jordan Crittenden Papers
Franklin Harper Elmore Papers
Edward Frost Papers
James Henry Hammond Papers

Samuel Houston Papers
Andrew Jackson Papers
William L. Marcy Papers
Duncan McArthur Papers
Miscellaneous Manuscripts Collection
     William Campbell Preston Papers
     James Hamilton, Jr., Papers
     James Hamilton[, Sr.,] Papers
     Robert Young Hayne Papers
     Waddy Thompson, Jr., Papers
James Louis Petigru Papers
Franklin Pierce Papers
Joel Roberts Poinsett Papers
James K. Polk Papers
Andrew Stevenson Papers
John Tyler Papers
Martin Van Buren Papers

Perkins Library, Duke University

Armistead Burt Papers
Francis Porteus Corbin Papers
James Hamilton, Jr., Papers
Alfred Huger Letterpress Books
Hugh Swinton Legaré Papers
George McDuffie Papers
Richard Singleton Papers

South Carolina Historical Society

Robert F. W. Allston Papers
Chesnut-Miller-Manning Papers
Langdon Cheves I Papers
Lynch Papers
Mitchell-Pringle Collection

South Caroliniana Library, University of South Carolina

James Hamilton Papers
James Henry Hammond Papers
Robert Y. Hayne Papers
George McDuffie Papers
Stephen D. Miller Papers
Beaufort T. Watts Papers
Williams-Miller-Chesnut-Manning Papers

Southern Historical Collection, University of North Carolina

John McPherson Berrien Papers
Elliott-Gonzales Papers
Franklin Harper Elmore Papers
Thomas Jefferson Green Papers
John Berkley Grimball Diary
James Hamilton Papers
Thomas Butler King Papers
William Lowndes Papers
Benjamin F. Perry Papers
Phillips-Myers Papers
John Rutledge Papers

State Historical Society of Wisconsin

Nathaniel Pitcher Tallmadge Papers

Texas State Library and Archives Commission

Adjutant General, General Correspondence, Navy Papers
Albert T. Burnley Papers
Memucan Hunt Papers
Treasury Papers of the Republic

PUBLISHED PRIMARY SOURCES

Adams, Charles Francis, ed. *Memoirs of John Quincy Adams, Comprising Portions of His Diary from 1795 to 1848.* 12 vols. New York: AMS Press, 1970.
Bassett, John Spencer, ed. *Correspondence of Andrew Jackson.* Vols. 3–6. Washington, D.C.: Carnegie Institution, 1931.
Binkley, William C., ed. *Official Correspondence of the Texas Revolution, 1835–1836.* Vol. 2. New York: D. Appleton-Century, 1936.
Carson, James Petigru, ed. *Life, Letters, and Speeches of James Louis Petigru: The Union Man of South Carolina.* Washington, D.C.: H. L. & J. B. McQueen, 1920.
Cutler, Wayne, ed. *Correspondence of James K. Polk.* Vol. 8. Knoxville: University of Tennessee Press, 1993.
Gulick, C. A., et al., eds. *The Papers of Mirabeau Buonaparte Lamar.* Vols. 1–5. Austin: Texas State Library, 1921–27.
Hopkins, James F., and Mary W. M. Hargreaves, eds. *The Papers of Henry Clay.* 10 volumes. Lexington: University of Kentucky Press, 1959–91.
Moser, Harold D., Daniel R. Hoth, and George H. Hoemann, eds. *The Papers of Andrew Jackson.* Vol. 5, *1821–1824.* Knoxville: University of Tennessee Press, 1980.
Roberts, Madge Thornall. *The Personal Correspondence of Sam Houston.* Vol. 1: *1839–1845.* Denton: University of North Texas Press, 1996.

Wallace, John William. *Cases Argued and Adjudged in the Supreme Court of the United States, December Term, 1863.* Vol. 1. Washington, D.C.: W. H. & O. H. Morrison, 1866.

Weaver, Herbert, ed. *Correspondence of James K. Polk.* Vol. 1. Nashville: Vanderbilt University Press, 1969.

Williams, Amelia W., and Eugene C. Barker, eds. *The Writings of Sam Houston, 1813–1863.* 8 vols. Austin: University of Texas Press, 1938–43.

Wilson, Clyde N., ed. *The Papers of John C. Calhoun.* Vols. 10–14. Columbia, S.C.: University of South Carolina Press, 1977–81.

Wiltse, Charles M., and Harold D. Moser, eds. *The Papers of Daniel Webster.* 14 vols. in 4 series plus general index. Hanover: University Press of New England, 1974–89.

Wright, Louis B., and Marion Tinling. *Quebec to Carolina in 1785–1786, Being the Travel Diary and Observations of Robert Hunter, Jr., a Young Merchant of London.* San Marino, Ca.: Huntington Library, 1943.

NEWSPAPERS AND PERIODICALS

Austin (Texas) City Gazette (1839–42)
Austin (Texas) Texas State Gazette (1850–56)
Austin (Texas) Western Advocate (1843–44)
Charleston Courier (1811–50)
Charleston Mercury (1822–57)
Clarksville (Texas) Northern Standard (1850)
Columbia (S.C.) Telescope (1826–39)
DeBow's Review (1846)
Houston Telegraph and Texas Register (1838–42)
Marshall (Texas) Texas Republican (1850)
Niles' Register (1820–44)
Newport (R.I.) Mercury (1790–1805)
South Carolina Legislative Journals (1819–23, 1834–37)
Washington (D.C.) Republican (1850)

GOVERNMENT DOCUMENTS

Benton, Thomas Hart, ed. *Abridgment of the Debates of Congress.* 16 vols. New York: D. Appleton, 1857–61.

Garrison, George P., ed. *Diplomatic Correspondence of the Republic of Texas.* 3 vols. American Historical Association *Annual Report for the Years 1907, 1908.* Washington: Government Printing Office, 1907–08.

Jenkins, William Sumner, ed. *Records of the States of the United States of America: A Microfilm Compilation.* Washington: Library of Congress Photoduplication Service, 1949.

South Carolina. *Journals of the Conventions of the People of South Carolina, Held in 1832, 1833, and 1852*. Columbia: R.W. Gibbes, 1860.

United Kingdom. Public Record Office. Foreign Office 75 (Texas). Vols. 1–2 (1840–41). Microfilm, Library of Congress.

United States. Congress. *Annals of the Congress of the United States*. Vols. 30–42. Washington: Gales and Seaton, 1817–24.

———. *The Congressional Globe*. Vols. 19–26. Washington: Blair and Rives, 1850–57.

———. *Register of the Debates in Congress*. Vols. 2–4. Washington: Gales and Seaton, 1827–28.

Winkler, Ernest William, ed. *Secret Journals of the Senate, Republic of Texas, 1836–1845*. Austin: Austin Printing Company, 1911.

SPEECHES AND PAMPHLETS

Hamilton, James. *An Eulogium of the Public Services and Character of Robert J. Turnbull, Esq. Delivered in St. Philip's Church, Charleston, on the 22d day of November, 1833, After the Laying of the Corner-Stone of the Monument Erected by the State Rights' Party to His Memory*. Charleston: A. E. Miller, 1834.

National and State Rights, Considered by the Hon. George McDuffie, Under the Signature of One of the People in Reply to the 'Trio,' with the advertisement prefixed to it, Generally Attributed to Major James Hamilton, Jr. when published in 1821. Charleston: W. S. Blain, 1830.

Secondary Sources

BOOKS, ESSAYS, THESES, AND DISSERTATIONS

Adams, Ephraim Douglass. *British Interests and Activities in Texas, 1838–1846*. Gloucester, Mass.: Peter Smith, 1963.

Adams, Henry. *John Randolph*. 1882. Reprint, New York: Fawcett Publications, 1961.

Adburgham, Alison. *Silver Fork Society: Fashionable Life and Literature from 1814 to 1840*. London: Constable, 1983.

Ames, Herman V., ed. *State Documents on Federal Relations: The States and the United States*. Vols. 1–6. Philadelphia: Department of History, University of Pennsylvania, 1900.

Ashworth, John. *"Agrarians" and "Aristocrats": Party Political Ideology in the United States, 1837–1846*. London: Royal Historical Society, 1983.

———. *Slavery, Capitalism, and Politics in the Antebellum Republic*. Vol. 1, *Commerce and Compromise, 1820–1850*. New York: Cambridge University Press, 1995.

Bailey, N. Louise, ed. *Biographical Directory of the South Carolina House of Representatives*. Vol. 4. Columbia: University of South Carolina Press, 1984.

Bailey, N. Louise, Mary L. Morgan, and Carolyn R. Taylor. *Biographical Directory of the South Carolina Senate, 1776–1985*. Vol. 2. Columbia: University of South Carolina Press, 1986.

Banner, James M., Jr. "The Problem of South Carolina." In *The Hofstadter Aegis: A Memorial*, edited by Stanley Elkins and Eric McKitrick, 60–93. New York: Alfred A. Knopf, 1974.

Barker, Nancy Nichols, trans. and ed. *The French Legation in Texas*. Vol. 1, *Recognition, Rupture, and Reconciliation*. Austin: Texas State Historical Association, 1971.

Bemis, Samuel Flagg. *John Quincy Adams and the Union*. New York: Alfred A. Knopf, 1956.

Biographical Directory of the American Congress, 1774–1971. Washington, D.C.: U.S. Government Printing Office, 1971.

Bleser, Carol, ed. *Secret and Sacred: The Diaries of James Henry Hammond, a Southern Slaveholder*. New York: Oxford University Press, 1988.

Bourne, Kenneth. *Palmerston: The Early Years, 1784–1841*. New York: Macmillan, 1982.

Brandon, Edgar Ewing. *A Pilgrimage of Liberty: A Contemporary Account of the Triumphal Tour of General Lafayette through the Southern and Western States in 1825, as Reported by the Local Newspapers*. Athens, Ohio: Lawhead Press, 1944.

Brant, Irving. *James Madison: Commander in Chief, 1812–1836*. Indianapolis: Bobbs-Merrill, 1961.

Bridenbaugh, Carl, and Jessica Bridenbaugh. *Rebels and Gentlemen: Philadelphia in the Age of Franklin*. New York: Oxford University Press, 1965.

Brock, William R. *Parties and Political Conscience: American Dilemmas, 1840–1850*. Millwood, N.Y.: KTO Press, 1979.

Broussard, James H. *The Southern Federalists, 1800–1816*. Baton Rouge: Louisiana State University Press, 1978.

Calhoun, Richard J., ed. *Witness to Sorrow: The Antebellum Autobiography of William J. Grayson*. Columbia: University of South Carolina Press, 1990.

Campbell, Randolph B. *An Empire for Slavery: The Peculiar Institution in Texas, 1821–1865*. Baton Rouge: Louisiana State University Press, 1989.

Chamberlain, Muriel E. *British Foreign Policy in the Age of Palmerston*. London: Longman Group, 1980.

———. *Lord Aberdeen: A Political Biography*. New York: Longman, 1983.

———. *Lord Palmerston*. Cardiff: GPC Books, 1987.

Channing, George Gibbs. *Early Recollections of Newport, R.I., from the Year 1793 to 1811*. Newport: A. J. Ward; Charles E. Hammett, Jr., and Boston: Nichols and Noyes, 1868.

Chaplin, Joyce E. *An Anxious Pursuit: Agricultural Innovation and Modernity in the Lower South, 1730–1815*. Chapel Hill: University of North Carolina Press, 1993.

Chase, Mary Katherine. *Negociations de la Republique du Texas en Europe, 1837–1845*. Paris: Librairie Ancienne Honore Champion, 1932.

Coclanis, Peter A. *The Shadow of a Dream: Economic Life and Death in the South Carolina Lowcountry, 1670–1920*. New York: Oxford University Press, 1989.

Cole, Arthur C. *The Whig Party in the South.* Washington, D.C.: American Historical Association, 1914.

Cole, Donald B. *Martin Van Buren and the American Political System.* Princeton: Princeton University Press, 1984.

Connor, Seymour V. *Adventure in Glory: The Saga of Texas, 1836–1849.* Austin: Steck-Vaughn, 1965.

Cooke, George Willis. *A History of The Clapboard Trees or Third Parish, Dedham, Mass., Now the Unitarian Parish, West Dedham, 1736–1886.* Boston: Geo. H. Ellis, 1887.

Cooper, William J., Jr. *The South and the Politics of Slavery, 1828–1856.* Baton Rouge: Louisiana State University Press, 1978.

Crane, Elaine Forman. *A Dependent People: Newport, Rhode Island, in the Revolutionary Era.* New York: Fordham University Press, 1985.

Crane, Virginia Glenn. "The Lynches of South Carolina: Traditional Elite and the New Family History." In *The American Family: Historical Perspectives*, edited by Jean E. Hunter and Paul T. Mason. Pittsburgh: Duquesne University Press, 1991.

Crook, Cornelia English. *Henry Castro: A Study of Early Colonization in Texas.* San Antonio: St. Mary's University Press, 1988.

Dangerfield, George. *The Era of Good Feelings.* New York: Harcourt, Brace, 1952.

Dethloff, Henry C. *A History of the American Rice Industry, 1685–1985.* College Station: Texas A&M University Press, 1988.

Dillon, Richard. *We Have Met the Enemy: Oliver Hazard Perry: Wilderness Commodore.* New York: McGraw-Hill, 1978.

Dutton, Charles J. *Oliver Hazard Perry.* New York: Longmans, Green, 1935.

Edgar, Walter B., ed. *Biographical Directory of the South Carolina House of Representatives.* Vol. 1, *Session Lists, 1692–1973.* Columbia: University of South Carolina Press, 1974.

Edgar, Walter B., and N. Louise Bailey, eds. *Biographical Directory of the South Carolina House.* Vol. 2. Columbia: University of South Carolina Press, 1977.

Edmonds, John W. and George T. Dexter. *Spiritualism.* Vol. 1. New York: Partridge & Brittan, 1853.

Ellet, Elizabeth F. *Women of the American Revolution.* Vol. 2. Philadelphia: George W. Jacobs, 1900.

Ellis, Richard E. *The Union at Risk: Jacksonian Democracy, States' Rights, and the Nullification Crisis.* New York: Oxford University Press, 1987.

Fischer, David Hackett. *The Revolution of American Conservatism: The Federalist Party in the Era of Jeffersonian Democracy.* New York: Harper & Row, 1965.

Ford, Lacy K., Jr. *Origins of Southern Radicalism: The South Carolina Upcountry, 1800–1860.* New York: Oxford University Press, 1988.

Fornell, Earl Wesley. *The Unhappy Medium: Spiritualism and the Life of Margaret Fox.* Austin: University of Texas Press, 1964.

Fox-Genovese, Elizabeth, and Eugene Genovese. *Fruits of Merchant Capital: Slavery and Bourgeois Property in the Rise and Expansion of Capitalism.* New York: Oxford University Press, 1983.

Frantz, Joe B. *Texas: A Bicentennial History.* New York: W. W. Norton, 1976.

Freehling, William W. *Prelude to Civil War: The Nullification Controversy in South Carolina, 1816–1836.* New York: Harper & Row, 1965.

———. *The Reintegration of American History.* New York: Oxford University Press, 1994.

———. *The Road to Disunion: Secessionists at Bay, 1776–1854.* New York: Oxford University Press, 1990.

———, ed. *The Nullification Era: A Documentary Record.* New York: Harper & Row, 1967.

Freidel, Frank. *Francis Lieber: Nineteenth-Century Liberal.* Baton Rouge: Louisiana State University Press, 1947.

Gaillardet, Frederic. *Sketches of Early Texas and Louisiana.* Translated and edited by James L. Shepherd III. Austin: University of Texas Press, 1966.

Gambrell, Herbert. *Anson Jones: The Last President of Texas.* 2nd ed. Austin: University of Texas Press, 1964.

Garden, Alexander. *Anecdotes of the Revolutionary War in America, with Sketches of Character of Persons the Most Distinguished, in the Southern States, For Civil and Military Purposes.* 1822. Reprint, Spartanburg: Reprint Company, 1972.

Garland, Hugh A. *The Life of John Randolph of Roanoke.* 2 vols. New York: D. Appleton, 1851.

Germany, George Patrick. "The South Carolina Governing Elite, 1820–1860." Ph.D. diss., University of California, Berkeley, 1972.

Glenn, Virginia Louise. "James Hamilton, Jr. of South Carolina: A Biography." Ph.D. dissertation, University of North Carolina, Chapel Hill, 1964. Note: This author also appears in this bibliography as Virginia Glenn Crane.

Godbold, E. Stanly, and Robert H. Woody. *Christopher Gadsden and the American Revolution.* Knoxville: University of Tennessee Press, 1982.

Green, Constance McLaughlin. *Washington: Village and Capital, 1800–1878.* Princeton: Princeton University Press, 1962.

Green, Edwin L. *George McDuffie.* Columbia, S.C.: State Company, 1936.

Goldfard, Russell M., and Clare R. *Spiritualism and Nineteenth-Century Letters.* Rutherford, N.J.: Fairleigh Dickinson University Press, 1978.

Goldman, Perry M., and James S. Young. *The United States Congressional Directories, 1789–1840.* New York: Columbia University Press, 1973.

Govan, Thomas Payne. *Nicholas Biddle: Nationalist and Public Banker, 1786–1844.* Chicago: University of Chicago Press, 1959.

Greb, Gregory Allen. "Charleston, South Carolina, Merchants, 1815–1860: Urban Leadership in the Antebellum South." Ph.D. diss., University of California, San Diego, 1978.

Green, Constance McLaughlin. *Washington: Village and Capital, 1800–1878*. Vol. 1. Princeton: Princeton University Press, 1962.

Greenberg, Kenneth S. *Honor and Slavery: Lies, Duels, Noses, Masks, Dressing as a Woman, Gifts, Strangers, Humanitarianism, Death, Slave Rebellions, the Proslavery Argument, Baseball, Hunting, and Gambling in the Old South*. Princeton: Princeton University Press, 1996.

———. *Masters and Statesmen: The Political Culture of American Slavery*. Baltimore: Johns Hopkins University Press, 1985.

Hamilton, James A. *Reminiscences of James A. Hamilton or, Men and Events, at Home and Abroad, During Three Quarters of a Century*. New York: Charles Scribner, 1869.

Hammond, Bray. *Banks and Politics in America from the Revolution to the Civil War*. Princeton: Princeton University Press, 1957.

Hargreaves, Mary W. M. *The Presidency of John Quincy Adams*. Lawrence: University Press of Kansas, 1985.

Hartley, Cecil B. *Heroes and Patriots of the South*. Philadelphia: G. G. Evans, 1860.

Head, John M. *A Time to Rend: An Essay on the Decision for American Independence*. Madison: State Historical Society of Wisconsin, 1968.

Hogan, William Ransom. *The Texas Republic: A Social and Economic History*. Norman: University of Oklahoma Press, 1946.

Holman, Hamilton. *Prologue to Conflict: The Crisis and Compromise of 1850*. Lexington: University of Kentucky Press, 1964.

Holt, Michael F. "The Election of 1840, Voter Mobilization, and the Emergence of the Second American Party System: A Reappraisal of Jacksonian Voting Behavior." In *A Master's Due: Essays in Honor of David Herbert Donald*, edited by William J. Cooper, Jr., Michael F. Holt, and John McCardell, 16–58. Baton Rouge: Louisiana State University Press, 1985.

———. *The Rise and Fall of the American Whig Party: Jacksonian Politics and the Onset of the Civil War*. New York: Oxford University Press, 1999.

Howe, Daniel Walker. *The Political Culture of the American Whigs*. Chicago: University of Chicago Press, 1979.

Huff, Archie Vernon, Jr. *Langdon Cheves of South Carolina*. Columbia, S.C.: University of South Carolina Press, 1977.

Jenkins, John H., gen. ed. *The Papers of the Texas Revolution, 1835–1836*. Vol. 7. Austin: Presidial Press, 1973.

Jenkins, John H., and Kenneth Kesselus. *Edward Burleson: Texas Frontier Leader*. Austin: Jenkins, 1990.

Jervey, Theodore D. *Robert Y. Hayne and His Times*. New York: Macmillan, 1909.

Johnston, Henry P. *The Yorktown Campaign and the Surrender of Cornwallis, 1781*. New York: Harper & Brothers, 1881.

Jones, Anson. *Memoranda and Official Correspondence Relating to the Republic of Texas, Its History and Annexation, Including a Brief Autobiography of the Author*. 1859. Reprint, Chicago: Rio Grande Press, 1966.

Jones, Howard. *To the Webster-Ashburton Treaty: A Study in Anglo-American Relations, 1783–1843*. Chapel Hill: University of North Carolina Press, 1977.

Jones, Wilbur Devereux. *Lord Aberdeen and the Americas*. Athens: University of Georgia Press, 1958.

Joseph, George L., Jr. "The Champlins of Newport: A Commercial History." Ph.D. diss., University of Connecticut, 1977.

Kaplanoff, Mark Dementi. "Making the South Solid: Politics and the Structure of Society in South Carolina, 1790–1815." Ph.D. diss., Cambridge University, 1979.

Kell, Carl Lewis. "A Rhetorical History of James Hamilton, Jr.: The Nullification Era in South Carolina, 1816–1834." Ph.D. diss., University of Kansas, 1971.

Kett, Joseph F. *Rites of Passage: Adolescence in America, 1790 to the Present*. New York: Basic Books, 1977.

Kibler, Lillian Adele. *Benjamin F. Perry: South Carolina Unionist*. Durham: Duke University Press, 1936.

Killens, John Oliver. *The Trial Record of Denmark Vesey*. Boston: Beacon Press, 1970.

Klein, Rachel N. *Unification of a Slave State: The Rise of the Planter Class in the South Carolina Backcountry, 1760–1808*. Chapel Hill: University of North Carolina Press, 1990.

Latham, Francis S. *Travels in the Republic of Texas, 1842*. Edited by Gerald S. Pierce. Austin: Encino Press, 1971.

Lesesne, J. Mauldin. *The Bank of the State of South Carolina: A General and Political History*. Columbia: University of South Carolina Press, 1970.

Lindley, James G. *South Carolina National: The First 150 Years*. New York: Newcome Society of the United States, 1985.

Lockey, Joseph Byrne. *Pan-Americanism: Its Beginnings*. New York: Macmillan, 1920.

Lofton, John. *Denmark Vesey's Revolt: The Slave Plot That Lit a Fuse to Fort Sumter*. Kent, Ohio: Kent State University Press, 1983. Originally published as *Insurrection in South Carolina: The Turbulent World of Denmark Vesey*. Antioch Press, 1964.

Mackenzie, Alexander Slidell. *The Life of Commodore Oliver Hazard Perry*. New York: Harper & Brothers, 1840.

Maissin, Eugene. *The French in Mexico and Texas, 1838–1839*. Translated and with introduction and notes by James L. Shepherd III. Salado, Texas: Anson Jones Press, 1961.

Margetson, Stella. *Victorian High Society*. New York: Holmes & Meier, 1980.

McCurry, Stephanie. *Masters of Small Worlds: Yeoman Households, Gender Relations, and the Political Culture of the Antebellum South Carolina Low Country*. New York: Oxford University Press, 1995.

McFaul, John M. *The Politics of Jacksonian Finance*. Ithaca: Cornell University Press, 1972.

McLoughlin, William G. *Rhode Island: A Bicentennial History*. New York: W. W. Norton, 1978.

Miller, Edmund Thornton. *A Financial History of Texas*. Austin: University of Texas Press, 1916.

Miller, John C. *Crisis in Freedom: The Alien and Sedition Acts*. Boston: Little, Brown, 1951.

Moore, John Hammond. *South Carolina Newspapers*. Columbia: University of South Carolina Press, 1988.

Moore, Robert Laurence. *In Search of White Crows: Spiritualism, Parapsychology, and American Culture*. New York: Oxford University Press, 1977.

Morison, Samuel Eliot. *"Old Bruin": Commodore Matthew C. Perry, 1794–1858*. Boston: Little, Brown, 1967.

Muir, Andrew Forest, ed. *Texas in 1837: An Anonymous, Contemporary Narrative*. Austin: University of Texas Press, 1958.

Munroe, John A. *Louis McLane: Federalist and Jacksonian*. New Brunswick: Rutgers University Press, 1973.

Murray, Paul. *The Whig Party in Georgia, 1825–1853*. Chapel Hill: University of North Carolina Press, 1948.

Nackman, Mark E. *A Nation within a Nation: The Rise of Texas Nationalism*. Port Washington, N.Y.: Kennikat Press, 1975.

Nance, Joseph Milton. *After San Jacinto: The Texas-Mexican Frontier, 1836–1841*. Austin: University of Texas Press, 1963.

———. *Attack and Counter-Attack: The Texas-Mexican Frontier, 1842*. Austin: University of Texas Press, 1964.

Nelson, Paul David. *Anthony Wayne: Soldier of the Early Republic*. Bloomington: Indiana University Press, 1985.

Nielsen, George Raymond. "The Indispensable Institution: The Congressional Party during the Era of Good Feelings." Ph.D. diss., University of Iowa, 1968.

Niven, John. *John C. Calhoun and the Price of Union: A Biography*. Baton Rouge: Louisiana State University Press, 1988.

———. *Martin Van Buren and the Romantic Age of American Politics*. New York: Oxford University Press, 1983.

Norton, Diane Cook. "A Methodological Study of the South Carolina Political Elite of the 1830's." Ph.D. diss., University of Pennsylvania, 1972.

Pancake, John S. *This Destructive War: The British Campaign in the Carolinas, 1780–1782*. University, Ala.: University of Alabama Press, 1985.

Paul, James C. N. *Rift in the Democracy*. Philadelphia: University of Pennsylvania Press, 1951.

Pearsall, Ronald. *The Table-Rappers*. London: Michael Joseph, 1972.

Pease, Jane H., and William H. Pease. *James Louis Petigru: Southern Conservative, Southern Dissenter*. Athens: University of Georgia Press, 1995.

———. *The Web of Progress: Private Values and Public Styles in Boston and Charleston, 1828–1843*. New York: Oxford University Press, 1985.

Pegg, Herbert Dale. *The Whig Party in North Carolina*. Chapel Hill: Colonial Press, 1968.

Perry, Benjamin Franklin. *Reminiscences of Public Men.* Greenville, S.C.: Shannon, 1889.

Perry, Thomas Sergeant, ed. *The Life and Letters of Francis Lieber.* Boston: James R. Osgood, 1882.

Peterson, Merrill D. *The Great Triumvirate: Webster, Clay, and Calhoun.* New York: Oxford University Press, 1987.

———. *Olive Branch and Sword: The Compromise of 1833.* Baton Rouge: Louisiana State University Press, 1982.

Pierce, Madge Evalene. "The Service of James Hamilton to the Republic of Texas." Master's thesis, University of Texas, 1933.

Pletcher, David M. *The Diplomacy of Annexation: Texas, Oregon, and the Mexican War.* Columbia: University of Missouri Press, 1973.

Potter, David M. *The Impending Crisis, 1848–1861.* New York: Harper & Row, 1976.

Price, Thomas Stephen. "Palmettos and Property: Historical Memory and Political Culture in Early National South Carolina." Ph.D. diss., University of Illinois at Chicago, 1994.

Rakove, Jack N. *The Beginnings of National Politics: An Interpretive History of the Continental Congress.* New York: Alfred A. Knopf, 1979.

Ratliff, Lucile. "The Diplomatic Relations of Texas and Mexico, 1836–1846." Master's thesis, East Texas State Teachers College, 1939.

Ratner, Sidney. *The Tariff in American History.* New York: D. Van Nostrand, 1972.

Ravenel, Harriott Horry Rutledge. *The Life and Times of William Lowndes of South Carolina, 1782–1822.* Boston: Houghton, Mifflin, 1901.

Reichstein, Andreas V. *Rise of the Lone Star.* Translated by Jeanne R. Willson. College Station: Texas A&M University Press, 1989.

Remini, Robert V. *Andrew Jackson.* 1966. Reprint, New York: Harper & Row, 1969.

———. *Andrew Jackson and the Course of American Freedom, 1822–1832.* New York: Harper & Row, 1981.

———. *Daniel Webster: The Man and His Time.* New York: W.W. Norton, 1997.

———. *Henry Clay: Statesman for the Union.* New York: W. W. Norton, 1991.

———. *Martin Van Buren and the Making of the Democratic Party.* 1951. Reprint, New York: W. W. Norton, 1970.

Richardson, Edgar P. *Washington Allston: A Study of the Romantic Artist in America.* New York: Thomas Y. Crowell, 1948.

Ridley, Jasper. *Lord Palmerston.* London: Constable, 1970.

Rippy, J. Fred. *Joel Roberts Poinsett: Versatile American.* Durham: Duke University Press, 1935.

Risjord, Norman K. *The Old Republicans: Southern Conservatism in the Age of Jefferson.* New York: Columbia University Press, 1965.

Roberts, Madge Thornall, ed. *The Personal Correspondence of Sam Houston.* Vol. 1, *1839–1845.* Denton: University of North Texas Press, 1996.

Rogers, George C., Jr. *Evolution of a Federalist: William Loughton Smith of Charleston, 1758–1812.* Columbia: University of South Carolina Press, 1962.

Ryerson, Richard Alan. *The Revolution Is Now Begun: The Radical Committees of Philadelphia, 1765–1776*. Philadelphia: University of Pennsylvania Press, 1978.

Salley, Alexander S., Jr. *Narratives of Early Carolina, 1650–1708*. New York: Charles Scribner's Sons, 1911.

Salley, Alexander S., Jr., and R. Nicholas Olsberg, eds. *Warrants for Lands in South Carolina, 1672–1711*. Columbia: South Carolina Department of Archives and History, 1973.

Schlesinger, Arthur M., Jr., and Roger Bruns. *Congress Investigates: A Documentary History, 1792–1974*. Volume 1. New York: Chelsea House, 1975.

Schmitz, Joseph William. *Texan Statecraft, 1836–1845*. San Antonio: Naylor, 1941.

Schweikart, Larry. *Banking in the American South from the Age of Jackson to Reconstruction*. Baton Rouge: Louisiana State University Press, 1987.

Sellers, Charles. *The Market Revolution: Jacksonian America, 1815–1846*. New York: Oxford University Press, 1991.

Sharp, James Roger. *The Jacksonians versus the Banks: Politics in the States after the Panic of 1837*. New York: Columbia University Press, 1970.

Shore, Lawrence. *Southern Capitalists*. Chapel Hill: University of North Carolina Press, 1986.

Siegel, Stanley. *The Poet President of Texas: The Life of Mirabeau B. Lamar, President of the Republic of Texas*. Austin: Pemberton Press, 1977.

———. *A Political History of the Republic of the Texas Republic, 1836–1845*. Austin: University of Texas Press, 1956.

Silverthorne, Elizabeth. *Ashbel Smith of Texas: Pioneer, Patriot, Statesman, 1805–1886*. College Station: Texas A&M University Press, 1982.

Sinha, Manisha. "The Counter-Revolution of Slavery." Ph.D. diss., Columbia University, 1994.

Sitterson, J. Carlyle. *Sugar Country: The Sugar Cane Industry in the South, 1753–1950*. Lexington: University of Kentucky Press, 1953.

Smith, Alfred Glaze, Jr. *Economic Readjustment of an Old Cotton State: South Carolina, 1820–1860*. Columbia: University of South Carolina Press, 1958.

Smith, Justin H. *The Annexation of Texas*. New York: Barnes & Noble, 1941.

South, Stanley A. *The General, the Major, and the Angel: The Discovery of General William Moultrie's Grave*. Research Manuscript Series No. 146. Columbia: Institute of Archeology and Anthropology, University of South Carolina, 1979.

Stafford, Vernon C. "The Diplomatic Service of William Kennedy to Texas." Master's thesis, Texas Technological College, 1950.

Stanwood, Edward. *American Tariff Controversies in the Nineteenth Century*. 2 vols. Boston: Houghton, Mifflin, 1904.

Starobin, Robert S., ed. *Denmark Vesey: The Slave Conspiracy of 1822*. Englewood Cliffs, N.J.: Prentice-Hall, 1970.

Stegmaier, Mark J. *Texas, New Mexico, and the Compromise of 1850: Boundary Dispute and Sectional Crisis*. Kent: Kent State University Press, 1996.

Stille, Charles J. *Major-General Anthony Wayne and the Pennsylvania Line in the Continental Army.* 1893. Reprint, Port Washington, N.Y.: Kennikat Press, 1968.

Sydnor, Charles S. *The Development of Southern Sectionalism, 1819–1848.* Baton Rouge: Louisiana State University Press, 1948.

Taussig, F. W. *State Papers and Speeches on the Tariff.* Cambridge: Harvard University [Press], 1893.

Temin, Peter. *The Jacksonian Economy.* New York: W. W. Norton, 1969.

Thompson, Edgar T. *Plantation Societies, Race Relations, and the South: The Regimentation of Populations.* Durham: Duke University Press, 1975.

Thornton, J. Mills III. *Politics and Power in a Slave Society: Alabama, 1800–1860.* Baton Rouge: Louisiana State University Press, 1978.

Tise, Larry E. *Proslavery: A History of the Defense of Slavery in America, 1701–1840.* Athens: University of Georgia Press, 1987.

Tussell, John B. B., Jr. *The Pennsylvania Line: Regimental Organization and Operations, 1776–1783.* Harrisburg: Pennsylvania Historical and Museum Commission, 1977.

Vipperman, Carl J. *William Lowndes and the Transition of Southern Politics, 1782–1822.* Chapel Hill: University of North Carolina Press, 1989.

Watson, Harry L. *Jacksonian Politics and Community Conflict: The Emergence of the Second American Party System in Cumberland County, North Carolina.* Baton Rouge: Louisiana State University Press, 1981.

———. *Liberty and Power: The Politics of Jacksonian America.* New York: Hill and Wang, 1990.

Wayland, Francis Fry. *Andrew Stevenson: Democrat and Diplomat, 1785–1857.* Philadelphia: University of Pennsylvania Press, 1949.

Weaver, Bobby D. *Castro's Colony: Empresario Development in Texas, 1842–1865.* College Station: Texas A&M University Press, 1985.

Weems, John Edward, and Jane Weems. *Dream of Empire: A Human History of the Republic of Texas, 1836–1846.* New York: Simon and Schuster, 1971.

Weir, Robert M. *"The Last of American Freemen": Studies in the Political Culture of the Colonial and Revolutionary South.* Macon: Mercer University Press, 1986.

Weld, Timothy Dwight. *American Slavery As It Is, Testimony of a Thousand Witnesses.* 1839. Reprint, New York: Arno Press and the New York Times, 1969.

Wender, Herbert. *Southern Commercial Conventions, 1837–1859.* Baltimore: Johns Hopkins Press, 1930.

Whitaker, Arthur P. *The Western Hemisphere Idea: Its Rise and Decline.* Ithaca: Cornell University Press, 1954.

White, Laura Amanda. *Robert Barnwell Rhett: Father of Secession.* New York: Century Co., 1931.

Wild, Philip Frederick. "South Carolina Politics: 1816–1833." Ph.D. diss., University of Pennsylvania, 1949.

Williams, George W. *History of Banking in South Carolina from 1712 to 1900.* Charleston: Walker, Evans & Cogswell, 1900.

Williams, John Hoyt. *Sam Houston: A Biography of the Father of Texas.* New York: Simon & Schuster, 1993.

Wiltse, Charles M. *Nationalist, 1792–1828.* Vol. 1 of *John C. Calhoun.* Indianapolis: Bobbs-Merrill, 1944.

———. *Sectionalist, 1840–1850.* Vol. 3 of *John C. Calhoun.* Indianapolis: Bobbs-Merrill, 1951.

Withey, Lynne Elizabeth. "Population Change, Economic Development, and the Revolution: Newport, Rhode Island, as a Case Study, 1760–1800." Ph.D. diss., University of California, Berkeley, 1976.

Woodman, Harold D. *King Cotton and His Retainers: Financing and Marketing the Cotton Crop of the South, 1800–1925.* Lexington: University of Kentucky Press, 1968.

Yoakum, H. *History of Texas from Its First Settlement in 1685 to Its Annexation to the United States in 1846.* 2 vols. 1855. Reprint, Austin: Steck, 1935.

Young, James Sterling. *The Washington Community, 1800–1828.* New York: Columbia University Press, 1966.

ARTICLES

Barker, Nancy Nichols. "Devious Diplomat: Dubois de Saligny and the Republic of Texas." *SWHQ* 72 (January 1969): 324–34.

Boucher, Chauncey S. "The Annexation of Texas and the Bluffton Movement in South Carolina." *Mississippi Valley Historical Review* 6 (June 1919): 3–33.

Bridenbaugh, Carl. "Colonial Newport as a Summer Resort." *Rhode Island Historical Society Collections* (January 1933): 1–23.

Callahan, M. Generosa. "Henri Castro and James Hamilton." *SWHQ* 69 (October 1965): 174–85.

Crane, Virginia Glenn. "Two Women, White and Brown, in the South Carolina Court of Equity, 1842–1845." *SCHM* 96 (July 1995): 198–220.

Delp, Robert W. "The Southern Press and the Rise of American Spiritualism, 1847–1860." *Journal of American Culture* 7 (1984): 88–95.

Gould, Christopher. "The South Carolina and Continental Associations: Prelude to Revolution." *SCHM* 87 (January 1986): 30–48.

Govan, Thomas Payne. "An Ante-Bellum Attempt to Regulate the Price and Supply of Cotton." *North Carolina Historical Review* 17 (October 1940): 302–12.

Haw, James. "The Rutledges, the Continental Congress, and Independence." *SCHM* 94 (October 1993): 232–51.

Johnson, Michael P. "Denmark Vesey and His Co-Conspirators." *William and Mary Quarterly,* 3rd ser., 58 (October 2001): 915–76.

Lander, Ernest M., Jr. "The Calhoun-Preston Feud, 1836–1842." *SCHM* 59 (January 1958): 24–37.

Laurent, Pierre Henri. "Belgium's Relations with Texas and the United States, 1839–1844." *SWHQ* 68 (October 1964): 220–36.

Moltke-Hansen, David. "Protecting Interests, Maintaining Rights, Emulating An-
cestors: U.S. Constitution Reflections on 'The Problem of South Carolina,'
1787–1860." *SCHM* 89 (July 1988): 160–82.

Moraud, Marcel. "The Diplomatic Relations of the Republic of Texas." *Rice Institute
Pamphlet* 43 (October 1956): 29–54.

Ochenkowski, J. P. "Origins of the Nullification Crisis." *SCHM* 83 (April 1982):
121–53.

Pease, Jane H., and William H. Pease. "The Economics and Politics of Charleston's
Nullification Crisis." *JSH* 47 (August 1981): 335–62.

Raiford, Norman Gasque. "South Carolina and the Second Bank of the United
States: Conflict in Political Principle or Economic Interest?" *SCHM* 72 (January
1971): 30–43.

Rippy, J. Fred. "Britain's Role in the Early Relations of the United States and Mexico." *Hispanic American Historical Review* 7 (February 1927): 2–24.

Rogers, George C., Jr. "South Carolina Federalists and the Origins of the Nullification Movement." *SCHM* 71 (January 1970): 17–32.

Rowland, Lawrence S. "'Alone on the River': The Rise and Fall of the Savannah
River Rice Plantations of St. Peter's Parish, South Carolina." *SCHM* 88 (July
1987): 121–50.

Stewart, James Brewer. "'A Great Talking and Eating Machine': Patriarchy, Mobilization and the Dynamics of Nullification in South Carolina." *Civil War History*
27 (September 1981): 197–220.

Stoney, Samuel Gaillard, ed. "Memoirs of Frederick Adolphus Porcher." *SCHM* 47
(January and April 1946): 32–52, 83–108.

Trautmann, Frederic. "South Carolina through a German's Eyes: The Travels of
Clara Von Gerstner, 1839." *SCHM* 85 (July 1984): 220–32.

Index